Guide to Microsoft® Virtual PC 2007 and Virtual Server 2005

Ron Carswell & Heidi Webb

Australia • Brazil • Japan • Korea • Mexico • Singapore • Spain • United Kingdom • United States

Guide to Microsoft® Virtual PC 2007 and Virtual Server 2005
Ron Carswell & Heidi Webb

Acquisitions Editor: Nick Lombardi

Senior Product Manager: Alyssa Pratt

Developmental Editor: Amanda Brodkin

Content Project Manager: Jill Braiewa

Quality Assurance: Green Pen Quality Assurance

Print Buyer: Julio Esperas

Editorial Assistant: Claire Jeffers

Art Director: Kun-Tee Chang

Compositor: International Typesetting and Composition

Copyeditor: Karen Annett

Proofreader: Harry Johnson

Indexer: Rich Carlson

© 2009 Course Technology, Cengage Learning

ALL RIGHTS RESERVED. No part of this work covered by the copyright herein may be reproduced, transmitted, stored or used in any form or by any means graphic, electronic, or mechanical, including but not limited to photocopying, recording, scanning, digitizing, taping, Web distribution, information networks, or information storage and retrieval systems, except as permitted under Section 107 or 108 of the 1976 United States Copyright Act, without the prior written permission of the publisher.

> For product information and technology assistance, contact us at
> **Cengage Learning Customer & Sales Support, 1-800-354-9706**
>
> For permission to use material from this text or product, submit all requests online at **cengage.com/permissions**
>
> Further permissions questions can be emailed to
> **permissionrequest@cengage.com**

ISBN-13: 978-1-4283-2195-3

ISBN-10: 1-4283-2195-0

Course Technology
25 Thomson Place
Boston, MA 02210
USA

Disclaimer
Course Technology Cengage Learning reserves the right to revise this publication and make changes from time to time in its content without notice.

The programs in this book are for instructional purposes only. They have been tested with care, but are not guaranteed for any particular intent beyond educational purposes. The author and the publisher do not offer any warranties or representations, nor do they accept any liabilities with respect to the programs.

Cengage Learning is a leading provider of customized learning solutions with office locations around the globe, including Singapore, the United Kingdom, Australia, Mexico, Brazil, and Japan. Locate your local office at: **international.cengage.com/region**

Cengage Learning products are represented in Canada by Nelson Education, Ltd.

For your lifelong learning solutions, visit **course.cengage.com**

Visit our corporate website at **cengage.com**

Printed in Canada
1 2 3 4 5 6 7 14 13 12 11 10 09 08

Brief Contents

INTRODUCTION	x
CHAPTER 1 **Overview of Virtualization Technology**	1
CHAPTER 2 **Configuring Virtual Machines in Virtual PC 2007**	33
CHAPTER 3 **Installing Microsoft Windows Vista and Server 2008 Operating Systems**	71
CHAPTER 4 **Implementing the Dovercorp.local Virtual Network**	109
CHAPTER 5 **Using Advanced Options and Troubleshooting in Virtual PC**	157
CHAPTER 6 **Implementing Virtual Server**	201
CHAPTER 7 **Using Microsoft VMRCplus**	249
CHAPTER 8 **Implementing the Classroom.local Virtual Network**	301
CHAPTER 9 **Classroom.local Virtual Network Infrastructure**	349
CHAPTER 10 **Implementing Security for the Classroom.local Virtual Network**	397
GLOSSARY	447
INDEX	453

Table of Contents

INTRODUCTION	x

CHAPTER 1
Overview of Virtualization Technology — 1

Introduction to Virtualization Technology	2
Uses for Virtualization Technology	4
Benefits of Virtualization	4
Drawbacks of Virtualization	5
Uses for Virtualization	6
Microsoft Virtualization Products	7
History	7
Virtual Machines	9
Emulated Hardware	10
Supported Operating Systems	11
Virtual Hard Disks	11
Virtual Networking	13
Virtual Machine Additions	17
Installing Microsoft VPC	18
Researching Microsoft Virtual PC 2007 on the Web	18
Installing Internet Connection Sharing	19
Installing Microsoft Virtual PC 2007	22
Viewing Virtual PC 2007 Help	24
Exploring a Virtual PC Blog	26
Chapter Summary	27
Key Terms	27
Review Questions	28
Case Projects	31

CHAPTER 2
Configuring Virtual Machines in Virtual PC 2007 — 33

Creating Virtual Machines	34
First Virtual Machine	34
Adding Additional Virtual Machines	40
Removing Virtual Machines	41
Configuring Global Virtual PC 2007 Settings	42
Restore at Start	42
Performance	43
Hardware Virtualization	44
Full-Screen Mode	44
Sound	45
Messages	46
Keyboard	47
Mouse	48
Security	49
Language	50
Managing Individual Virtual Machine Settings	51
Virtual Machine Name	52
Memory	52

Hard Disks	54
Undo Disks	55
CD/DVD Drive	56
Floppy Disk	56
COM Ports	57
LPT1	58
Networking	59
Sound	60
Mouse	61
Shared Folders	61
Display	62
Close	63
Chapter Summary	66
Key Terms	66
Review Questions	66
Case Projects	70

CHAPTER 3
Installing Microsoft Windows Vista and Server 2008 Operating Systems — 71

Installing Operating Systems in Virtual PC 2007	72
Initial Text Screens	72
Overview of Operating System Installation	75
DVDs and ISO Images	75
Overview: Installing Windows Vista Business	75
Installing Virtual Machine Additions	90
Shared Folders	92
Mouse Integration	93
Drag and Drop	94
Clipboard Integration	95
Time Synchronization	96
Arbitrary Video Resolutions	96
Customized Video Drivers	97
Closing the Virtual Machine	97
Cloning Virtual Machines	98
Issues with Cloning	98
Using Sysprep	98
Chapter Summary	102
Key Terms	102
Review Questions	103
Case Projects	106

CHAPTER 4
Implementing the Dovercorp.local Virtual Network — 109

The Dovercorp.local Virtual Network	110
Server01 Role—Domain Controller	111
Server02 Role—File Server	112
Client01 Role—Desktop Client	112
Operating System Requirements	112

Table of Contents

Implementing the Dovercorp.local Virtual Network — 115
  Dovercorp.local Network Diagram — 115
  Installing Operating Systems for the Dovercorp.local Virtual Machines — 117
  Verifying the IP Addressing on the Dovercorp.local Network — 122
  Configuring the Windows Firewall — 127
  Verifying IP Connectivity — 130

Implementing Active Directory Domain Services — 132
  Overview of Active Directory Domain Services Installation — 132
  Joining the Domain — 147

Chapter Summary — 150

Key Terms — 150

Review Questions — 151

Case Projects — 155

CHAPTER 5
Using Advanced Options and Troubleshooting in Virtual PC — 157

Performance Optimization — 158
  CPU — 158
  Memory — 159
  Hard Disk — 160

Implementing the Advanced Disk Options — 168
  Undo Disks — 168
  Differencing Disks — 170
  Linked Disks — 171

Dynamic Disks and Fault Tolerance — 179
  Additional Virtual Hard Disks — 179
  Dynamic Disk Conversion — 180
  Fault-Tolerant Storage — 182

Troubleshooting Virtual PC Installations — 192

Chapter Summary — 194

Key Terms — 194

Review Questions — 195

Case Projects — 198

CHAPTER 6
Implementing Virtual Server — 201

Overview of Virtual Server — 202
  Virtual Server Architecture — 202
  Virtual Machines — 203
  Emulated Hardware — 205
  Supported Operating Systems — 205
  Virtual Machine Additions — 205
  Differences Between Virtual PC and Virtual Server — 207

Installing Virtual Server — 209

Configuring Virtual Server — 212
  Server Properties — 213
  Administration Web Site Properties — 216
  CPU Resource Allocation — 218
  Event Viewer — 219

Implementing Virtual Networks	220
Internal Network	221
Network Adapter on the Physical Computer	221
Microsoft Loopback Adapter	221
Internet Connection Sharing	222
Virtual Machine Network Services Driver	223
DHCP Server	223
Creating a Virtual Network	223
Virtual Disks in Virtual Server	227
Dynamically Expanding	227
Fixed Size	228
Linked to a Hard Disk	228
Differencing	228
Enable Undo Disks	229
Virtual Floppy Disk	230
Creating a Virtual Disk	230
Implementing Virtual Machines	234
Creating a Virtual Machine	234
Running a Virtual Machine in Virtual Server	236
Chapter Summary	243
Key Terms	244
Review Questions	245
Case Projects	249

CHAPTER 7
Using Microsoft VMRCplus   249

Overview of VMRCplus	250
Key Features	252
Installing and Configuring VMRCplus	253
Creating and Running Virtual Machines	257
Creating the First Virtual Machine	257
Installing an Operating System for the First Virtual Machine	261
Installing Virtual Machine Additions for the First Virtual Machine	262
VMRCplus Managers	266
The Virtual Machine Manager	266
Working with Selected Virtual Machines	273
Using the Console Manager	281
Using the Virtual Disks Manager	283
Implementing Virtual Networks	289
Chapter Summary	294
Key Terms	295
Review Questions	295
Case Projects	299

CHAPTER 8
Implementing the Classroom.local Virtual Network   301

Describing the Classroom.local Virtual Network	302
Server-01 Role—Domain Controller	303
Server-02 Role—Infrastructure Server	304

Server-03 Role—File Server	304
Client-01 Role—Desktop Client	304
Client-02 Role—Desktop Client	304
Operating System Requirements	304
Implementing the Classroom.local Network	**308**
Classroom.local Network Diagram	308
Installing Operating Systems	309
Configuring the Child Servers	309
Virtual Machine Additions	320
Verifying the IP Addressing on the Classroom Network	321
Configuring the Windows Firewall	323
Verifying IP Connectivity	326
Implementing Active Directory Domain Services	**328**
Joining the Domain	330
Configuring DNS Services for Classroom.local	**333**
Overview of DNS Queries	333
Forwarding Name Resolution Requests	335
DNS Zones	336
Dynamic Update	338
Creating a Secondary DNS Server	340
Chapter Summary	**343**
Key Terms	**344**
Review Questions	**344**
Case Projects	**348**

CHAPTER 9
Classroom.local Virtual Network Infrastructure   349

Analyzing Traffic	**350**
Creating an Alias List	351
Filtering Packets	352
Capturing Data Between Two Computers	352
Reconfiguring a Virtual Network	357
Installing the Dynamic Host Configuration Protocol	**358**
Authorizing a DHCP Server	359
DHCP Process	359
Managing DHCP	360
Creating Scopes	361
Scope Options	363
Viewing DHCP Traffic in Microsoft Network Monitor	364
Implementing Routing	**369**
Routing Tables	369
Routing Protocols	371
Static Routing	371
Dynamic Routing	372
Network Policy and Access Services	373
Reconfiguring the Classroom.local Virtual Network for Routing	374
Revising the DHCP Relay Agent	386

Chapter Summary	389
Key Terms	389
Review Questions	391
Case Projects	395

CHAPTER 10
Implementing Security for the Classroom.local Virtual Network — 397

Using Active Directory Domain Services	398
Active Directory Concepts	398
Active Directory User and Computer Accounts	400
Active Directory Security Groups	403
Active Directory Organizational Units	406
Active Directory Sites	407
Applying Group Policy	414
Security Group Filtering	416
Policy Inheritance	416
Blocking Inheritance and No Override	417
Using the Group Policy Management Console	417
Using Resultant Set of Policy	418
Implementing IP Security	423
IPSec Protocols	423
IPSec Modes	424
Negotiation Phases	428
Phase II or Quick Mode Negotiation	430
How IPSec Works	431
End-to-End Security Between Specific Hosts	432
Creating IPSec Policies	432
Chapter Summary	439
Key Terms	440
Review Questions	442
Case Projects	446

GLOSSARY	**447**
INDEX	**453**

Introduction

Welcome to *Guide to Microsoft® Virtual PC 2007 and Virtual Server 2005*. This book emphasizes the use of the latest Microsoft software products: Virtual PC 2007, Virtual Server 2005, Windows Vista Business, and Windows Server 2008. Steps are provided to create two virtual environments. The first virtual environment is pictured in Figure 1. The host uses Microsoft Vista Business. The guest machines run either Microsoft Server 2008 or Windows Vista Business in a networked virtual environment.

In later chapters another network is introduced that supports advanced topics such as IPSec and routing, as pictured in Figure 2. This second virtual environment uses Windows Server 2008, Windows Vista Business, and Virtual Server 2005. The two virtual environments support a wide range of topics that are presented in the Course Technology Cengage Learning MCSA/MCSE series.

In addition, this book contains information about VMRCplus, which was developed by Microsoft as an alternative to the Virtual Server Administration Web site used by Virtual Server 2008. VMRCplus does not replace every function of the Virtual Server Administration Web site, but it does provide useful features that the Web site does not have. For example, VMRCplus can generate the configurations for multiple child virtual machines from a parent virtual machine.

VMRCplus also provides a Windows GUI that is easier to use than the Virtual Server Administration Web site for configuring and managing guest virtual machines. The virtual machines are displayed in a tabbed window, which makes it easy to jump from virtual machine to virtual machine when working with multiple running virtual machines.

Microsoft released the latest development version for Windows Server 2008, Release Candidate 0 (RC0), during the development of this book. In this book, the discussions, activities, and screen shots all reflect the appearance and functionality of Windows Server 2008 (RC0).

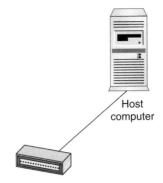
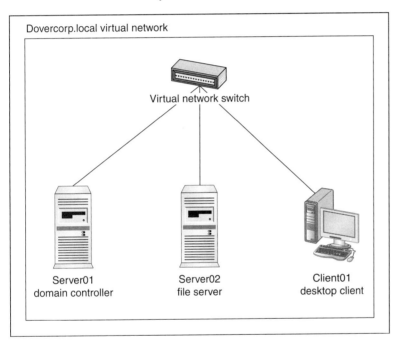

Figure 1 First virtual environment

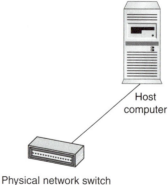
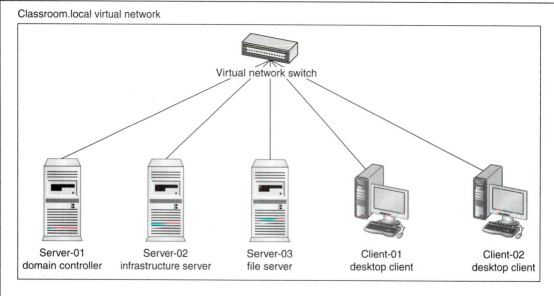

Figure 2 Second virtual environment

Intended Audience This book introduces the features of Microsoft Virtual PC 2007 and Virtual Server 2005. It assumes that students have previously used a personal computer with the Windows XP or Windows Vista operating systems.

The book focuses on the effective use of Microsoft Virtual PC 2007 or Virtual Server 2005 to implement virtual networks for the various activities in the MCSE/MCSA Guide series:

- *MCSE Guide to Microsoft Windows XP Professional*
- *MCSE Guide to Managing a Windows Server 2003 Environment*
- *MCSE/MCSA Guide to Installing and Managing Microsoft Windows XP Professional and Windows Server 2003*
- *MCSE Guide to Managing a Windows Server 2003 Environment, Enhanced*
- *MCSE Guide to Managing a Windows Server 2003 Network*

- *MCSE Guide to Managing a Windows Server 2003 Network, Enhanced*
- *MCSE Guide to Microsoft Windows Vista Professional*

Appendix A is available online at www.course.com and as part of the Instructor's Resources CD. Information is presented in Appendix A, Installing Fedora Core 8, which makes this text useful for the installation of Linux for the following texts:

- *Guide to Parallel Operating Systems with Microsoft Windows XP and Linux*
- *Getting Started with Linux: Novell's Guide to CompTIA's Linux+*
- *SUSE Linux Enterprise Server Administration*
- *Guide To Operating Systems, Enhanced Edition*
- *Linux+ Guide to Linux Certification*

The book provides a conceptual presentation of each Microsoft Virtual PC 2007 and Virtual Server 2005 feature. For each feature, step-by-step instructions and activities support the use of Microsoft Virtual PC 2007 and Virtual Server 2005 to accomplish activities that would otherwise require multiple physical computers.

As numerous colleges are using the MCSE/MCSA Guide series from Course Technology Cengage Learning, this text provides guidance for implementing virtual environments for the activities in these texts. Use of the techniques in the *Guide to Microsoft® Virtual PC 2007 and Virtual Server 2005* will enable students to gain the advantages of virtual technology while reducing the capital outlays of colleges for multiple computer systems.

To best understand the material in this book, you should have a working knowledge of operating in a workgroup or Active Directory domain environment.

Chapter Descriptions There are 10 chapters in this book, as follows:

Chapter 1, "Overview of Virtualization Technology," introduces virtualization technology, describing how users can benefit from virtualization technology. Next, you will examine examples of virtualization technology in use. The chapter concludes with the installation of Microsoft Virtual PC 2007.

Chapter 2, "Configuring Virtual Machines in Virtual PC 2007," starts by providing information that you will use to create the proper virtual machine for each guest operating system. The chapter concludes with a discussion of the settings that are available in both the New Virtual Machine Wizard and the Virtual PC Console. With proper management of memory, undo disks, security, shared folders, and networking, virtual machines on a host operating system can provide an efficient and productive work environment.

Chapter 3, "Installing Microsoft Windows Vista and Server 2008 Operating Systems," starts with an overview of the steps involved in installing an operating system in a virtual machine. The chapter concludes with the installation of Microsoft Windows Vista Business and Windows Server 2008.

Chapter 4, "Implementing the Dovercorp.local Virtual Network," starts with a description of the Dovercorp.local virtual network, which includes three virtual machines and proceeds with installation and configuration of the three virtual machines. The last task implements directory services to provide centralized security management of the virtual machines and other network objects.

Chapter 5, "Using Advanced Options and Troubleshooting in Virtual PC," discusses a range of actions available to increase the performance of virtual machines. This chapter spotlights trouble spots related to virtual machine optimization while addressing common errors to help you avoid installation issues. Also, you will learn how to preserve the integrity of data during a malfunction.

Chapter 6, "Implementing Virtual Server," prepares you to install and use Virtual Server 2005. As part of mastering Virtual Server, you will learn to link virtual networks, virtual hard disks, virtual machines, and more.

Chapter 7, "Using Microsoft VMRCplus," outlines the skills that you will need to use VMRCplus, an alternative to the Virtual Server Administration Web site. The chapter concludes with the creation and management of virtual machines with VMRCplus.

Chapter 8, "Implementing the Classroom.local Virtual Network," describes the Classroom .local virtual demonstration network, which features five virtual machines. After defining the five guests, you will install and configure them. The last task implements directory services and DNS to provide centralized security management of the guests and other network objects.

Chapter 9, "Classroom.local Virtual Network Infrastructure," continues building the network infrastructure. You will download a tool from Microsoft that lets you access detailed information about the contents of packets, which helps you troubleshoot the network. To reduce the administration burden and complexity of configuring hosts on a TCP/IP-based network, you will add a role to support dynamic IP addressing. Finally, you will implement routing, which is the process of moving a data packet from its local network to a remote network based on the address of the remote network.

Chapter 10, "Implementing Security for the Classroom.local Virtual Network," focuses on using security policy to deliver managed computing environments Lastly, the chapter implements a framework of open standards to ensure private, secure communications over Internet Protocol (IP) networks.

Features and Approach *Guide to Microsoft® Virtual PC 2007 and Virtual Server 2005* differs from virtualization support books in its unique hands-on approach and its orientation to building demonstration virtualization networks. To help you comprehend how to use Microsoft virtualization products with Microsoft operating systems, this book incorporates the following features:

- **Chapter Objectives** Each chapter begins with a detailed list of the concepts to be mastered. This list gives you a quick reference to the chapter's contents and is a useful study aid.

- **Activities** Activities are incorporated throughout the text, giving you practice in setting up, managing, and troubleshooting a network system. The Activities give you a strong foundation for carrying out network administration tasks in the real world. Because of the book's progressive nature, completing the Activities in each chapter is essential before moving on to the end-of-chapter materials and subsequent chapters.

- **Chapter Summaries** Each chapter's text is followed by a summary of the concepts introduced in that chapter. These summaries are a helpful way to recap and revisit the ideas covered in each chapter.

- **Key Terms** All of the terms within the chapter that were introduced with boldfaced text are gathered together in the Key Terms list at the end of the chapter. This provides you with a method of checking your understanding of all the terms introduced.

- **Review Questions** The end-of-chapter assessment begins with a set of Review Questions that reinforces the ideas introduced in each chapter. Answering these questions will ensure that you have mastered the important concepts.
- **Case Projects** Finally, each chapter closes with a section that proposes certain situations. You are asked to evaluate the situations and recommend the course of action to be taken to remedy the problems described. This valuable tool will help you sharpen your decision-making and troubleshooting skills.

Text and Graphic Conventions Additional information and exercises have been added to this book to help you better understand what is being discussed in the chapter. Icons throughout the text alert you to these additional materials. The icons used in this book are described below.

Tips offer extra information on resources, how to attack problems, and time-saving shortcuts.

Notes present additional helpful material related to the subject being discussed.

The Caution icon identifies important information about potential mistakes or hazards.

Each Activity in this book is preceded by the Activity icon.

Case Project icons mark the end-of-chapter case projects, which are scenario-based assignments that ask you to independently apply what you have learned in the chapter.

Instructor's Resources The following supplemental materials are available when this book is used in a classroom setting. All of the supplements available with this book are provided to the instructor on a single CD-ROM.

Electronic Instructor's Manual The Instructor's Manual that accompanies this textbook includes additional instructional material to assist in class preparation, including suggestions for classroom activities, discussion topics, and additional projects.

Solutions are provided for the end-of-chapter material, including Review Questions, and where applicable, Activities and Case Projects. Solutions to the Practice Exams are also included.

PowerPoint presentations This book comes with Microsoft PowerPoint slides for each chapter. These are included as a teaching aid for classroom presentation, to make available to students on the network for chapter review, or to be printed for classroom distribution. Instructors, please feel at liberty to add your own slides for additional topics you introduce to the class.

Figure files All of the figures and tables in the book are reproduced on the Instructor's Resource CD, in bitmap format. Similar to the PowerPoint presentations, these are included as a teaching aid for classroom presentation, to make available to students for review, or to be printed for classroom distribution.

Minimum Lab Requirements

Recommended network:

The students will have access to multiple computers labeled Host01–Host16. The Host computers will need Internet access.

Hardware/software configurations for the Host computers:

For the first five chapters, install Microsoft Vista Business on a partition with a minimum of 100 GB. As a part of the installation, create the Student user account with a password of Secret1. Create a second partition with a minimum of 100 GB for a future installation of Windows Server 2008.

For the remaining chapters, install Windows Server 2008 in the second partition. Create a password of Secret1 for the Administrator account. Use the Windows Server 2008 host starting with Chapter 6.

The required hardware configuration follows:

- Pentium 800 MHz (1 GHz or higher is recommended)
- 3 GB (4 GB or higher to complete routing lab activities)
- 200 GB of free space
- DVD-ROM
- One network interface card networked with access to the Internet.

Acknowledgments

Ron Carswell

This text is a product of the talents of many individuals. First, I wish to say thanks to the staff at Course Technology Cengage Learning. More specifically, I would like to thank my project manager, Alyssa Pratt, for her patience and help. Development editor Amanda Brodkin provided the inspiration to mold my thoughts clearly and concisely.

I would also like to thank my wife, Coleen, for the numerous hours devoted to proofing the text and testing each lab activity. Her insight, from a student perspective, enhanced the quality of this text.

Heidi Webb

Thanks to Ron for his wonderful support and guidance through the years. He has been a great friend and mentor. Special thanks go to the great team at Course Technology Cengage Learning for believing in this project. As always, my family was there to support me during this project. I especially want to thank my husband Dennis for his help in keeping things quiet when I needed to meet my deadlines.

Last, we would like to thank the following reviewers for their help in pulling this book together: Jim Black, Marjorie Deutsch, Ronald Handlon, Jeff Palmer, and Daniel Ziesmer.

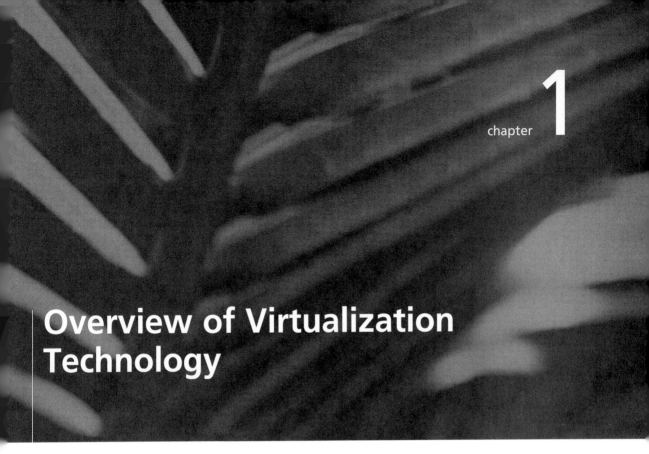

chapter 1

Overview of Virtualization Technology

After reading this chapter and completing the exercises, you will be able to:

- Describe virtualization technology
- Describe uses of virtualization technology
- Describe Microsoft virtualization products
- Install Microsoft Virtual PC 2007

Virtualized systems—systems that appear to be real but are actually simulations—are used in many environments. Airline pilots use flight simulators for flight practice and testing, whereas computer games such as Sim City let the player create a virtual city in a game environment that feels real, but actually exists only in the hardware and software of the game.

In the IT world, **virtualization** refers to the use of virtualization software that allows the physical hardware of a single PC to run multiple operating systems simultaneously in **virtual machines (VMs)**. The virtualization software simulates enough hardware to create an environment that allows an unmodified **guest operating system** (the one running inside a VM) to be run in isolation on a **host operating system** (the one running on the physical computer system).

This text presents the information that you will need to successfully use the two Microsoft virtualization products—Microsoft Virtual PC 2007 (VPC) and Microsoft Virtual Server 2005 (VS). Virtualization software is available from other manufacturers as well.

To help you get a grasp of virtualization, the chapter starts with a description of virtualization technology, illustrating how users can benefit from virtualization technology. Next, you will examine examples of virtualization technology in use. Then, you will learn about the VPC product. The chapter concludes with the installation of VPC. The chapter provides guidance on resources that are available to help you use the VPC product.

Chapter 1 through Chapter 5 present information on the use of VPC. The remaining chapters present information on VS.

Introduction to Virtualization Technology

Virtualization technology uses software to simulate a physical environment that includes virtual hardware on which you can install and interact with a number of operating systems (OSs). With virtualization technology, you can run a range of OSs on top of an OS.

Figure 1-1 shows various Microsoft OSs on the Microsoft Windows Vista desktop. From top to bottom are Windows XP Professional, Windows 2000 Professional, Windows NT Workstation, and DOS 6.22. Each OS runs on top of the virtual hardware provided by the virtualization program. Each OS is isolated from the other OSs.

You could use combinations of operating systems other than the one shown in the figure—for example, you could run multiple copies of Windows Server 2003 on top of Microsoft Windows XP Professional.

Figure 1-2 shows a high-level overview of how virtualization works. At the base layer, you see the hardware within the physical computer. This hardware includes the system board, memory, disk, network, and other hardware components. Above the hardware is the host operating system.

The virtualization software runs within the host OS and provides the virtual platform for the VMs. An **emulated hardware system** (imitating the function of a computer system) is provided within each VM for each guest OS. The OS and software within each VM are unaware of the other VMs and have full access to the virtual platform.

Introduction to Virtualization Technology **3**

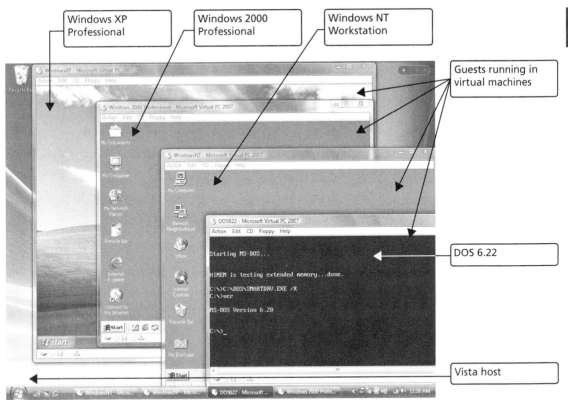

Figure 1-1 Various operating systems on Microsoft Windows Vista desktop

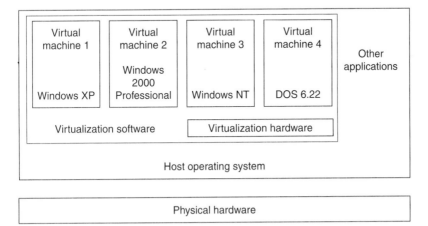

Figure 1-2 Virtual machine technology

4 Chapter 1 Overview of Virtualization Technology

Figure 1-3 presents another view of the four guest operating systems and their relation to the host operating system. Windows Vista, the host operating system, controls the physical computer. The virtualization software creates the four VMs that permit the execution of the guest operating systems. The VMs contain the operating systems that were displayed in Figure 1-1.

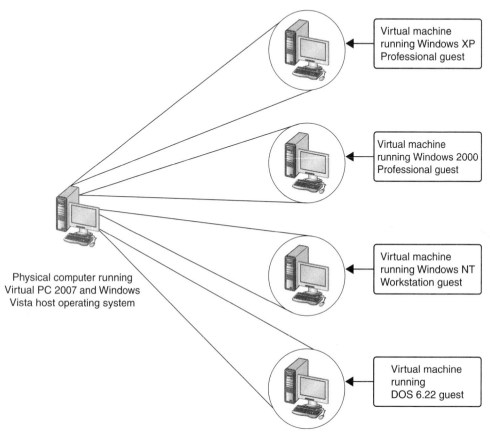

Figure 1-3 Multiple guests running on top of host

Uses for Virtualization Technology

At this point, you are probably wondering how and why virtualization is used. The sections that follow provide the answers to these questions.

Benefits of Virtualization

The benefits of virtualization include improvements in hardware utilization, provisioning, and flexibility.

Increased Hardware Utilization You probably realize that your computer has available processor cycles. These cycles could be used to accomplish additional computing activities. Think about many servers running at less than full capacity—perhaps at 10 to 20 percent of available processor cycles. In many data centers, servers struggle to reach even 10 percent of their capacity for processor cycles. As hardware continues to gain additional power, thanks to multicore processors available in new computer systems, the problem will become worse. These wasted processor cycles could be put to use.

Virtualization allows the **consolidation** of low utilization systems—multiple OSs on a single computer system. Consolidation results in a need for fewer systems that have higher rates of utilization. The resulting reduction in the number of servers (which must be purchased and maintained) translates to cost savings.

Many businesses are using, or evaluating, virtualization technology in their data centers. Whether used for server consolidation, redundancy, or flexibility, the benefits are too great to ignore. The majority of consolidation projects today are focusing on replacing a number of existing underutilized systems with a more modern server using virtualization.

Users of multiple stand-alone computers could consolidate these desktop computers. For example, you might have a computer running an application on Windows 98, another running Windows NT Workstation, and so on. Moving these OSs and applications to VMs on a single desktop computer would be a more efficient way to gain the same range of OSs.

Rapid Provisioning If you need to install a new OS in the physical world, you would need to purchase a new computer, install an additional hard drive, create a partition on the existing hard drive, or remove and replace your existing OS. Virtualization permits the installation of the new OS on an existing computer system without disrupting the previous OS. Because each VM exposes the same emulated hardware, you might be able to save time by copying a standard OS image to this computer. Your standard image could be available in a library of previously installed VMs.

System Flexibility VMs provide amazing operational flexibility. You can quickly change memory, storage, and network resources with a reboot of the VM. You can also close the VM—put it into a saved state—which stops the VM from using any system resources, but allows the VM to be restored quickly to a current state at a later time.

Drawbacks of Virtualization

Virtualization, for all its benefits, does have its downside. The drawbacks of using virtualization software include drain on performance, limited scalability, and common hardware. In many cases, the benefits will overcome the drawbacks. You will need to weigh the benefits against the drawbacks carefully when making your decision to use virtualization.

Performance No matter how you approach the subject, virtualization software adds a certain amount of overhead to the computer system. For most situations, this overhead is acceptable and is justified by the benefits of virtualization.

Determining the overall performance impact of virtualization including overhead is hard to do. Generally speaking, virtualization software impacts processor and memory performance by only a negligible amount. Virtualization adds a more significant impact to disk and networking performance. Video performance within the VM will have the most significant impact on the performance of the VM.

You might experience a performance impact while installing an OS into a VM. This occurs because the installation stresses the emulated virtual disk as files are copied from the CD/DVD.

Scalability Microsoft VPC and VS are designed to be scalable applications with the ability to run multiple VMs in the same physical computer system. However, these programs do have a number of limitations. All VMs are uniprocessor, are limited by the amount of physical memory of the host system, and can run only 32-bit OSs.

Common Hardware Common hardware—the availability of a single hardware configuration—provides both benefits and drawbacks when it comes to virtualization. Rapid provisioning and system flexibility are benefits of common hardware. However, if the OS and applications that you want to virtualize are not capable of running on the system hardware or require other hardware, you are out of luck. You cannot add new or different hardware to the VM.

Uses for Virtualization

Now that you can describe the benefits and drawbacks of virtualization, you need to learn how virtualization is applied. In the sections that follow, you will discover potential ways that you can use virtualization. These usages include application development, training, documentation, and help desk support.

Application Development and Testing Virtualization allows software developers to run multiple VMs rather than multiple physical machines. When developing and testing an application, the developer might need a network of machines: a database server, a transaction server, and a client. Virtualization could be used to run this network on one physical machine. By using rapid provisioning, the developers can quickly and economically create the necessary network infrastructure. Developers can repeatedly test software inside of VMs with the ability to quickly return to a clean, known state after each test.

Training VMs are great tools for implementing training and learning. Training people about new OSs and computer applications involves extensive amounts of time and hardware.

For example, if you were training students to become network administrators, you would need to provide students with access to demonstration networks. You would need to acquire enough hardware to supply isolated computer systems and the network infrastructure to provide an authentic training environment for each student. Either you or your students would have to install the OSs and configure the computer systems appropriately.

In many training situations, the students will be changing the system configuration. Of course, the students might accidentally do something wrong. In either case, you or your students would periodically need to reinstall the OSs and reconfigure the computer systems after each student completes the required assignments. These conditions can require a lot of time and money.

Virtualization provides flexibility in the training environment by:

- Reducing the amount of hardware required for the necessary training environment. Complete training networks are running on a computer system for each student.

- Providing for instant restoration of the training environment. By using undo disks and differencing disks, any changes a student makes can be discarded, resulting in a convenient return to the original environment.

- Permitting training environments to be easily and quickly created for other training classes. With VMs, you could load the VMs for multiple classes. Students could bring up the specific training environment that they need.

Sales Demonstrations Selling technology products, including software and hardware, requires demonstrating the value of your application to others, answering the question, "How can your product solve a customer's problem?" Effectively applying your product to a customer's unique situation can be a challenge. Often, a proper demonstration requires a significant network infrastructure and amount of preparation. Sometimes, nontechnical users are performing the demonstration. Performing the demonstration in the customer's environment can exacerbate these challenges.

Virtualization can help overcome these problems. You can create a complete network infrastructure—tailored to the customer's specifications—on a single laptop. After creating this environment, you can replicate it for other users to demonstrate with ease.

Help Desks Help desks must support several varieties of hardware and software configurations. The combinations of multiple Windows versions and various application versions become unwieldy.

Help desk personnel must maintain multiple computers or restart their computers to support people who use various configurations. They might not have access to a configuration that a customer is using, and so they guess or fly blind. Thus, customer satisfaction suffers.

With virtualization, help desks are better able to duplicate users' environments, including the OSs and applications. These environments are built in advance and installed on each help desk computer system. For example, help desk personnel who use Windows Vista and VPC can still support previous Windows OSs. To save time, they can simply start a prebuilt virtual machine from a saved state, which takes seconds, and then continue the call.

Microsoft Virtualization Products

Microsoft provides two virtualization products. Virtual PC 2007 is the current version of the desktop product. For servers, Microsoft currently markets Virtual Server 2005 R2 SP1 (which, for simplicity, is called Virtual Server 2005).

In the sections that follow, you will learn about Microsoft Virtual PC 2007. Microsoft Virtual Server 2005 is covered in detail starting with Chapter 6.

History

Virtual PC 2007, as shown in Figure 1-4 on the next page, is based on technology that Microsoft purchased from Connectix in 2003. Connectix was a pioneer in the development of VMs for personal computer systems. Initially, Connectix developed a product that enabled Windows-based applications to run on the Apple Macintosh platform. In 2001, Connectix ported this technology to Windows and created Virtual PC for Windows. Microsoft Virtual PC 2004, the predecessor of Virtual PC 2007, was the first Windows-based version of this technology to be released by Microsoft. Microsoft Virtual PC 2007 is considered to be a desktop virtualization product.

8 Chapter 1 Overview of Virtualization Technology

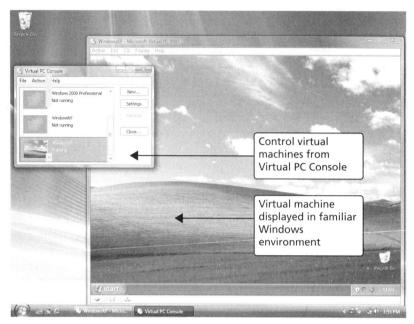

Figure 1-4 Virtual PC 2007

Microsoft Virtual Server 2005, as shown in Figure 1-5, was first released in August 2005 and was the first server virtualization product to be released by Microsoft. Virtual Server 2008 will be released within Windows Server 2008, which is Microsoft's current server operating system.

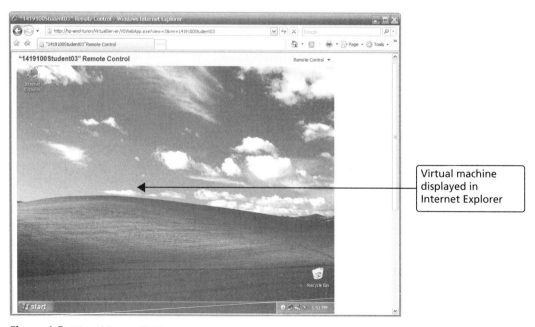

Figure 1-5 Virtual Server 2005

Virtual Machines

Each VM acts like a stand-alone computer system, with its own video, keyboard, mouse, hard disk, CD/DVD, and network card. The virtualization software—VPC or VS—provides virtualized hardware for the hard disk, CD/DVD, and network card as shown in Figure 1-6. The video, keyboard, and mouse are used by the foreground, or active, VM.

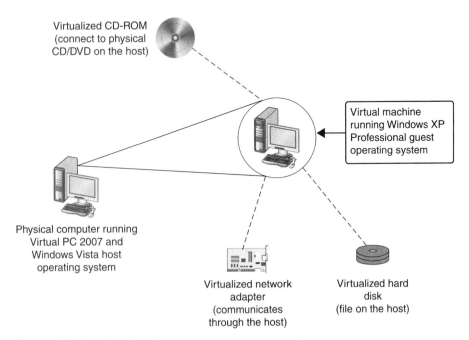

Figure 1-6 Virtualized hardware

What hardware is commonly presented to the guest OS? An OS interacts with a number of hardware components. Figure 1-7 on the next page shows the various settings available in VPC. Hardware components provided by VPC and emulated by VMs are as follows:

- *Memory*—Limited by the amount of physical memory in the physical machine
- *Hard disk*—Access up to three virtual hard disks with a default of 16,384 MB (maximum of 130,577 MB)
- *CD/DVD*—Mount one CD/DVD drive to an IDE port
- *Floppy disk*—Detected automatically
- *Communication ports (COM1, COM2)*—Map to the physical ports in the host
- *Printer ports (LPT1)*—Map to one printer port
- *Networking*—Support for one to four network adapters
- *Sound*—Support for one Creative Labs sound card
- *Mouse*—Provides two-button mouse with scroll button

- *Graphics adapter*—Support for S3 Trio 32/64 PCI (resolutions up to 1600 × 1200 at 16-bit graphics)
- *Display*—Support for one display device

Specific information for these and other settings used by VPC is detailed in Chapter 2. VS uses similar hardware components that are defined in Chapter 6.

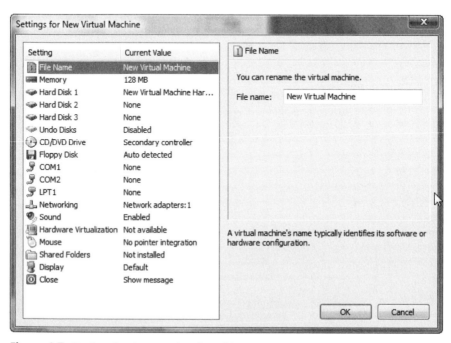

Figure 1-7 Settings for the new virtual machine

Emulated Hardware

When you are considering the hardware requirements for a given OS, you might need to consider the specific hardware that is emulated by VPC. Table 1-1 provides a list of these devices.

Table 1-1 Emulated devices in VPC

Component or device	Virtual machine emulated hardware
BIOS	AMI BIOS
Chipset	Intel 440BX
Sound card	Creative Labs Sound Blaster 16 ISA Plug and Play
Network adapter	Intel/DEC 21140A 10/100
Video card	S3 Trio 32/64 PCI

Supported Operating Systems

VPC supports desktop OSs. Supported host OSs include Windows Vista Business, Windows Vista Enterprise, Windows Vista Ultimate, Windows XP Professional, or Windows XP Tablet PC Edition. Supported guest OSs include the host OSs, plus Windows 98, Windows 98 Second Edition, and Windows Millennium Edition (Windows Me).

VPC can run most x86 OSs, in addition to the supported OSs, in a VM environment. Can you run Windows Server OSs in VPC? Yes, the OS dialog box includes Windows NT Server, Windows 2000 Server, and Windows Server 2003. By choosing "Other," you can install other OSs, such as a Linux distribution.

How is the supported OS different than the nonsupported OS? Microsoft provides support for the installation and use of the supported OS. If you choose to run a nonsupported OS, you are on your own. For example, if you decide to run a Linux distribution, you need to know what configurations need to be made in Linux to match the emulated hardware provided by VPC.

Virtual Hard Disks

Each virtual machine in VPC is provided with two IDE controllers (a primary and a secondary). The virtual CD/DVD is attached to one of the two controllers. You could attach a total of three virtual hard disks to the two controllers.

Virtual hard disks are files stored on the hard disk of the physical computer. To the VM, the virtual hard disk looks and acts like an entire hard disk separate from that of the host. See Figure 1-8.

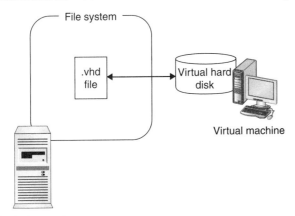

Figure 1-8 Virtual hard disks

Any operation that the guest OS performs is mapped back to the data stored within the **.vhd** file extension (the .vhd extension stands for *virtual hard disk*). A virtual hard disk is a special file that contains multiple files—all of the files that you would typically find on a computer system, such as OS files, personal settings, Windows Registry, menus, programs, data files, and more. VPC formats, reads, and writes to the .vhd file as if it were a hard disk.

When accessing a .vhd file, a guest OS running within a VM cannot access any area of the host's physical disk outside of the .vhd file. This is true even for low-level operations, including partitioning and formatting of the virtual hard drive.

VPC includes five options for the creation and use of virtual hard disks: dynamically expanding, fixed size, linked to a hard disk, differencing, and enable undo disks. You will learn about each of these options in the sections that follow.

Dynamically Expanding The size of the virtual hard disk expands as data is written to the .vhd file. The .vhd file starts at about 135 KB in size and grows from there until the limit that you specified is reached. The dynamically expanding option is the recommended (and default) option that is suitable for most OS installations.

Fixed Size This option limits the .vhd file to the size that you specify. When the .vhd file is created, the file is allocated to the specified limit. For example, if you create a 5-GB fixed size .vhd, the space allocated will be 5 GB. This option might yield higher performance than the others, but it uses more hard disk space on your host computer.

Linked to a Hard Disk You will use this option if you want your VM to use an existing physical hard disk. You configure the VM to point to the existing physical hard disk. You must use the entire hard disk. You cannot link to a volume on the disk. The VM operates at the physical hard disk level—not at the logical volume level.

Differencing When you create a differencing virtual hard disk, you are asked to specify an existing virtual hard disk, called the **parent** virtual hard disk, to which the differencing virtual hard disk points. When the VM uses this differencing (or **child**) virtual hard disk, the changes are stored in the differencing hard disk.

Consider a situation in which you configure parent and child disks for a WinXP_01 virtual computer, as shown in Figure 1-9. VPC will boot from the parent disk. As changes occur, the changes are written to the child disk.

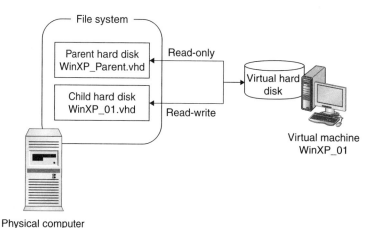

Figure 1-9 Differencing disks

The main benefit of differencing disks is speed. Differencing disks can speed up the creation of multiple VMs. In Chapter 8 you will use these techniques to create three VMs from one parent. You will install Windows Server 2008 on the parent VM and use differencing disks for the four servers. Recall that OS installation is time consuming. You will need to install the Windows Server 2008 only once for the parent. This will reduce the time to install the servers to one-third of the time.

Enable Undo Disks If you select the enable undo disks option, any changes made when a VM runs are saved to an undo disk (a file with a **.vud** extension). The .vud file is a temporary file and is separate from the .vhd file. When the VM is shut down, you have the option to delete the changes, commit the changes to the .vhd file, or save the changes for another time. Deleting the changes removes the .vud file. The enable undo disks option can only be selected when the VM is not running.

In Figure 1-10, you see an undo disk setup for a VM. The VM will be started from the .vhd disk. The changes are written to the .vud disk. When the VM is shut down, you can choose between deleting, merging, and saving the changes.

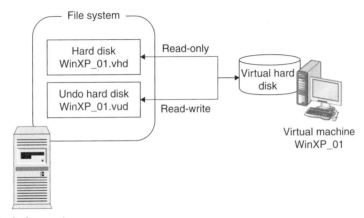

Figure 1-10 Undo disks

This option is useful in situations where you want to start with a pristine OS configuration. After changes are made to the configuration, the changes are deleted; this approach is especially useful in program testing. Likewise, this option can be used in training classes where multiple students complete the same training activity.

Virtual Networking

With **virtual networking**, you can connect a VM to another VM to share files, surf the Web, and more. It is important to know how to use virtual networking so that you can make the best choices for a given situation.

VPC loads a software driver, called the **Virtual Machine Network Services Driver**, on your host OS. This driver is bound to each adapter in use. Figure 1-11 on the next page shows this software adapter in the Local Area Connection Properties dialog box.

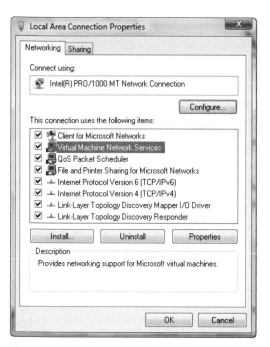

Figure 1-11 Local Area Connection Properties dialog box with Virtual Machine Network Services Driver

The purpose of the Virtual Machine Network Services Driver is to route Ethernet frames between VMs and (optionally) the network to which the host computer is connected. Figure 1-12 shows how this works. Each VM believes that it has up to four separate physical adapters. All Ethernet frames are intercepted by the virtual machine Network Services Driver. Based on the net- work configuration, the Ethernet frames are routed between the VMs or to the host's physical adapter.

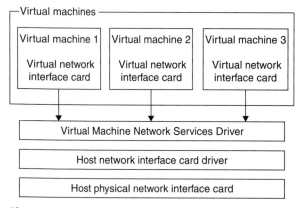

Figure 1-12 Virtual network architecture

VPC includes several options for the creation and use of virtual networking, which are described in the sections that follow.

Local Networking With the local option, all of the VMs communicate over a local network. The VMs will not have access to any network resources on the host computer system.

Shared Networking The shared networking option lets you access network resources through the host computer system with isolation for the VM from the network of the host computer system. The first VM network adapter can be assigned to a shared network, as shown in Figure 1-13. This shared network includes a virtual **Dynamic Host Configuration Protocol (DHCP)** server (which provides the IP configuration for the VM), and a virtual **Network Address Translation (NAT)** server (which translates IP addresses between the virtual network and the host's physical network). The VMs on the shared network will be assigned to the 192.168.0.0 network. For example, the shared network adapter (or gateway) in Figure 1-13 is 192.168.0.1 and the guest machine is 192.168.0.2. The host adapter i192.168.25.10 is shown for illustrative purposes.

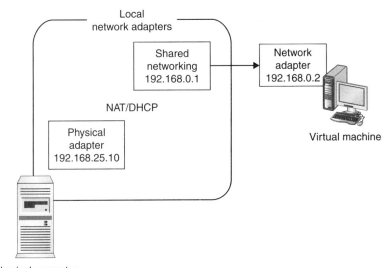

Physical computer

Figure 1-13 Shared network architecture

Network Adapter on the Physical Computer With the network adapter on the physical computer option, the VM is connected directly to the network served by the physical adapter of the host computer system. See Figure 1-14 on the next page. The VM will appear as if it were physically connected to the physical network with addresses on the same network as the physical network. If the physical network uses DHCP, the VM will receive an IP address configuration from the physical network's DHCP server.

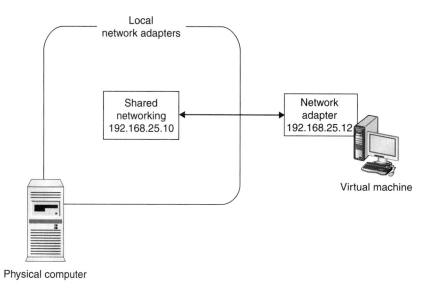

Figure 1-14 Network adapter on the physical computer

Microsoft Loopback Adapter Microsoft Windows Vista ships with a built-in network interface driver called the **Microsoft Loopback Adapter** that lets you create a local-only network interface device. This adapter can be extremely useful when you want to create multiple virtual networks, as shown in Figure 1-15. You install a Microsoft Loopback Adapter in the host computer for each virtual network that you will need. Then, you configure the VMs to access the virtual network supported by the Microsoft Loopback Adapter. You will need to assign network IP addresses for the machines on each virtual network.

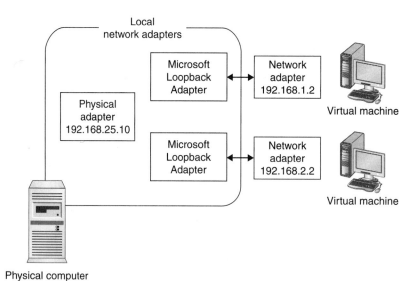

Figure 1-15 Microsoft Loopback Adapter

Virtual Machine Additions

One of the most important features in VPC is **Virtual Machine Additions** (**VMA**). VMA is software that you install in the guest OS that helps provide a boost in performance and added features within your VMs.

"Virtual Machine Additions" is a single noun. Therefore, a singular verb is required.

Performance Improvements If you are running Windows NT 4, Windows 2000, or Windows XP as a guest OS inside a VM, performance will be enhanced significantly with VMA.

Mouse Integration Prior to installing VMA, you must press the right Alt key to free the mouse in order to move it from a window within a VM. After installing VMA, you can move freely between the host OS windows and VM windows. VMA tracks the location of the mouse pointer and makes it active in the appropriate window.

Clipboard Integration VMA allows Clipboard integration. You can cut or copy from a VM to the host OS. Of course, you can cut or copy from the host OS to a VM. However, you cannot cut, copy, and paste from one VM to another. You can use the menus for the cut, copy, or paste operations, or use the equivalent shortcut keys: CTRL+X for cut, CTRL+C for copy, and CTRL+V for paste. This feature is not available in Virtual Server.

Drag and Drop Similar to the Clipboard integration, you can drag and drop from the host OS to a VM or vice versa. However, you cannot drag and drop between VMs. This feature is not available in VS.

Time Synchronization When VMA is installed, the system clocks of the VMs will be synchronized with the host machine's clock. This is important if you need to process files between the VMs.

Arbitrary Video Resolutions VMA allows you to select an arbitrary video resolution. This means that you can resize a VM window. This is significant. You will not need to adjust the screen resolution within the VM to change the size of the window displayed on the host computer. The text will shrink or grow as the window size is changed. This feature is not available in VS.

Customized Video Drivers VMA automatically installs video drivers that are optimized for the OS running in the VM. VMA provides better graphical performance and access to additional video RAM (from 4 MB to 8 MB).

Shared Folders VMA makes it easy to share folders between the host OS and the VMs. As shown in Figure 1-16 on the next page, you map a folder in the host OS to a drive letter in the VM. For example, the folder named Shared Folder, which resides on the host OS, is mapped to the Z drive on the VM. This feature is not available in VS.

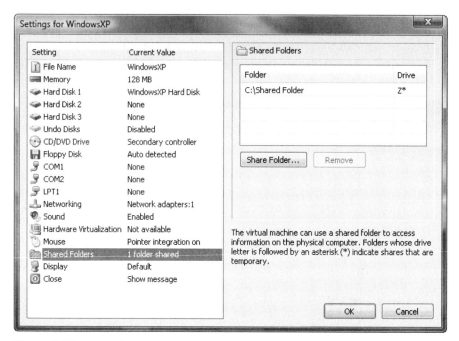

Figure 1-16 Shared folders

Installing Microsoft VPC

Before installing VPC, you should complete two important tasks. After accomplishing these two tasks, you will install Virtual PC 2007 on your host OS.

1. Visit the Microsoft Virtual PC 2007 Web page to research up-to-the-minute information about VPC.
2. Create an Internet-ready networking environment with Internet Connection Sharing.

After installing VPC, you will locate additional information that will assist you with the use of Virtual PC 2007. You will take a quick look at the Virtual PC 2007 Help pages. Lastly, you will surf to the blog pages for Ben Armstrong, the program manager on the core virtualization team at Microsoft.

Researching Microsoft Virtual PC 2007 on the Web

In this section, you will complete an activity to research information on VPC. You will find this information helpful when you install and use VPC.

Activity 1-1: Researching Microsoft Virtual PC 2007

Time Required: 10 minutes

Objective: Research Microsoft Virtual PC 2007 on the Web.

Description: In this activity, you will visit the Microsoft Virtual PC 2007 Web page and locate information on Microsoft Virtual PC 2007. This activity is useful if you want to learn more about Microsoft Virtual PC 2007.

1. If necessary, log on to your Host PC with a username of **Student** and a password of **Secret1**.
2. To launch the Microsoft Internet Explorer browser, click **Start** and then click **Internet**.

If you have another Web browser installed (for example, Mozilla Firefox), click **Start**, click **All Programs**, and then click **Internet Explorer**.

3. Type **Microsoft Virtual PC 2007** in the Live Search text box, and then press **Enter**.
4. To access the Microsoft Virtual PC 2007 Web page, click the **Microsoft Virtual PC 2007** link.

There are numerous links from which to choose. You want the home Web page for Microsoft Virtual PC 2007.

5. Click the **Read the product overview** button.
6. Click each of the navigational buttons (**Overview, Benefits, Key Features, Additional Information**, and **Product Specifications**), reading the information about Microsoft Virtual PC on each page.
7. Close the open windows.
8. Leave the computer logged on for the next activity.

Installing Internet Connection Sharing

You will most likely want your VMs to have access to the Internet for OS updates. With **Internet Connection Sharing (ICS)**, which is included in the Microsoft Vista OS, you can connect one or more VMs to the Internet using the Internet connection provided by the host computer. See Figure 1-17. ICS is the preferred Microsoft method for VMs to access the Internet.

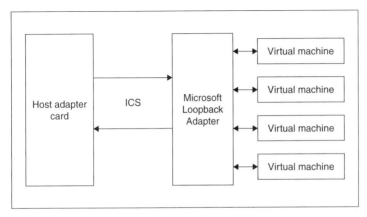

Figure 1-17 Internet Connection Sharing

The host computer needs two network connections:

- The local area network connection, automatically created by installing a network adapter in your host computer, connects to the computers on your main network.
- The other network adapter is provided by the Microsoft Loopback Adapter—a built-in network interface driver that lets you create a local-only network interface device.

The local area connection connects to the main network that provides Internet access for the host computer. ICS links the local area connection in the host computer to the Microsoft Loopback Adapter. The Microsoft Loopback Adapter then connects to the local area connection within each VM.

You need to ensure that ICS is enabled on the connection that has the Internet connection. By doing this, the shared connection can connect your VMs to the main network and gain access to the Internet.

ICS provides the services required by your VMs to access both the main network and virtual network shared by the VMs. These services are as follows:

- *Network Address Translation (NAT)*—Translates an IP address used within one network (in this case, the virtual network) to an IP address known within another network (in this case, the main network)
- *IP addressing*—Provides the IP address, subnet mask, and gateway address for each VM
- *Name resolution services*—Enables host names to be resolved to IP addresses

Activity 1-2: Installing Internet Connection Sharing

Time Required: 10 minutes

Objective: Configure ICS to connect the network adapter in the host computer to the Microsoft Loopback Adapter, which is used by each VM.

Description: In this activity, you will install a Microsoft Loopback Adapter. Next, you will enable ICS. This activity is useful if you want to permit the VMs to access the Internet.

1. If necessary, log on to your Host PC with a username of **Student** and a password of **Secret1**.

2. If the Microsoft Loopback Adapter has been previously installed, click **Start**, right-click **Computer**, click **Properties**, click **Device Manager**, click **Continue**, expand **Network adapters**, right-click **Microsoft Loopback Adapter**, click **Uninstall**, click **OK**, and then close the open windows.

3. To open the Add Hardware dialog box, click **Start**, click **Control Panel**, click **Classic View**, and then double-click **Add Hardware**.

4. When the User Account Control dialog box opens, click **Continue**.
5. Click **Next**, click the **Install the hardware that I manually select from a list (Advanced)** option button, and then click **Next**.
6. To select the Network adapters entry, scroll the Common hardware types list, click **Network adapters** (see Figure 1-18), and then click **Next**.

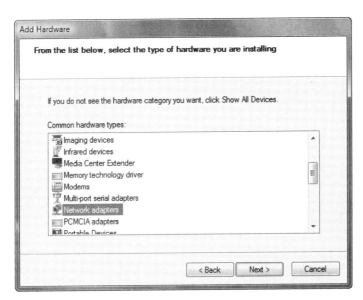

Figure 1-18 Select network adapters

7. To select the Microsoft Loopback Adapter, click **Microsoft** under Manufacturer, scroll the Network Adapter list, scroll and click **Microsoft Loopback Adapter**, and then click **Next**.
8. To install the Microsoft Loopback Adapter, click **Next**.
9. Wait for the installation to complete, and then click **Finish**.
10. To display the Network and Sharing Center, double-click **Network and Sharing Center**.
11. To display the Local Area Connection Properties dialog box, click the **View status** link for the Local Area Connection entry, and then click **Properties**.
12. When the User Account Control dialog box opens, click **Continue**.
13. To remove TCP/IPv6, clear the **Internet Protocol Version 6 (TCP/IPv6)** check box.

14. To enable ICS, click the **Sharing** tab, check the **Allow other network users to connect through this computer's Internet connection** check box (see Figure 1-19), click **OK**, and then click **Close**.

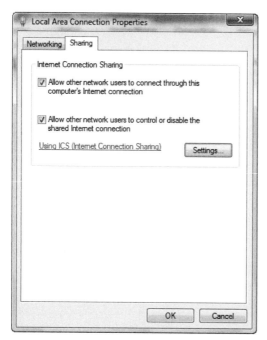

Figure 1-19 Enable Internet Connection Sharing

 Under Windows Vista, your Microsoft Loopback Adapter is hard configured to use 192.168.0.1. This is problematic if your external network is configured to use the 192.168.0.xxx subnet—but unfortunately there is nothing that you can do about this except to change your main network settings. (This text uses a host IP address on the 192.168.25.xxx network for exactly this reason.)

15. Close the open windows.
16. Leave the computer logged on for the next activity.

Installing Microsoft Virtual PC 2007

In this section, you will complete an activity to install Virtual PC 2007. The configuration and use of Virtual PC 2007 is covered in Chapter 2

Activity 1-3: Installing Microsoft Virtual PC 2007

Time Required: 10 minutes

Objective: Install Microsoft Virtual PC 2007.

Description: In this activity, you will access the Microsoft Virtual PC 2007 Web page and download Microsoft Virtual PC 2007. VPC is a free product available from this Web page. Next, you will install Microsoft Virtual PC 2007.

1. If necessary, log on to your Host PC with a username of **Student** and a password of **Secret1**.
2. To uninstall a previous installation of Microsoft Virtual PC 2007, click **Start**, click **Control Panel**, and then click the **Control Panel Home** link. Under the Programs link, click the **Uninstall a program** link, right-click **Microsoft Virtual PC 2007**, click **Uninstall**, click **Yes**, click **Allow**, wait for the uninstall to complete, and then close the open window.
3. To launch the Internet Explorer browser, click **Start**, and then click **Internet**.

If you have another Web browser installed (such as Firefox), click **Start**, click **All Programs**, and then click **Internet Explorer**.

4. Type **Microsoft Virtual PC 2007** in the Live Search text box, and then press **Enter**.
5. To access the Microsoft Virtual PC 2007 Web page, click the **Microsoft Virtual PC 2007** link.

There are numerous links from which to choose. You want the home Web page for Microsoft Virtual PC 2007 (the same Web page that you accessed in Step 4 of Activity 1-1).

6. To access the Microsoft Download Center, scroll and click the **Download now** link, scroll and click the **Microsoft Download Center** link located at the end of the sentence "To get Virtual PC 2007, download it via the …".
7. Scroll and locate the **32 BIT\setup.exe** (or **64 BIT\setup.exe**) file (see Figure 1-20 on the next page), and then click the **Download** button.

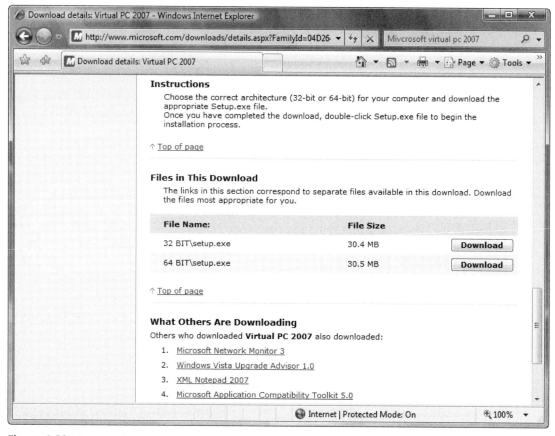

Figure 1-20 Download details

8. To run the setup, click the **Run** button.
9. Wait for the download to complete.
10. When the User Account Control dialog box opens, click **Continue**.
11. Click **Next**, click the **I accept the terms in the license agreement** option button, click **Next** twice, and then click the **Install** button.
12. Wait for the installation to complete, and then click **Finish**.
13. Close the open window.
14. Leave the computer logged on for the next activity.

Viewing Virtual PC 2007 Help

In this section, you will complete an activity to view Virtual PC 2007 Help pages. You will find this information helpful when you configure and use Virtual PC 2007.

Activity 1-4: Exploring Microsoft Virtual PC 2007 Help

Time Required: 5 minutes

Objective: Research information on Microsoft Virtual PC 2007.

Requirements: Completion of Activity 1-3.

Description: In this activity, you will explore the Microsoft Virtual PC 2007 Help. This activity is useful if you want to locate the answer to a question regarding the use of Microsoft Virtual PC 2007.

1. If necessary, log on to your Host PC with a username of **Student** and a password of **Secret1**.
2. To launch the Virtual PC Console, click **Start**, point to **All Programs**, and then click **Microsoft Virtual PC**.
3. If the New Virtual Machine Wizard appears, click **Cancel**.
4. To access the Virtual PC Help, click **Help** on the Virtual PC Console menu, and then click **Virtual PC Help**.
5. To access the Virtual PC Overview, click the **Contents** tab, expand **Virtual PC**, and then expand the **Concepts About Virtual PC** topic (see Figure 1-21).

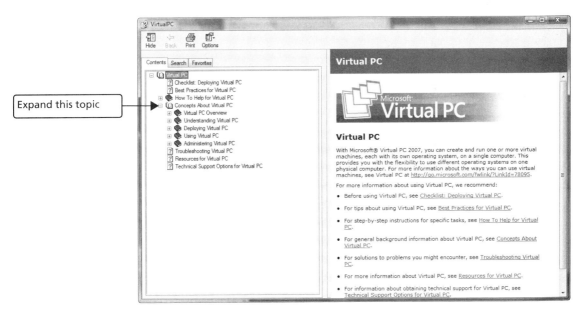

Figure 1-21 Expanded Virtual PC Help

6. Read the topics under **Virtual PC Overview**, **Understanding Virtual PC**, and **Using Virtual PC**.
7. Close the open windows.
8. Leave the computer logged on for the next activity.

Exploring a Virtual PC Blog

In this section, you will complete an activity to explore a blog supporting Virtual PC 2007. You will find this information helpful when you need to troubleshoot Virtual PC 2007 problems.

Activity 1-5: Exploring a Virtual PC Blog

Time Required: 5 minutes

Objective: Explore information on Virtual PC 2007 from a blog.

Description: In this activity, you will access the blog for Virtual PC 2007 maintained by Ben Armstrong. This activity is useful if you want to locate the answer to a question regarding the use of Microsoft Virtual PC 2007.

1. If necessary, log on to your Host PC with a username of **Student** and a password of **Secret1**.
2. To launch the Internet Explorer browser, click **Start**, click **All Programs**, and then click **Internet Explorer**.

If you have another Web browser installed (such as Firefox), click **Start**, click **All Programs**, and then click **Internet Explorer**.

3. Type **Virtual PC Guy's Weblog** in the Live Search text box, and then press **Enter**.
4. To access Ben Armstrong's Virtual PC Guy's WebLog, click the **Virtual PC Guy's WebLog** link.

There are numerous links from which to choose. You want the home Web page for Ben Armstrong's blog. Pick the one that does not have a : (colon) followed by a subject.

5. Scroll down and read information about Ben Armstrong in the left frame.

The information available on Ben Armstrong's blog will vary from day to day.

6. Scroll up and type **vista handy tip** in the Search box, and then press **Enter**.
7. Explore through the entries of interest to you.
8. Close the open windows.
9. Log off and shut down the computer.

Chapter Summary

- Virtual machine technology allows multiple operating systems to run concurrently on a single PC.
- VM technology greatly reduces hardware requirements for application development and testing, training, sales demonstrations, and help desks. It provides a way for developers to test multiple applications, gives students freedom to make changes that can be corrected or reset if needed, and allows support personnel to work with a variety of hardware and software configurations.
- The Microsoft Virtual PC 2007 desktop virtualization product features shared networking, file sharing, and mouse and keyboard integration, and provides an emulated sound card.
- Microsoft Virtual Server 2005 is a virtualization product that primarily supports server OSs.
- Microsoft Virtual PC 2007 is installed from the Web. To access information on VPC, you can access Help; for additional troubleshooting information, you can access a Virtual PC blog.

Key Terms

child—A new virtual hard disk that stores the changes when using differencing disks.

consolidation—Combining multiple OSs on a single computer system, resulting in higher rates of utilization.

Dynamic Host Configuration Protocol (DHCP)—Protocol for assigning dynamic IP addresses to computers on a network.

emulated hardware system—Duplicates the functions of one system with a different system.

guest operating system—An operating system running within a virtual machine.

host operating system—The OS that controls the physical computer system on which the virtual environment runs.

Internet Connection Sharing (ICS)—Allows the sharing of a single computer's Internet connection with other computers on the same local area network. With VMs, ICS enables one or more VMs to connect to the Internet using the connection provided by the host computer.

Microsoft Loopback Adapter—Built-in network interface driver shipped with Microsoft Windows Vista that allows the creation of a local-only network interface device and is useful when creating multiple virtual networks.

Network Address Translation (NAT)—Conversion of an Internet Protocol address (IP address) used within one network to a different IP address known within another network.

parent—An existing virtual hard disk. When using differencing, the parent is used to start the VM with changes made to the differencing disk.

.vhd—The file extension for the virtual hard disk file. This special file contains multiple files typically found on a computer system, including OS files, personal settings, Windows Registry, menus, programs, and data files.

virtual machine—The software that simulates enough hardware to allow multiple OSs to be set up on a host OS.

Virtual Machine Additions—Software that increases performance and adds important features to the guest machine; one of the most important features in Virtual PC 2007 that is not installed by default.

Virtual Machine Network Services Driver—Driver installed during the installation of Microsoft Virtual PC 2007 that routes Ethernet frames between VMs; frames can optionally be routed to the host computer's network.

virtual networking—The ability to connect a VM to another VM to share files, surf the Web, and more.

virtualization—The use of software to allow physical hardware to run multiple OS images in VMs at the same time.

.vud—The extension for the temporary file used as an undo disk. This file allows you to commit changes to the .vhd file, save the changes for later, or delete the changes and remove the .vud file.

Review Questions

1. With virtual machine technology, moving from one OS to another is accomplished by _____.
   a. Rebooting the system
   b. Pressing the F2 key
   c. Clicking the other OS window
   d. Logging off the system

2. The guest OS on a VM _____.
   a. Is the one running the physical computer system
   b. Is required to supply at least half of the hardware to function properly
   c. Is the one running inside the VM
   d. Is considered to be the actual VM

3. Which of the following are considered benefits in using virtualization? (Choose all that apply.)
   a. Increased hardware utilization
   b. Rapid provisioning
   c. System flexibility
   d. Hardware can be added to the new VM

4. Which of the following are considered common uses for virtualization? (Choose all that apply.)
   a. Application and program testing
   b. Training
   c. Sales demonstrations
   d. Help desks

5. Which of the following are considered drawbacks in using virtualization? (Choose all that apply.)
   a. All VMs are uniprocessor
   b. Rapid provisioning
   c. Each VM has the same set of fixed hardware
   d. Only 32-bit OSs can be run

6. The Microsoft products that are provided for virtualization are _____. (Choose all that apply.)
   a. Virtual PC 2008
   b. Virtual 2007
   c. Virtual PC 2007
   d. Virtual Server 2005

7. Virtual machine technology is intended to _____. (Choose all that apply.)
   a. Allow multiple OSs to run concurrently on a single PC
   b. Reduce hardware requirements for application development
   c. Allow support personnel to work with various software configurations
   d. Facilitate sales demonstrations of software applications

8. Virtual hard disks are _____ that are stored on the hard disk of the physical computer.
   a. Files
   b. Directories
   c. Virtual CD/DVDs
   d. Temporary files

9. A virtual hard disk has a file extension of _____.
   a. .vdd
   b. .vrd
   c. .vvd
   d. .vhd

10. The guest OS cannot _____.
    a. Access any area of the host's physical disk outside the .vhd file
    b. Partition the virtual hard drive
    c. Format the virtual hard drive
    d. Access a floppy disk
11. The undo disk has a file extension of _____.
    a. .vdd
    b. .vvd
    c. .vud
    d. .vhd
12. When an undo disk is enabled and the VM shuts down, the user can _____. (Choose all that apply.)
    a. Commit changes to the .vhd file
    b. Delete changes
    c. Save changes for another time
    d. Remove the .vhd file
13. Virtual networking _____.
    a. Is not available with VMs
    b. Allows multiple VMs to share files
    c. Refers to two computers working independently
    d. Requires no special software adapter
14. The Virtual Machine Network Services Driver _____.
    a. Is automatically installed with Microsoft Virtual PC 2007
    b. Intercepts none of the Ethernet frames
    c. Is used to route Ethernet frames between VMs and optionally between the VM and the host computer's network
    d. Is a hardware adapter
15. The Microsoft Loopback Adapter _____. (Choose all that apply.)
    a. Is a built-in interface drive that ships with Microsoft Windows Vista
    b. Enables the creation of a local-only network interface device
    c. Is extremely useful when creating multiple virtual networks
    d. Is installed in the host computer for each virtual network that is needed

16. One of the most important features in Virtual PC 2007 is the _____.
    a. Microsoft Loopback Adapter
    b. Network Adapter
    c. Virtual Machine Additions
    d. Virtual Machines Network Services Driver
17. Features provided by Virtual Machine Additions include _____. (Choose all that apply.)
    a. Drag and drop
    b. Network improvements
    c. Mouse integration
    d. Clipboard integration
18. Features provided by Virtual Machine Additions include _____. (Choose all that apply.)
    a. Performance improvements
    b. Time synchronization
    c. Arbitrary video resolutions
    d. Shared folders
19. Internet Connection Sharing _____. (Choose all that apply.)
    a. Is provided by Vista
    b. Connects one or more VMs to the host computer
    c. Is the preferred Microsoft method for VMs to access the Internet
    d. Requires two network connections
20. To acquire Virtual PC 2007, you must _____.
    a. Purchase it from a local computer store
    b. Purchase it from Microsoft
    c. Download it from the Virtual PC 2007 Web site
    d. Copy it from the Vista installation disk

Case Projects

Case 1-1: Adopting Virtual Machine Technology

Your manager, Craig, has been reading about virtual machine technology. He has received a request for 10 new PCs to run a Linux application for the Engineering Department at your company, which contracts to build roads and highways. The engineers have located an open source engineering program that enables the engineers to design structural highway systems. The engineering program requires 128 MB of RAM and 20 GB of hard disk space. Linux will require

512 MB of RAM and 20 GB of hard disk space. The engineering program has a text interface. The engineers have one-year-old PCs that run Windows Vista Business with 4 GB of memory, 250-GB hard drives, and the fastest processors available. Craig wants you to write a report on the possibility of using Virtual PC 2007 on the existing Windows Vista Business PCs to run the Linux application. Because the engineers are technically savvy, your report must provide the technical reasons for your recommendation.

Case 1-2: Using Virtualization Technology

Your college's computer club is considering showcasing various software projects they have been working on during the semester. Seven projects have progressed to a presentable state. Projects range from stand-alone game programs to transaction/database applications. The club's president is attempting to avoid the logistics of transporting 14 computer systems to multiple presentation sites. Also, she wants the presenters to bring up their applications with a minimum of transition time. The computer club has access to a new computer with 4 GB of RAM and two 500-GB hard disks. Provide a recommendation on the advisability of using Virtual PC 2007.

Case 1-3: Exploring Features of Virtual PC 2007

A local technology training academy wants to investigate the use of virtualized multiple desktop OSs. Their concern is reducing the costs to set up and maintain the computers for the 16 classes that are taught, which range from Microsoft Office 2007 to Microsoft Windows Server 2008. Analyze the features of Virtual PC 2007 that will permit the training firm to reduce the costs of keeping the classroom computers up to date, and summarize your analysis in a concise but technically detailed report.

chapter 2

Configuring Virtual Machines in Virtual PC 2007

After reading this chapter and completing the exercises, you will be able to:

- Create virtual machines
- Set global Virtual PC 2007 options
- Configure individual virtual machine settings

In the previous chapter, you learned about the Microsoft Virtual PC 2007 Console. In this chapter, you will learn to use the Virtual PC Console to bring your virtual machines (VMs) to life.

First, you will learn to use the New Virtual Machine Wizard to specify information that Virtual PC will need to create the proper VM for each chosen guest operating system (OS). You will learn to specify such items as the amount of random access memory (RAM) to allocate.

Virtual PC has a series of options that, when configured, affect the operation of all of the executing VMs. For example, the decisions that you make control the action of VMs or impact the performance of your executing VMs. To get the best performance from VPC, you will learn to set these properly.

Each VM that you create has settings that control various functions and features. Some of the settings are available in the New Virtual Machine Wizard, and all are available in Virtual PC Console. With proper management of memory, undo disks, security, shared folders, and networking, VMs on a host operating system can be productive work environments.

Creating Virtual Machines

The first step in using virtualization software is to plan which operating systems you need to run. The decisions you make here impact the number of VMs that can be run simultaneously in RAM. You might be planning to build a virtual network with two or more VMs running at the same time. Because the amount of physical RAM is critical, you will need to balance the amount of physical RAM available against the performance needs for each VM.

This section introduces you to the steps involved in creating a VM; you will perform these steps later in the chapter in the activity sections.

First Virtual Machine

In Chapter 1, you installed Microsoft Virtual PC 2007. The next task is to start creating VMs. When you launch Virtual PC 2007 for the first time, the New Virtual Machine Wizard runs. You will use this wizard to create your first VM. This section walks you through the contents of the New Virtual Machine Wizard.

For any VM, regardless of the specific settings, creating a working VM incorporates these general steps:

1. Specify the name and location of the .vmc virtual machine configuration file.
2. Select the operating system to be installed.
3. Review the amount of RAM and increase it, if additional applications are required.
4. Specify the name and location of the .vhd virtual hard disk file.
5. Review the configuration.

Virtual PC 2007 creates a shortcut for the VM in a folder (for example, C:\Users\Student\AppData\Roaming\Microsoft\Windows), which is used to propagate the list of VMs displayed within the Virtual PC 2007 Console.

 You can specify an existing virtual disk. Because the VMs reside in .vhd files, the files can be shared and copied. If you will be installing an operating system in the future, select the option to create a new VM.

The wizard begins by prompting you to select one of three options, as illustrated in Figure 2-1. These options specify how you will create the first VM.

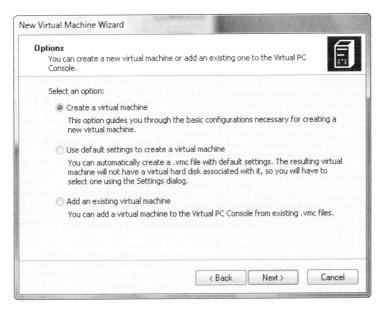

Figure 2-1 Virtual machine options

If you select the first option, Create a virtual machine, you will be using the wizard to create the **virtual machine configuration (.vmc)** file.

The second option, Use default settings to create a virtual machine, lets you create a VM without a virtual disk. This option requires you to specify the location of the .vhd file in the Settings dialog box at a later time.

If you select the third option, Add an existing virtual machine, you will specify an existing .vmc file as the new VM. This .vmc file could be copied when the .vhd file was copied or moved.

After you have worked with VMs for some time, you will most likely copy and share .vmc and .vhd files. When copying and sharing these files, you will use the second and third options. You will learn the specifics of copying VMs in Chapter 3.

In this chapter, you will use the first option to create a VM. After selecting the first option, you specify the name for the VM, as shown in Figure 2-2 on the next page. The name of the VM typically reflects the OS it is emulating. For example, the VM shown in Figure 2-2 is named Vista. If you will be building a network of Vista VMs, you would want to number the VMs sequentially: Vista01, Vista02, Vista03, and so on.

By default, the wizard creates the VM configuration file in the My Virtual Machines folder in Documents (for example, C:\Users\Student\Documents\My Virtual Machines). Both the .vmc and .vhd files and folder have the name that you specified in the wizard.

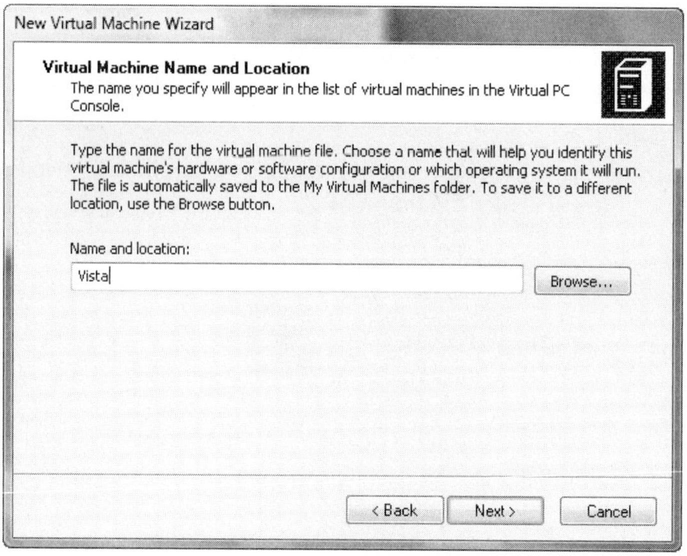

Figure 2-2 Naming the virtual machine

The OS dialog box then lets you specify the operating system (note that the previous step only named the VM; it did not associate the operating system with the VM). Because you specified the characters *Vista* in the previous dialog box, the wizard defaults to Windows Vista, as shown in Figure 2-3. If you specify My Vista, Vista88, or any other name containing the characters *Vista*, the wizard defaults to Windows Vista.

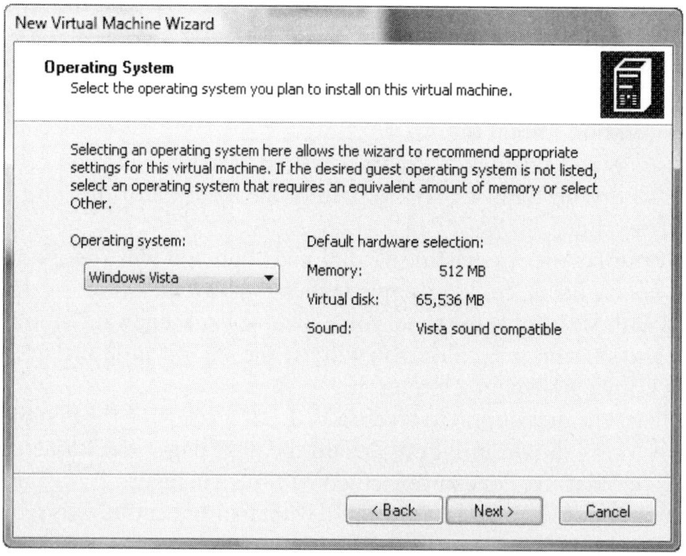

Figure 2-3 Windows Vista in Operating System dialog box

For each operating system, Virtual PC 2007 provides a default hardware selection, as summarized in Table 2-1. This information is useful when planning for the mix of operating systems you will be running at one time. You will need to have sufficient resources, particularly physical memory and hard disk space, to support whatever configuration you plan.

Table 2-1 Operating systems default hardware selections

Operating system	Memory required	Virtual disk space required	Sound card emulated
Windows 98	64 MB	16,384 MB	Sound Blaster compatible
Windows NT Workstation, Windows NT Server	64 MB	8,192 MB	Sound Blaster 16 compatible
Windows 2000	128 MB	16,384 MB	Sound Blaster 16 compatible
IBM OS/2	64 MB	2,048 MB	Sound Blaster 16 compatible
Windows XP	128 MB	65,536 MB	Sound Blaster 16 compatible
Windows Vista	512 MB	65,536 MB	Vista sound compatible
Windows 2000 Server	256 MB	16,384 MB	Sound Blaster 16 compatible
Windows Server 2003	256 MB	65,536 MB	Sound Blaster 16 compatible
Windows Server 2008	512	65,536 MB	Vista sound compatible
Other	128 MB	16,384 MB	Sound Blaster 16 compatible

If your operating system is not listed, select Other, and then change the memory and virtual disk size.

Next, the wizard presents the Memory dialog box, which lets you configure the VM's RAM. You need to change this setting if you plan to run a large number of applications. The Adjusting the RAM option button lets you change the memory setting from the recommended RAM, as shown in Figure 2-4 on the next page. You can move the slider or type numbers in the MB text box. The operating system type that you selected determines the default memory allocation, which you can change either in the wizard or after creating the VM.

After adjusting the RAM, you must add a new or existing virtual hard disk using the Virtual Hard Disk Options dialog box, as shown in Figure 2-5 on the next page. Because this is a new VM, you select the A new virtual hard disk option button. Of course, if you had an existing .vhd file, you would retain the An existing virtual hard disk option button.

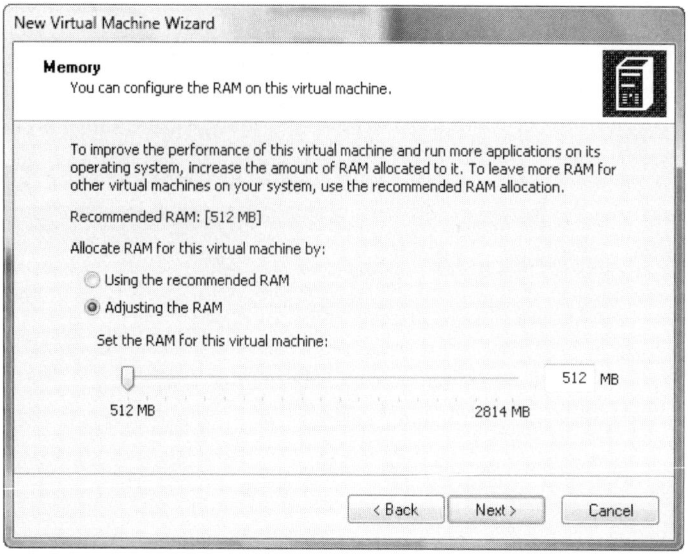

38 Chapter 2 Configuring Virtual Machines in Virtual PC 2007

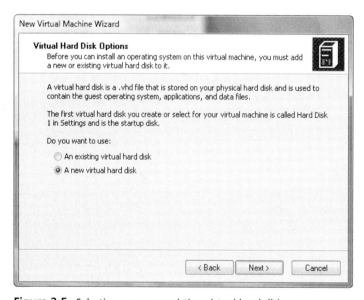

Figure 2-4 Adjusting the RAM

Figure 2-5 Selecting a new or existing virtual hard disk

Next, you create the virtual hard disk. Figure 2-6 shows the default size and location settings, which are controlled in the Virtual Hard Disk Location dialog box of the wizard. These defaults are adequate for most VMs.

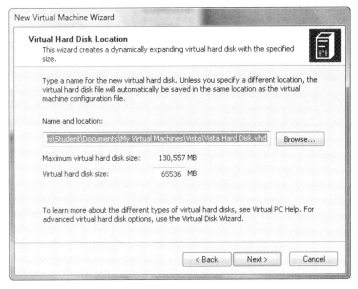

Figure 2-6 Specifying the .vhd location

Finally, the Completing the New Virtual Machine Wizard dialog box summarizes the VM settings. See Figure 2-7. Review this summary box carefully. If you need to make a correction, click Back until you reach the appropriate dialog box. Otherwise, clicking Finish closes the wizard and saves the .vmc configuration file.

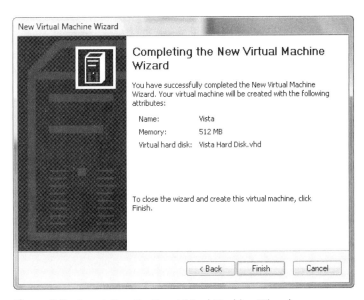

Figure 2-7 Completing the New Virtual Machine Wizard

Activity 2-1: Adding the First Virtual Machine

Time Required: 5 minutes

Objective: Use the New Virtual Machine Wizard to create the first VM.

Requirements: Completion of Activity 1-3.

Description: In this activity, you will start Microsoft Virtual PC 2007 and use the New Virtual Machine Wizard to create your first VM.

1. Log on to your Host PC with a username of **Student** and a password of **Secret1**.
2. To launch the Virtual PC Console, click **Start**, point to **All Programs**, and then click **Microsoft Virtual PC**.
3. To start the New Virtual Machine Wizard, click **Start**, click **Microsoft Virtual PC**, and then click **Next**.
4. To start the creation of a VM, ensure the **Create a virtual machine** option button is selected, and then click **Next**.
5. To name the VM, type **Vista01** (or Vista02, or Vista03, or whatever name you choose) in the Name and location text box, and then click **Next**.

If you discover that the VM name you have chosen has been previously used by you or another student, use the next number in sequence. For example, if you or a previous student has used Vista01, use Vista02, and so on.

6. Confirm that the default operating system is Windows Vista, and then click **Next**.

Contact your instructor if the default OS is not Windows Vista.

7. Confirm that the RAM allocation is **512 MB**, and then click **Next**.
8. To create a new virtual hard disk in the default location, click the **A new virtual hard disk** option button, and then click **Next** twice.
9. Review the VM attributes, and then click **Finish**.
10. Leave the computer logged on for the next activity.

Adding Additional Virtual Machines

After creating your first VM, you need to create the additional VMs that you require. You accomplish this by clicking New in the Virtual PC Console, as shown in Figure 2-8, and continuing with the New Virtual Machine Wizard. The New Virtual Machine Wizard only runs automatically when no guests are listed in the Virtual PC 2007 Console.

Figure 2-8 Virtual PC Console

Removing Virtual Machines

When you have completed the project that used the VMs, you might want to clean up the list of VMs listed in the Virtual PC Console. To remove an existing VM, click on the guest in the Virtual PC 2007 Console and click Remove. Removing a VM does not remove the .vmc and .vhd files. If you need to remove these files, locate the files in Windows Explorer and delete them. By default, the files are located under Documents in the My Virtual Machines folder. The folder will be the name that you assigned to the VM.

Activity 2-2: Adding and Removing a Virtual Machine

Time Required: 10 minutes

Objective: Add and remove VMs.

Requirements: Completion of Activity 1-3.

Description: In this activity, you will add a VM and remove the VM from the Virtual PC Console. Next, you will add the existing .vmc file to Virtual PC Console. This activity is useful if you need to readd the .vmc file for a previously removed VM.

1. If necessary, log on to your Host PC with a username of **Student** and a password of **Secret1**.
2. If necessary, to start Microsoft Virtual PC 2007, click **Start**, and then click **Microsoft Virtual PC**.
3. To start the New Virtual Machine Wizard and add a VM, click **New** and then click **Next**.
4. To create a VM, retain the **Create a virtual machine** option button, and then click **Next**.
5. To name the VM, type **Test1** (or Test2, or Test3, or whatever name you choose) in the Name and location text box, and then click **Next**.

6. To select an operating system, click the Operating system list box arrow, click **Windows XP,** and then click **Next.**
7. To practice adjusting the RAM, click the **Adjusting the RAM** option button, type **256** in the MB text box, and then click **Next.**
8. To specify a new virtual hard disk file, click the **A new virtual hard disk** option button, and then click **Next.**
9. To practice adjusting the size of the new virtual hard disk file, type **16384** in the MB text box, and then click **Next.**
10. Review the settings and click **Finish.**
11. To remove the Test1 VM, click **Test1** (or the name you used for your VM) in the Virtual PC Console, click **Remove,** and then click **Yes.**
12. To create a new VM with an existing virtual hard disk, click **New,** click **Next,** click the **Add an existing virtual machine** option button, click **Next,** click **Browse,** double-click the **Test1** (or Test2, Test3, and so on) folder, click **Test1** (or Test2, Test3, and so on), click **Open,** click **Next,** click **Finish,** and then click **OK.**

Use the instructions in Step 12 to create a VM for a copied .vhd file.

13. Leave the computer logged on for the next activity.

Configuring Global Virtual PC 2007 Settings

When setting up your VMs, you need to apply global and local settings, or options. Global options apply to all of the VMs, whereas local settings apply to individual VMs.

In this section, you will learn about global options, including settings for restoring, performance, hardware virtualization, screen mode, sound, and more. You change these settings using the Virtual PC Options dialog box, which is accessed using the File, Options menu.

The Virtual PC Options dialog box is illustrated in Figure 2-9. The dialog box is divided into two panes. The left pane contains each option with its current setting. As you click each entry in the left pane, the right pane changes to display the selections for that option. After completing your selections, click OK to save the changes and close the dialog box. If you change your mind about your selections, click Cancel.

Restore at Start

If you were running any VMs when you previously closed Virtual PC 2007, you could restore those VMs using the Restore at Start option (see Figure 2-9). The default setting restores virtual machines when Virtual PC is started.

Configuring Global Virtual PC 2007 Settings

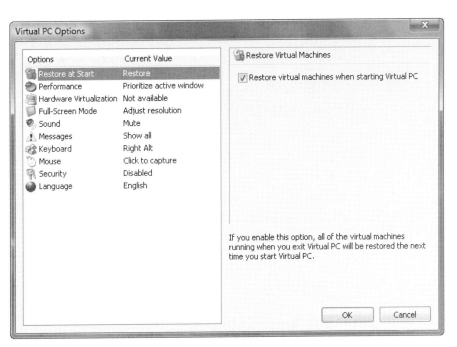

Figure 2-9 Available selection for the Restore at Start option

When you use this option, all VMs that were open when Virtual PC 2007 was closed at the end of the previous session are restored to their previous state the next time that Virtual PC 2007 opens. This is useful when you need to close your VMs quickly to complete another task and then return to your VMs.

Performance

You get your VMs to run faster by tweaking the Performance options. Figure 2-10 on the next page illustrates the defaults that provide maximum performance under most conditions.

To select how you want CPU time to be allocated between VMs, choose one of the following:

- To allocate all running VMs equal CPU time, you would use the All running virtual machines get equal CPU time option.
- To allocate more CPU time to the active VM than the background ones, select the Allocate more CPU time to the virtual machine in the active window option.
- So that VMs in the background do not have any CPU time, use the Pause virtual machines in inactive windows option.

You can also specify how you want CPU time to be allocated between the VMs and the host operating system. When all VMs are running in the background, choose one of the following:

- To give process priority to the host operating system, select the Give processes on the host operating system priority option.
- To give process priority to the VMs, select the Run Virtual PC at maximum speed option.

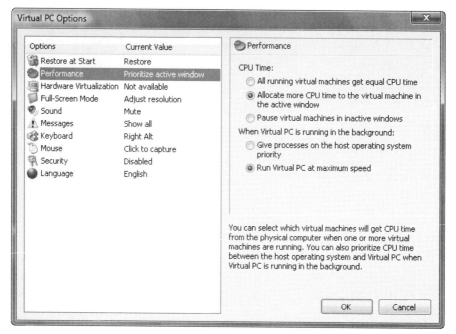

Figure 2-10 Available selections for the Performance option

Hardware Virtualization

Over the past few years, both Intel and AMD have implemented hardware that enables and is optimized for virtualization. Computer systems with the Intel-VT or AMD Pacifica chips have virtualization hardware. In systems with this virtualization hardware, you can enable hardware virtualization for all VMs. These systems experience performance gains related to memory utilization and input/output.

Full-Screen Mode

If the Full-Screen Mode option is configured to use video resolution matching, the screen resolution of a VM running in full-screen mode adjusts to match the host operating system. For example, if the host operating system is configured to use 1024 × 768 and the guest operating system is using 800 × 600, when in full-screen mode, the 1024 × 768 will be used.

To coordinate full-screen video resolution with the host operating system, check or clear the Adjust screen resolution so the host operating system is the same as the guest operating system check box, as shown in Figure 2-11.

When running your VMs, you might want to swap between window mode and full-screen mode. To change the screen mode of a VM, you do one of the following in the VM window:

- To change from window mode to full-screen mode, click the Action menu, and then click Full-Screen Mode, or press right Alt+Enter.

- To change from full-screen mode to window mode, press right Alt+Enter.

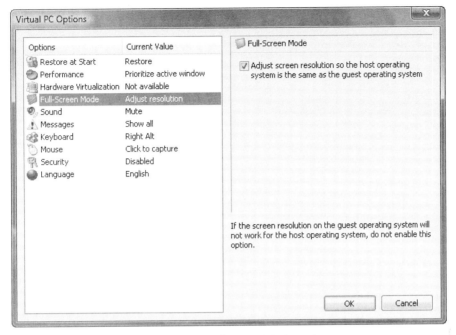

Figure 2-11 Available selection for the Full-Screen Mode option

Sound

You can turn sound on or off for each VM. If enabled on the VM, the foreground VM will be heard through the speakers. However, if enabled on the VM, the sound from the background VMs also can be heard through the speakers. You might not want to hear the sound from all of the VMs at the same time.

The Mute the sound for virtual machines in inactive windows option (see Figure 2-12 on the next page) blocks all sounds generated by background VMs. You should use this option when running multiple VMs that generate sound.

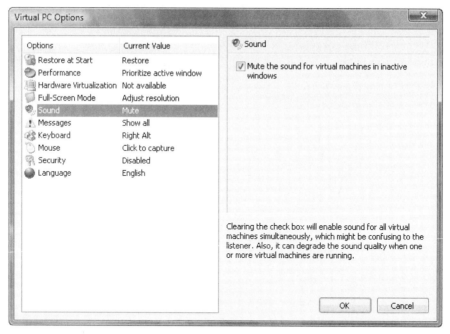

Figure 2-12 Available selection for the Sound option

Messages

Virtual PC 2007 displays messages for errors, warnings, and informational feedback. By default, all messages are displayed; however, you can suppress the display of all Virtual PC 2007 warning and information messages. As shown in Figure 2-13, you control the message display using the Don't show any messages check box.

Another option lets you suppress Virtual PC 2007 messages individually. When a message appears, it might have a Don't show this message again check box. Selecting this option prevents the same message from appearing in the future. If you later decide that you want to see these suppressed messages, you can use the Reset Messages button to show all messages you had previously suppressed in Virtual PC 2007.

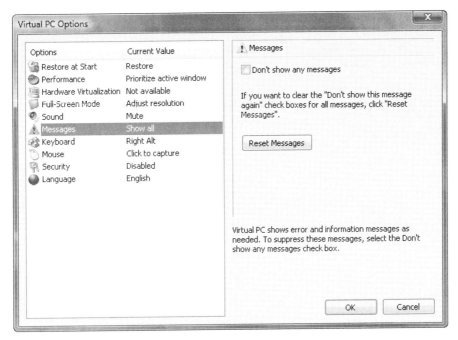

Figure 2-13 Available selection for the Messages option

Keyboard

The Keyboard option allows you to select the host key. By default, this is the right Alt key. The host computer listens for the host key. When the host key is pressed, the VM recognizes that the key combination is intended for the host operating system.

In general, the keyboard works the same for a VM as it does for the physical computer. However, you might have already considered the special case of Ctrl+Alt+Delete. This three-finger combination does not work in a VM because the key combination is reserved by the host operating system to perform a system shutdown. This problem is solved by the use of the host key. The Ctrl+Alt+Delete becomes host key+Delete.

To change the Current host key box, as shown in Figure 2-14 on the next page, you click the current host key name to select it (Right Alt in the figure), and then, on the keyboard, you press the key that you want to use as the host key. The name of the new host key is displayed in the Current host key box.

By default, Virtual PC 2007 supports the use of Windows key combinations only on the guest operating system. The default option works with the applications on the active VM. Using the Allow Windows key combinations list box arrow, you can allow key combinations to be recognized only on the host operating system, only on the guest operating system, or only in full-screen mode on the guest operating system. If you wanted to test an application on the guest by preventing any use of the Windows key combinations by the guest, you would select the On host operating system option.

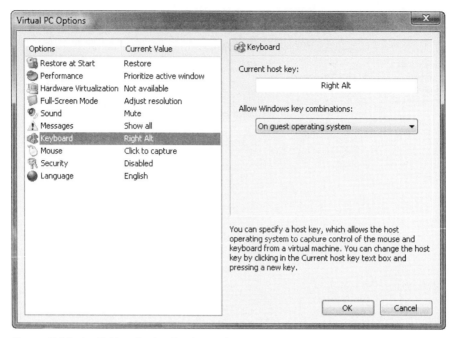

Figure 2-14 Available selection for the Keyboard option

Mouse

You can control the way that you use the mouse pointer within a VM by configuring the method for capturing the mouse pointer in the VM window. You control this by selecting one of two options in the Virtual PC Options dialog box, as shown in Figure 2-15:

- The Clicking in the virtual machine window option button controls the mouse pointer when you click in any VM window.
- The Moving the pointer into the virtual machine window option button controls the mouse pointer whenever you move the pointer over any VM window.

After the pointer is captured, you can release it from the VM using the host key (by default, right Alt).

For the best utilization of the mouse pointer, you should install Virtual Machine Additions, which you learned about in Chapter 1.

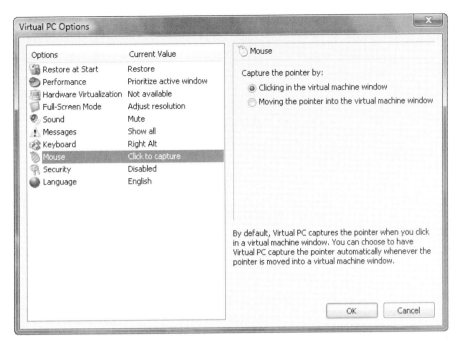

Figure 2-15 Available selections for the Mouse option

Security

If you are setting up your Virtual PC 2007 environment to be used by others, you should enable security. By default, security is not enabled. If you want to enable security, you can require that a user have administrator privileges for the areas shown in Figure 2-16 (on the next page).

You enable security in these areas:

- Options—Set global options that are presented in this chapter.
- Settings—Configure VM settings and virtual disk options.
- New Virtual Machine Wizard—Run the New Virtual Machine Wizard.
- Virtual Disk Wizard—Run the Virtual Disk Wizard.

In your day-to-day use of your VMs, you do not need to be overly concerned with these security settings. However, if you were building a set of VMs for use, for example, by various personnel, you might want to lock down your VM security options. You should turn off the ability to tinker with VM settings. Also, users would have no need to run either of the two wizards to create additional VMs and virtual hard disks.

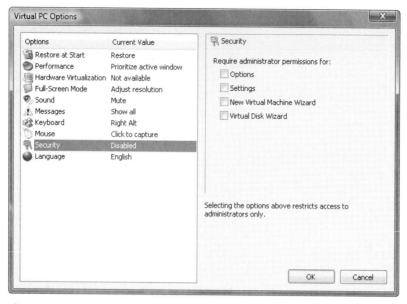

Figure 2-16 Available selections for the Security option

Language

When you installed Virtual PC, you specified the language to be used in the user interface. You can change the language by using the Language option, as shown in Figure 2-17. The languages available in Virtual PC 2007 are English, French, German, Japanese, Italian, and Spanish. Changing the language affects only the Virtual PC 2007 interface; no change is made for the language used by the guest operating system or the host.

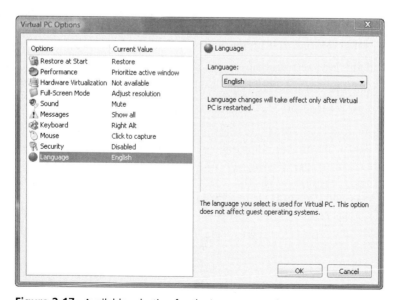

Figure 2-17 Available selection for the Language option

You must restart Virtual PC 2007 for a change of language to take effect.

Activity 2-3: Setting Global Options

Time Required: 5 minutes

Objective: Configure settings for all your VMs.

Requirements: Completion of Activities 2-1 and 2-2.

Description: In this activity, you will configure settings for all of your VMs.

1. If necessary, log on to your Host PC with a username of **Student** and a password of **Secret1**.
2. If necessary, to start Microsoft Virtual PC 2007, click **Start**, and then click **Microsoft Virtual PC**.
3. To open the Virtual PC Options dialog box, click the **File** menu, and then click **Options**.
4. To avoid starting VMs when Virtual PC 2007 starts, clear the **Restore virtual machines when starting Virtual PC** check box.
5. To reset the messages that are displayed in Virtual PC 2007, click **Messages**, click **Reset Messages**, and then click **OK**.
6. To capture the pointer by moving the pointer, click **Mouse**, and then click **Moving the pointer into the virtual machine window** option button.
7. Click **OK**.
8. Leave the computer logged on for the next activity.

Managing Individual Virtual Machine Settings

Now that you are familiar with the configuration settings that affect all of your virtual machines, you can begin to learn about changing the configuration of individual machines. Some local options are similar to global options, whereas others are available only for individual VMs. Local settings for individual VMs include options for filename, memory, hardware virtualization, sound, and more.

You access the configuration settings for an individual VM by selecting the VM in the Virtual PC 2007 Console and then clicking Settings. Figure 2-18 (on the next page) shows the settings for a VM in the Settings dialog box.

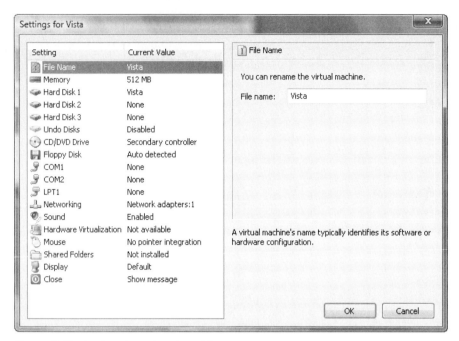

Figure 2-18 Settings for a virtual machine

Virtual Machine Name

You can change a VM's name by clicking File Name in the Settings dialog box, as shown in Figure 2-18, and then replacing the existing filename with the new name. If you misname a VM during creation, you can quickly change the name to correct the mistake.

When you rename a VM, the following elements are updated:

- The name of the VM configuration (.vmc) file
- The name of the VM shortcut, which changes the VM name shown in the list of VMs in Virtual PC 2007 Console
- The display name of the VM window

Changing the File Name setting does not change the name of the VM folder and the .vhd file.

If you manually rename a VM folder or .vhd file in Windows Explorer, Virtual PC 2007 cannot locate the VM. To correct this problem, remove the VM and add the renamed .vhd file using the New Virtual Machine Wizard.

Memory

You might want one VM to use more memory than the default settings provide. This is particularly true if you intend to run large applications on the VM. The host operating system and each open VM all share the same physical memory. You need to allocate enough memory to a VM to run the guest operating system well, but you do not want to allocate so much as to diminish the operations of the host operating system. Virtual PC 2007 requires about 32 MB overhead for each VM. You cannot exceed the amount of physical memory on the host computer.

You need to consider the effect of paging on VMs and the host computer. Recall that paging is the use of hard disk space to temporarily hold overflow pages from RAM. If you do not have enough memory allocated, you will see excessive paging, which causes processing to slow.

Virtual PC 2007 differs from other applications in how it uses memory. Most applications use memory in a fashion that allows the operating system to "page them out" when it needs to use their memory for something else. Doing this does cause things to be slower—but it does permit more applications to run.

However, Virtual PC 2007 holds the memory that it uses for each VM so that the host operating system cannot reclaim it—no matter how much it needs it—while the VM is running.

If a guest operating system needs to page excessively, then it is going to cause that VM to run slowly. But if the host operating system needs to page excessively, then everything (VMs included) will run slowly.

Adding more memory speeds processing as paging is reduced. However, after you have the memory required by the operating systems and applications available, adding even more memory does not make the system run any faster.

You cannot change the memory allocation if the VM is running or is in a saved state.

You can adjust the amount of memory that a VM uses by clicking Memory, and either typing the number of megabytes in the RAM text box or moving the slider until the RAM text box displays the number of megabytes. See Figure 2-19.

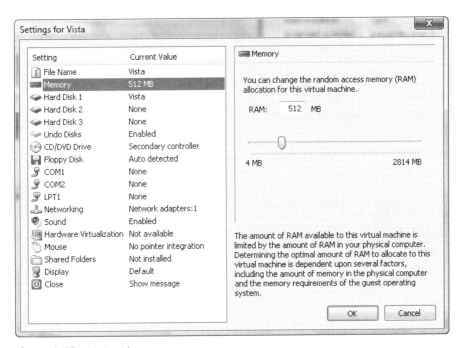

Figure 2-19 Settings for Memory

Hard Disks

You can have up to three emulated hard disks per VM, as shown in Figure 2-20. Recall that each of the emulated hard disks is stored on the host computer as a .vhd file.

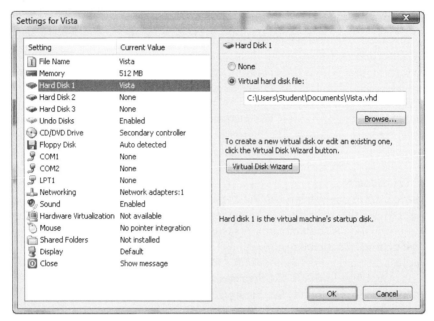

Figure 2-20 Settings for hard disks

You could use the three virtual hard disks in these ways:

- Hard Disk 1—This is the VM's start-up disk. For most installations, only this disk is required.
- Hard Disk 2—If you run out of hard disk space on Hard Disk 1, you can use this disk for the overflow of files.
- Hard Disk 3—If you need additional disk space, you can use this disk.

You could use Hard Disk 2 or Hard Disk 3 to access files in the virtual disk of another computer. The other VM cannot be running.

Virtual PC 2007 has a virtual disk wizard that accomplishes a number of activities for a selected hard disk, including the following:

- Creating a new virtual disk
- Reviewing the current settings—filename and location, file type, size, and version number
- Compacting the dynamically expanding virtual disk
- Converting a dynamically expanding virtual disk to a fixed-size virtual disk

After creating a new virtual hard disk, you will need to associate the created .vhd file with Hard Disk 2 or Hard Disk 3. You do this by clicking the Hard Disk (2 or 3) option in the Settings dialog box, clicking the Virtual hard disk file option button, and then clicking the Browse button to locate the .vhd file.

TIP You can gain additional flexibility by adding virtual hard disks, as needed. You might want to use a test virtual hard disk while testing an application. Remove the test virtual hard disk and attach the production hard disk when the application is completed.

Undo Disks

If you want to run a VM and reverse the changes made to the associated virtual disks, you should use the Undo Disks option; Figure 2-21 shows the Enable undo disks check box. You can control whether changes are made to the virtual hard disk, and if so, when the changes are made.

When you use undo disks, any changes you make to the virtual hard disk are saved to the undo disk files, not the original virtual hard disks. When you shut down the VM, you will select one of the following options:

- Save the undo file—Defer the decision on the undo file.
- Delete the undo file—Erase the undo file, leaving the original virtual hard disk as it was.
- Commit the changes—Save the changes to the original virtual disk.

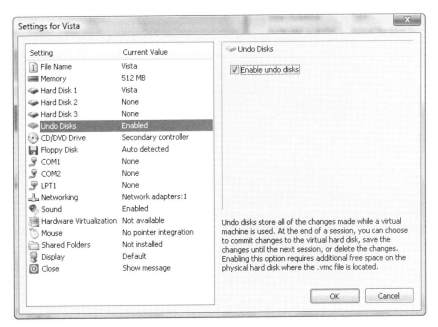

Figure 2-21 Settings for Undo Disks

You cannot selectively enable undo disks. Your decision applies to all of the hard disks in use by the VM. In other words, you cannot selectively delete or commit the changes on individual hard disks; you can only do so for all disks in a VM.

The undo disk file is created in the same folder as the VM configuration (.vmc) file. Prior to using undo disks, you must use Windows Explorer to verify that sufficient disk space is available on the host computer system.

CD/DVD Drive

If you are having problems installing a CD/DVD drive for your VM, you can change from the secondary IDE controller (the default as shown in Figure 2-22) to the primary IDE controller by clearing the Attach CD or DVD drive to Secondary IDE controller check box.

Only one CD/DVD drive can be used in Virtual PC 2007.

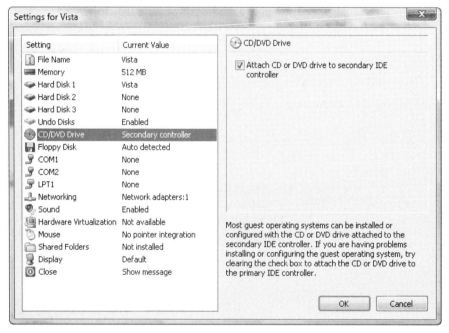

Figure 2-22 Settings for CD/DVD Drive controller

Floppy Disk

When you select the Automatically detect floppy disk option, which is the default setting shown in Figure 2-23, the VM automatically controls the floppy disk.

With this setting enabled, Virtual PC 2007 spends valuable processing time checking for the presence of a floppy disk. You can clear the Automatically detect floppy disk check box and avoid this performance hit.

Alternatively, you can capture the floppy drive in the VM when you are ready to access the floppy drive. To do so, locate the floppy disk icon on the status bar at the bottom of the VM window. Right-click the floppy disk icon, and then click Control Physical Drive A: to use a floppy disk inserted in the physical computer's floppy drive.

Managing Individual Virtual Machine Settings   **57**

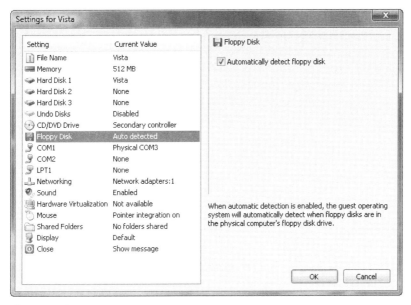

Figure 2-23 Settings for Floppy Disk

COM Ports

If you have a modem connected to the host computer and you want to use it on a VM, select the appropriate COM setting and specify the port on the host computer to which the modem is attached. For example, associate COM1 in the VM with COM3 in the host machine.

Figure 2-24 shows an example of these settings for a modem on a COM port.

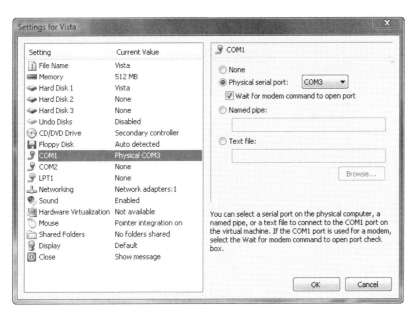

Figure 2-24 Settings for COM1 port

It is a good idea to check the Wait for modem command to open port check box. This simplifies the use of communication ports on the host operating system. When a program running on the VM attempts to access the COM port, the port is captured. This option causes Virtual PC 2007 to wait for an AT modem command to be sent for the port. If the program using the COM port times out after capturing the port, the port is released to the host operating system.

There are four possible settings for a COM port:

- None—No device is connected. This is the default setting.
- Physical serial port—Use either the COM1 or COM2 serial port on the VM as described previously. Associate COM1, COM2, COM3, or COM4 on the host computer to either COM1 or COM2 on the VM.
- Named pipe—Create a serial connection between two VMs. Use a local named pipe path in the form of \\.\pipe\mypipename. This serial connection simulates a null modem cable.
- Text file—Send COM port output from the VM to a text file. You can use this option to debug communications programs.

LPT1

Figure 2-25 shows that you can connect a VM to a printer through the LPT1 port on the physical computer. Only the LPT1 printer port is supported. After the parallel port is captured, the connected printer is accessible to the VM. You would use this setup to permit the applications running on the VM to print documents and reports.

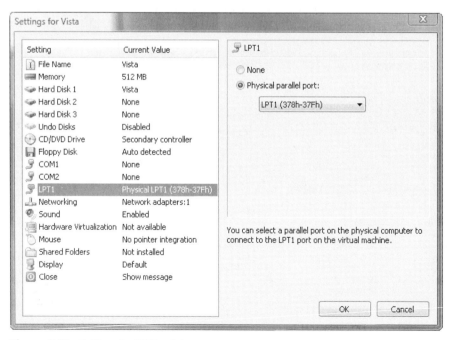

Figure 2-25 Settings for LPT1 printer port

Networking

You can specify up to four emulated network adapters to be used by a VM. With up to four adapters, you can build complex networks. For example, a guest operating system could route between network segments. See Figure 2-26 for the four adapters, which can be configured as indicated. You can assign each emulated adapter to one of the following settings:

- Not connected—Networking is not available on this adapter. You would use this option when either the guest or host computer is not on a network.
- Local only—Networking only is enabled between VMs. You would use this option when the adapter will not require access to the host computer.
- Network adapter on the physical computer—The network adapter is connected directly to the adapter on the host. You would use this option when you need the guest and host to be on the same physical network.
- Microsoft Loopback Adapter—The network adapter is connected to a Microsoft Loopback Adapter installed in the host computer. You would use this option when you need to create multiple virtual networks between the VMs.
- Shared networking (NAT)—The network adapter is connected to a virtual network created by Virtual PC 2007. Only the first adapter can be assigned to Shared networking (NAT). You would use this option when you need to connect the VM to a network that includes virtual DHCP and Network Address Translation servers.

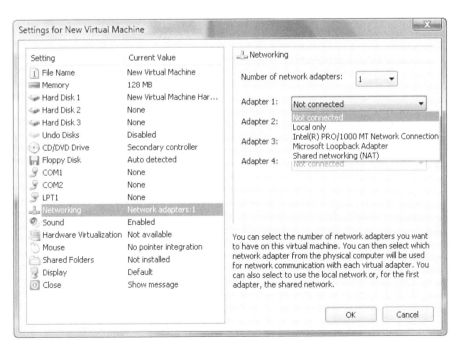

Figure 2-26 Settings for network adapters

Refer to the "Virtual Networking" section in Chapter 1 for additional information on the use of the various networking choices.

Problems with Shared Networking Shared networking in a virtual environment involves a number of potential problems. Recall that in Chapter 1, you installed Internet Connection Sharing, which overcomes the problems described here. If DHCP is available on the host's physical network and network isolation is not necessary, the network adapter on the physical computer setting is generally preferred.

Virtual PC 2007 provides a virtual DHCP server that provides the IP configuration for each VM that uses shared networking. The provided IP address is on the 192.168.131.0 network; individual VMs are assigned a value from 192.168.131.1 to 192.168.131.253. The IP address for the default gateway is 192.168.131.254. The IP address of the DNS server is the IP address of the host computer.

Virtual PC 2007 does not provide an interface to manually specify the IP network assigned by the virtual DHCP server. You are stuck with the 192.168.131.0 network. This becomes a problem if the host computer is on the 192.168.131.0 network. Because you cannot have two interfaces on the same network, you must change the network address of the host computer. To use Shared networking, you should configure the operating system installed on the VM to obtain an IP address from a DHCP server automatically.

Shared networking does not support inbound port mapping. External computers are unable to access a server running in the VM or any ports on the VM. Shared networking also does not support networking between VMs or from the host operating system to the VM.

Internet connectivity when using Shared networking has its own set of issues. With shared networking, the VM shares the Internet connection that is set up on the host operating system, regardless of whether the host is connected through a modem or a local area network (LAN).

- Some networking software, such as chat programs, might not work correctly under Shared networking because they require a static IP address.
- Users who are not administrators or members of the administrators group on the host operating system will be unable to send or receive pings or other Internet Control Message Protocol (ICMP)–based network traffic when shared networking is activated.

Sound

You can enable sound on each VM. The Enable sound card setting of each VM controls whether an emulated sound card is available on the VM. See Figure 2-27. By default, the sound card is enabled. If you have only one VM that requires an emulated sound card, clear the Enable sound card check box on all of the other VMs.

Managing Individual Virtual Machine Settings

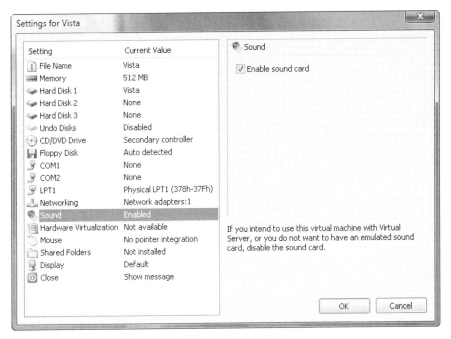

Figure 2-27 Settings for sound

If you anticipate running your VM using Virtual Server 2005, you must disable the sound card. Virtual Server 2005 does not support emulated sound cards.

Mouse

After you install Virtual Machine Additions, you can move the mouse pointer freely between a VM window and the host operating system. The default setting for mouse control is Use pointer integration.

Shared Folders

You can share folders between the host computer system and a VM. To share a folder, use the Share Folders setting to open the Browse for Folder dialog box. You will be able to select the folder that you need from the host computer system. See Figure 2-28 (on the next page).

You can select a drive letter or accept the default drive letter; drive letters are assigned in reverse order (Z then Y, and so on). If you anticipate needing to share files frequently between the VM and the host system, check the Share every time check box. Temporary shares are indicated by an asterisk after the drive letter.

Unlike the mapping of drive letters for network shares, this shared folder mapping only occurs between the VM and the host computer system. No other computers have access to this private share.

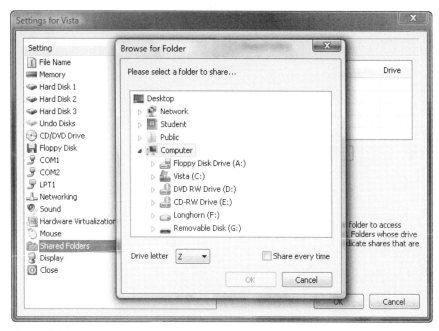

Figure 2-28 Browse for Folder

Display

You have a number of options that control the display of the VM, as shown in Figure 2-29.

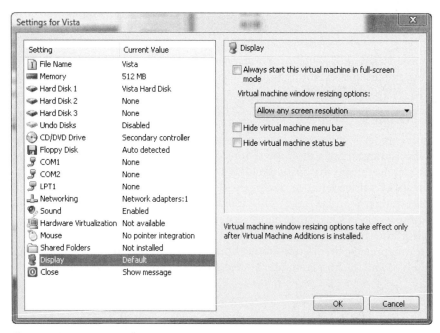

Figure 2-29 Settings for Display

You can choose to start the VM in full-screen mode, or you can set the display resizing options for the VM by selecting options for allowing any screen resolution, only using standard screen resolutions, or using guest operating system screen resolution, which prevents the sizing of VM windows.

Virtual PC 2007 supports the following standard resolutions:

- 640 × 480
- 800 × 600
- 1024 × 768
- 1152 × 864
- 1280 × 1024
- 1600 × 1200

You can control whether the menu or status bar is visible or hidden by checking the appropriate check box:

- Hide virtual machine menu bar—Controls whether the menu bar is displayed at the top of the VM window
- Hide virtual machine status bar—Controls whether the status bar is displayed at the lower-left corner of the VM window

Close

Finally, you can control the way that the VM can be shut down by choosing from one of three options:

- Save state—Automatically saves the state of the VM. The next time the VM is run, it will start from where it was saved.
- Shut down—Initiates a shut down as if you had selected Shut down in Windows.
- Turn off—Immediately shuts down the VM without saving any open files or operating system settings. This would be equivalent to pulling the power plug on a personal computer.

You must select one of these three options to close the VM. See Figure 2-30 (on the next page).

If you know in advance how you will be shutting down the VM, you can click the Automatically close without a message and option button. You must also select from the choices in the Show message with these options at close setting. The Close setting offers an additional Show message option, Turn off and delete changes, which is available when you are using undo disks.

Chapter 2 Configuring Virtual Machines in Virtual PC 2007

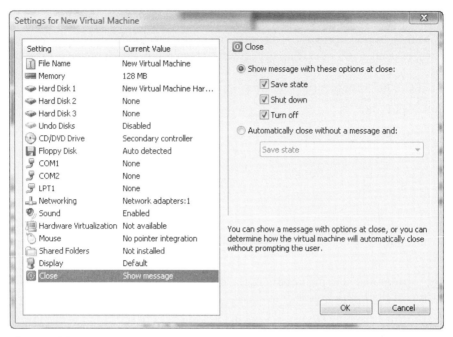

Figure 2-30 Settings for close messages

Activity 2-4: Setting Individual Virtual Machine Settings

Time Required: 10 minutes

Objective: Set configuration settings for one of your VMs.

Requirements: Completion of Activities 2-1, 2-2, and 2-3.

Description: In this activity, you will practice configuring settings for one of your VMs.

1. If necessary, log on to your Host PC with a username of **Student** and a password of **Secret1**.

2. If necessary, to start Microsoft Virtual PC 2007, click **Start**, and then click **Microsoft Virtual PC**.

3. To configure individual VM settings, click **Test1** (or Windows XP if you have previously completed Activity 2-4), and then click **Settings**.

4. To change the filename, click **File Name**, and then in the File name text box, replace Test1 with **Windows XP**.

5. To practice changing the memory, click **Memory**, and then type **192** in the MB text box.

6. To practice enabling undo disks, click **Undo Disks**, and then check the **Enable undo disks** check box.

7. To practice gaining performance relative to use of the floppy disk, click **Floppy Disk**, and then clear the **Automatically detect floppy disk** check box.
8. To practice using the Microsoft Loopback Adapter in the host computer, click **Networking** and then click **Microsoft Loopback Adapter** from the Adapter 1 drop-down list.
9. To practice setting the display to use only standard screen resolutions, click **Display**, click the VM window resizing options list box arrow, and click **Only use standard screen resolutions**.
10. To practice setting the close options, turn off the VM and delete the changes in the undo disks, click **Close**, click the **Automatically close without a message and** option list box arrow, and then click **Turn off and delete changes**.
11. Click **OK**.
12. Leave the computer logged on for the next activity.

Activity 2-5: Creating an Additional Virtual Machine

Time Required: 5 minutes

Objective: Use the New Virtual Machine Wizard to create a VM.

Requirements: Completion of Activity 2-1.

Description: In this activity, you will start Microsoft Virtual PC 2007 and use the New Virtual Machine Wizard to create a VM for use in Chapter 3.

1. If necessary, log on to your Host PC with a username of **Student** and a password of **Secret1**.
2. If necessary, to start Microsoft Virtual PC 2007, click **Start**, and then click **Microsoft Virtual PC**.
3. To add a VM, click **New** and then click **Next**.
4. To create a VM, retain the **Create a virtual machine** option button, and then click **Next**.
5. To name the VM, type **Longhorn1** (or Longhorn2, Longhorn3, and so on) over New Virtual Machine in the Name and location text box, and then click **Next**.
6. To select an operating system, click the **Operating system** drop-down menu and click **Other**, and then click **Next**.
7. To adjust the memory, click **Adjusting the RAM** option button, type **512** in the RAM text box, and then click **Next**.
8. To set the Virtual Hard Disk options, click the **A new virtual hard disk** option button, click **Next**, type **65536** in the **Virtual hard disk size** text box, and then click **Next**.
9. Review the attributes and click **Finish**.
10. To configure settings for the Longhorn VM, click **Longhorn1** and click **Settings**.

11. To set the network adapter to use the Microsoft Loopback Adapter, click **Networking**, click the **Adapter 1** drop-down list arrow, and then click **Microsoft Loopback Adapter**.
12. To turn off sound, click **Sound**, clear the **Enable sound card** check box, and then click **OK**.
13. Close the Virtual PC Console.
14. Log off and shut down the computer.

Chapter Summary

- You use the New Virtual Machine Wizard to create your first VM when Virtual PC 2007 is first launched. The wizard has three options for creating a VM and the corresponding files.
- Use the memory and hard disk requirements in Table 2-1 when planning to run multiple operating systems at one time. Adjustments to the memory and other settings can be made in the wizard or after the VM is created.
- Virtual PC 2007 lets you apply globally many options to enhance performance, customize settings, and save current machine states and settings. Options that can be applied globally to all VMs include settings for restore at start, performance, hardware virtualization, screen mode, sound, messages, keyboard, mouse, and security.
- Within Virtual PC 2007, you can configure settings for individual VMs. These settings manage VM name, hard disks, CD/DVD drive, floppy disk, COM ports, LPT1, networking, folder sharing, and close, along with many of the settings that can be applied globally.

Key Terms

virtual machine configuration (.vmc) file—The file that stores the VM configuration information.

Review Questions

1. Choosing the Use default settings to create a VM in the New Virtual Machine Wizard allows you to _____.
    a. Use the wizard to create the .vmc file
    b. Specify an existing .vmc file
    c. Create a VM without a virtual disk
    d. Does not exist as a choice

2. When planning to use Virtual PC 2007 and a mix of operating systems running simultaneously, planning for proper resources such as _____ and _____ is important.
   a. Physical memory, hard disk space
   b. Application purchases, operating systems
   c. Manpower, electrical outlets
   d. Physical memory, operating systems
3. When Virtual PC 2007 is closed, the current session _____.
   a. Is always lost no matter how you close the session
   b. Can be saved if the Save state and save changes option is chosen
   c. Will always be saved no matter which option is chosen
   d. Is still active
4. When interacting with a CPU-intensive application in a VM, for optimal performance, you should select the _____ option.
   a. All running virtual machines get equal CPU time
   b. Allocate more CPU time to the virtual machine in the active window
   c. Pause virtual machines in active windows
   d. Accelerate virtual machines in active windows
5. When allocating CPU time between VMs, the choice Pause virtual machines in inactive window will _____.
   a. Not allocate any CPU time to all running virtual machines
   b. Allocate the active virtual machine more CPU time than the background ones
   c. Allocate CPU time to the machines in the background only
   d. Not allocate any CPU time to the virtual machines in the background
6. Changing the screen mode of a VM can be done by _____. (Choose all that apply.)
   a. Clicking the Action menu, and then clicking Full-Screen mode
   b. Pressing left Alt+Enter
   c. Clicking the Action menu, and then clicking screen mode
   d. Pressing right Alt+Enter
7. You should _____ when you hear multiple, overlapping sounds coming from the speakers.
   a. Select the sound icon on the host operating system
   b. Select the Mute the sound for virtual machines in active windows option
   c. Select the Mute the sound for virtual machines in inactive windows option
   d. Do nothing, it is handled automatically and never a problem

8. By default in Virtual PC 2007, all messages _____.
   a. Are suppressed and must be activated before they can be displayed
   b. Are printed
   c. Are stored
   d. Are displayed

9. The default host key for the host operating system is _____.
   a. Right Alt key
   b. Left Alt key
   c. Right Ctrl key
   d. Left Ctrl key

10. The best utilization of the mouse pointer occurs after the installation of _____.
    a. Microsoft Vista operating system
    b. Virtual Machine Additions
    c. Virtual PC 2007
    d. Virtual Server 2005

11. In Virtual PC 2007, security is _____.
    a. Set in the New Virtual Machine Wizard
    b. Automatically enabled; the user doesn't need to set it
    c. Not enabled and needs to be set
    d. The same as the security on the host system

12. Languages available for the Virtual PC 2007 interface include _____. (Choose all that apply.)
    a. German
    b. Portuguese
    c. Spanish
    d. English

13. When a VM is renamed, the following elements are updated: _____. (Choose all that apply.)
    a. The name of .vmc file
    b. The name of the VM shortcut, which changes the VM name shown in the list of VMs in Virtual PC 2007 Console
    c. The display name in the VM window
    d. The name of the .vhd file

14. Virtual PC 2007 requires about _____ MB overhead of memory for each VM.
    a. 64
    b. 128
    c. 32
    d. 512
15. The total number of emulated disks you can have is _____.
    a. 1
    b. 2
    c. 3
    d. 4
16. When undo disks are enabled, you can _____. (Choose all that apply.)
    a. Reverse changes made to associated virtual disks
    b. Control if and when changes are made to the virtual hard disk
    c. Save the undo file, which will defer the decision on the undo file
    d. Delete the undo file, which will erase the undo file
17. Networking on a VM can be done by specifying emulated adapters, which you can assign with the _____ setting. (Choose all that apply.)
    a. Not connected
    b. Local
    c. Microsoft Loopback Adapter
    d. Shared networking
18. With shared networking, the VM _____. (Choose all that apply.)
    a. Can function as a Web server
    b. Can network with other VMs
    c. Shares the Internet connection that is set up on the host operating system
    d. Automatically obtains an IP address from a DHCP server
19. With shared folders, _____. (Choose all that apply.)
    a. Sharing occurs between the host computer system and a VM
    b. Sharing occurs between multiple VMs
    c. You share by selecting Share Folder
    d. Mapping of drive letters functions the same as for network shares

20. To shut down a VM running Windows Vista Business, you choose the _____ option. (Choose all that apply.)
    a. Save state
    b. Shut down
    c. Turn off
    d. Sleep

Case Projects

Case 2-1: Calculating Virtual Machine Memory

The student lab will be set up using virtual machines next semester. The computers in the student lab have 1 GB of memory. Lab staff have asked that you participate in the planning phase prior to the setup of the VMs. They have determined they want to run Vista Business as a host operating system, with one instance of Windows XP and two instances of Windows Server 2003 running in virtual mode. What is your recommendation for memory? Show your calculations.

Case 2-2: Identifying Performance Problems

A former classmate, Ricardo, is having problems with the VMs on his laptop; it seems it takes forever for some of the applications to finish. You don't have time to fix the problems; however, a checklist of performance-tuning ideas might help Ricardo isolate the problem. Create a list of the settings that should be checked or possibly reset and identify what those settings should be. Put the list of settings in the order that you feel would be most logical.

Case 2-3: Configuration Requirements

You have been asked to set up the VMs in a new training lab. The training classes use the sets of applications with the requirements indicated in Table 2-2.

Table 2-2 Requirements for training lab

Guest operating system(s)	Application	Special requirements
Windows XP	Office XP	Discard changes made after lesson completion
Windows Vista	Office 2007	Discard changes made after lesson completion
Windows Server 2003	None	Network three VMs on a local network
Windows Server 2003	None	Discard changes made after lesson completion
Windows Vista	Office 2007	Use files in folder on host operating system

Prepare a detailed report indicating how you will configure the VMs to meet the requirements as outlined in Table 2-2.

chapter 3

Installing Microsoft Windows Vista and Server 2008 Operating Systems

After reading this chapter and completing the exercises, you will be able to:

- Install the most current Microsoft client and server operating systems
- Install and use Virtual Machine Additions
- Clone existing virtual machines

In this chapter, you will learn how to install Microsoft's newest operating systems into Virtual PC 2007 virtual machines. Installing an OS can be an intricate process because of the many decisions you need to make during the installation. First you will learn about the steps involved in installing an operating system to help familiarize yourself with the various dialog boxes and windows that are part of the installation of a modern Windows operating system.

After you have reviewed the concepts behind OS installation, you will install your first guest OS, Microsoft Windows Vista Business. These steps occur starting in Activity 3-1. In later activities, you will install Microsoft Server 2008, previously known as the Longhorn server.

To get the full benefits of Microsoft's virtual machines, you must install Virtual Machine Additions. Finally, you will learn a technique to reduce the time to install multiple operating systems in virtual machines.

Installing Operating Systems in Virtual PC 2007

In Chapter 1, you installed Virtual PC. You created your first virtual machine and customized many settings for VPC in Chapter 2. Now you will begin to experiment with the true benefit of VPC, namely, its capacity for running multiple operating systems on a single host PC.

Before installing the Vista Business and Microsoft Server 2008 operating systems, you must have the installation DVDs for these two programs available so that you can complete the chapter's activities.

The first step in installing an OS in VPC is to start the virtual machine previously created for the intended OS. Virtual PC displays a number of initial text screens requiring the proper responses.

Initial Text Screens

You can bypass these initial text screens by inserting the OS installation CD/DVD and pressing a key on the keyboard when the "Press any key to boot from CD or DVD" message appears. The timing for this task can be a bit tricky! You might miss this message or VPC might not display this message and go directly from the BIOS screen to the PXE Boot Screen.

You will need to know how to interact with these initial text screens to install an operating system. Also, you might need to make a change in the BIOS. For example, you might want to use the numeric keypad and might want to turn the Num Lock on.

BIOS Setup Utility
When the virtual machine starts, you will see a BIOS screen that resembles the BIOS screen of a physical computer. If you press the Delete key when the BIOS screen is displayed, you can display the BIOS Setup Utility, as shown in Figure 3-1. There are not many reasons to access the operating system setup utility screen. However, you might want to turn on the Num Lock to use the numeric keypad. To turn on Num Lock within the BIOS Setup Utility, press the right arrow, press the down arrow twice, press Enter, press the down arrow, press the + key, press the F10 key, and then press Enter.

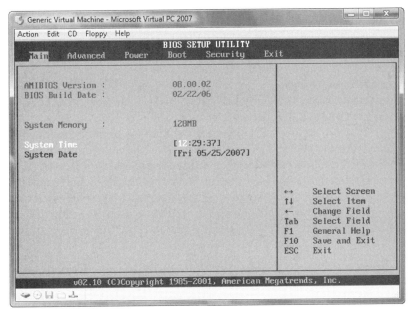

Figure 3-1 BIOS Setup Utility

PXE Boot The network adapter emulated by VPC is capable of booting using the **Preboot Execution Environment (PXE)**. VPC will display a screen for the PXE Boot Agent, as shown in Figure 3-2. PXE is pronounced "pixie." The PXE Boot Agent allows a workstation to boot from a server on a network prior to booting the operating system on the local hard drive.

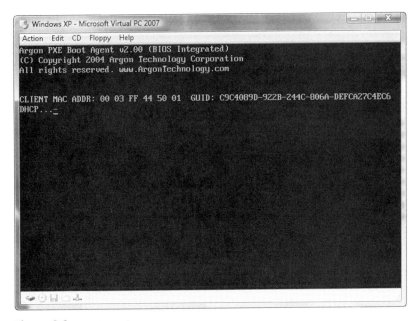

Figure 3-2 PXE Boot Agent

When the appropriate network infrastructure is present, you can perform a network installation of a guest operating system. In a network installation, the files for the installation of an OS are copied from a network server rather than from an installation CD/DVD. In addition to being faster, you have the option to preconfigure the installation files, which results in a consistent deployment of the operating systems.

For example, with Microsoft Remote Installation Services (RIS), you can set up new client computers remotely by using a RIS network shared folder as the source of the Windows operating system files. You can install operating systems on remote boot-enabled client computers by connecting the computer to the virtual network, starting the guest computer, booting off a PXE ROM and logging on with a valid user account.

From a practical perspective, a PXE installation in a virtual environment is rarely necessary given the ease of duplicating and distributing the operating system installation (to be discussed in further detail later in the chapter). Normally, the PXE Boot Agent simply times out, and the virtual machine proceeds to the next step, which instructs the user that the CD/DVD is missing.

Reboot and Select Proper Boot Device You will receive the message shown in Figure 3-3 when the OS installation CD/DVD media has not been inserted into the CD/DVD drive. Open the CD/DVD drive and insert the CD/DVD media. Click CD on the menu, click Use Physical Drive D: (or whichever drive letter is being used), and then press Enter.

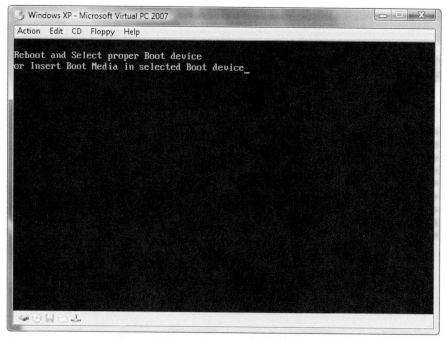

Figure 3-3 Missing CD/DVD media

Overview of Operating System Installation

You can install an operating system, such as Microsoft Vista, from a DVD. In this section, you will install Microsoft Vista as your first virtual machine.

DVDs and ISO Images

Operating system installation CD/DVDs are formatted with an **ISO 9660 file system**. ISO 9660 is a standard published by the International Organization for Standardization (ISO) that defines a file system for CD-ROM and DVD-ROM media. Thus, an **ISO image (.iso)** is an image of the entire contents of an ISO 9660 file system, which equates to the contents of a CD or DVD disk. The advantage of this file is that all individual files and folders within the file system are contained within a single .iso file, making it an attractive alternative to physical media for the distribution of software, and simplifying distribution of software over the Internet.

Most often installers will choose to install an operating system from either an .iso file (copied to a hard drive), or the more common CD/DVD. Because the hard drive is still faster than current optical drives, you will experience a performance boost when using the .iso file on a hard drive.

Overview: Installing Windows Vista Business

You can install Windows Vista Business using several methods—all are valid. The method you choose depends on your needs and your hardware/software environment. In this text, you will use the simplest form of installation—directly from the Windows Vista Business DVD.

Activity 3-1 (later in this chapter) provides detailed installation steps. This section assumes that you have created an empty virtual machine following the steps in Chapter 2.

The general steps to install Vista in an existing virtual machine are explained in this section. You will perform the actual installation in the activities sections later in the chapter.

Start the Vista virtual machine. Insert the Vista DVD. If necessary, click the CD menu and instruct VPC to use the physical drive where the DVD is located.

A black window, shown in Figure 3-4 on the next page, appears momentarily while a small number of files on the DVD are read into RAM.

Unlike previous versions of Microsoft Windows, Windows Vista does not have a noticeable text mode phase of the setup. On first boot, the **Windows Preinstallation Environment (WinPE)** loads into RAM and provides a basic graphical user interface (GUI) for the first phase of setup. See Figure 3-5 (on the next page). WinPE does not expect any user interaction at this point in the installation; there are no icons or menus. WinPE is built from Windows Vista components. However, WinPE is not a full-featured operating system like Windows Vista.

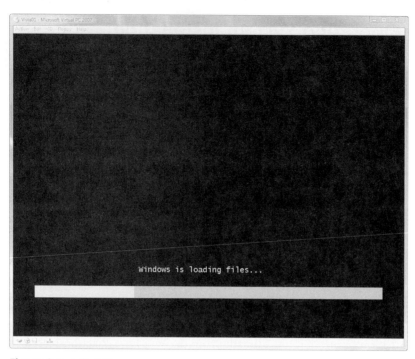

Figure 3-4 Initial file copy

Figure 3-5 WinPE initial GUI

After a few moments, you will see the dialog box to configure the regional settings. See Figure 3-6. Some versions of Vista have multiple language capabilities, in which case you would choose from one of the languages or dialects. The time and currency formats are different from country to country. For example, Vista supports various time and currency formats. In the United States, the currency is dollars ($) and in Great Britain, it is pounds (£). Finally, you could choose an alternate keyboard pattern, perhaps Dvorak. Review the regional settings and make any necessary changes.

Figure 3-6 Regional settings dialog box

Next, you will see the Install now button, as shown in Figure 3-7 on the next page. This screen also includes links for accessing basic information on installation and for repairing your computer.

After clicking the Install now button, you will see the Type your product key for activation dialog box, shown in Figure 3-8 on the next page, where you enter your product key. You will need to uncheck the Automatically activate Windows when I'm online check box. Respond No to the question, "Do you want to enter your product key now?"

Product activation is a license validation procedure used by Microsoft and other vendors. Specifically, product activation refers to a method that confirms a unique installation ID number generated from the hardware serial numbers and an ID number specific to the product's license (a product key). The installation ID is sent to Microsoft to verify the authenticity of the product key and determine that the product key is not being used for multiple installations.

78 Chapter 3 Installing Microsoft Windows Vista and Server 2008 Operating Systems

Figure 3-7 Dialog box with Install now button

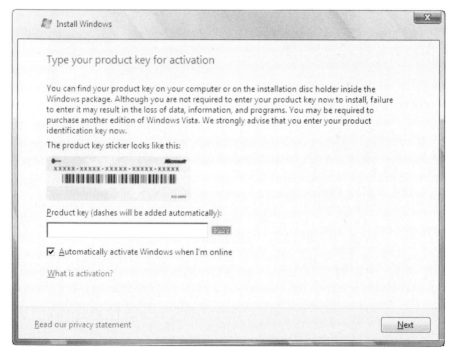

Figure 3-8 Entering the product key

Entering the product key identifies to the setup program the specific copy and version of Vista that you are installing. If you install Vista without typing a product key, you can run Vista for a 30-day evaluation. You can provide the key at a later time. On the 31st day, Vista runs Microsoft Internet Explorer and asks you to purchase a product key.

TIP There is an officially supported way to turn the 30-day evaluation period into 120 days. You can "rearm" the trial period for another 30 days, and do so up to three times. Here's how: Click Start, type cmd into the Start Search box, and then press Ctrl+Shift+Enter. Type slmgr -rearm and then press Enter. Shut down and restart Vista. Be sure to rearm Vista again within 30 days. This feature was built in to Vista by Microsoft, and the company has confirmed that extending the evaluation period is not a violation of Vista's end user agreement.

Because you did not enter a product key, you will be presented, as shown in Figure 3-9, with all versions available on the DVD. The Windows Vista Business DVD includes multiple versions of the operating system; Home Basic, Home Premium, Ultimate, Home Basic N, Business N, and Starter versions of Vista are all included on the Vista DVD. You can choose one of the different Vista versions because the product key is the only thing that tells the setup process what version of Vista it should install. You will need to check the I have selected the edition of Windows that I purchased check box.

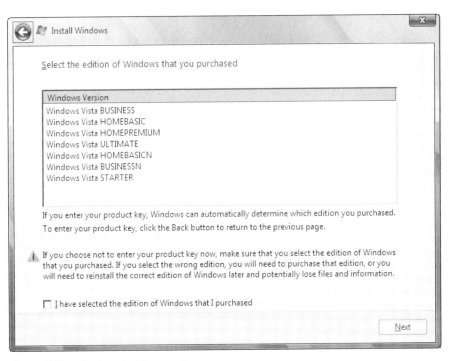

Figure 3-9 Selecting the Vista version

Next, you will need to accept the license terms. See Figure 3-10. You need to check the I accept the license terms check box. If you choose to reject the license terms, the install will be aborted.

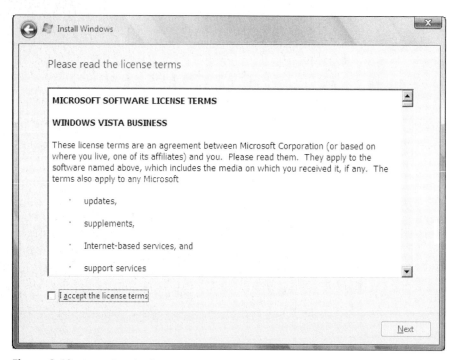

Figure 3-10 Accepting the license terms

Figure 3-11 shows the installation type dialog box. Click the Custom (Advanced) installation type button. The Upgrade button is disabled because you are installing the software into a new virtual machine without a previous operating system.

In the next step, you will need to make decisions about the partitions on your virtual hard disk. See Figure 3-12. If you are content with allocating all of the available space within the virtual hard drive, click Next. Doing so will create one partition on all of the available space.

If your virtual hard disk has existing partitions, you can choose to delete these partitions. Or, perhaps you need to create additional partitions. In either case, clicking the Drive options (advanced) link presents advanced partitioning options, as shown in Figure 3-13. Options to Delete, Format, or Extend an existing volume are now available. You can carve out a partition in the unallocated space by selecting New.

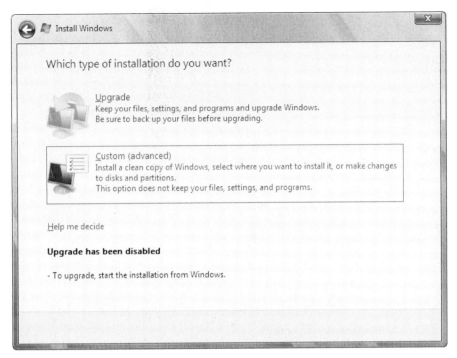

Figure 3-11 Choosing the installation type

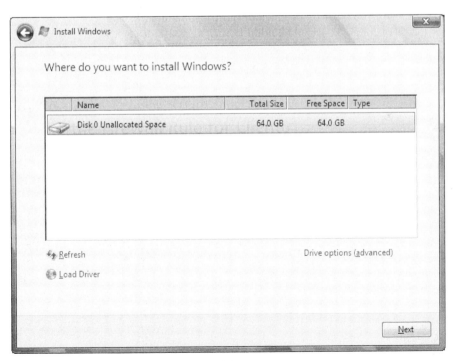

Figure 3-12 Selecting the installation partition

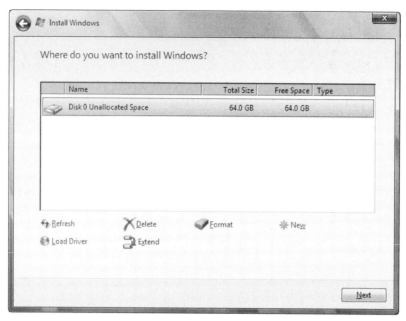

Figure 3-13 Advanced partitioning options

After you specify the installation partition, the install process copies and expands files from the Vista installation DVD to the virtual hard disk. The setup next installs updates for the guest operating system, then restarts the VM. See Figure 3-14.

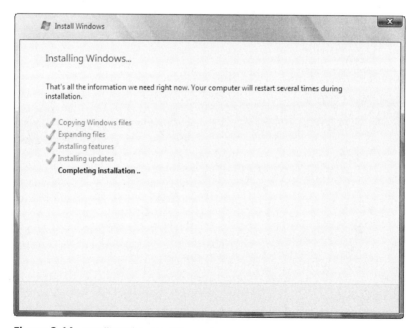

Figure 3-14 Installing the operating system

You will see a black screen that asks you to wait while Windows prepares to start for the first time. Now comes a long waiting period—potentially up to 30 minutes—during which the installation process configures the operating system. Again, the exact time depends on the physical hardware available. From time to time, you will see black screens. After this long wait, the virtual machine will reboot once again. Next, you will see a black screen. Don't panic! After a few moments, you will see a small colored circle.

Eventually, you are prompted to enter a username and a password for the first user of the guest operating systems. See Figure 3-15. This user account will have the rights and privileges of an administrator. This text uses a username of Student and a password of Secret1.

Figure 3-15 Entering the username and password

Next, you will name the guest computer in the dialog box shown in Figure 3-16 on the next page. The setup program generates a name for the computer—based on the username you entered (for example, if you entered Student as a username, then the setup program would automatically name the computer something meaningless like Student-PC). You should change the system-generated name to one that is meaningful within your network. This text will provide specific names for the virtual machines that you will create. Selecting a desktop background is also completed in this screen.

As with any OS installation, you must specify how to handle updates for Windows Vista. Figure 3-17 on the next page shows the Microsoft Windows Update (Automatic Updates) options for Vista. You can choose between three options: recommended settings, important updates, or defer a decision. You should choose important updates because this choice provides improved security and reliability. Recommended updates can address noncritical problems and help enhance your computing experience.

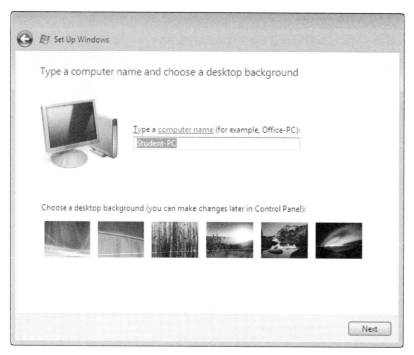

Figure 3-16 Naming the computer

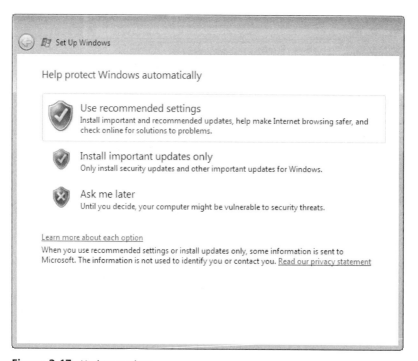

Figure 3-17 Update options

You will need to change the time and date settings unless you live in the Pacific time zone, which is the installed default setting. Figure 3-18 shows the dialog box to select the time zone. Adjust the date and time as needed.

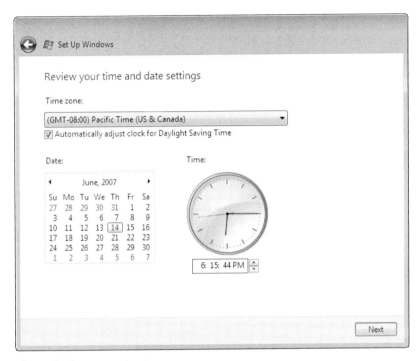

Figure 3-18 Setting the time zone

The first time you connect to a network, you must choose a network location. See Figure 3-19 on the next page. Establishing the location automatically sets the appropriate security settings for the type of network to which you are connected. Choosing a network location can help ensure that your computer is set to the appropriate security levels.

Although the dialog box lists three options, in reality, there are only two network locations:

- Private (Home or Work)—The computer is connected to a network that has some level of protection from the Internet and contains known or trusted computers. Examples are home networks or small office networks that are located behind an Internet gateway device that provides firewalling against incoming traffic from the Internet.
- Public (Public location)—The computer is connected to a network that has a direct connection to the Internet. Examples are public Internet access networks such as those found in airports, libraries, and coffee shops.

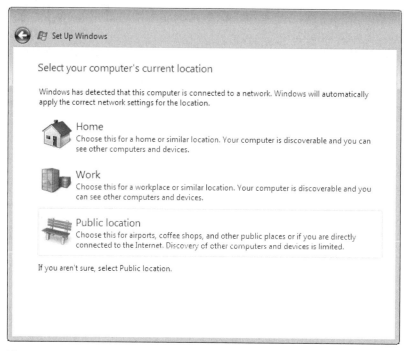

Figure 3-19 Selecting the computer's location

A Thank You window appears after you have completed the installation. You are now ready to click Start to begin using the operating system within the VM. Now that you are familiar with the steps required to install your first VM, you can perform the actual installation.

In the next two activities, you will install Vista Business and Windows Server 2008.

Activity 3-1: Installing Microsoft Vista Business

Time Required: 60–90 minutes

Objective: Install Microsoft Vista Business into the virtual machine created in Activity 2-1.

Requirements: Completion of Activity 2-1, and the Microsoft Vista Business DVD. If this activity has been previously completed, adjust the computer name.

Description: In this activity, you will start Microsoft Virtual PC 2007 and install Microsoft Vista Business in a virtual machine.

1. If necessary, log on to your Host PC with a username of **Student** and a password of **Secret1**.
2. To start Microsoft Virtual PC 2007, click **Start**, and then click **Microsoft Virtual PC**.
3. Insert the Microsoft Vista Business DVD into the DVD drive.
4. If the Autoplay window appears, close the window.

Overview of Operating System Installation

If necessary, substitute the name used in Activity 2-1 for Vista01 in the following steps.

5. To start the Vista virtual machine, click **Vista01**, and then click the **Start** button in the Virtual PC 2007 Console.
6. To mount the DVD and start the installation, click the **CD** menu, and then click **Use Physical Drive D**. If necessary, click the **Action** menu, click **Reset**, and then click **Reset**.
7. Wait for Vista to load files.
8. When the WinPE GUI is displayed, click the mouse in the virtual machine window.
9. Review the regional settings and then click **Next**.
10. To start the installation, click the Install now button.
11. Wait for Vista to load files.

At some time during the installation, the message indicating that Virtual Machine Additions is not installed on this virtual machine might appear. If it does, check the Don't show this message again check box, and then click OK.

12. To indicate that you want to install an evaluation copy of Vista and when the Type your product key for activation dialog box opens, uncheck the **Automatically activate Windows when I'm online** check box, click **Next**, and then click **No**.
13. When the Select the edition of Windows that you purchased dialog box opens, click **Windows Vista Business**, check the **I have selected the edition of Windows that I purchased** check box, and then click **Next**.
14. When the Please read the license terms dialog box opens, check the **I accept the license terms** check box, and then click **Next**.
15. When the Which type of installation do you want? dialog box opens, click **Custom (advanced)**.
16. When the Where do you want to install Windows? dialog box opens, click **Next**.
17. Wait for the installation of Windows to complete and restart.
18. Ignore the Press any key to boot from CD or DVD message.
19. Wait while Windows prepares to start for the first time and to complete installation.
20. Wait for the Windows screen with the small, animated circle to appear.

21. When the Choose a user name and picture dialog box opens, type **Student** in the Type a user name (for example, John) text box, press **Tab**, type **Secret1** in the Type a password (recommended) text box, press **Tab**, type **Secret1** in the Retype your password text box, and then click **Next**.

If The passwords do not match message appears, type **Secret1** in the Type a password (recommended) text box, press **Tab**, type **Secret1** in the Retype your password text box, and then click **Next**.

22. When the Type a computer name and choose a desktop background dialog box opens, type **Vista01** (or Vista02, Vista03, and so on) in the Type a computer name (for example, Office-PC) text box, and then click **Next**.
23. When the Help protect Windows automatically dialog box opens, click **Install important updates only**.
24. To set the time zone, click the Time zone drop-down menu, click the appropriate time zone, review the date and time, and then click **Next**.
25. When the Select your computer's current location dialog box opens, click **Work**, and then click **Start**.
26. Wait for Vista to check the computer's performance.
27. Wait for the Password screen, type **Secret1**, and then press **Enter**.
28. Wait for Vista to prepare your desktop.
29. When the Welcome Center window opens, close the Welcome Center window.
30. To shut down the virtual machine, click **Start**, click the arrow next to the Lock button, and then click **Shut Down**.
31. Leave the host computer logged on for the next activity.

Now that you have installed Vista Business, a desktop product, you are ready to install Server 2008, a server product. Although the server product fits different needs, the installations are very similar.

Activity 3-2: Installing Microsoft Windows Server 2008 in a Virtual Machine

Time Required: 60–90 minutes

Objective: Install Microsoft Windows Server 2008.

Requirements: Completion of Activity 2-5 and the Microsoft Windows Server 2008 DVD. If this activity has been previously completed, adjust the computer name.

Description: In this activity, you will install Microsoft Server 2008.

1. If necessary, log on to your Host PC with a username of **Student** and a password of **Secret1**.
2. To start Microsoft Virtual PC 2007, click **Start**, and then click **Microsoft Virtual PC**.
3. Insert the Microsoft Windows Server 2008 DVD into the DVD drive.
4. If the Autoplay window opens, close the window.

If necessary, substitute the name used in Activity 2-5 for Longhorn1 in the following steps.

5. To start the Longhorn virtual machine, click **Longhorn1** and then click the **Start** button in the Virtual PC 2007 Console.
6. To mount the DVD and start the installation, click the **CD** menu, and then click **Use Physical Drive D**. If necessary, click the **Action** menu, click **Reset**, and then click **Reset**.
7. Wait for Windows to load files.
8. To activate the virtual machine, click in the **Longhorn1** virtual machine window.

At some time during this installation, the Virtual Machine Additions is not installed on this virtual machine dialog box might appear. If it does, check the **Don't show this message again** check box, and then click **OK**.

9. Verify the regional settings and then click **Next**.
10. Click the **Install now** button.
11. To indicate that this virtual machine is using an evaluation copy, wait for the Type your product key for activation dialog box to open, uncheck the **Automatically activate Windows when I'm online** check box, click **Next**, and then click **No**.
12. To indicate which version to install, click **Windows Server 2008 Standard** (Full Installation), check the **I have selected the edition of Windows that I purchased** check box, and then click **Next**.
13. Check the **I accept the license terms** check box, and then click **Next**.
14. Click the **Custom (advanced)** icon.
15. To accept the Default allocation, click **Next**.
16. Wait for Windows to copy and expand files, install features and updates, and restart to complete the installation.
17. Ignore the Press any key to boot from CD or DVD message.
18. Wait while Windows prepares to start for the first time and to complete the installation.

19. Wait while Windows prepares your desktop.
20. When the user's password must be changed before logging on the first time message appears, click OK. Type **Secret1** in the New password text box, press **Tab**, type **Secret1** in the Confirm password text box, press **Enter**, and then click **OK**.
21. To set the time zone, click the **Set time zone** link, review the date and time, click the **Change time zone** button, click the appropriate zone, and then click **OK**. Click **OK** to close the Date and Time dialog box.
22. To provide a static address, click the **Configure networking** link, right-click **Local Area Connection**, click the **Properties**, clear the **Internet Protocol Version 6 (TCP/IPv6)** check box, click the **Internet Protocol Version 4 (TCP/IPv4)** line, click the **Properties** button, click the **Use the following IP address** option button, type **192.168.0.101** in the IP address text box, press **Tab** twice, type **192.168.0.1** in the **Default gateway** text box, press **Tab** twice, type **192.168.0.101** in the **Preferred DNS server** text box, click **OK**, click **Close**, and then close the **Network Connections** window.
23. To provide a computer name, click the **Provide computer name and domain** link, click the **Change** button, type **Longhorn1** (or Longhorn2, Longhorn3, and so on) in the Computer name text box, click **OK** twice, click **Close**, and then click the **Restart Now** button.
24. Wait for the virtual machine to restart.
25. Ignore the Press any key to boot from CD or DVD message.
26. Press the **right Alt+Delete** key combination and log on to your Longhorn virtual machine with the username **Administrator** and a password of **Secret1**.
27. Check the **Do not show this window at logon** check box, and then click **Close**.
28. Close any open windows.
29. To shut down the server, click **Start**, click the arrow next to the Lock button, click **Shut Down**, click the **Option** drop-down menu, click **Operating System: Reconfiguration (Planned)**, and then click **OK**.
30. Leave the computer logged on for the next activity.

Installing Virtual Machine Additions

You learned about Virtual Machine Additions in Chapter 1. Until you install Virtual Machine Additions, you will periodically see the message shown in Figure 3-20. You should install Virtual Machine Additions on applicable Microsoft operating systems to gain the features the add-in provides and to avoid the Virtual Machine Additions message.

To free the mouse pointer, press the right Alt key. The left Alt key is assigned to regular Alt key functions.

Figure 3-20 Virtual Machine Additions message

Activity 3-3: Installing Virtual Machine Additions

Time Required: 10 minutes

Objective: Install Virtual Machine Additions into the virtual machine containing the Vista Business guest created in Activity 3-1.

Requirements: Completion of Activity 3-1.

Description: In this activity, you will install Virtual Machine Additions in the guest Microsoft Vista Business OS in a virtual machine. This activity is useful if you want to use the features of Virtual Machine Additions.

1. If necessary, log on to your Host PC with a username of **Student** and a password of **Secret1**.
2. If necessary, to start Microsoft Virtual PC 2007, click **Start,** and then click **Microsoft Virtual PC.**

If necessary, substitute the name used in Activity 2-1 for Vista01 in the following steps.

3. If necessary, to start the Vista virtual machine, click **Vista01** and then click **Start.**
4. If necessary, wait for the Password screen, type **Secret1,** and then press **Enter.**

To stop the Welcome Center from showing each time Vista starts, clear the **Run at startup** check box, and close the Welcome Center window.

5. To install the Virtual Machines Additions in a guest operating system, press the **right Alt** key, click the **Action** menu, click **Install or Update Virtual Machine Additions**, and then click **Continue**.
6. Click **Run setup.exe**.
7. When the User Account Control dialog box opens, click **Continue**.
8. Click in the virtual machine window, and click **Next**.
9. Wait for the installation to complete, and then click **Finish**.
10. When requested to restart your system, click **Yes**.
11. Wait for Vista to restart.
12. Log on to your virtual machine with a username of **Student** and a password of **Secret1**.
13. Leave the computer logged on for the next activity.

Virtual Machine Additions provides a number of features. You will learn about seven of the most useful options, including folder sharing, mouse integration, drag and drop, Clipboard integration, time synchronization, arbitrary video resolutions, and customizing video drivers, in the following sections of the chapter. Also, you will learn about options to shut down your virtual machine.

Shared Folders

To access files that are stored on your host computer, you can use the Shared Folders feature. Folder sharing allows a virtual machine to access files on the host operating system as if it were a mapped network drive. A shared folder on the host operating system can be shared among more than one virtual machine simultaneously. Files within the folders can be opened for writing only by one virtual machine at a time; however, files can be opened for reading by more than one virtual machine at the same time.

This feature provides an easy way to transfer files between virtual machines. Using the shared folder on the host operating system as an intermediary between virtual machines, you can transfer files from one virtual machine to another.

When creating a shared folder, you must assign it a drive letter that is not already being used by a drive or device in the virtual machine. If two drives or devices are assigned to the same drive letter, the shared folder will not appear in the virtual machine.

Activity 3-4: Using Shared Folders

Time Required: 5 minutes

Objective: Use shared folders to access a file on the host computer.

Requirements: Completion of Activities 3-1 and 3-3. If this activity has been previously completed, adjust the folder and filenames.

Description: In this activity, you will access a file in a shared folder on the host operating system. This activity is useful if you want to read or write a file on the physical computer from a virtual machine.

1. If necessary, log on to your Host PC with **Student** and a password of **Secret1**.
2. If necessary, to start Microsoft Virtual PC 2007, click **Start**, and then click **Microsoft Virtual PC**.

 If necessary, substitute the name used in Activity 2-1 for Vista01 in the following steps.

3. If necessary, to start the Vista virtual machine, click **Vista01** and then click **Start**.
4. If necessary, wait for the Password screen, type **Secret1**, and then press **Enter**.
5. To create a folder on the host operating system, click **Start** in the host computer, click **Computer**, double-click **Local Disk (C:)**, right-click in the white space in the right pane, point to **New**, click **Folder**, type **My Shared Folder** as the folder name, and then press **Enter**.
6. To create a file in the My Shared Folder on the host operating system, double-click **My Shared Folder**, right-click in the white space in the right pane, point to **New**, click **Text Document**, type **Action Log** as the document name, press **Enter**, and then close the Computer window.
7. To map the My Shared Folder on the host operating system, return to the Virtual PC Console, click **Vista01**, click the **Settings** button, click **OK**, click **Shared Folders**, click the **Share Folder** button, expand **Local Disk (C:)**, click My **Shared Folder**, click **OK**, and then click **OK**.
8. To access the shared folder, click **Start** in the Vista01 virtual machine, click **Computer**, double-click **Disconnected Network Drive (Z:)**, double-click **Action Log**, confirm that Action Log opened in Notepad, type **Writing action note** in Notepad, click the **File** menu, click **Save**, click the **File** menu, and then click **Exit**.
9. To verify that the text was written to the file in the shared folder on the host operating system, click **Start** in the host computer, click **Computer**, double-click **Local Disk (C:)**, double-click **My Shared Folder**, double-click the Action Log shortcut, and verify that Action Log opened in Notepad and the text Writing action note is visible. Close Notepad, and then close the Computer window.
10. Return to the Vista01 virtual machine, and close the Computer window.
11. Leave the computer logged on for the next activity.

Mouse Integration

You use the keyboard and a mouse to control a virtual machine much as you would a physical computer.

In general, the keyboard works the same for a virtual machine as it does for a physical computer, with a few exceptions. You learned about some of these exceptions, such as the Ctrl+Alt+Delete combination, earlier in this book.

When Virtual Machine Additions is installed and the mouse setting for that virtual machine is set to use pointer integration, you can move the pointer freely in and out of each virtual machine window.

Drag and Drop

You most likely have used drag and drop to move files within the Computer window. To copy a file or folder to a virtual machine, you point to the file or folder to be copied from the host operating system, and then drag the file or folder to a location on the virtual machine. To copy a file or folder from a virtual machine, you point to the file or folder to be copied from the virtual machine, and then drag the file or folder to a location on the host operating system.

Beware of the following restrictions:

- You cannot use the right mouse button to move a file or folder or to cancel a copy action.
- You cannot use the right mouse button to copy a file or folder outside of the virtual machine window.
- You can use drag-and-drop copying to paste data to folder and desktop locations only. You cannot paste data to other locations such as the Run dialog box or an application.
- Dragging and dropping large files will cause VPC to stop responding temporarily until the process is complete.

Activity 3-5: Using Drag and Drop to Copy Files

Time Required: 5 minutes

Objective: Use drag and drop to copy a file from the host computer to the virtual machine.

Requirements: Completion of Activities 3-1, 3-3, and 3-4. If this activity has been previously completed, adjust the filenames.

Description: In this activity, you will copy a file on the host operating system to the Vista01 virtual machine.

1. If necessary, log on to your Host PC with **Student** and a password of **Secret1**.
2. If necessary, to start Microsoft Virtual PC 2007, click **Start**, and then click **Microsoft Virtual PC**.

If necessary, substitute the name used in Activity 2-1 for Vista01 in the following steps.

3. If necessary, to start the Vista virtual machine, click **Vista01** and then click **Start**.
4. If necessary, wait for the Password screen, type **Secret1**, and then press **Enter**.

5. To open the Documents window on the Vista01 guest operating system, click **Start**, click **Computer**, double-click **Local Disk (C:)**, and then click **Documents**.
6. To open the My Shared Folder window on the host computer, click **Start**, click **Computer**, double-click **Local Disk (C:)**, and then double-click **My Shared Folder**.
7. Position the Computer windows so both are visible.
8. To copy the Action Log file on the host computer to the Vista01 virtual machine, point to the **Action Log** file, click and drag the **Action Log** file to the Computer window in the Vista01 virtual machine, and then release the mouse button.
9. If you receive the Item already exists message, click the **Replace** button.
10. Close the two Computer windows.
11. Leave the computer logged on for the next activity.

Clipboard Integration

You can copy and paste text and graphics between applications running on the host operating system and the virtual machine.

To transfer graphics or text, you use the copy and paste functions just as you would when copying and pasting data between applications on the host operating system. Text selections are copied unformatted. Text formatting—such as bold, italic, or paragraph style—is not transferred.

Activity 3-6: Copying Text Using Clipboard Integration

Time Required: 5 minutes

Objective: Use the Clipboard to copy text from an application on the guest computer to an application on the Vista01 virtual machine.

Requirements: Completion of Activities 3-1 and 3-3. If this activity was previously completed, adjust the filenames.

Description: In this activity, you will copy text from an application on the host operating system to an application on the Vista01 virtual machine.

1. If necessary, log on to your Host PC with **Student** and a password of **Secret1**.
2. If necessary, to start Microsoft Virtual PC 2007, click **Start**, and then click **Microsoft Virtual PC**.

If necessary, substitute the name used in Activity 2-1 for Vista01 in the following steps.

3. If necessary, to start the Vista virtual machine, click **Vista01** and then click **Start**.
4. If necessary, wait for the Password screen, type **Secret1**, and then press **Enter**.

5. To open Notepad on the host computer, click **Start** on the host computer, type **notepad** in the Start Search text box, and then click **Notepad**.
6. To open Notepad on the Vista01 guest computer, click in the **Vista01** virtual machine, click **Start** on the guest computer, type **notepad** in the Start Search text box, and then click **Notepad**.
7. Position the Notepad windows so both are visible. The application windows are sized relative to the operating system windows.
8. To create text in the host Notepad application, click in the host Notepad window, and then type **Be the First to Experience Windows Vista**.
9. To copy the text to the Clipboard, click the **Edit** menu, click **Select All**, click the **Edit** menu, and then click **Copy**.
10. To paste text in the Vista01 Notepad application, click in the guest Notepad window, click the **Edit** menu, and then click **Paste**.
11. Verify that the text was copied and pasted.
12. Close the two Notepad windows. When prompted to save the changes, click **Don't Save**.
13. Leave the computer logged on for the next activity.

Time Synchronization

The clock used in your virtual machine is automatically synchronized with the clock used by the host operating system. This coordination becomes important when you move or copy files from virtual machines to the host or vice versa. Synchronizing system clocks means you do not need to be concerned that timestamps on the files are incorrect.

Arbitrary Video Resolutions

When you are interacting with multiple virtual machines on your host computer's desktop, you will want to size the virtual machines to fit attractively on the host computer's desktop.
You must complete the following two steps to accomplish this:

- Personalize the display resolution on the host computer—For example, set the host computer's screen resolution to 1280 × 1024 or the largest that your monitor will support.
- Dynamically resize the virtual machine window—Resizing the window of a virtual machine adjusts the screen resolution of the guest operating machine.

If you will be working only in one virtual machine, you might want to maximize the video for that virtual machine. To maximize the video, press right Alt+Enter. You will not see the host operating system nor can you interact with it. To toggle back, use the same key combination.

Activity 3-7: Resizing Virtual Machine Windows

Time Required: 5 minutes

Objective: Resize a virtual machine window.

Requirements: Completion of Activities 3-1 and 3-3.

Description: In this activity, you will resize the window on the Vista01 virtual machine.

1. If necessary, log on to your Host PC with **Student** and a password of **Secret1**.
2. If necessary, to start Microsoft Virtual PC 2007, click **Start**, and then click **Microsoft Virtual PC**.

If necessary, substitute the name used in Activity 2-1 for Vista01 in the following steps.

3. If necessary, to start the **Vista** virtual machine, click **Vista01** and then click **Start**.
4. If necessary, wait for the Password screen, type **Secret1**, and then press **Enter**.
5. To resize the virtual machine window, point to the lower-right corner of the Vista01 window, click and drag the window to a smaller window size, and then release the mouse button.
6. Wait for the window to adjust the video resolution.
7. Verify that the text and icons are proportionally resized.
8. To shut down the virtual machine, click **Start**, click the arrow next to the Lock button, and then click **Shut Down**.
9. Leave the computer logged on for the next activity.

Customized Video Drivers

The S3 Trio 64 video drivers of the guest operating system may recognize only 2 MB or 4 MB of **video RAM (VRAM)** by default. Installing Virtual Machine Additions allows the guest operating system to use 8 MB of VRAM. VRAM uses separate pins for the processor and the video circuitry, providing the video circuitry with a back door to the video RAM. This increase provides higher resolutions with increased color depth for the guest operating system.

Closing the Virtual Machine

When you have completed working with your virtual machines, you can either shut down the guest operating system using the operating system's shutdown method, or you can use a Virtual Machine Additions option. This option involves shutting down the virtual machine by clicking the Action menu, and then clicking Close. You would then select an option from the Virtual PC Close options. For example, when closing Vista with the close defaults, you would see: Save state, Shut down Windows Vista, or Turn off.

Cloning Virtual Machines

When using multiple virtual machines with the same operating system product, you can save time by cloning a previously installed virtual machine. **Cloning** is the task of copying a full image of a hard disk from one virtual machine to create a new virtual machine. Cloning saves time setting up new machines by eliminating the installation of the operating system and each individual application.

Sysprep is a Microsoft program that prepares a Microsoft Windows operating system for cloning. To create a clone, prepare the virtual machine with Sysprep and copy the .vhd file to a new .vhd file, as shown in Figure 3-21.

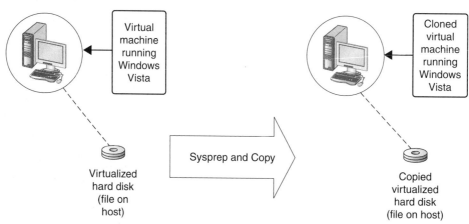

Figure 3-21 Copying .vhd to create a clone

You will learn how to prepare a virtual machine for cloning in the following sections.

Issues with Cloning

Users refer to computers and user accounts using the computer or user account name, but the operating system internally refers to accounts by their **security identifiers** (**SIDs**). SIDs are unique alphanumeric strings and should never be reused.

Cloned machines all have identical SIDs, which violates the concept of never reusing an SID. Note that just changing the computer name does not change the computer SID. In addition, the Administrator account for all of the cloned machines will have the same SID.

According to Microsoft, if you have duplicate SIDS, you will encounter problems. You can expect to experience future security issues as you position your virtual machines in networks.

When used on an operating system before cloning, Sysprep resolves the SID problem by generating a new SID when the new cloned installations are started. Using Sysprep, you can create a clone that bypasses the file copies, configurations, and starts with the Windows Welcome. This speeds up the installation of virtual machines with identical operating systems.

Using Sysprep

Sysprep was copied to the virtual hard disk during the installation of Vista. The tool prepares an installation of Windows for duplication, removing all system-specific information from an installed Windows image, including the computer security identifier (SID).

You run Sysprep from a command line with the appropriate switches, as shown in Figure 3-22. The /oobe switch instructs the Windows installation to run Windows Welcome the next time the computer boots. The oobe stands for "out of box experience." The oobe is required by Microsoft when a manufacturer markets a personal computer with a preinstalled Windows product. The /generalize switch instructs Sysprep to remove system-specific data, including unique security IDs (SIDs). After the unique system information is removed, the computer shuts down.

Figure 3-22 Running Sysprep

Although Sysprep enables you to skip the file copies and other time-consuming activities related to installing a new VM, you will need to repeat these tasks for each cloned installation:

- Complete the region setup.
- Provide a product key.
- Accept the license terms.
- Create a user account.
- Name the computer.
- Select an update option.
- Verify the time zone, date, and time.
- Select a computer location.

This abbreviated task list is easier to do than starting from scratch with the Vista installation DVD. You have duplicated the "out of box experience."

Activity 3-8: Cloning a Virtual Machine (Optional)

Time Required: 45 minutes

Objective: Clone a virtual machine.

Requirements: Completion of Activity 3-1. If Activity 3-8 has been previously completed, adjust the computer, folder, and filenames.

Description: In this activity, you will use Sysprep with your Vista01 virtual machine. Next, you will copy the .vhd file to create a clone. Then, you will configure the clone from the Windows Welcome.

1. If necessary, log on to your Host PC with **Student** and a password of **Secret1**.
2. If necessary, to start Microsoft Virtual PC 2007, click **Start,** and then click **Microsoft Virtual PC.**

If necessary, substitute the name used in Activity 2-1 for Vista01 in Steps 3 through 8.

3. If necessary, to start the Vista virtual machine, click **Vista01** and then click **Start.**
4. If necessary, wait for the Password screen, type **Secret1,** and then press **Enter.**
5. To open a command prompt window, click **Start,** type **cmd** in the Start Search text box, and then press **Enter.**
6. To launch the Sysprep program, type **cd \windows\system32\sysprep**, press **Enter,** type **sysprep /oobe /generalize,** and then press **Enter.**
7. When the User Account Control dialog box opens, click **Continue.**
8. Wait for Sysprep to complete and the Vista01 virtual machine to shut down.

If necessary, substitute the name used in Activity 2-1 for Vista01 in the following steps and use Vista02 or Vista03, Vista04, and so on for the new Vista02 machine.

9. To create a folder for the new Vista02 virtual machine, click **Start** in the host operating system, click **Computer,** click **Documents,** double-click **My Virtual Machines,** right-click in the white space in the right pane, point to **New,** click **Folder,** type **Vista02** as the new folder, and then press **Enter.**
10. To copy the Vista01.vhd file, double-click the **Vista01** folder, right-click the **Vista01 Hard Disk,** click **Copy,** click the Back button to My Virtual Machines, right-click the **Vista02** folder, and then click **Paste.**
11. Wait for the file to finish copying.

12. To rename the .vhd file, double-click the **Vista02** folder, right-click the **Vista01 Hard Disk**, click **Rename**, type **Vista02 Hard Disk** over Vista01 Hard Disk, and then press **Enter**.
13. To start the New Virtual Machine Wizard, return to the Virtual PC Console, and then click **New**.
14. To provide a name for the virtual machine, click **Next** twice, type **Vista02** in the Name and location text box, and then click **Next**.
15. Review the default operating system, which should be Vista, and then click **Next**.
16. Review the RAM memory allocation, which should be 512 MB, and then click **Next**.
17. To specify the virtual hard disk in the default location, retain the **An existing virtual hard disk** option button, click **Next**, click the **Browse** button, double-click **Vista02**, click **Vista02 Hard Disk**, click **Open**, and then click **Next**.
18. Review the virtual machine attributes, and then click **Finish**.
19. To start the Vista02 virtual machine, double-click the **Vista02** icon.
20. Wait for Vista to start for the first time.
21. Wait for the Windows screen with the small animated circle.
22. Wait for Vista to restart.
23. Review the regional settings, and then click **Next**.
24. To indicate that you want to install an evaluation copy of Vista, when the Type your product key for activation dialog box opens, clear the Automatically activate Windows when I'm online check box, and then click **Next**.
25. When the Please read the license terms dialog box opens, check the **I accept the license terms** check box, and then click **Next**.
26. When the Choose a user and picture dialog box opens, type **Another** in the Type a user name (for example, John) text box, press **Tab**, type **Secret1** in the Type a password (recommended) text box, press **Tab**, type **Secret1** in the Retype your password text box, and then click **Next**.
27. If The passwords do not match message appears, type **Secret1** in the Type a password (recommended) text box, press **Tab**, type **Secret1** in the Retype your password text box, and then click **Next**.
28. When the Type a computer name and choose a desktop background dialog box opens, type **Vista02** in the Type a computer name (for example, Office-PC) text box, and then click **Next**.
29. When the Help protect Windows automatically dialog box opens, click **Install important updates only**.
30. Review the time zone, date, and time, and then click **Next**.
31. When the Select your computer's current location dialog box opens, click **Work**.
32. When the Thank You message appears, click **Start**.
33. Wait for the Password dialog box to appear, click **Student**, type **Secret1**, and then press **Enter**.

34. To shut down the virtual machine, click **Start**, click the arrow next to the Lock button, and then click ***Shut Down***.
35. Log off and shut down the host computer.

Chapter Summary

- You can install an operating system in several different ways. The method of installation is determined by the hardware and software environment being used. The method you used to install the Windows Vista Business operating system in this chapter was the simplest form of installation. You also installed Windows Server 2008.

- Installing Virtual Machine Additions removed the recurring message and added features. By configuring and using the VMA features, you customized the environment and improved its ease of use. The features for shared folders allowed file sharing among virtual machines, and mouse integration allowed better access between virtual machines and the host operating system.

- Cloning existing virtual machines demonstrated the use of the Sysprep tool. You learned the importance of the SID number and why a virtual machine needs to be prepped before cloning.

Key Terms

cloning—The process of replicating or copying the entire contents of a partition on a hard disk drive (or the virtual hard disk .vhd file) by creating an image of the hard disk drive.

ISO 9660 file system—An international format standard for CD-ROM and DVD-ROM media adopted by the International Organization for Standardization (ISO).

ISO image (.iso)—A copy or duplicate of an ISO 9600 file system.

Preboot Execution Environment (PXE)—The environment that allows a workstation to boot from a server on a network prior to booting the operating system on the local hard drive.

security identifiers (SIDs)—A unique alphanumeric string that the operating systems uses for user accounts. These are not changed when the computer name is changed or the computer is cloned unless the operating system is prepared prior to cloning.

Sysprep—A software tool used to prepare a Windows operating system for duplication. It removes all system-specific information from an installed Windows image, including the computer security identifier (SID).

video RAM (VRAM)—A special type of RAM (DRAM) used in high-speed video applications. Video RAM uses separate pins for the processor and the video circuitry, providing the video circuitry with a back door to the video RAM.

Windows Preinstallation Environment (WinPE)—A basic version of the operating system that is loaded into RAM when Windows Vista is first installed. It provides a basic GUI for the first phase of setup and is built from Windows Vista components.

Review Questions

1. The full benefits of virtual machines can be achieved by _____.
   a. Using Microsoft Vista
   b. Avoiding Microsoft Server 2008
   c. Installing Virtual Machine Additions
   d. Ignoring initial start-up screens in the virtual machines

2. PXE _____. (Choose all that apply.)
   a. Is an acronym for Preboot Execution Environment
   b. Is an acronym for Pre Extended
   c. Is pronounced "pixie"
   d. Allows a workstation to boot from a server on a network prior to booting the operating system on the local hard drive

3. An ISO image _____. (Choose all that apply.)
   a. Is another name for a floppy disk
   b. Is simple to retrieve from the Internet
   c. Is a disk image of an ISO 9660 file system
   d. Has a file extension of .iso

4. Windows Vista does not have _____.
   a. A noticeable text mode phase of the setup
   b. A GUI interface
   c. A full-featured operating system
   d. A Windows Preinstallation Environment

5. WinPE is an acronym for _____.
   a. Windows Preview
   b. Windows Preinstallation Editor
   c. Windows Priority Environment
   d. Windows Preinstallation Environment

6. The Windows Vista 30-day evaluation can be officially extended _____.
   a. Once
   b. Twice
   c. Three times
   d. Never; after 31 days you must purchase a product key

7. Shared folders allow a virtual machine _____. (Choose all that apply.)
   a. To share files simultaneously with other virtual machines
   b. To easily transfer files between virtual machines
   c. To open files for writing at the same time as other virtual machines
   d. To open files for writing but not at the same time as other virtual machines
8. The keyboard combination that does not work because of the interaction between the host operating system and the virtual machine is _____.
   a. Right Alt+Delete
   b. Shift+Alt+Delete
   c. Ctrl+Alt+Delete
   d. Shift+Right+Delete
9. Setting the mouse for pointer integration use will allow you to _____.
   a. Use a mouse only in the virtual machine window
   b. Disable the mouse
   c. Require special mapping of the keyboard to use the mouse
   d. Move the pointer freely in and out of each virtual machine window
10. To copy a file or folder from a virtual machine, _____.
    a. Point to the file or folder to be copied from the virtual machine and then drag the file or folder to a location on the host operating system
    b. Point to the file or folder to be copied from the virtual machine and then click the left Alt+Ctrl key combination
    c. Use the right mouse button to move the file or folder to the host operating system
    d. Use the right mouse button to copy the file or folder to the host operating system
11. To copy a file or folder to a virtual machine, _____.
    a. Point to the file or folder to be copied from the host operating system and then click the left Alt+Ctrl key combination
    b. Point to the file or folder to be copied from the host operating system and then drag the file to a location on the virtual machine
    c. Use the right mouse button to move the file or folder to the host operating system
    d. Use the right mouse button to copy the file or folder to the host operating system

12. To transfer text from an application on the host machine to an application on the virtual machine, _____.
    a. Use the Edit menu host on the host machine to copy the text to the Clipboard and then use the Edit menu in the virtual machine to paste the text from the Clipboard
    b. Use the Edit menu on the host machine to copy the text to the Clipboard and then use the left Alt+Ctrl key combination to paste the text from the Clipboard
    c. Point to the text to be copied from the host operating system and then drag the text to a location on the virtual machine
    d. Point to the text to be copied from the application on the host operating system and then drag the text to an application on the virtual machine

13. Text selections are copied _____.
    a. Unformatted
    b. Completely formatted
    c. Partially formatted with only paragraph style kept
    d. Partially formatted with bold and italic text, but no paragraph style

14. Time synchronization _____. (Choose all that apply.)
    a. Needs to be handled manually
    b. Is automatically synchronized by the virtual machine, with the clock used by the host operating system
    c. Is not available manually or automatically
    d. Is not a concern; the timestamps will be correct

15. Virtual Machine Additions must be installed _____. (Choose all that apply.)
    a. To allow the guest operating system to use 2 MB of VRAM
    b. To allow the guest operating system to use 4 MB of VRAM
    c. To allow the guest operating system to use 8 MB of VRAM
    d. To provide higher resolutions with increased color depth for the guest operating systems

16. Cloning is _____. (Choose all that apply.)
    a. A task that involves creating a copy of a full image of a hard disk from one virtual machine to create a new virtual machine
    b. Used to save time setting up new machines by eliminating the installation of the operating system and each individual application
    c. Started by preparing the virtual machine to be copied by using Sysprep
    d. Not recommended because of the amount of time it takes

17. Sysprep is _____.
    a. An industry term for system preparation of computer networks
    b. An application used for the preparation of file sharing
    c. A Microsoft tool used on an operating system before cloning to resolve SID problems by generating a new SID
    d. A security feature on Microsoft Vista machines

18. SIDs are _____. (Choose all that apply.)
    a. Unique alphanumeric strings used by the operating system to refer to user accounts
    b. Identical on cloned machines if they have not been properly prepped
    c. Future security problems in networks of virtual machines if they are identical
    d. Able to be changed by the user

19. Duplication _____. (Choose all that apply.)
    a. Is also referred to as imaging
    b. Enables you to capture a customized Windows image that you can reuse
    c. Is not recommended for any operating system
    d. Requires preparation

20. /oobe _____. (Choose all that apply.)
    a. Instructs the Windows installation to run Windows Welcome the next time the computer boots
    b. Stands for "out of box experience"
    c. Is required by Microsoft when a manufacturer markets a personal computer with a preinstalled Windows product
    d. Instructs Sysprep to remove system-specific data, including unique SIDs

Case Projects

Case 3-1: Presenting Virtual Machine Additions

Your college computer club is reluctant to mess up a good thing and has opted to stay away from Virtual Machine Additions. Write a short presentation on the features you learned about in this chapter. List the benefits of VMA and how these features can make the virtual machine easier to use. Your presentation should be no more than two pages in length and should persuade your fellow club members to install VMA.

Case 3-2: Working with Shared Folders

Your college computer club has just finished installing Virtual Machine Additions, thanks to your convincing work in Case 3-1. Now they need to transfer the club records from the host operating system to the new virtual machine. Write out a procedure that specifies the proper transfer of files and folders from the host operating system to the new virtual machines.

Case 3-3: Cloning

Your supervisor, Craig, is pleased with the work you have done so far with the virtual machines; however, he is still reluctant to try cloning existing operating systems. He has asked you to create a short report on the benefits of cloning a machine. Your report should address any issues that need to be taken care of prior to the procedure.

Implementing the Dovercorp.local Virtual Network

chapter 4

After reading this chapter and completing the exercises, you will be able to:

- Describe the Dovercorp.local virtual network
- Install the Dovercorp.local virtual network
- Implement directory services for the Dovercorp.local virtual network

In the previous three chapters, you learned about the features and uses of Microsoft Virtual PC 2007. In this chapter, you will put your knowledge to work as you build a demonstration network for a fictitious vehicle leasing company, Dover Leasing.

First, you will describe the Dovercorp.local virtual network, which will include three virtual machines. Microsoft includes **server roles** with Windows Server 2008. In Windows Server 2008, a server role describes the primary function of the server. The advantage of working with server roles is that you only have to install the services that are really necessary for the task of a server, which makes server management easier when dealing with updates or troubleshooting, for example. You will define the roles for the three virtual machines with the operating systems requirements. You will also define the IP addressing scheme to ensure accurate communications between the virtual machines.

Next, you will install and configure the three virtual machines. To ensure that the virtual machines can communicate in a network, you will test the connectivity using communication utilities.

The last task implements **directory services** to provide centralized security management of the virtual machines and other network objects. As part of this task, you will join the three virtual machines into a cohesive network.

The Dovercorp.local Virtual Network

Dover Leasing is a fictitious company headquartered in Boston. Dover Leasing leases a wide range of executive cars. In the past, the company has relied on several independent desktop computers to manage their assets. Dover Leasing has grown, and management has come to realize that the company could benefit by implementing a network. As the IT manager for Dover Leasing, implementing the Dovercorp.local network will be your responsibility.

As a user of Microsoft software, Dover Leasing will build its network around Microsoft Windows Server 2008, previously known as Longhorn Server. Dover implements Microsoft Vista Business as its desktop operating system of choice.

Although there are a number of ways to implement a virtual network, the network design implemented in this chapter focuses on the three roles found in all networks. The initial network diagram is shown in Figure 4-1. Server01 and Server02 are virtual machines running Windows Server 2008. The virtual machine Client01 is a desktop computer running Microsoft Vista Business. These virtual machines will communicate with one another over a local virtual network.

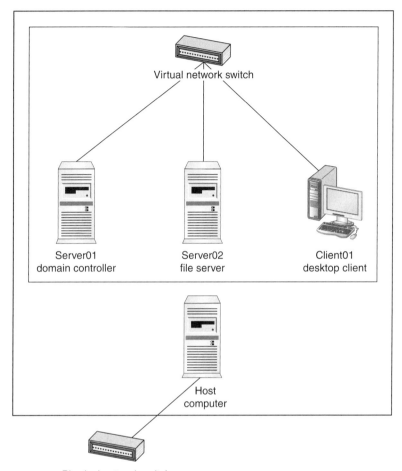

Figure 4-1 Initial network diagram for Dovercorp.local

Begin by discovering the role of these computers and operating systems requirements in the Dovercorp.local network.

Server01 Role—Domain Controller

Server01 is the virtual machine that manages the Dovercorp.local domain. A **domain** is a logical group of computers that shares access to network resources with centralized administration and security policies. Server01 is the **domain controller**—the server that responds to security authentication requests (logging on, checking permissions, and so on) within the Windows Server 2008 domain. The domain controller is the server that essentially makes networking (at least in a secure function) possible. **A directory service** is a software application that stores and organizes information about a computer network's users and network resources; it also allows network administrators to manage users' access to the resources. **Active Directory Domain Services** is the native directory service included with Microsoft Windows Server 2008. You will implement the domain controller role by promoting Server01 to function as a domain controller.

Active Directory Domain Services uses the **Domain Name System (DNS)** to maintain domain-naming structures and to locate network resources. DNS does this by translating the common names that people readily understand (such as *www.microsoft.com*) to the IP addresses that computers understand (such as 207.46.193.254). DNS maintains databases of IP addresses for host names. Active Directory Domain Services is designed to take advantage of DNS's powerful capabilities, so Active Directory Domain Services names must follow standard DNS naming conventions. You will implement the DNS role on Server01 for the Dovercorp.local domain as part of establishing Server01 as a domain controller (installing the Active Directory Domain Services service).

Domain names used on local networks that are not registered for use on the Internet should use invalid top-level names, such as .local.

Server02 Role—File Server

Server02 serves as a **file server**, meaning it is the computer system that is responsible for the central storage and management of data files so that other computers on the Dovercorp.local network can access these files. To take advantage of Active Directory Domain Services security features, you will need to join Server02 to the Dovercorp.local domain. As a domain member, Server02 can coordinate the security access of its files with the domain controller (Server 01).

Client01 Role—Desktop Client

Client01 is a desktop client that will use software applications to access various system resources, including folders and files on the network file server. Server01, with Active Directory Domain Services and DNS, helps locate network resources and controls security access to these network resources. Server02 holds the data files that Client01's applications require.

Operating System Requirements

When planning for RAM and hard disk space requirements, you need to take into consideration the role that the particular virtual machine will be playing in your network. Table 4-1 presents a summarization for these two critical variables for the virtual machines in the Dovercorp.local network.

Table 4-1 Operating system requirements

Virtual machine	Role	Operating system	RAM requirement	Virtual hard disk requirement	Operating system hard disk requirement
Server01	Domain controller	Windows Server 2008	640 MB	65,536 MB	65,536 MB
Server02	File server	Windows Server 2008	512 MB	65,536 MB	16,384 MB
Client01	Desktop	Windows Vista Business	512 MB	65,536 MB	65,536 MB

Two configuration settings stand out when compared to the Microsoft recommendations presented in Table 2-1 in Chapter 2. Because Server01 serves as a domain controller, it requires 640 MB of RAM to run Windows Server 2008. Table 2-1 shows that Server 2008 requires

512 MB of RAM; the extra 128 MB of RAM for Server01 will provide better performance for this specialized application server. Because Server02 is a file server, special partition allocations are recommended. Although you will create a virtual hard disk of 65536 MB for Server02, you will allocate only 16384 MB for the operating system. This is done to split the operating system files from the data files. After you install the operating system, you will need to create additional volumes for the data files; you will create these volumes in Chapter 5. Another benefit of using a data partition is simplified backup of the data files. Repairing or replacing the operating system can be accomplished without disturbing the data files stored on the second partition in the virtual hard drive.

You will use the information in Table 4-1 to complete Activity 4-2, in which you create the three virtual machines.

If your host machine has sufficient memory resources, consider increasing the amount of memory to improve the performance of your virtual machines. Remember to adhere to the rules of memory allocation highlighted in Chapter 2.

Activity 4-1: Removing Existing Virtual Machines

Time Required: 10 minutes

Objective: Remove existing virtual machines.

Requirements: Completion of Activity 2-1.

Description: In this activity, you will clean up the virtual environment by removing the existing virtual machines.

1. If necessary, log on to your host PC with a username of **Student** and a password of **Secret1**.
2. If necessary, to start Microsoft Virtual PC 2007, click **Start**, and then click **Microsoft Virtual PC**.
3. To remove the first virtual machine, click the first virtual machine in the Virtual PC console, click **Remove**, and then click **Yes**.
4. Repeat Step 3 for the remaining virtual machines.
5. To open Windows Explorer, click **Start**, click **Computer**, click **Documents**, and then double-click **My Virtual Machines**.
6. To remove the folder for each virtual machine, click and hold **Shift**, right-click the first folder, click **Delete**, and then click the **Yes** button.
7. Repeat Step 6 for the remaining folders in My Virtual Machines.
8. Close the Computer window.
9. Leave the computer logged on for the next activity.

Activity 4-2: Creating the Dovercorp.local Virtual Machines

Time Required: 10 minutes

Objective: Create the virtual machines.

Requirements: Completion of Activities 1-2 and 4-1.

Description: In this activity, you will create the virtual machines (Server01, Server02, and Client01) for the Dovercorp.local domain.

1. If necessary, log on to your host PC with a username of **Student** and a password of **Secret1**.
2. If necessary, to start Microsoft Virtual PC 2007, click **Start**, and then click **Microsoft Virtual PC**.

Creating Virtual Machine Server01

3. To start the creation of a virtual machine, click **New**, click **Next**, confirm that the **Create a virtual machine** option button is selected, and then click **Next**.
4. To provide a name for the virtual machine, type **Server01** in the Name and location text box, and then click **Next**.
5. To specify the Windows Server 2008 operating system, click the **Operating system** drop-down list arrow, click **Other**, and then click **Next**.
6. To specify the RAM allocation, click the **Adjusting the RAM** option button, type **640** in the MB text box, and then click **Next**.
7. To create a new virtual hard disk in the default location, click the **A new virtual hard disk** option button, click **Next**, type **65536** in the Virtual hard disk size text box, and then click **Next**.
8. Review the virtual machine attributes, and then click **Finish**.
9. To configure the network adapter, click the **Settings** button, click **Networking**, click the **Adapter 1** drop-down menu, and then click **Microsoft Loopback Adapter**.
10. To disable sound, click **Sound**, clear the **Enable sound card** check box, and then click **OK**.

Creating Virtual Machine Server02

11. Repeat Steps 3–10, replacing Server01 with Server02. Set the RAM to 512 MB in Step 6.

Creating Virtual Machine Client01

12. To start the creation of the last virtual machine, click **New**, click **Next**, confirm that the **Create a virtual machine** option button is selected, and then click **Next**.
13. To provide a name for the virtual machine, type **Client01** in the Name and location text box, and then click **Next**.
14. To specify the operating system, click the **Operating system** drop-down menu, click **Windows Vista**, and then click **Next**.

15. To use the recommended RAM, retain the **Using the recommended RAM** option button, and then click **Next**.
16. To create a new virtual hard disk in the default location, click the **A new virtual hard disk** option button, click **Next**, review the Virtual Hard Disk allocation, and then click **Next**.
17. Review the virtual machine attributes, and then click **Finish**.
18. To configure the network adapter, click the **Settings** button, click **Networking**, click the **Adapter 1** drop-down menu, click **Microsoft Loopback Adapter**, and then click **OK**.
19. Leave the computer logged on for the next activity.

Implementing the Dovercorp.local Virtual Network

Before you install the three operating systems for the Dovercorp.local network, you must define the communications scheme.

Dovercorp.local Network Diagram

Figure 4-2 shows the virtual devices for the network.

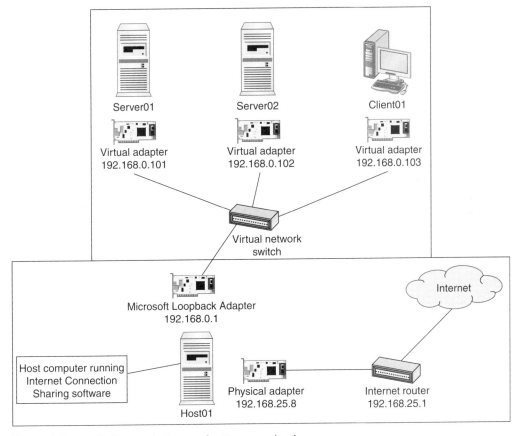

Figure 4-2 Detailed network diagram for Dovercorp.local

Locate the virtual network switch in the middle of the diagram. The three virtual machines, Server01, Server02, and Client01, access the Dovercorp.local virtual network through this virtual switch. The host computer, Host01, contains a Microsoft Loopback Adapter, which was installed to permit an Internet connection using Internet Connection Sharing. This Microsoft Loopback Adapter also participates as a member of the virtual network.

The host computer runs the Internet Connection Sharing (ICS) software, which was discussed and installed in Chapter 1. With ICS, you can connect the three virtual machines to the Internet using the Internet connection provided by the host computer. ICS routes packets between the two network adapters on the host—the physical network adapter and the Microsoft Loopback Adapter. In addition, ICS supports DNS name resolution, which is used to resolve the computers on the Internet to IP addresses.

To ensure reliable communication between the virtual machines, the two servers require **static IP addressing**, in which the computer uses the IP address assigned by an administrator. With static IP addressing, each virtual machine is assigned a unique static IP address; for example, Server01 has 192.168.0.101. By using static IP addresses, you always know the IP address configurations for the virtual machines. This simplifies the configuration and testing of your virtual machines. The IP address configurations for the three virtual machines and the host computer are presented in Table 4-2. All Internet-bound traffic travels through the gateway at IP address 192.168.0.1. Because all of the virtual machines will access the future DNS service on Server01, the DNS for the three virtual machines is 192.168.0.101.

Table 4-2 Summary of IP addressing

Virtual machine/ computer	Adapter type	Assigned IP address	Subnet mask	Gateway address	DNS address
Server01	Virtual adapter	192.168.0.101	255.255.255.0	192.168.0.1	192.168.0.101
Server02	Virtual adapter	192.168.0.102	255.255.255.0	192.168.0.1	192.168.0.101
Client01	Virtual adapter	192.168.0.103	255.255.255.0	192.168.0.1	192.168.0.101
Host01	Microsoft Loopback Adapter	192.168.0.1	255.255.255.0	Provided by ICS	Provided by ICS
Host01	Physical adapter	192.168.25.4 Provided by Internet router	255.255.255.0	192.168.25.1 Provided by Internet router	192.168.25.1 Provided by Internet router

The host computer, Host01, has two network adapters: the Microsoft Loopback Adapter and a physical adapter. Recall from Chapter 1 that ICS connects the two adapters. Therefore, Host01, with two network adapters, has IP addresses on both networks. ICS uses 192.168.0.1 for the IP address of the gateway from the virtual network. The IP configuration on the physical network to network 192.168.25.0 was provided dynamically by the Internet router. For the current lease, Host01 has a physical network IP address of 192.168.25.4 with a gateway IP address and DNS of 192.168.25.1.

> The IP addresses for the physical adapter on the host network are included here for illustration purposes only. The IP configuration for your host computer will be determined by your physical network's IP addressing scheme.

Installing Operating Systems for the Dovercorp.local Virtual Machines

In the activities that follow, you will install the operating systems for the three virtual machines. Although you gained experience installing these operating systems in the activities in Chapter 3, you should pay special attention to the configurations in these activities. Failure to do so might make future activities difficult or impossible to complete.

Activity 4-3: Installing Microsoft Server 2008 in Virtual Machines

Time Required: 180–240 minutes

Objective: Install Microsoft Server 2008.

Requirements: Completion of Activities 4-1 and 4-2 and the Microsoft Server 2008 DVD.

Description: In this activity, you will install Microsoft Server 2008 on two virtual machines: Server01 and Server02.

1. If necessary, log on to your Host PC with a username of **Student** and a password of **Secret1**.
2. To start Microsoft Virtual PC 2007, click **Start,** and then click **Microsoft Virtual PC.**

Installing Windows Server 2008 in Server01

3. To start the server virtual machine, click **Server01,** and then click **Start.**
4. Insert the Microsoft Windows Server 2008 DVD into the CD/DVD drive.
5. To mount the DVD and start the installation, click the **CD** menu, click **Use Physical Drive D,** click the **Action** menu, click **Reset,** and then click **Reset** again.
6. Wait for Windows to load files.
7. To activate the virtual machine, click in the Server01 virtual machine.

> At some time during this installation, the Virtual Machine Additions is not installed on this virtual machine message box might appear. If this occurs, check the Don't show this message again check box, and then click OK.

8. When the regional dialog box opens, verify the language, time and currency, and keyboard. Correct as needed, and then click **Next.**
9. Click the **Install now** link.

10. To indicate that this virtual machine is using an evaluation copy, wait for the Type your product key for activation dialog box, clear the **Automatically activate Windows when I'm online** check box, click **Next**, and then click **No**.

11. To indicate the version to install, click **Windows Server 2008 Enterprise (Full Installation)**, check the **I have selected the edition of Windows that I purchased** check box, and then click **Next**.

12. When the Please read the license terms dialog box opens, check the **I accept the license terms** check box, and then click **Next**.

13. To start the installation, click **Custom (advanced)**, and then click **Next**.

14. Wait for Windows to copy and expand files, install features and updates, and restart to complete the installation.

15. Ignore the Press any key to boot from CD or DVD message.

16. Wait while Windows prepares to start for the first time and to complete the installation.

17. To activate the virtual machine, click in the Server01 virtual machine.

18. When the user's password must be changed before logging on the first time message appears, click **OK**. Type **Secret1** in the New password text box, press **Tab**, type **Secret1** in the Confirm password text box, press **Enter**, and then click **OK**.

19. To set the time zone, click the **Set time zone** link, click the **Change time zone** button, click the appropriate time zone, review the date and time and change if needed, and then click **OK** twice.

20. To open the Local Area Connection properties dialog box, click the **Configure networking** link, right-click **Local Area Connection**, click **Properties**, clear the **Internet Protocol Version 6 (TCP/IPv6)** check box, click **Internet Protocol Version 4 (TCP/IPv4)**, and then click the **Properties** button.

21. To provide an IP configuration, click the **Use the following IP address** option button, type **192.168.0.101** in the IP address text box, press **Tab** twice, type **192.168.0.1** in the Default gateway text box, press **Tab** twice, type **192.168.0.101** in the Preferred DNS server text box, click **OK**, click **Close**, and then close the Network Connections window.

22. To provide a computer name, click the **Provide computer name and domain** link, click the **Change** button, type **Server01** in the Computer name text box, click **OK** twice, click **Close**, and then click the **Restart Now** button.

23. Wait for the virtual machine to restart.

24. Ignore the Press any key to boot from CD or DVD message.

25. Press **right Alt+delete** and log on to your Server01 virtual machine with a username of **Administrator** and a password of **Secret1**.

26. To enable network discovery and file sharing, click **Start**, right-click **Network**, click **Properties**, click the **Network discovery** drop-down arrow, click the **Turn on network discovery** option button, click the **Apply** button, click the **No, make the network that I am connected to a private network** link, click the **File sharing** drop-down arrow, click the **Turn on file sharing** option button, click the **Apply** button, and then close the Network and Sharing Center window.

27. Click the **Do not show this window at logon** check box and close the Initial Configuration Tasks window.

28. To shut down the server, click in the virtual machine window, click **Start**, click the arrow next to the Lock button, click **Shut Down**, click the **Option** drop-down menu, click **Operating System: Reconfiguration** (**Planned**), and then click **OK**.

Installing Windows Server 2008 in Server02

29. Repeat Steps 3–20 using Server02 in place of Server01.

30. To allocate the disk partition for the operating system, click the **Drive options** (**advanced**) link, click the **New** link, type **16384** in the MB text box, and then click **Apply**.

31. Wait for the partition to be allocated, click the **Format** link, click **OK**, and then click **Next**.

32. Repeat Steps 14 through 19 using Server02 in place of Server01.

33. To open the Local Area Connection properties dialog box, click the **Configure networking** link, right-click **Local Area Connection**, click **Properties**, clear the **Internet Protocol Version 6 (TCP/IPv6)** check box, click **Internet Protocol Version 4 (TCP/IPv4)**, and then click the **Properties** button.

34. To provide an IP configuration, click the **Use the following IP address** option button, type **192.168.0.102** in the IP address text box, press **Tab** twice, type **192.168.0.1** in the Default gateway text box, press **Tab** twice, type **192.168.0.101** in the Preferred DNS server text box, click **OK**, click **Close**, and then close the Network Connections window.

35. Repeat Steps 22–28 using Server02 in place of Server01.

36. Leave the computer logged on for the next activity.

Activity 4-4: Installing Microsoft Vista Business

Time Required: 90–120 minutes

Objective: Install Microsoft Vista Business.

Requirements: Completion of Activities 4-1 and 4-2 and the Microsoft Vista Business DVD.

Description: In this activity, you will install Microsoft Vista Business in virtual machine Client01.

1. If necessary, log on to your Host PC with a username of **Student** and a password of **Secret1**.

2. If necessary, to start Microsoft Virtual PC 2007, click **Start**, and then click **Microsoft Virtual PC**.

3. Insert the Microsoft Vista Business DVD into the DVD drive.

4. If the Autoplay window opens, close the window.

5. To start the Vista virtual machine, click **Client01**, and then click the **Start** button in the Virtual PC 2007 Console.

120 Chapter 4 Implementing the Dovercorp.local Virtual Network

6. To mount the DVD and start the installation, click the **CD** menu, click **Use Physical Drive D**, click the **Action** menu, click **Reset**, and then click **Reset**.
7. Wait for Vista to load files.
8. When the splash is displayed, click the mouse in the virtual machine window.
9. When the regional dialog box opens, verify the language, time and currency, and keyboard. Correct as needed, and then click **Next**.
10. To start the installation, click the **Install now** link.
11. Wait for Vista to load files.

NOTE At some time during this installation, the Virtual Machine Additions is not installed on this virtual machine message box will appear. When this occurs, check the Don't show this message again check box, and then click OK.

12. To indicate that you want to install an evaluation copy of Vista and when the Type your product key for activation dialog box opens, clear the **Automatically activate Windows when I'm online** check box, click **Next**, and then click **No**.
13. When the Select the edition of Windows that you purchased dialog box opens, click **Windows Vista Business**, check the **I have selected the edition of Windows that I purchased** check box, and then click **Next**.
14. When the Please read the license terms dialog box opens, check the **I accept the license terms** check box, and then click **Next**.
15. When the **Which type of installation do you want?** dialog box opens, click **Custom (advanced)**.
16. When the **Where do you want to install Windows?** dialog box opens, click **Next**.
17. Wait for Windows to copy and expand files, install features and updates, and then restart to complete the installation.
18. Ignore the Press any key to boot from CD or DVD message.
19. Wait while Windows prepares to start for the first time and complete installation.
20. When the Choose a user and picture dialog box opens, type **Student** in the Type a username (for example, John) text box, press **Tab**, type **Secret1** in the Type a password (recommended) text box, press **Tab**, type **Secret1** in the Retype your password text box, and then click **Next**.
21. When the Type a computer name and choose a desktop background dialog box opens, type **Client01** in the Type a computer name (for example, Office-PC) text box, and then click **Next**.
22. When the Help protect Windows automatically dialog box opens, click **Install important updates only**.
23. To set the time zone, click the **Time zone** drop-down menu, click the appropriate time zone, review the date and time and correct as needed, and then click **Next**.

24. When the Select your computer's current location dialog box opens, click **Work**, and then click **Start**.
25. Wait for the Password screen, type **Secret1**, and then press **Enter**.
26. Wait for Vista to prepare your desktop and set Personalized Settings.
27. Wait for Vista to complete configuration and to download and install updates. Click the **Restart now** button, wait for the updates to be configured, and then logon with a username of **Student** and a password of **Secret1**.
28. If the Welcome Center window opens, close the Welcome Center window.
29. Click **Start**, click **Control Panel**, click the **View network status and tasks** link under Network and Internet, click the **View status** link under Network (Private network), and then click the **Properties** button.
30. When the User Account Control dialog box opens, click the **Continue** button.
31. To provide an IP configuration, clear the **Internet Protocol Version 6 (TCP/IPv6)** check box, click **Internet Protocol Version 4 (TCP/IPv4)**, click the **Properties** button, click the **Use the following IP address** option button, type 192.168.0.103 in the IP address text box, press **Tab** twice, type 192.168.0.1 in the Default gateway text box, press **Tab** twice, type 192.168.0.101 in the Preferred DNS server text box, click **OK**, and then click **Close** twice.
32. To enable File sharing, click the **File sharing** drop-down arrow, click the **Turn on file sharing** option button, and then click the **Apply** button.
33. When the User Account Control dialog box opens, click the **Continue** button.
34. When the Do you want to turn on file sharing for all public networks? message appears, click **No, make the network that I am connected to a private network**.
35. Close the Network and Sharing Center window.
36. To shut down the virtual machine, click **Start**, click the arrow next to the Lock button, and then click **Shut Down**.

Activity 4-5: Installing Virtual Machine Additions

Time Required: 10 minutes

Objective: Install Virtual Machine Additions into the virtual machines.

Requirements: Completion of Activities 4-1 through 4-4.

Description: In this activity, you will install Virtual Machine Additions into the three virtual machines.

1. If necessary, log on to your Host PC with a username of **Student** and a password of **Secret1**.
2. If necessary, to start Microsoft Virtual PC 2007, click **Start**, and then click **Microsoft Virtual PC**.

Installing Virtual Machine Additions in Server01

3. To start the virtual machine, click **Server01**, and then click **Start**.
4. Log on to your virtual machine with a username of **Administrator** and a password of **Secret1**.
5. To install the Virtual Machines Additions in a guest operating system, press right **Alt**, click the **CD** menu, click **Release Physical Drive D:**, click the **Action** menu, click **Install or Update Virtual Machine Additions**, and then click the **Continue** button.
6. When the Autoplay window opens, click **Run setup.exe**.
7. Click in the virtual machine, and then click **Next**.
8. Wait for the installation to complete, and then click **Finish**.
9. When requested to restart your system, click **Yes**.
10. Wait for **Server01** to restart.
11. Log on to your virtual machine with a username of **Administrator** and a password of **Secret1**.

Installing Virtual Machine Additions in Server02

12. Repeat Steps 3–11 using Server02 in place of Server01.

Installing Virtual Machine Additions in Client01

13. To start the virtual machine, click **Client01**, and then click **Start**.
14. Log on to your virtual machine with a username of **Student** and a password of **Secret1**.
15. If the Welcome Center window opens, close the Welcome Center window.
16. To install the Virtual Machine Additions in a guest operating system, press right **Alt**, click the **CD** menu, click **Release Physical Drive D:**, click the **Action** menu, click **Install or Update Virtual Machine Additions**, and then click the **Continue** button.
17. When the Autoplay window opens, click **Run setup.exe**.
18. When the User Account Control dialog box opens, click the **Continue** button.
19. Click in the virtual machine, and then click **Next**.
20. Wait for the installation to complete, and then click **Finish**.
21. When requested to restart your system, click **Yes**.
22. Log on to your virtual machine with a username of **Student** and a password of **Secret1**.
23. Leave the computer logged on for the next activity.

Verifying the IP Addressing on the Dovercorp.local Network

If the IP configurations are not correct, the virtual machines will not communicate with each other. You will need to check the IP configuration for each virtual machine and for the host computer. The host computer is included because it runs ICS and is the virtual network's gateway to the Internet.

To check the IP configuration, you can run the ipconfig command from a command prompt. You can open a command prompt by clicking Start, typing cmd in the Start Search text box, and then pressing Enter. You will check the IP configuration of your virtual machines in Activity 4-6.

The IP configuration for the Server01 virtual machine is presented in Figure 4-3. To ensure proper communication, you need to verify these entries: The IPv4 address should be 192.168.0.101, the subnet mask should be 255.255.255.0 (this was entered when the Tab key was pressed), the default gateway should be 192.168.0.1, and the DNS entry should be 192.168.0.101.

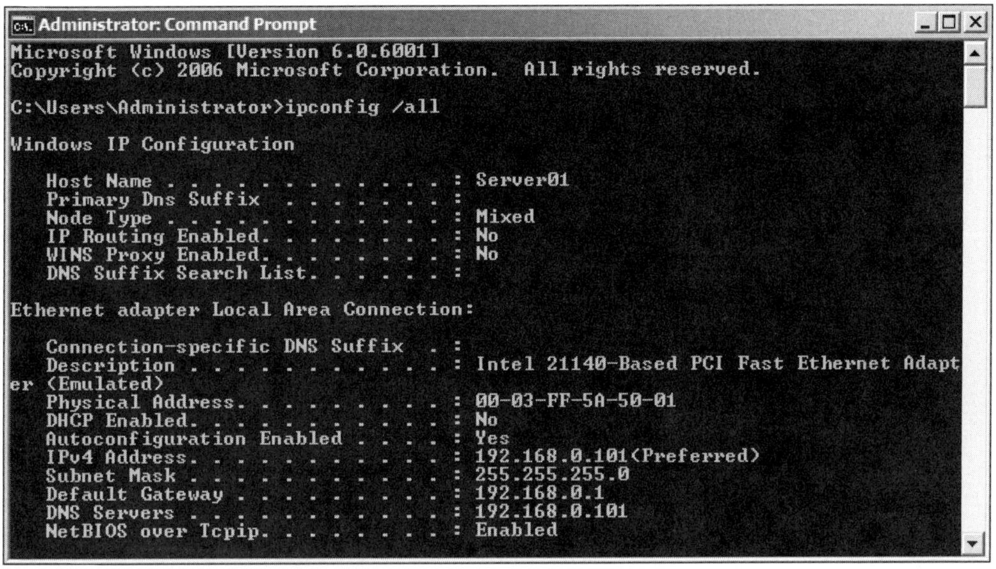

Figure 4-3 IP configuration for Server01

The IP configuration for the Server02 virtual machine is shown in Figure 4-4 (on the next page). As with Server01, you need to verify these entries: The IPv4 address should be 192.168.0.102, the subnet mask should be 255.255.255.0, the default gateway should be 192.168.0.1, and the DNS entry should be 192.168.0.101.

The IP configuration for the Client01 virtual machine is shown in Figure 4-5 (on the next page). You will need to verify these entries as well: The IPv4 address should be 192.168.0.103, the subnet mask should be 255.255.255.0, the default gateway should be 192.168.0.1, and the DNS entry should be 192.168.0.101.

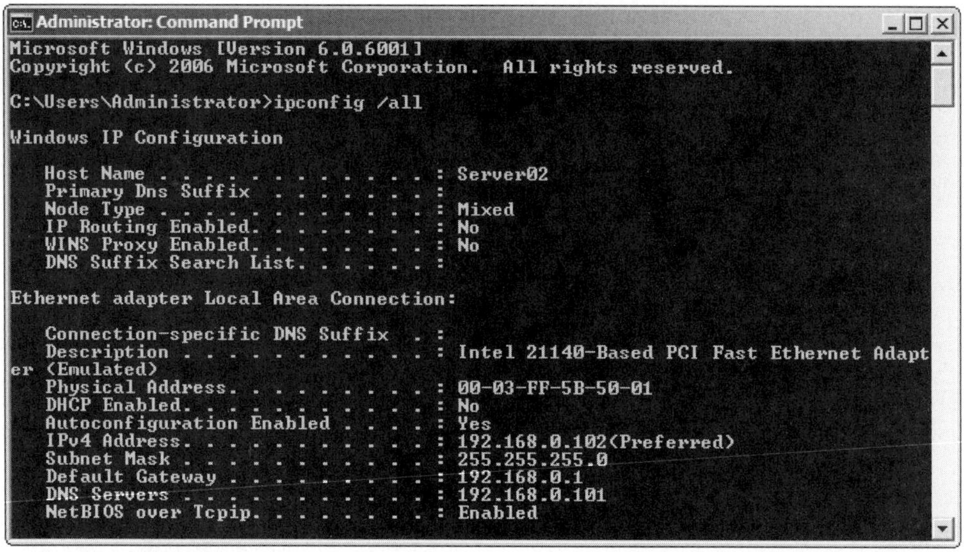

```
Administrator: Command Prompt

Microsoft Windows [Version 6.0.6001]
Copyright (c) 2006 Microsoft Corporation.  All rights reserved.

C:\Users\Administrator>ipconfig /all

Windows IP Configuration

    Host Name . . . . . . . . . . . . : Server02
    Primary Dns Suffix  . . . . . . . :
    Node Type . . . . . . . . . . . . : Mixed
    IP Routing Enabled. . . . . . . . : No
    WINS Proxy Enabled. . . . . . . . : No
    DNS Suffix Search List. . . . . . :

Ethernet adapter Local Area Connection:

    Connection-specific DNS Suffix  . :
    Description . . . . . . . . . . . : Intel 21140-Based PCI Fast Ethernet Adapter (Emulated)
    Physical Address. . . . . . . . . : 00-03-FF-5B-50-01
    DHCP Enabled. . . . . . . . . . . : No
    Autoconfiguration Enabled . . . . : Yes
    IPv4 Address. . . . . . . . . . . : 192.168.0.102(Preferred)
    Subnet Mask . . . . . . . . . . . : 255.255.255.0
    Default Gateway . . . . . . . . . : 192.168.0.1
    DNS Servers . . . . . . . . . . . : 192.168.0.101
    NetBIOS over Tcpip. . . . . . . . : Enabled
```

Figure 4-4 IP configuration for Server02

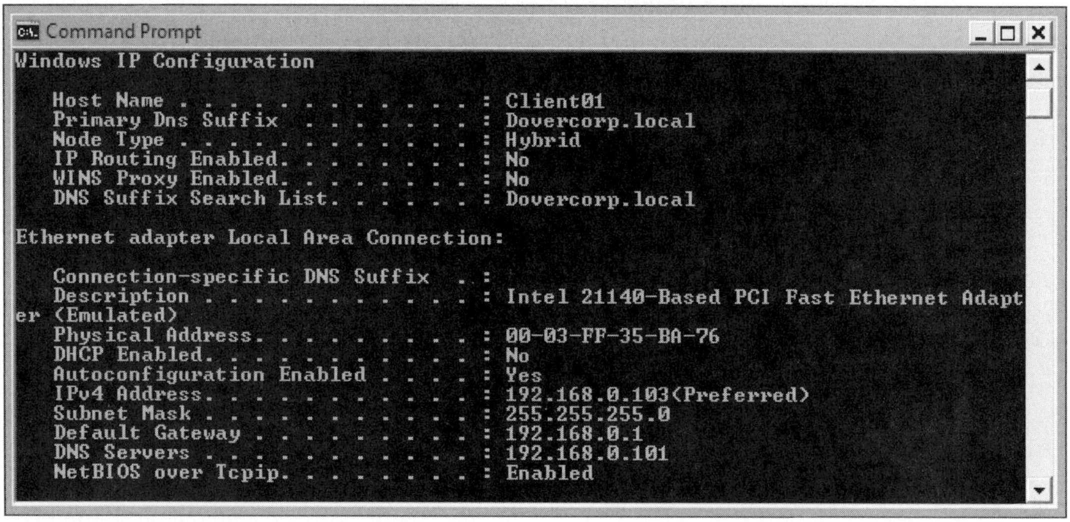

```
Command Prompt

Windows IP Configuration

    Host Name . . . . . . . . . . . . : Client01
    Primary Dns Suffix  . . . . . . . : Dovercorp.local
    Node Type . . . . . . . . . . . . : Hybrid
    IP Routing Enabled. . . . . . . . : No
    WINS Proxy Enabled. . . . . . . . : No
    DNS Suffix Search List. . . . . . : Dovercorp.local

Ethernet adapter Local Area Connection:

    Connection-specific DNS Suffix  . :
    Description . . . . . . . . . . . : Intel 21140-Based PCI Fast Ethernet Adapter (Emulated)
    Physical Address. . . . . . . . . : 00-03-FF-35-BA-76
    DHCP Enabled. . . . . . . . . . . : No
    Autoconfiguration Enabled . . . . : Yes
    IPv4 Address. . . . . . . . . . . : 192.168.0.103(Preferred)
    Subnet Mask . . . . . . . . . . . : 255.255.255.0
    Default Gateway . . . . . . . . . : 192.168.0.1
    DNS Servers . . . . . . . . . . . : 192.168.0.101
    NetBIOS over Tcpip. . . . . . . . : Enabled
```

Figure 4-5 IP configuration for Client01

The IP configuration for the host computer is shown in Figure 4-6. The host computer, which runs ICS, has two network adapters. The Microsoft Loopback Adapter is the link between the virtual machines and the host machine. As ICS is installed, it completes the IP configuration for the Microsoft Loopback Adapter. Verify the entries for this adapter: The IPv4 address should be 192.168.0.1 and the subnet mask should be 255.255.255.0. The other adapter is the physical adapter in the host computer. The entries for this adapter reflect the IP configuration for your actual host network. For illustration purposes, the IP configuration is as follows: The IPv4 address is 192.168.25.4, the subnet mask is 255.255.255.0, the default gateway is 192.168.25.1, and the DNS entry is 192.168.25.1. The IP address 192.168.25.1 is the address of the Internet router.

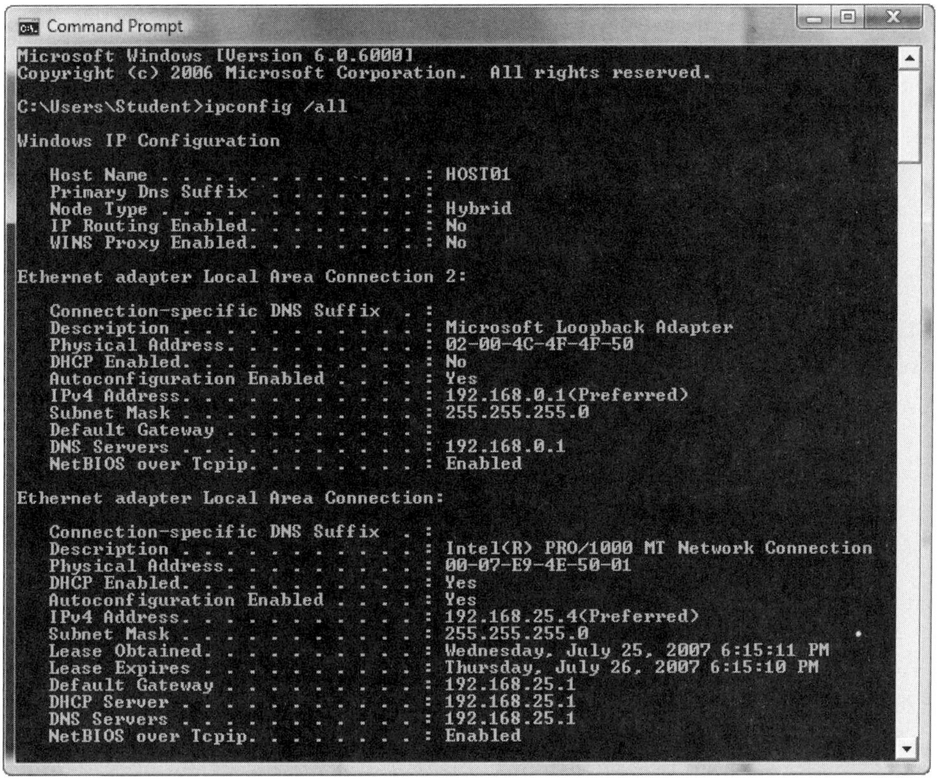

Figure 4-6 IP configuration for Host01

Activity 4-6: Verifying IP Configurations

Time Required: 10 minutes

Objective: Verify the IP configurations for the virtual machines.

Requirements: Completion of Activities 4-1 through 4-5.

Description: In this activity, you will use the ipconfig command to verify that the IP configuration is correct on each virtual machine and the host computer.

1. If necessary, log on to your host PC with a username of **Student** and a password of **Secret1**.
2. If necessary, to start Microsoft Virtual PC 2007, click **Start**, and then click **Microsoft Virtual PC**.

Verifying IP Configuration for Server01

3. If necessary, to start the Server01 virtual machine, click **Server01**, and then click **Start**.
4. If necessary, log on to your virtual machine with a username of **Administrator** and a password of **Secret1**.
5. To open a command prompt window, click **Start**, and then click **Command Prompt**.
6. To execute the ipconfig command, type **ipconfig /all**, and then press **Enter**.
7. Scroll the window and verify that the IP configuration matches Figure 4-3 for the IP addresses. If there are discrepancies for the IP addresses, contact your instructor.

To see more of the ipconfig results, drag the bottom of the command prompt window down to enlarge the window.

8. To close the command prompt window, type **exit** and then press **Enter**.

Verifying IP Configuration for Server02

9. Repeat Steps 3–6 using Server02 in place of Server01.
10. Scroll the window and verify that the IP configuration matches Figure 4-4 for the IP addresses. If there are discrepancies for the IP addresses, contact your instructor.
11. To close the command prompt window, type **exit**, and then press **Enter**.

Verifying the IP Configuration for Client01

12. If necessary, to start the Client01 virtual machine, click **Client01**, and then click **Start**.
13. If necessary, log on to your virtual machine with a username of **Student** and a password of **Secret1**.
14. To open a command prompt window, click **Start**, type **cmd** in the Start Search text box, and then press **Enter**.
15. To execute the ipconfig command, type **ipconfig /all**, and then press **Enter**.
16. Scroll the window and verify that the IP configuration matches Figure 4-5 for the IP addresses. If there are discrepancies for the IP addresses, contact your instructor.
17. To close the command prompt window, type **exit**, and then press **Enter**.

Verifying the IP Configuration for the Host Computer

18. To open a command prompt window on the host computer, click **Start** on the host computer, type **cmd** in the Start Search text box, and then press **Enter**.
19. To execute the ipconfig command, type **ipconfig /all**, and then press **Enter**.
20. Scroll the window and verify that the IP configuration resembles Figure 4-6 for the IP addresses.

 The IP addresses for the host network were provided for illustration purposes only. The IP configuration for your host computer will be determined by your physical network IP addressing scheme.

21. To close the command prompt window, type **exit**, and then press **Enter**.

22. Leave the computer logged on for the next activity.

Configuring the Windows Firewall

A personal firewall controls network traffic to and from your computer, permitting or denying communications based on your established security settings. Windows Firewall, Microsoft's personal firewall software, provides protection against network attacks for computers on which it is enabled. Windows Firewall does this by checking all communications that cross the network connection and selectively blocking certain communications.

Because Windows Firewall monitors all aspects of the communications that cross its path, it is considered a **stateful firewall**. It keeps track of the state of network connections (such as TCP streams and UDP communications) traveling across it. The firewall is programmed to identify legitimate packets for various types of connections. Only packets matching a known connection state are allowed by the firewall; others are rejected. An attempt by someone on the Internet trying to connect to your computer is called an **unsolicited request**. When your computer gets an unsolicited request, Windows Firewall blocks the connection.

Windows Firewall is designed to monitor and manage both incoming and outgoing traffic. For example, you can configure Windows Firewall to block all traffic sent to specific ports, such as the well-known ports used by virus software, or to specific addresses containing either sensitive or undesirable content.

In brief, the default behavior of the Windows Firewall is to:

- Block all incoming traffic unless it is solicited or it matches a configured rule.
- Allow all outgoing traffic unless it matches a configured rule.

The default blocking behavior can sometimes cause a problem. The ping command is commonly used to check connectivity between two computers. It involves sending an Echo Request using an **Internet Control Message Protocol (ICMP)** message. ICMP is a message control and error-reporting protocol used to announce network errors, time-outs, and congestion. The ping command is chiefly used by networked computers' operating systems to send error messages—indicating, for instance, that a requested service is not available or that a host could not be reached. The Echo Request message sends a packet of data to another computer and expects that data to be sent in return in an Echo Reply. Windows Firewall rejects this Echo Request because this is unsolicited data.

Network administrators must change the File and Printer Sharing (Echo Request – ICMPv4-In) rule in Windows Firewall to permit the ICMP request to be accepted. Figure 4-7 (on the next page) shows Windows Firewall with Advanced Security window. In Activity 4-7, you will set this rule for your three virtual machines and the host computer.

To open the Windows Firewall with Advanced Security snap-in, you must click Start, click Control Panel, click Control Panel Home, click the System and Maintenance link, click the Administrative Tools link, and double-click the Windows Firewall with Advanced Security shortcut.

128   Chapter 4   Implementing the Dovercorp.local Virtual Network

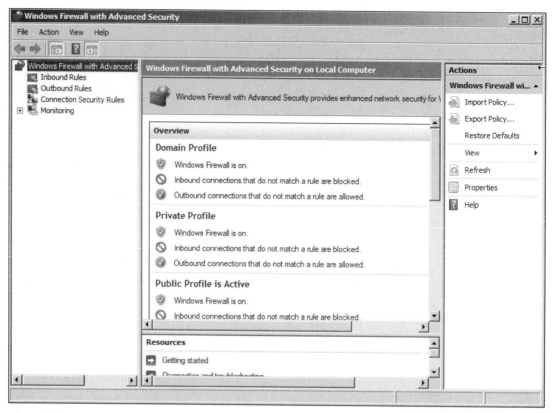

Figure 4-7 Windows Firewall with Advanced Security window

Figure 4-8 shows the location of the File and Printer Sharing (Echo Request – ICMPv1-In) rule. Notice that the pane was scrolled down.

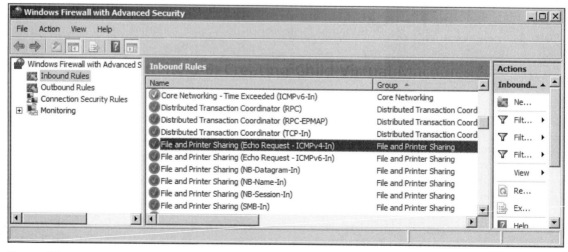

Figure 4-8 Windows Firewall—Inbound Rules

Activity 4-7: Setting the ICMP Rules

Time Required: 10 minutes

Objective: Set the ICMP rules to permit the Echo Request.

Requirements: Completion of Activities 4-1 through 4-6.

Description: In this activity, you will enable the Echo Request rule in Windows Firewall, which permits the ping command to function correctly.

1. If necessary, log on to your Host PC with a username of **Student** and a password of **Secret1**.
2. If necessary, to start Microsoft Virtual PC 2007, click **Start**, and then click **Microsoft Virtual PC**.

Setting the Firewall Rule for Server01

3. If necessary, to start the Server01 virtual machine, click **Server01**, and then click **Start**.
4. If necessary, log on to your virtual machine with a username of **Administrator** and a password of **Secret1**.
5. To open the Windows Firewall with Advanced Security snap-in, click **Start**, click the **Administrative Tools** link, and double-click the **Windows Firewall with Advanced Security** shortcut.
6. To modify the inbound rule for ICMP, click **Inbound Rules** in the left pane, scroll and double-click the **File and Printer Sharing (Echo Request – ICMPv4-In)** rule (the one with the gray check mark), click the **Enabled** check box, and then click **OK**.
7. Close the open windows.

Setting the Firewall Rule for Server02

8. Repeat Steps 3–7 using Server02 in place of Server01.

Setting the Firewall Rule for Client01

9. If necessary, to start the Client01 virtual machine, click **Client01**, and then click **Start**.
10. If necessary, log on to your virtual machine with a username of **Student** and a password of **Secret1**.
11. To open the Windows Firewall with Advanced Security snap-in, click **Start**, click **Control Panel**, click the **System and Maintenance** link, scroll and click the **Administrative Tools** link, and double-click the **Windows Firewall with Advanced Security** shortcut.
12. When the User Account Control dialog box opens, click the **Continue** button.
13. To modify the inbound rule for ICMP, click **Inbound Rules** in the left pane, scroll and double-click the **File and Printer Sharing (Echo Request – ICMPv4-In)** rule (the one with the gray check mark), click the **Enabled** check box, and then click **OK**.
14. Close the open windows.

Setting the Firewall Rule for Host

15. To open the Windows Firewall with Advanced Security snap-in on the host, click **Start** on the host computer, click **Control Panel**, click the **System and Maintenance** link, scroll and click the **Administrative Tools** link, and double-click the **Windows Firewall with Advanced Security** shortcut.

16. When the User Account Control dialog box opens, click the **Continue** button.

17. To modify the inbound rule for ICMP, click **Inbound Rules** in the left pane, scroll and double-click the first **File and Printer Sharing (Echo Request – ICMPv4-In)** rule (the one with the gray check mark), click the **Enabled** check box, and then click **OK**.

18. Close the open windows.

19. Leave the computer logged on for the next activity.

Verifying IP Connectivity

Now that you have set the firewall rules, you will test IP connectivity between the three virtual machines and the host computer using ICMP. For this test, you use the ping command, as shown in Figure 4-9. You will conduct the testing in Activity 4-8.

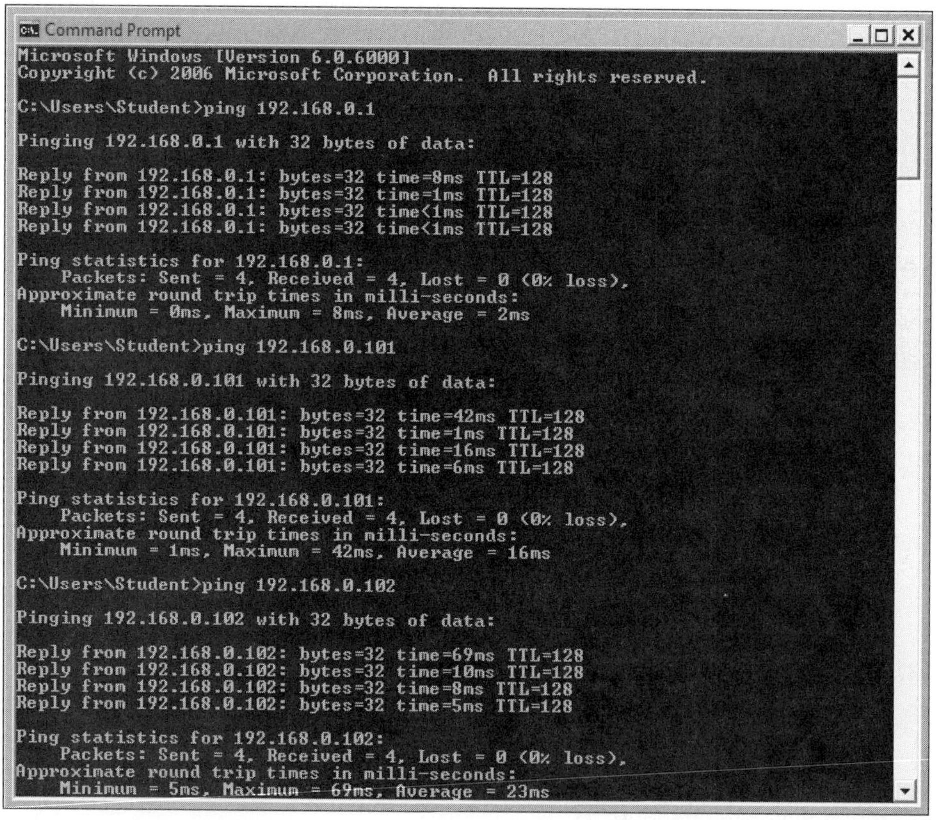

Figure 4-9 Ping test results

You will first select one of the virtual machines. In this case, the Client01 computer was used. In sequence, issue a ping command to the remaining machines—host (ping 192.168.0.1), Server01 (ping 192.168.0.101), and then Server02 (ping 192.168.0.102). There is no need to issue a ping 192.168.0.103 because this would contact the Client01 virtual machine.

Activity 4-8: Verifying IP Connectivity

Time Required: 10 minutes

Objective: Verify IP connectivity from the Client01 virtual machine.

Requirements: Completion of Activities 4-1 through 4-7.

Description: In this activity, you will verify IP connectivity between the Client01 virtual machine and the other virtual machines (Server01 and Server02) and the host computer.

1. If necessary, log on to your Host PC with a username of **Student** and a password of **Secret1**.
2. If necessary, to start the Microsoft Virtual PC 2007, click **Start**, and then click **Microsoft Virtual PC**.
3. If necessary, to start the Server01 virtual machine, click **Server01**, and then click **Start**. If necessary, log on to the Server01 virtual machine with a username of **Administrator** and a password of **Secret1**.
4. If necessary, to start the Server02 virtual machine, click **Server02**, and then click **Start**. If necessary, log on to the Server02 virtual machine with a username of **Administrator** and a password of **Secret1**.
5. If necessary, to start the Client01 virtual machine, click **Client01**, and then click **Start**.
6. If necessary, log on to the Client01 virtual machine with a username of **Student** and a password of **Secret1**.
7. To open a command prompt window for the Client01 VM, click **Start**, type **cmd** in the Start Search text box, and then press **Enter**.
8. To execute the first command, type **ping 192.168.0.1** and then press **Enter**. Verify that you can ping the gateway. If you cannot reach the gateway, contact your instructor.
9. To execute the second command, type **ping 192.168.0.101** and then press **Enter**. Verify that you can ping Server01. If you cannot reach Server01, contact your instructor.
10. To execute the third command, type **ping 192.168.0.102** and then press **Enter**. Verify that you can ping Server02. If you cannot reach Server02, contact your instructor.
11. Leave the computer logged on for the next activity.

Implementing Active Directory Domain Services

Active Directory Domain Services provides a directory service that you can use for centralized, secure management of your network. Installing Active Directory Domain Services on Server01 establishes that computer as the domain controller for the Dovercorp.local network.

In the sections that follow, you preview the process for creating a domain controller. You will create a domain controller on Server01 in Activity 4-9.

Overview of Active Directory Domain Services Installation

The first action is to add a role for Server01, which you accomplish by clicking the Add roles link in the Server Manager, as shown in Figure 4-10.

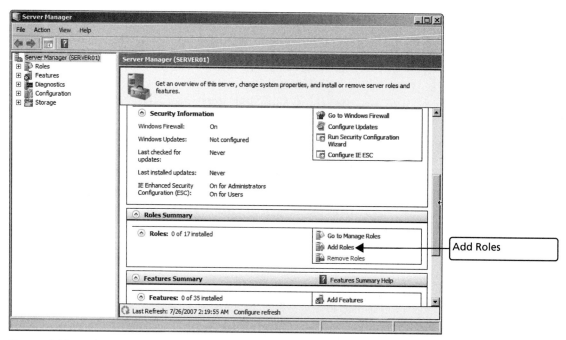

Figure 4-10 Server Manager

The Add Roles Wizard provides a dialog box, as shown in Figure 4-11, where you choose the new role for your server—Active Directory Domain Services. If you need additional information about a role, click the role. An explanation—in this case, DNS Server—appears in the upper-right corner. Notice that DNS, which will be needed, can be installed with the installation of Active Directory Domain Services. Advance through the Add Roles Wizard by clicking Next twice and clicking Install.

Figure 4-12 shows the status of the installation of Active Directory Domain Services.

Implementing Active Directory Domain Services **133**

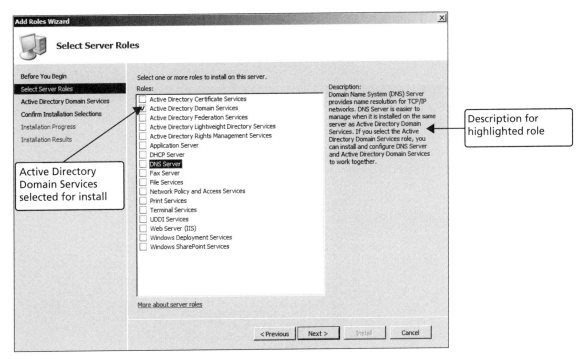

Figure 4-11 Select Server Roles—Active Directory Domain Services

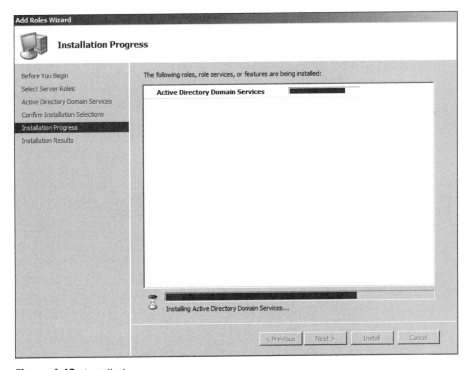

Figure 4-12 Installation progress

Figure 4-13 shows the installation results, indicating that the installation of the role service was successful, but notice that Active Directory Domain Services has not been installed. The Active Directory Domain Services Installation Wizard still needs to run.

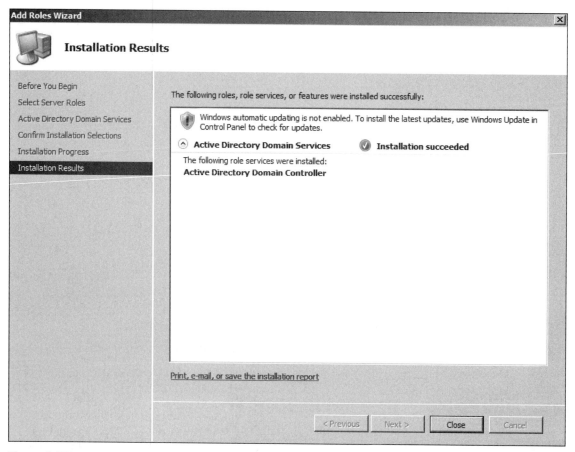

Figure 4-13 Installation results

After the Active Directory Domain Services Installation Wizard runs, you are returned to the Server Manager, as shown in Figure 4-14. Because you have a role installed, you have a role to manage. Clicking the Go to Manage Roles link advances to the Roles view.

Figure 4-15 shows the Roles view, including a summary for Active Directory Domain Services. Clicking the Go to Active Directory Domain Services link advances to Active Directory Domain Services Role view.

The message shown in Figure 4-16 (on page 136) states that the server has not been promoted to a domain controller. You are prompted to run the Active Directory Domain Services Installation Wizard. Clicking this link starts the Active Directory Domain Services Installation Wizard.

In Figure 4-17 (on page 136), you see the initial welcome dialog box for the Active Directory Domain Services Installation Wizard. Clicking Next starts the installation process.

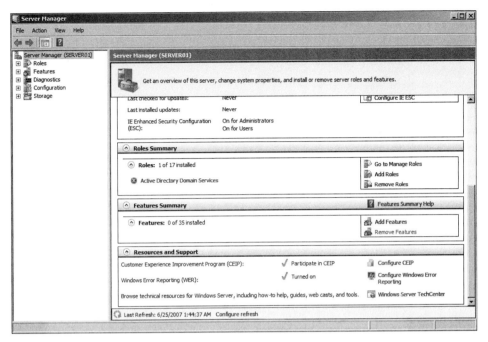

Figure 4-14 Server Manager

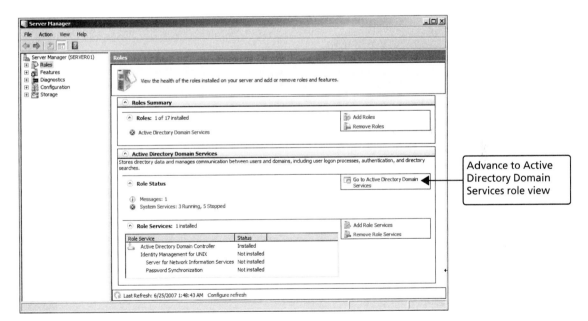

Figure 4-15 Server Manager—Roles

136 Chapter 4 Implementing the Dovercorp.local Virtual Network

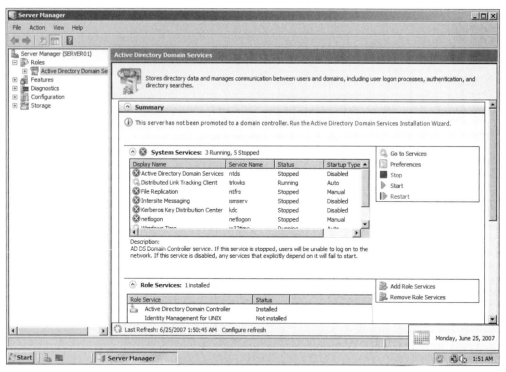

Figure 4-16 Server Manager—Active Directory Domain Services

Figure 4-17 Active Directory Domain Services installation

In Figure 4-18, you make decisions regarding forests and domains. A **forest** is a logical collection of domains. Because you are building a single domain, you select Create a new domain in a new forest.

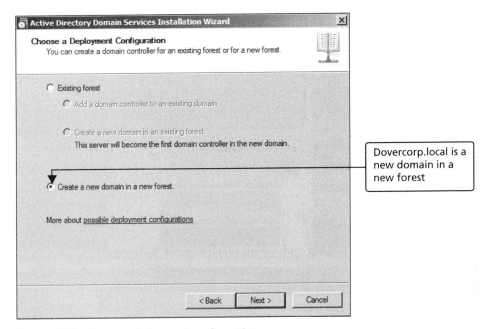

Figure 4-18 Choose a deployment configuration

You will enter Dovercorp.local as your DNS name. See Figure 4-19 (on the next page). Because you have one forest with one domain, the DNS name is called the forest root domain.

Domain controllers can run different versions of Windows Server operating systems. The Active Directory Domain Services functional level of a domain or forest depends on which versions of Windows Server operating systems you run on the domain controllers in the domain or forest. The domain or forest's advanced features are related to its functional level.

Figure 4-20 on the next page shows the selection for the forest functional level. The functional levels for Windows Server 2003 and Windows Server 2008 remain the same. By selecting a functional level of Windows Server 2003, you create a network where you could create additional domain controllers using existing Windows Server 2003 operating systems.

138 Chapter 4 Implementing the Dovercorp.local Virtual Network

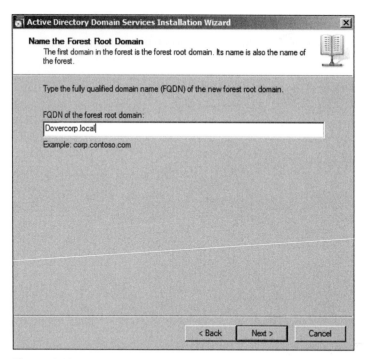

Figure 4-19 Name the forest root domain

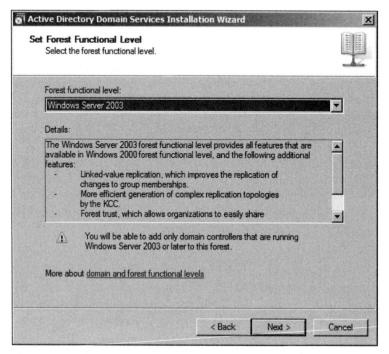

Figure 4-20 Forest functional level

Figure 4-21 shows the setting for the domain functional level. Again, Windows Server 2003 is chosen as the functional level to match the forest functional level.

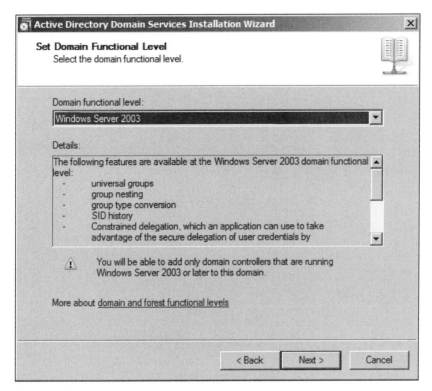

Figure 4-21 Domain functional level

You are given the option to permit the Active Directory Domain Services Installation Wizard to install DNS. DNS must be running on the network prior to installing the Active Directory Domain Services or installed with Active Directory Domain Services. Using the wizard to install the DNS server in an Active Directory Domain Services environment simplifies the installation process, which can be complicated if you are installing manually. See Figure 4-22 on the next page for the DNS server information.

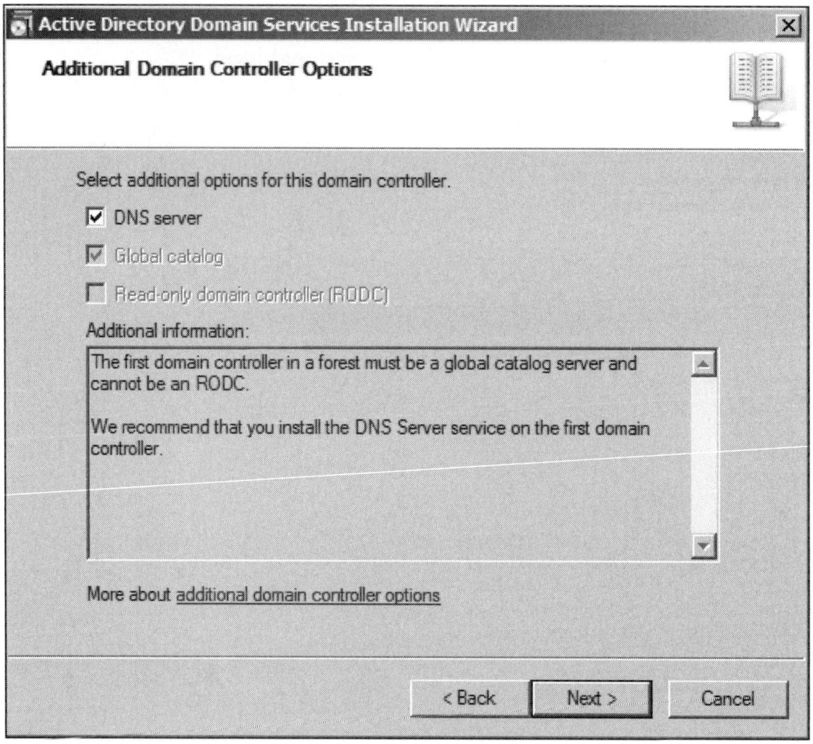

Figure 4-22 Additional domain controller options

The Dovercorp.local network has only one DNS server, which is being installed on Server01. Because there is only one DNS server in the network and a delegation is not required, you can safely ignore the warning message shown in Figure 4-23.

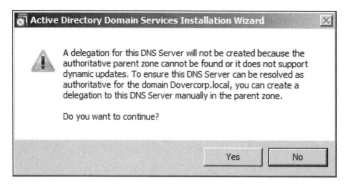

Figure 4-23 Delegation of DNS

If Server01 had multiple physical hard drives, the folders, shown in Figure 4-24, could be balanced across these physical hard drives. In your virtual environment, the default choices are satisfactory.

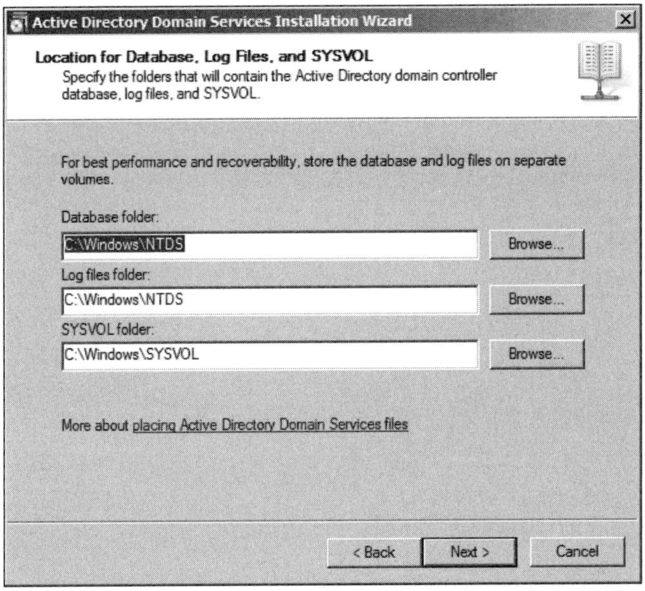

Figure 4-24 File locations

You can set up Active Directory Domain Services to restore the Directory Services databases from a backup. In Figure 4-25, the passwords for use by the Restore Mode Administrator account are entered for this possible restoration. The Restore Mode Administrator account is a special account to be used when the Directory Services databases are restored from a backup.

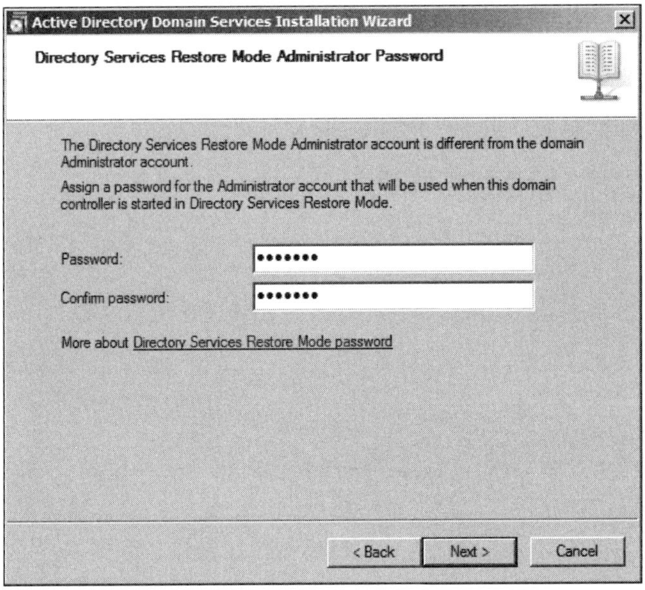

Figure 4-25 Restore mode password

Finally, the Summary screen indicates that the Active Directory Domain Services configuration has been completed. See Figure 4-26. If you change your mind about one of the settings you selected, the wizard would allow you to back up and make the change.

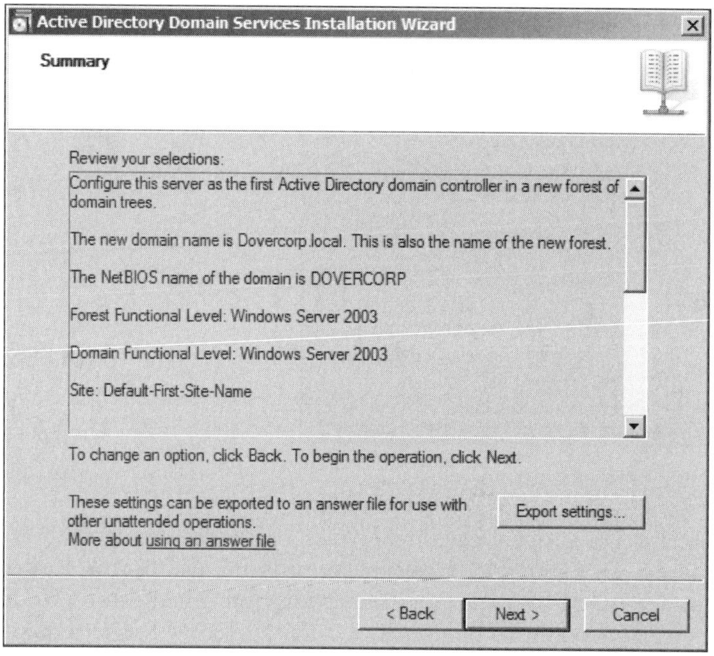

Figure 4-26 Installation summary

In Figure 4-27, you see the installation progress. Installation takes a few minutes and is a good time to take a break. The progress text changes to indicate the current activity.

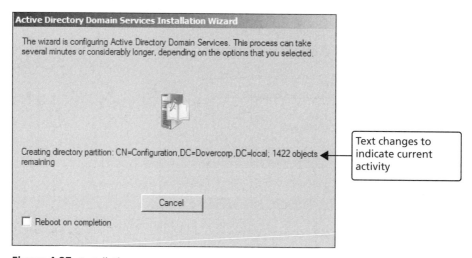

Figure 4-27 Installation progress

The wizard completes with a dialog box indicating that the installation is final. Figure 4-28 provides a brief summary of the activity. The virtual machine will restart to change to its new role—domain controller.

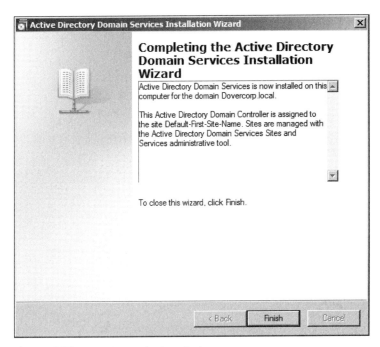

Figure 4-28 Completing the installation

After you complete the installation, you should view the results of your efforts. Active Directory Users and Computers is an administrative tool used for viewing the objects stored in Active Directory. Figure 4-29 shows Active Directory Users and Computers expanded to show the Domain Controllers node for the domain controller that you just created.

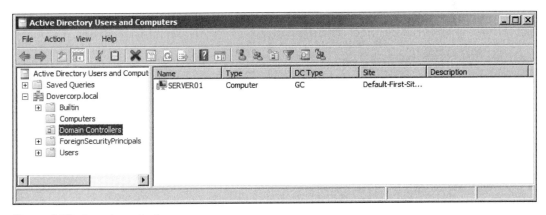

Figure 4-29 Domain controllers

You view the users and security groups by clicking the Users node. Figure 4-30 shows the default users and security groups. Default users are the user accounts that permit access to the domain resources. Default user accounts are represented by an icon with a single head. An example of a default user account is the Administrator account. To simplify administration, users are grouped into security groups, which are represented by icons with two heads. Consider the Domain Users security group. This security group will contain the user accounts for those users who require access to network resources within the domain.

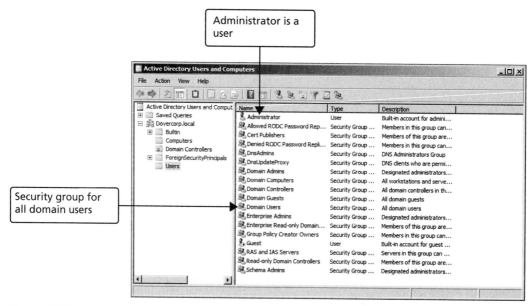

Figure 4-30 Users and security groups

Although these users and groups might have names similar to those you might find on a local computer, they are, in fact, different because they will provide access to resources across the entire domain, and not just on one computer.

Activity 4-9: Creating a Domain Controller

Time Required: 45–60 minutes

Objective: Promote a virtual machine to a domain controller.

Requirements: Completion of Activities 4-1 through 4-8.

Description: In this activity, you will change the role of Server01 to establish it as a domain controller.

1. If necessary, log on to your Host PC with a username of **Student** and a password of **Secret1**.

2. If necessary, to start Microsoft Virtual PC 2007, click **Start,** and then click **Microsoft Virtual PC**.

3. If necessary, to start the Server01 virtual machine, click **Server01**, and then click **Start**.
4. If necessary, log on to the Server01 virtual machine with a username of **Administrator** and a password of **Secret1**.
5. Insert the Windows Server 2008 DVD. When the Autoplay window opens, close the window.
6. If the Server Manager does not appear, click **Start**, point to **Administrative Tools**, and click **Server Manager**.
7. To start the installation of Active Directory Domain Services, click the **Add** roles link, click **Server Roles**, check the **Active Directory Domain Services** check box, and then click **Next**.
8. Review the Introduction to Active Directory Domain Services, and then click **Next**.
9. Review the Confirm Installation Selections, and then click **Install**.
10. Review the Installation Results, and then click **Close**.
11. When the Server Manager window opens, click the **Go to Roles** link.
12. When the role status is displayed, click the **Go to Active Directory Domain Services** link.
13. When Active Directory Domain Services is displayed, click the **Run the Active Directory Domain Services Installation Wizard** (dcpromo.exe) link.
14. Review the Welcome to the Active Directory Domain Services Installation Wizard dialog box, and then click **Next**.
15. To specify the forest and domain, click the **Create a new domain in a new forest** option button, and then click **Next**.
16. Type **Dovercorp.local** in the FQDN of the forest root domain name text box, and then click **Next**.
17. Wait for the forest name and NetBIOS name to be verified.
18. Click the **Forest functional level** drop-down list arrow, click **Windows Server 2003**, and then click **Next**.
19. Retain the domain functional level setting, and then click **Next**.
20. Wait for the Examining DNS configuration progress to complete.
21. Retain the **DNS Server** check box, and then click **Next**.
22. Wait for the Examining DNS configuration progress to complete.
23. Review the delegation message, and then click **Yes**.
24. Review the file locations, and then click **Next**.
25. To set the directory services restore password, type **Secret1** in the Password text box, press **Tab**, type **Secret1** in the Confirm password text box, and then click **Next**.
26. Review the summary, and then click **Next**.
27. Wait for the installation to complete.

To check on the installation activities, watch the messages in the center of the Active Directory Domain Services Installation Wizard dialog box. Depending on the speed of the host processor, this part of the installation could take up to 30 minutes.

28. Review the Completing the Active Directory Domain Services Installation Wizard, and then click **Finish**.
29. When requested, click the **Restart Now** button.
30. Wait for the virtual machine to restart. You will see a black screen as the configuration of Active Directory Domain Services finishes.
31. Log on to the Server01 virtual machine with a username of **Administrator** and a password of **Secret1**.
32. Wait for the snap-ins to be added to the console and the roles summary to be updated in Server Manager and then click the **Roles** node.
33. To verify the correctness of your domain controller, click **Start**, click **Command Prompt**, type **dcdiag /fix**, and then press **Enter**.
34. Scroll to the line Doing Primary tests, and review the lines looking for tests that were passed.

If you have questions about the results, discuss them with your instructor.

35. Close the command prompt window.
36. Click the Server Manager (Server01) node, click the **Do not show me this console at logon** check box, and then close the Server Manager window.
37. To view the domain controller, click **Start**, point to **Administrative Tools**, click **Active Directory Users and Computers**, expand **Dovercorp.local**, and then click **Domain Controllers**.
38. To view the users and security groups, click **Users**, and then review the users and security groups.
39. To establish the forwarder for Internet host name resolution, click **Start**, point to **Administrative Tools**, click **DNS**, click the **SERVER01** node, right-click **Forwarders** in the right pane, click **Properties**, click the **Edit** button, type **192.168.0.1** over the <Click here to add an IP address or DNS Name> entry, and then click **OK** twice.
40. Leave the computer logged on for the next activity.

Joining the Domain

For a virtual machine to access the network resources of the Dovercorp.local domain, the virtual machine must be a member of the domain. This process is called *joining a domain*. In this process, you will contact the domain controller from a virtual machine and request to become a member.

The process varies from one operating system to another. But in each case, you will use the Computer Name/Domain Changes dialog box, as shown in Figure 4-31. You first enter the name of the domain to which the virtual machine should be joined.

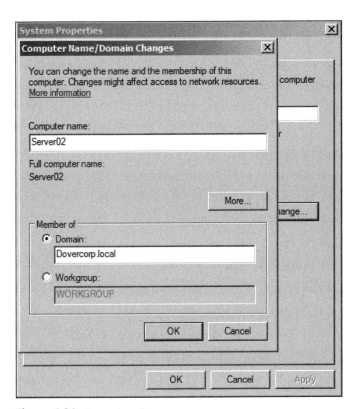

Figure 4-31 Enter domain name

To join the VM to the domain, you will need to know the user ID and password of an account that has the right to join computers to the domain. After entering the user ID and password, and waiting briefly, you will see a "Welcome to the domain" message.

After you have joined all of the computers to the domain, you can view the computer accounts in Active Directory Users and Computers by clicking the Computers node, as shown in Figure 4-32.

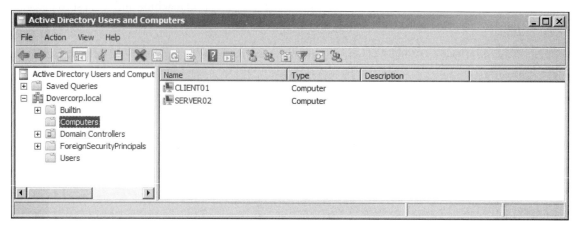

Figure 4-32 Computers shown in Active Directory Users and Computers

Activity 4-10: Joining Computers to the Domain

Time Required: 20 minutes

Objective: Join virtual machines to the Dovercorp.local domain.

Requirements: Completion of Activities 4-1 through 4-9.

Description: In this activity, you will add Server02 and Client01 to the Dovercorp.local domain.

1. If necessary, log on to your Host PC with a username of **Student** and a password of **Secret1**.
2. If necessary, to start Microsoft Virtual PC 2007, click **Start**, and then click **Microsoft Virtual PC**.
3. If necessary, to start the Server01 virtual machine, click **Server01**, and then click **Start**.
4. If necessary, log on to the Server01 virtual machine with a username of **Administrator** and a password of **Secret1**.

Joining Server02 to the Domain

5. If necessary, to start the Server02 virtual machine, click **Server02**, and then click **Start**.
6. If necessary, log on to the Server02 virtual machine with a username of **Administrator** and a password of **Secret1**.
7. To verify that DNS can resolve the IP address of Server01, click **Start**, click **Command Prompt**, type **ping server01**, and then press **Enter**.

If you have questions about the results, discuss them with your instructor.

8. Close the command prompt window.
9. To launch Server Manager, click **Start**, point to **Administrative Tools**, and then click **Server Manager**.
10. To change the domain name, click **Server Manager (Server02)**, click the **Change System Properties** link, click the **Change** button, click the **Domain** option button, type **Dovercorp.local** in the Domain text box, and then click **OK**.
11. When the Windows Security dialog box opens, type **Administrator**, type **Secret1** as the password, and then click **OK**.
12. Wait for the Welcome to the Dovercorp.local domain message to appear, and click **OK**.
13. To restart the virtual machine, click **OK**, click **Close**, and then click the **Restart Now** button.
14. Wait for the virtual machine to restart.

Joining Client01 to the Domain

15. If necessary, to start the Client01 virtual machine, click **Client01**, and then click **Start**.
16. If necessary, log on to the Client01 virtual machine with a username of **Student** and a password of **Secret1**.
17. To open a command prompt window, click **Start**, type **cmd** in the Start Search text box, and then press **Enter**.
18. To verify that DNS can resolve the IP address of Server01, type **ping server01**, and then press **Enter**.

If you have questions about the results, discuss them with your instructor.

19. Close the command prompt window.
20. To open the System Properties dialog box, click **Start**, right-click **Computer**, click **Properties**, and then click the **Advanced system settings** link.
21. When the User Account Control dialog box opens, click the **Continue** button.
22. To change the domain name, click the **Computer Name** tab, click the **Change** button, click the **Domain** option button, type **Dovercorp.local** in the Domain text box, and then click **OK**.

23. When the Windows Security dialog box opens, type **Administrator**, type **Secret1** as the password, and then click **OK**.
24. Wait for the Welcome to the Dovercorp.local domain message to appear, and then click **OK**.
25. To restart the virtual machine, click **OK**, click **Close**, and then click the **Restart Now** button.
26. Wait for the virtual machine to restart.

Chapter Summary

- You learned how to set up a virtual network using the example of the Dovercorp.local network, which you implemented for a fictitious leasing company. Implementing the network required information about each computer's role and operating system requirements.
- The process of implementing the Dovercorp.local network started with information provided on the detailed network diagram. The implementation required reviewing the IP addresses, installation of operating systems on virtual machines, and installation of Virtual Machine Additions.
- Prior to implementing Active Directory Domain Services, you verified IP configurations and set the File and Printer Sharing (ICMP) rule in Windows Firewall. The ping command verified IP connectivity between each of the virtual machines and the host computer.
- To provide centralized, secure management of the network, you installed Active Directory Domain Services. First, the Add Roles Wizard created the new role for the server, and then you used the Active Directory Domain Services Installation Wizard to complete the installation of the domain controller.

Key Terms

Active Directory Domain Services—The native directory service included with Microsoft Windows Server 2008.

directory services—A service on a network that acts as a repository of information about users, devices, and other services on a network.

domain—A collection of computers that shares access to network resources with centralized administration and security policies.

domain controller—A server that responds to security requests within a domain.

Domain Name System (DNS)—A system for converting host names and domain names into IP addresses on the Internet or on local networks that use the TCP/IP protocol.

file server—A file storage device on a local area network that is accessible to all users on the network.

forest—A logical collection of domains.

Internet Control Message Protocol (ICMP)—A message control and error-reporting protocol used to announce network errors, time-outs, and congestion. ICMP is the basis of the ping command.

server roles—A description of one or more functions of the server.

stateful firewall—A firewall that keeps track of the state of network connections (such as TCP streams) traveling across it. Only packets that match a known connection state are allowed by the firewall; others are rejected.

static IP addressing—An addressing scheme in which the computer uses the IP address assigned by an administrator. Each virtual machine is assigned a unique, unchanging IP address.

unsolicited request—Incoming traffic that does not correspond to either traffic sent in response to a request by the computer or unsolicited traffic that has been specified as allowed.

Review Questions

1. A logical group of computers that shares access to network resources with centralized administration is known as a _____.

    a. Server
    b. Directory
    c. Domain
    d. Region

2. A centralized means of storing, managing, and accessing information about network objects is accomplished with a(n) _____.

    a. Directory service
    b. Active service
    c. DSN
    d. File server

3. The native directory service included with Microsoft Windows Server 2008 is _____.

    a. DNS
    b. Active Directory Domain Services
    c. An active file server
    d. An active domain

4. A file server is responsible for _____. (Choose all that apply.)
   a. The central storage of data files
   b. The management of data files
   c. The logical configuration of a group of computers
   d. Maintaining domain name structures
5. In the Dovercorp.local network, the domain controller is _____.
   a. Server01
   b. Server02
   c. Client01
   d. The host computer
6. In the Dovercorp.local network, the file server is _____.
   a. Server01
   b. Server02
   c. Client01
   d. The host computer
7. In the Dovercorp.local network, the role of Client01 is _____.
   a. The domain controller
   b. The host computer
   c. The file server
   d. The desktop client
8. In the Dovercorp.local network, the data files that Client01's applications require can be found on _____.
   a. Server01
   b. Server02
   c. Client01
   d. The host computer
9. The RAM is increased from 512 MB to 640 MB on the domain controller to _____.
   a. Enlarge the virtual hard drive
   b. Split the operating system files from the data files
   c. Simplify the backup of the data files
   d. Improve performance for this specialized application server

10. The hard disk requirements for the Server02 OS were decreased to _____.
    a. Repair the virtual hard drive
    b. Split the operating system files from the data files
    c. Simplify the backup of the data files
    d. Provide for better performance for this specialized application server
11. ICS routes packets between the _____.
    a. Physical network adapter and Microsoft Loopback Adapter
    b. DNS adapter and host computer
    c. Host computer and physical network adapter
    d. Microsoft Loopback Adapter and DNS adapter
12. For the virtual machines to communicate with each other, _____.
    a. The IP addresses must be identical
    b. Each virtual machine IP address needs to be in the same network
    c. The IP address of the host computer needs to be in the same network
    d. The IP addresses are not important
13. When IP configurations are checked, the host computer _____. (Choose all that apply.)
    a. Is included in the check because it runs ICS
    b. Is not included in the check
    c. Is included in the check because it is the gateway to the Internet
    d. Is included in the check because it is the domain controller
14. The command to check IP configurations is _____.
    a. check IP
    b. IP check
    c. ipconfiguration
    d. ipconfig /all
15. The default behavior of Windows Firewall is to _____. (Choose all that apply.)
    a. Block all incoming traffic unless it is unsolicited or it matches a configured rule
    b. Allow all incoming traffic
    c. Allow all outgoing traffic unless it matches a configured role
    d. Block all outgoing traffic unless it matches a configured role

16. The ICMP request _____. (Choose all that apply.)
    a. Is an Echo Request that sends a packet of data to another computer
    b. Expects that data is sent in return to an Echo Reply
    c. Will be rejected by a Windows Firewall that has default settings
    d. Will be accepted after the File and Printer Sharing rule is set in Windows Firewall
17. IP connectivity between virtual machines and the host computer can be tested by using the _____ command.
    a. IP
    b. ipconfig /all
    c. ping
    d. png
18. Centralized, secure management of your network can be provided by _____.
    a. The host computer
    b. Active Directory Domain Services
    c. Client01
    d. Support central
19. A logical collection of domains is known as a _____.
    a. Network
    b. Computer
    c. Forest
    d. Territory
20. For a virtual machine to access network resources of a local domain, it must _____. (Choose all that apply.)
    a. Be a member of the domain
    b. Be a domain controller
    c. Be a server
    d. Contact the domain controller and request to become a member

Case Projects

Case 4-1: Designing a Virtual Network
Your manager, Susan, has asked you to provide a high-level design for a virtual network for the company you work at part-time as an intern. The network will need one domain controller and two file servers for the six client computers. Provide a diagram of your suggested network, including details about system roles, memory requirements, and security settings.

Case 4-2: Summarizing IP Addressing for a Virtual Network
Using Table 4-2 as a guide, create a summary table of IP addressing for the local network you designed in Case 4-1.

Case 4-3: Testing Connectivity
Prepare a written procedure to test connectivity for the local network you designed in Case 4-1. Your procedure must test by both host name and IP address.

Using Advanced Options and Troubleshooting in Virtual PC

chapter 5

After reading this chapter and completing the exercises, you will be able to:

- Optimize virtual machine performance
- Deploy advanced disk alternatives
- Implement dynamic disks and fault tolerance
- Troubleshoot Virtual PC 2007 installations

In the previous chapter, you built the Dovercorp.local virtual network. Now you are ready to improve the network's performance and add features.

You can take a number of actions to increase the performance of your virtual machines. You will learn which options to use to make your virtual machines hum.

The various options for customizing virtual hard drives can be confusing. This chapter highlights trouble spots related to virtual machine optimization, addressing common errors to help you avoid installation issues. Also, you will learn how to establish **fault tolerance**, the ability of a computer to preserve the integrity of data during a malfunction.

Performance Optimization

Simply put, computer systems lacking adequate system resources run dismally. Virtual machines suffer the same limitations. System resources such as CPU processing cycles, memory, and hard disk access are critical to performance optimization. The general guideline for assigning these resources is "more is better." But how much is enough?

The authors of this text ran the virtual environment on an older computer with a 3.2-GHz Pentium 4 processor and 4 GB of RAM. Disk storage resides on a 250-GB IDE hard drive.

CPU, memory, and hard disk specifications can vary wildly. The following sections outline the resources you will need to optimally run multiple virtual machines.

CPU

Microsoft recommends at least a 1-GHz processor for running Virtual PC 2007 on the host computer. Running multiple virtual machines and applications will negatively affect performance. When you run more than one machine at a time, you'll have to make decisions on how to allocate processing cycles to maximize performance. You learned about these options in Chapter 2.

You select performance options from the Virtual PC Options dialog box, as shown in Figure 5-1.

Table 5-1 explains the performance allocation options for distributing CPU time among virtual machines.

You can also specify how you want CPU time to be allocated among the virtual machines and the host operating system. When all virtual machines are running in the background, choose one of the options from Table 5-2.

In Activity 5-3, you will measure and compare the time to run a provided PowerShell script under each of the combinations described in Table 5-1 and Table 5-2. **PowerShell** is a command-line shell designed and developed by Microsoft for system administrators. The shell includes an interactive prompt and a scripting environment. The PowerShell script provided for use with this chapter manipulates a 10,000-element array to consistently stress the CPU.

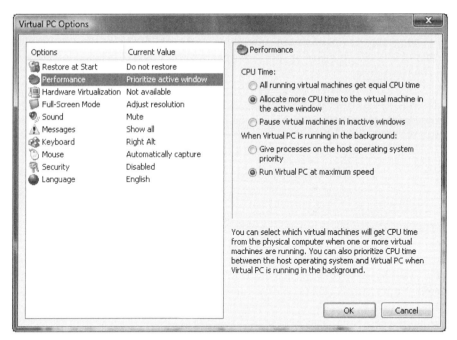

Figure 5-1 Virtual PC performance options

Table 5-1 CPU allocation among virtual machines

CPU time priority	CPU time option
Equal CPU time	All running virtual machines get equal CPU time
More CPU time for foreground	Allocate more CPU time to the virtual machine in the active window
No CPU time for background	Pause virtual machines in inactive windows

Table 5-2 CPU priorities between host and guest

Background priority	Background option
Host priority	Give processes on the host machine priority
Guest priority	Run virtual machine at maximum speed

Memory

Increasing RAM is one of the best ways to enhance performance on any computer. If you don't have enough RAM, the operating system will need to swap running data to the hard disk, which can diminish performance. In Chapter 4, you set up a virtual network with three guest machines. In Chapter 2, you learned how to calculate memory requirements for multiple operating systems. Remember to add overhead for the hosts and guests—128 MB for the host and 32 MB for each guest. Table 5-3 shows the calculations for the Dovercorp.local virtual network. This virtual environment requires a minimum of 2400 MB. If your computer system has less than 2400 MB of memory, performance will be sluggish because of the swapping of pages to the hard disk.

Table 5-3 Memory requirements for the Dovercorp.local network

Host/guest computer	Role	Operating system	Memory	Total memory
Host01	Host	Windows Vista Business	512 MB + 128 MB	640 MB
Server01	Domain controller	Windows Server 2008	640 MB + 32 MB	672 MB
Server02	File server	Windows Server 2008	512 MB + 32 MB	544 MB
Client01	Desktop	Windows Vista Business	512 MB + 32 MB	544 MB

If a host computer with a 32-bit processor has 4 GB of RAM installed, the system memory that is reported in the System window in Windows Vista is less than you might expect. For example, Vista might report 3,327 MB of system memory on a computer that has 4 GB of memory installed (4,096 MB).

The reduction in available system memory depends on the devices that are installed in the computer. For example, if you have a video card that has 256 MB of onboard memory, that memory must be mapped within the first 4 GB of address space. If 4 GB of system memory is already installed, part of that address space must be reserved by the graphics memory mapping. Graphics memory mapping overwrites a part of the system memory. These conditions reduce the total amount of system memory that is available to the operating system. However, to avoid potential driver compatibility issues, the 32-bit versions of Windows Vista limit the total available memory to 3,327 MB.

Hard Disk

There are no specific hard disk settings in Virtual PC 2007. However, you can improve the performance of your hard disks. The disk images used in Virtual PC 2007 are not sequentially organized files. They resemble files used by databases. Virtual PC 2007 utilizes 2-MB blocks, which are accessed from an allocation table. This approach provides flexibility in the reading and writing of files, but does use processor cycles to locate the block where a file is located.

The operations of Virtual PC 2007 can be disk intensive. Addressing the following maintenance items can increase the performance of your virtual machine's hard drives:

- Store .vhd files appropriately.
- Eliminate the page file.
- Defragment the drives.
- Zero the free space on virtual disks.
- Compress the virtual hard disk.

VHD File Storage None of the Virtual PC 2007 files should be stored on or accessed from a network server. If you need a .vhd file located on a network server, copy the file from the network server to your local physical hard drive first. If you have multiple physical hard disks, place your .vhd files and host operating system files on separate spindles.

File Paging If you have provided a sufficient amount of memory, the virtual machine will not write RAM pages to the hard disk. You can get better performance from your virtual machines and save disk space by eliminating the page file. Figure 5-2 shows options for eliminating the page file.

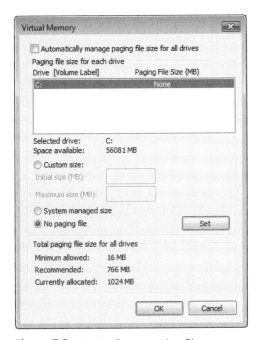

Figure 5-2 Setting for no paging file

Defragmentation Fragmentation is the distribution of files over noncontiguous memory locations and occurs when the host operating system cannot allocate enough contiguous space to store a complete file. Instead, the operating system puts parts of the file in gaps between other files. These gaps exist because the gaps formerly held a file that the operating system subsequently deleted.

Fragmentation causes a slowdown in the reading and writing of data. The time needed for the disk heads to move between fragments and waiting for the disk platter to rotate into position is increased. For many common operations, a heavily fragmented hard disk can be a performance bottleneck for the entire computer.

To solve this problem on your physical hard disk (host operating system), you run a program called the Disk Defragmenter, as shown in Figure 5-3 on the next page. You would click Start in the host operating system, type defrag in the Start Search text box, right-click Disk Defragmenter, and then click Run as administrator. You would then click the Defragment now button and wait for the disk to be defragged. Disk Defragmenter is a utility that is included with Microsoft Windows.

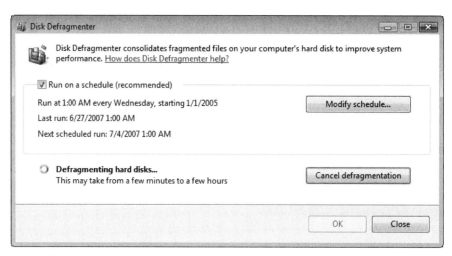

Figure 5-3 Disk Defragmenter

Zeroing Free Space When files are deleted by the guest within a virtual hard disk, the space formerly occupied by the deleted files is not available for reuse by additional files. This unrecovered space can grow very large. After a .vhd file expands, it doesn't shrink. To solve this space usage problem, you can do two things:

- Zero the free space on the .vhd with the Virtual Disk Precompactor.
- Compact the hard disk with the Compact it option in the Virtual Disk Information and Options from the Virtual Disk Wizard.

You use the Virtual Disk Precompactor to zero out the free space before you compact a dynamically expanding virtual hard disk. Using the Precompactor should result in a smaller compacted virtual hard disk. To use the Precompactor, you must first capture the image file Virtual Disk Precompactor.iso. This capture is initiated by clicking the CD menu and then clicking Capture ISO Image. Navigate to the location of the file by clicking Computer, double-clicking Local Disk (C:), double-clicking the Program Files folder, double-clicking the Microsoft Virtual PC folder, and then double-clicking the Virtual Machine Additions folder. The file, accessed through the Virtual Machine Additions folder, is shown in Figure 5-4. To launch the AutoPlay, click the Virtual Disk Precompactor.iso and then click the Open button.

Figure 5-4 Precompactor.iso

When the AutoPlay window opens, click Run precompact.exe. See Figure 5-5. When the Would you like to prepare the virtual hard disk(s) for compaction? message appears, click Yes. Next, a progress bar showing the progress of the compaction appears. Remember to clear the c:\temp directory, Microsoft Internet Explorer's temporary Internet files, and the event logs prior to shutdown.

Figure 5-5 AutoPlay for Precompactor

Compacting To use the Compactor, click a hard disk from the Virtual PC Settings dialog box and then click the Virtual Disk Wizard. From the Disk Options dialog box, select Edit an existing virtual disk. Locate the .vhd file on the hard disk and select Compact it, as shown in Figure 5-6 on the next page.

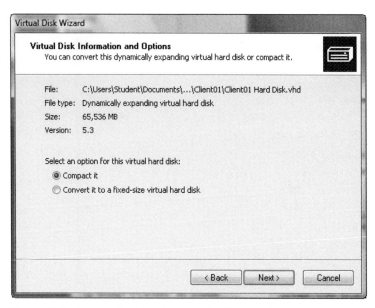

Figure 5-6 Compact it option for Virtual Disk Wizard

You need to specify whether to replace the .vhd file or save the file in another location. The dialog box points out the potential danger of replacing the .vhd file. See Figure 5-7. Microsoft recommends saving a copy of the virtual hard disk rather than replacing it in case errors occur during compacting.

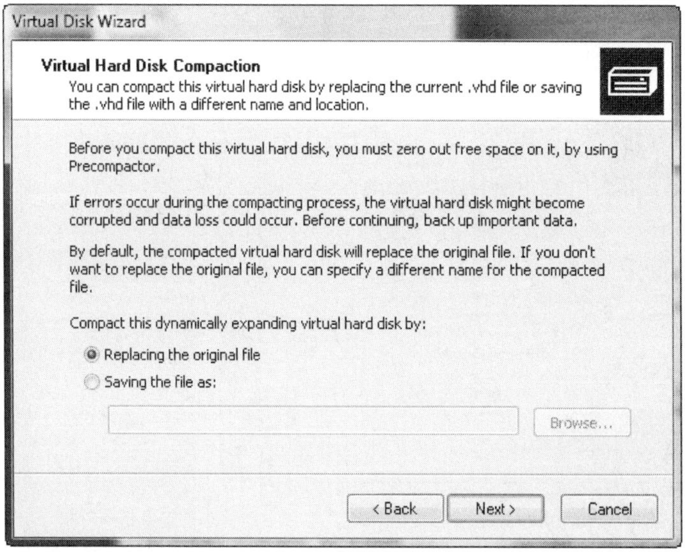

Figure 5-7 Virtual Hard Disk Compaction

Note: Defragging the physical hard disk and compacting a virtual hard disk can use a large percentage of processor resources. It is recommended that you take a production computer offline prior to initiating these activities.

Activity 5-1: Installing an Application in a Virtual Machine

Time Required: 10 minutes

Objective: Download and install an application in a virtual machine.

Requirements: Completion of Activities 4-1 through 4-8.

Description: In this activity, you will download and install the PowerShell program on the Client01 virtual machine.

1. If necessary, log on to your Host PC with a username of **Student** and a password of **Secret1**.
2. If necessary, to start Microsoft Virtual PC 2007, click **Start**, and then click **Microsoft Virtual PC**.
3. If necessary, to start the Server01 virtual machine, click **Server01**, and then click **Start**.
4. If necessary, log on to your virtual machine with a username of **Administrator** and a password of **Secret1**.
5. If necessary, to start the Client01 virtual machine, click **Client01**, and then click **Start**.
6. If necessary, log on to the Client01 virtual machine with a username of **Student** and a password of **Secret1**.
7. To launch Internet Explorer, click **Start**, and then click **Internet**.
8. Type **PowerShell** in the Live Search text box, and then press **Enter**.
9. If the Microsoft Phishing Filter dialog box opens, click the **Turn on automatic Phishing Filter (recommended)** option button, and then click **OK**.
10. To open the PowerShell download page, click the **Windows PowerShell** link. Scroll and click the **Download Windows PowerShell 1.0** link.
11. Scroll down and click the **x86: Windows Vista RTM (or x64: Windows Vista RTM)** link.
12. To begin Windows validation, scroll and click the **Continue** button.
13. If the Information Bar dialog box opens, click **Close**.
14. To install the Windows Genuine Advantage add-on, click the **This website wants to install...** link, and then click **Install ActiveX Control**.
15. When the User Account Control dialog box opens, click the **Continue** button.
16. When the Internet Explorer Add-on Installer–Security Warning dialog box opens, click **Install**.
17. When the Web page is refreshed, click the **Download** button, and then click **Open**.
18. Wait for the copy to complete.

19. When the Internet Explorer Security dialog box opens, click the **Allow** button.
20. When the User Account Control dialog box opens, click the **Continue** button.
21. When the Windows Update Standalone Installer dialog box opens, click **OK**.
22. Wait for the update to install and then click **Close**.
23. Close the Internet Explorer window.
24. Leave the computer logged on for the next activity.

Activity 5-2: Running a PowerShell Script

Time Required: 10 minutes

Objective: Copy and execute a PowerShell script that manipulates a 10,000-element array to consistently stress the CPU.

Requirements: Completion of Activity 5-1.

Description: In this activity, you will type the array script using Notepad and execute the script from the PowerShell prompt on the Client01 virtual machine. **PowerShell** is a command line shell and scripting language. This script will be used in Activity 5-3.

1. If necessary, log on to your Host PC with a username of **Student** and a password of **Secret1**.
2. If necessary, to start Microsoft Virtual PC 2007, click **Start**, and then click **Microsoft Virtual PC**.
3. If necessary, to start the Client01 virtual machine, click **Client01**, and then click **Start**.
4. If necessary, log on to the Client01 virtual machine with a username of **Student** and a password of **Secret1**.
5. To open Notepad, click **Start**, point to **All Programs**, click **Accessories**, and then click **Notepad**.
6. Type **$Msg="Writing array - Please wait"** and press **Enter**.
7. Type **$Msg** and press **Enter**.
8. Type **$NumArray = (1..10000)** and press **Enter**.
9. Type **$x = @()** and press **Enter**.
10. Type **foreach ($num in $NumArray) {$x+=$num * 7}** and press **Enter**.
11. Type **$x** and press **Enter**.
12. To save the PowerShell script, click **File**, click **Save As**, click **Student** in the Save As line, click the **Save as type** drop-down arrow, **click All Files**, type **array.ps1** in the File name text box, and then click **Save**.
13. To start PowerShell, click **Start**, type **PowerShell** in the Start Search text box, right-click **Windows PowerShell**, and then click **Run as administrator**.
14. When the User Account Control dialog box opens, click the **Continue** button.
15. To change the folder location of the script, type **cd \users\student** and press **Enter**.

16. To permit saved scripts to execute, type **set-executionpolicy Unrestricted** at the PS C:\users\Student command prompt, and then press **Enter**.
17. To execute and time the saved array script, type **Measure-Command {.\array}** and then press **Enter**.
18. Wait for the script to complete.
19. Leave the command prompt window open for the next activity.
20. Leave the computer logged on for the next activity.

Activity 5-3: Studying Effects of Performance Options

Time Required: 10 minutes

Objective: Study the effects of varying performance options.

Requirements: Completion of Activities 5-1 and 5-2.

Description: In this activity, you will alter the performance options, execute the array script, and record the execution times in Table 5-4.

Table 5-4 Results for performance study

	All running virtual machines get equal CPU time	Allocate more CPU time to the virtual machine in the active window	Pause virtual machines in inactive window
Give processes on the host operating system priority			
Run Virtual PC at maximum speed			

1. If necessary, log on to your Host PC with a username of **Student** and a password of **Secret1**.
2. If necessary, to start Microsoft Virtual PC 2007, click **Start**, and then click **Microsoft Virtual PC**.
3. If necessary, to start the Client01 virtual machine, click **Client01**, and then click **Start**.
4. If necessary, to start the Server01 virtual machine, click **Server01**, and then click **Start**.
5. If necessary, to start the Server02 virtual machine, click **Server02**, and then click **Start**.
6. If necessary, log on to the Client01 virtual machine with a username of **Student** and a password of **Secret1**.
7. To review the performance setting, return to the Virtual PC Console click the **File** menu, click **Options**, and then click **Performance**.
8. Click the **Give processes on the host operating system priority** option button.
9. Click the **All Running virtual machines get equal CPU time** option button and then click **OK**.

10. Switch to the Windows PowerShell window.
11. Press the **up arrow** to repeat the last command, and then press **Enter**.
12. Record the TotalMilliseconds.
13. To set the next performance setting, return to the Virtual PC Console, click **File**, click **Options**, and then click **Performance**.
14. Click the **Allocate more CPU time to the virtual machine in the active window** option button, and then click **OK**.
15. Return to the Windows PowerShell window.
16. Press the **up arrow** and then press **Enter**.
17. Record the TotalMilliseconds.
18. To set the next performance setting, return to the Virtual PC Console, click **File**, click **Options**, and then click **Performance**.
19. Click the **Pause virtual machines in inactive windows** option button, and then click **OK**.
20. Return to the Windows PowerShell window.
21. Press the **up arrow** and then press **Enter**.
22. Record the TotalMilliseconds.
23. To set the next performance setting, return to the Virtual PC Console, click **File**, click **Options**, and then click **Performance**.
24. Click the **Run Virtual PC at maximum speed** option button, click the **All virtual machines get equal CPU time** option button, and then click **OK**.
25. Repeat Steps 10 through 22.
26. How did the results vary? On a sheet of paper, document your impression of the results that were recorded.
27. To close the PowerShell window, type **exit** and press **Enter**.
28. Log off and shut down the Client01 virtual machine.
29. Leave the computer logged on for the next activity.

Implementing the Advanced Disk Options

In Chapter 2, you learned how to configure the settings for the disk options for virtual machines. Disk options specify how changes to the virtual hard disk files are saved. In this section, you will learn about additional options and how to apply these options to the virtual machines in the Dovercorp.local network.

Undo Disks

Recall that when you use Undo Disks, any changes you make to the virtual hard disk are saved to the undo disk files, not the original virtual hard disks. Figure 5-8 shows the setting for Undo Disks with the Enable undo disks check box checked.

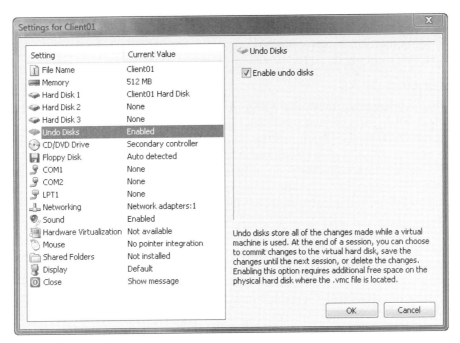

Figure 5-8 Undo Disks enabled

When you shut down the virtual machine, you will select one of the following options (as shown in Figure 5-9):

- *Commit changes to the virtual hard disk*—Saves the changes to the original virtual disk
- *Save undo disk changes*—Defers the decision on the undo file
- *Delete undo disk changes*—Erases the undo file, leaving the original virtual hard disk as it was prior to its use

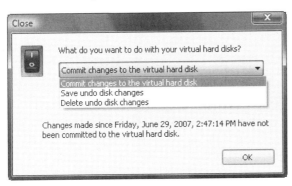

Figure 5-9 Undo disks choices

You cannot selectively enable undo disks. Your decision applies to all of the virtual machine's hard disks. In other words, you cannot selectively delete or commit the changes on individual hard disks; you can only do so for all disks in a virtual machine.

Differencing Disks

Recall that a differencing virtual hard disk stores changes to a specific virtual hard disk. You must specify an existing virtual hard disk, called the parent virtual hard disk, to which the differencing virtual hard disk points. When the VM uses this differencing (or child) virtual hard disk, the changes are stored in the differencing hard disk.

From a basic functional standpoint, differencing disks appear to be very similar to undo disks—both are used to isolate changes in separate physical hard disks. However, differencing disks are created for individual virtual hard disks. Undo disks operate at the level of the entire virtual machine—all virtual hard disks used by the virtual machine are enabled for undo.

You can use Virtual PC in situations that require rapid and frequent operating system reconfiguration. For example, you can use it for development and testing, product demonstrations, or training. You can build a base virtual machine. You can use differencing disks to create a variety of configurations from one base disk.

To create a differencing disk, use the Virtual Disk Wizard. Start the Virtual Disk Wizard from the File menu on the Virtual PC Console. Follow the wizard steps to the Virtual Hard Disk Options dialog box, where you select the Differencing option shown in Figure 5-10.

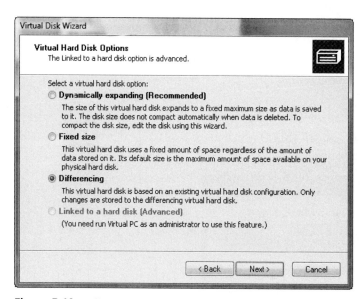

Figure 5-10 Differencing option

The next task is to browse to the location of the parent hard disk to link the differencing disk (or child disk) to the parent disk. Figure 5-11 shows the name and location of a parent hard disk.

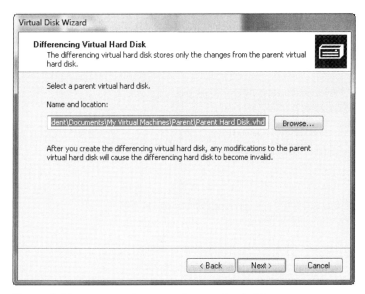

Figure 5-11 Name and location of parent hard disk

Linked Disks

The linked disks option stores changes to an existing physical hard disk. You configure the virtual machine to point to the existing physical hard disk. You must use the entire hard disk; you cannot link to a volume on the disk. The virtual machine operates at the physical hard disk level—not at the logical volume level.

To create a linked disk, use the Virtual Disk Wizard. You will need to use the Run as administrator option when launching Microsoft Virtual PC. To do this, click Start, right-click Microsoft Virtual PC, click Run as Administrator, and when the User Account Control dialog box opens, click the Continue button. Start the Virtual Disk Wizard from the File menu on the Virtual PC Console. Follow the steps of the wizard to the Virtual Hard Disk Options, where you select the Linked to a hard disk (Advanced) option, as shown in Figure 5-12 on the next page. Notice that a warning is displayed when this option is selected. A linked disk bypasses virtual disks and allows a virtual machine to use an actual disk on your host operating system. The message warns you about the potential loss of data on your primary hard disk—the only safe choice is to link to a secondary hard disk that will only be used by virtual machines.

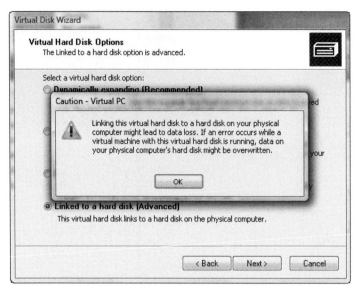

Figure 5-12 Linked to a hard disk option with warning

Figure 5-13 shows the selection of the physical drive. By default, the created virtual hard drive that is linked to the physical drive is read-only.

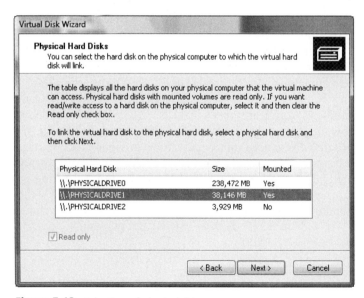

Figure 5-13 Selection of physical drive

Using sysprep The System Preparation (sysprep) tool prepares an installation of Windows for duplication. When you use differencing virtual hard disks, you are duplicating the parent virtual hard disk. The sysprep program was copied to the virtual hard disk when you installed Windows Server 2008. Sysprep removes all system-specific information from an installed Windows image, including the computer security identifier (SID).

You run sysprep from a command line with the appropriate switches, as shown in Figure 5-14. The /oobe switch instructs the Windows installation to run Windows Welcome the next time the computer boots. The oobe stands for "out-of-box experience" and is required by Microsoft when a manufacturer markets a personal computer with a preinstalled Windows product. The /generalize switch instructs sysprep to remove system-specific data, including unique security IDs (SIDs). After the unique system information is removed, the computer shuts down.

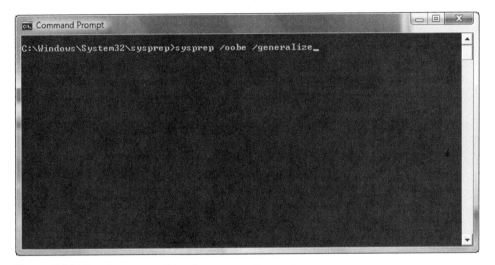

Figure 5-14 Running sysprep from the command prompt

Out-of-Box Experience When you first start a guest machine that has been sysprepped, you duplicate the out-of-box experience that occurs when a user first turns on a new computer with a Windows operating system installed. The user typically must follow similar steps to set up the new computer.

Although sysprep enables you to skip the file copies and other time-consuming activities related to installing a new virtual machine, you will need to repeat these tasks for each differenced installation:

- Complete the region setup.
- Provide a product key.
- Accept the license terms.
- Name the computer.
- Verify the time zone, date, and time.

This abbreviated task list is easier to accomplish than starting from scratch with the Windows Server 2008 installation DVD. These steps enable you to duplicate the "out-of-box experience."

Activity 5-4: Using Undo Disks

Time Required: 10 minutes

Objective: Study the effect of the Undo Disks option.

Requirements: Completion of Activity 3-1.

Description: In this activity, you will enable Undo Disks for the Client01 virtual machine, make a change to the desktop, and discard the change.

1. If necessary, log on to your Host PC with a username of **Student** and a password of **Secret1**.
2. If necessary, to start Microsoft Virtual PC 2007, click **Start**, and then click **Microsoft Virtual PC**.
3. If necessary, log off and shut down the Client01 virtual machine.
4. To enable the Undo Disks option, click **Client01**, click the **Settings** button, click **Undo Disks**, check the **Enable undo disks** check box, and then click **OK**.
5. To start the Client01 virtual machine, click **Client01**, and then click **Start**.
6. Log on to the Client01 virtual machine with a username of **Student** and a password of **Secret1**.
7. To change the desktop background, click **Start**, click **Control Panel**, click **Control Panel Home**, click the **Change desktop background** link, click a new wallpaper of your choice, click **OK**, and then close the Control Panel window.
8. Shut down the Client01 virtual machine.
9. When the Close dialog box opens, click the **What do you want to do with your virtual hard disks?** drop-down list arrow, click **Delete undo disk changes**, and then click **OK**.
10. To start the Client01 virtual machine, click **Client01**, and then click **Start**.
11. Log on to the Client01 virtual machine with a username of **Student** and a password of **Secret1**.
12. Verify that the desktop background reverted to the previous background.
13. Shut down the Client01 virtual machine.
14. When the Close dialog box opens, click the drop-down list arrow and click **Delete undo disk changes**, and then click **OK**.
15. To disable the Undo Disks option, click **Client01** in the Virtual PC Console, click **Settings**, click **Undo Disks**, clear the **Enable undo disks** check box, and then click **OK**.
16. Leave the computer logged on for the next activity.

Activity 5-5: Creating a Parent Virtual Machine

Time Required: 60–90 minutes

Objective: Create a parent virtual machine.

Requirements: Completion of Activity 3-2.

Description: In this activity, you will create the parent for the two virtual machines that will be differenced in Activity 5-6.

1. If necessary, log on to your Host PC with a username of **Student** and a password of **Secret1**.
2. If necessary, to start Microsoft Virtual PC 2007, click **Start**, and then click **Microsoft Virtual PC**.
3. To start the New Virtual Machine Wizard and add a virtual machine, click **New** and then click **Next**.
4. To create a virtual machine, retain the **Create a virtual machine** option button, and then click **Next**.
5. To name the virtual machine, type **Parent** in the Name and location text box, and then click **Next**.
6. To select an operating system, click the **Operating system** drop-down list arrow, click **Other**, and then click **Next**.
7. To adjust the RAM, click the **Adjusting the RAM** option button, type **512** in the MB text box, and then click **Next**.
8. To specify a new virtual hard disk file, click the **A new virtual hard disk** option button, and then click **Next** twice.
9. Review the settings and click **Finish**.
10. To start the new virtual machine, click **Parent**, and then click **Start**.
11. Insert the Microsoft Windows Server 2008 DVD into the CD/DVD drive.
12. If necessary, click the **CD** menu, and click **Use Physical Drive D:**.
13. To reset the virtual machine, click the **Action** menu, click **Reset**, and then click **Reset**.
14. Wait for Windows to load files.
15. To activate the virtual machine, click in the parent virtual machine.
16. Verify the regional settings and then click **Next**.
17. Click the **Install now** link.
18. To indicate that this virtual machine is using an evaluation copy, wait for the Type your product key for activation dialog box to open, clear the **Automatically activate Windows when I'm online** check box, click **Next**, and then click **No**.
19. To indicate which version to install, click **Windows Server 2008 Standard**, check the **I have selected the edition of Windows that I purchased** check box, and then click **Next**.

20. Check the **I accept the license terms** check box and then click **Next**.
21. Click the **Custom (advanced)** icon.
22. To accept the Default allocation, click **Next**.
23. Wait for Windows to copy and expand files, install features and updates, and restart.
24. Wait while Windows prepares to start for the first time and to complete the installation.
25. When requested to change the password, click **OK**, and then reset the Password to Secret1. Click **OK** to continue.
26. To set the time zone, click the **Set time zone** link, review the date and time, click the **Change time zone** button, click the appropriate time zone, and then click **OK** twice.
27. To provide a computer name, click the **Provide computer name and domain** link, click the **Change** button, type **Parent** in the Computer name text box, click **OK** twice, click **Close**, and then click the **Restart Now** button.
28. Wait for the virtual machine to restart.
29. Ignore the Press any key to boot from CD or DVD message.
30. Log on to your parent virtual machine with a username of **Administrator** and a password of **Secret1**.
31. To open a command prompt window, click **Start**, and then click **Command Prompt**.
32. To launch the sysprep program, type **cd \windows\system32\sysprep**, press **Enter**, type **sysprep /oobe /generalize**, and then press **Enter**.
33. Wait for sysprep to complete and the parent virtual machine to shut down.
34. To change the file attribute to read-only for the parent virtual machine, click **Start** in the host operating system, click **Computer**, click **Documents**, double-click **My Virtual Machines**, double-click the **Parent** folder, right-click **Parent Hard Disk**, click **Properties**, check the **Read-only** check box, and then click **OK**.
35. Close the Computer window.
36. Leave the computer logged on for the next activity.

Activity 5-6: Creating Child Virtual Machines

Time Required: 10 minutes

Objective: Study the creation of differencing disks.

Requirements: Completion of Activity 5-5.

Description: In this activity, you will create two child virtual machines by differencing from the parent virtual machine.

1. If necessary, log on to your Host PC with a username of **Student** and a password of **Secret1**.

2. If necessary, to start Microsoft Virtual PC 2007, click **Start**, and then click **Microsoft Virtual PC**.
3. Maximize the Virtual PC Console.
4. To start the Virtual Disk Wizard, click the **File** menu, click **Virtual Disk Wizard**, and then click **Next** three times.
5. To provide a name and location for the virtual machine, click the **Browse** button, double-click **My Virtual Machines**, type **Child01** in the File name text box, click **Save**, and then click **Next**.
6. To use a differencing hard disk, click the **Differencing** option button, and then click **Next**.
7. To specify the parent, click the **Browse** button, double-click the **Parent** folder, click the **Parent Hard Disk**, and then click **Open**.
8. Click **Next**, click **Finish**, and then click **Close**.
9. To start the New Virtual Machine Wizard and add a virtual machine, click **New**, and then click **Next**.
10. To create a virtual machine, retain the **Create a virtual machine** option button, and then click **Next**.
11. To specify the name for the virtual machine, type **Child01**, and then click **Next** twice.
12. To adjust the RAM allocation, click the **Adjusting the RAM** option button, type **512** in the MB text box, and then click **Next**.
13. To specify the child virtual hard disk, retain the **An existing virtual hard disk** option button, click **Next**, click the **Browse** button, click **Child01**, click **Open**, and then click **Next**.
14. Review the virtual machine attributes, and then click **Finish**.
15. Repeat Steps 4 through 14 using Child02 in place of Child01.
16. Leave the computer logged on for the next activity.

Activity 5-7: Running the Child Virtual Machines

Time Required: 30–45 minutes

Objective: Complete the out-of-box experience for the two child virtual machines.

Requirements: Completion of Activities 5-5 and 5-6.

Description: In this activity, you will run the two child virtual machines and experience the out-of-box experience.

1. If necessary, log on to your Host PC with a username of **Student** and a password of **Secret1**.
2. If necessary, to start Microsoft Virtual PC 2007, click **Start**, and then click **Microsoft Virtual PC**.

3. To start the Child01 virtual machine, double-click **Child01** in the Virtual PC Console.
4. Wait for Windows Server 2008 to start for the first time and restart to complete the configuration.
5. Wait for the configuration to complete.

You will see a black screen for 10–15 minutes.

6. Wait for the Set Up Windows dialog box to open, review the regional settings, and then click **Next**.
7. To indicate that you want to install an evaluation copy of Windows Server 2008 and when the Type your product key for activation dialog box opens, clear the **Automatically activate Windows when I'm online** check box, and then click **Next**.
8. When the Please read the license terms dialog box opens, check the **I accept the license terms** check box, and then click **Next**.
9. When the Type a computer name dialog box opens, type **Child01** in the Type a computer name (for example, Office-PC) text box, and then click **Start**.
10. When requested to change the password, click **OK**, and then set the Password to **Secret1**. Click **OK** to continue.
11. If necessary, wait and log on to your Child01 virtual machine with a username of **Administrator** and a password of **Secret1**.
12. Wait for the Initial Configuration Tasks window to open.
13. To provide a static address for Child01, click the **Configure networking** link, right-click **Local Area Connection**, click **Properties**, clear the **Internet Protocol Version 6 (TCP/IPv6)** check box, click **Internet Protocol Version 4 (TCP/IPv4)**, click the **Properties** button, click the **Use the following IP address** option button, type **192.168.0.105** in the IP address text box, press **Tab** four times, type **192.168.0.101** in the Preferred DNS server text box, click **OK**, click **Close**, and then close the Network Connections window.
14. Repeat Steps 3 through 12 using Child02 in place of Child01.
15. To provide a static address for Child02, click the **Configure networking** link, right-click **Local Area Connection**, click **Properties**, clear the **Internet Protocol Version 6 (TCP/IPv6)** check box, click **Internet Protocol Version 4 (TCP/IPv4)**, click the **Properties** button, click the **Use the following IP address** option button, type **192.168.0.106** in the IP address text box, press **Tab** four times, type **192.168.0.101** in the Preferred DNS server text box, click **OK**, click **Close**, and then close the Network Connections window.

16. To shut down the Child01 virtual machine, click **Start**, click the arrow next to the Lock button, click **Shut Down**, click the **Option** drop-down list arrow click **Operating System: Reconfiguration (Planned)**, and then click **OK**.

17. Repeat Step 16 for Child02.

18. Leave the computer logged on for the next activity.

Dynamic Disks and Fault Tolerance

When you create a virtual hard disk in Virtual PC, it behaves just like a physical hard drive. Just as with a physical hard disk, you can partition the virtual hard disk into one or more partitions.

Basic disks use normal partition tables, first supported by MS-DOS and then supported by all of the versions of the Windows operating systems. A disk initialized for basic storage is called a basic disk. A basic disk contains basic volumes, such as primary partitions and extended partitions with logical drives. A **volume** is a fixed amount of storage on a disk. When the operating systems were installed, they partitioned and formatted the virtual hard drives as a part of the installation.

Microsoft introduced dynamic storage with the Windows XP Professional, Windows 2000, and Windows Server 2003 operating systems. A disk initialized for dynamic storage is called a **dynamic disk**, which contains dynamic volumes. These dynamic volumes provide features that might not be available when using basic storage. For example, support for fault tolerance volumes in Windows Server 2008 requires dynamic disks. Also, with dynamic storage, you can perform disk and volume management without the need to restart Windows.

Fault tolerance is the ability of a computer to preserve the integrity of data during a system malfunction. The data is written to two or more hard drives. If one of the hard drives becomes unavailable, the data can be read from another hard drive or re-created from the remaining hard drives.

Unless each of the virtual hard disks is stored on a separate physical hard disk, true fault tolerance cannot be achieved in a virtual environment because all of the virtual hard disks (even in a fault-tolerant configuration) reside on a single point of failure—the single physical disk.

In the sections that follow, you will learn to implement two fault-tolerant storage methods.

Additional Virtual Hard Disks

To implement fault tolerance, you need additional virtual hard disks. Use the Virtual Disk Wizard to create these additional virtual hard disks. After the virtual hard disks are created, mount them to the virtual machine from the Settings dialog box, as shown in Figure 5-15 on the next page.

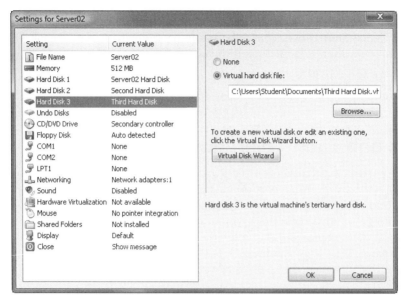

Figure 5-15 Mounting virtual hard disks

Dynamic Disk Conversion

Before you can implement fault tolerance, you must convert the existing basic disks to dynamic disks using the Disk Management tool in Windows Server 2003. To access Disk Management, click Start, and then click Administrative Tools and Computer Management. Figure 5-16 shows Disk Management.

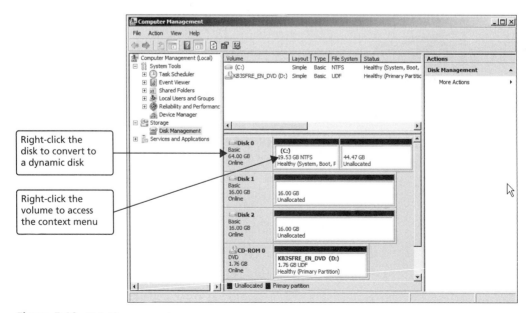

Figure 5-16 Disk Management

Before the disks can be managed by Disk Management, they must be initialized. The next time you launch Disk Management after adding new virtual hard disks with the Virtual Disk Wizard, the dialog box shown in Figure 5-17 will open. Use the MBR (Master Boot Record) for the partition table.

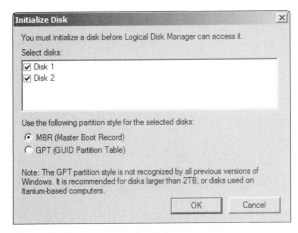

Figure 5-17 Initializing hard disks

Right-click the first hard disk to be converted and then click Convert to Dynamic Disk, as shown in Figure 5-18.

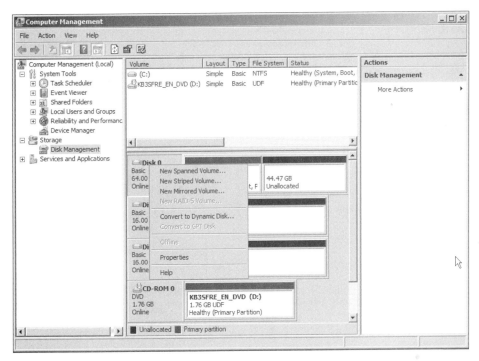

Figure 5-18 Selecting the first basic disk to convert

Disk Management will prompt for permission to convert the other basic disks. Check the remaining basic disks, as shown in Figure 5-19, and click OK. Disk Management presents a list of the hard drives to convert. After reviewing the list of hard drives to be converted, click Convert.

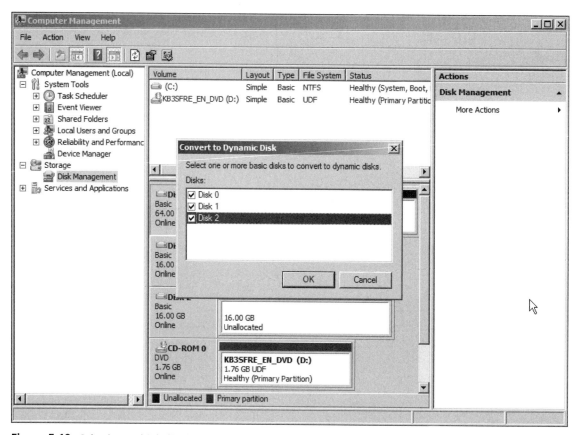

Figure 5-19 Selecting multiple hard disks to convert

The conversion from basic to dynamic is a one-way street. After converting, there is no easy way to revert back to basic without losing the contents of the volume.

Fault-Tolerant Storage

Windows Server 2008 supports two software-based, fault-tolerant storage options. In the following sections, you will learn how to implement these two options to protect data.

RAID-1 A **mirrored volume**, or **RAID-1** volume, is a fault-tolerant volume whose data is duplicated on two physical disks. **RAID** is short for Redundant Array of Independent (or Inexpensive) Disks, a category of disk drives that employ two or more drives in combination for fault tolerance and performance. In a mirrored volume, all of the data on one volume is copied to another disk to provide data redundancy. If one of the disks fails, the data can still be accessed from the remaining disk. A mirrored volume cannot be extended. Conceptually simple, RAID-1 is popular for those users who require fault tolerance and don't need top-notch read performance.

If you lose part of a mirror set (for example, as a result of hardware failure), Windows Server 2008 will display a message indicating that a disk that is part of a fault-tolerant volume can no longer be accessed. The drive will still be usable, but you won't have the mirroring capability. You will need to break the mirror set. To break the mirror set, from within Disk Management, click the mirrored volume and select Break Mirror from the Fault Tolerance menu. After replacing the failed hard drive, the mirror can be re-created.

Figure 5-20 shows two unallocated areas on separate hard drives that will be linked together by mirroring. The first volume has its data duplicated on the second drive. If either drive fails, the other continues to function as a single drive until the failed drive is replaced. When requested by a system administrator, the operating system can rebuild the mirror.

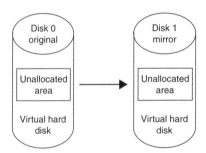

Figure 5-20 Picture of RAID-1

From the Disk Management pane, right-click the first available disk area to be allocated, as shown in Figure 5-21 on the next page. Select New Mirrored Volume.

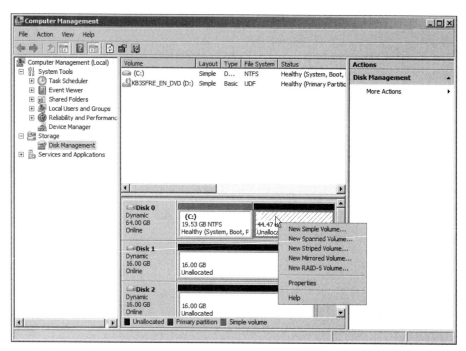

Figure 5-21 Location of first available disk area for RAID-1 with menu

Select an additional unallocated area on another hard drive to create the mirror. Indicate the amount of space to be mirrored, which should match the allocation in the original volume. Figure 5-22 shows the results of these actions.

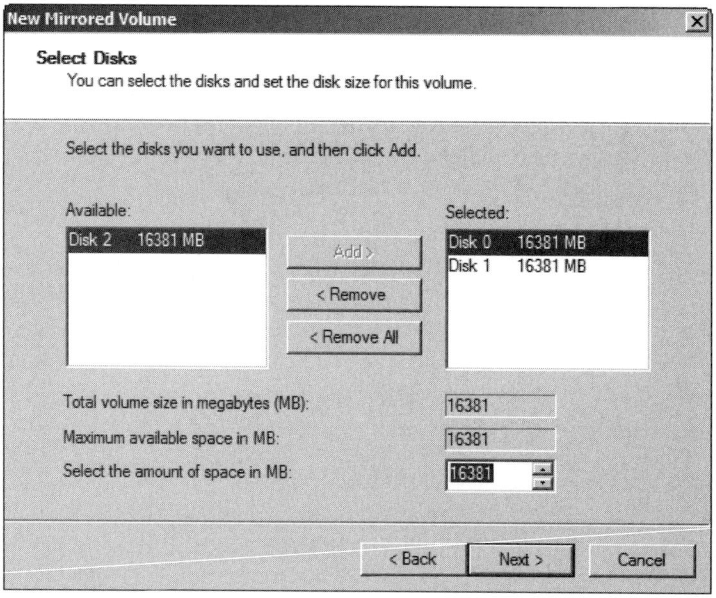

Figure 5-22 Completed selections for mirrored disks

After a brief period of time, the two areas will format simultaneously, as shown in Figure 5-23.

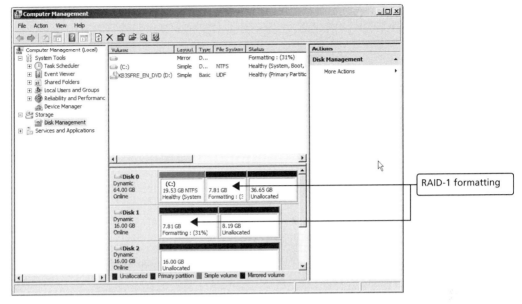

Figure 5-23 Formatting mirror

RAID-5 A RAID-5 volume is a fault-tolerant volume whose data is **striped** (which means that a body of data is divided into blocks and the blocks are spread across several volumes) across an array of three or more disks. **Parity** (a calculated value that can be used to reconstruct data after a failure) is also striped across the disk array. If a physical disk fails, the portion of the RAID-5 volume that was on that failed disk can be re-created from the remaining data and the parity. A RAID-5 volume cannot be mirrored or extended.

Figure 5-24 shows three unallocated areas on separate hard drives that are linked together. Using Microsoft's software-based **RAID-5**, both data and parity information are striped across three or more volumes. Fault tolerance is maintained by ensuring that the parity information for any given block of data is placed on a drive separate from that used to store the data itself. If one of the areas becomes unavailable because of a hardware failure, the data (and/or parity) from the remaining drives is used by the operating system to reconstruct the data. After replacing the failed drive and when requested by a system administrator, the operating system can rebuild the drive.

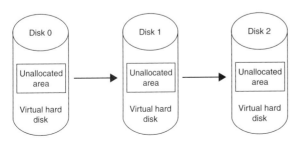

Figure 5-24 RAID-5 diagram

To implement RAID-5 fault tolerance, you right-click the first available disk area to be allocated in the Disk Management pane, as shown in Figure 5-25. Select New RAID-5 Volume.

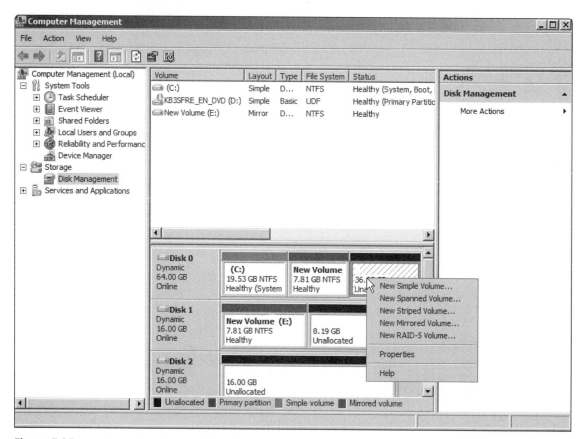

Figure 5-25 Location of the first available disk area for RAID-5 with menu

Select two or more additional unallocated areas, up to 32 areas, on other hard drives. Indicate the amount of space to be allocated, which should match the allocation in the original volume. Figure 5-26 shows the results of these actions.

Dynamic Disks and Fault Tolerance **187**

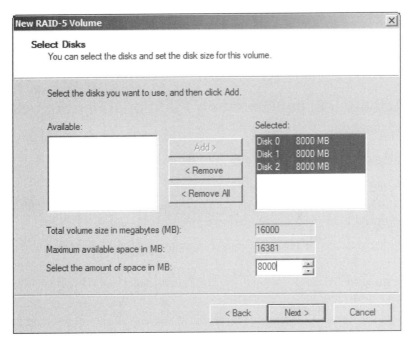

Figure 5-26 Completed selections for RAID-5

After a brief period of time, multiple areas will format simultaneously, as shown in Figure 5-27.

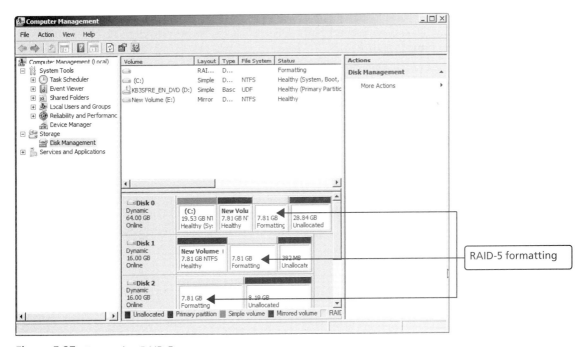

Figure 5-27 Formatting RAID-5

With RAID-5, you can recover the stripe set with parity if a single drive fails. You'll know that a stripe set with parity drive has failed when you see a system error message stating that a disk that is part of a fault-tolerant volume can no longer be accessed. If you see this message, you should repair or replace the failed drive. Afterward, you can attempt to regenerate the stripe set.

Activity 5-8: Implementing Additional Hard Drives

Time Required: 10 minutes

Objective: Create a second and third hard drive for Server02.

Requirements: Completion of Activity 3-2.

Description: In this activity, you will implement the second hard disk and third hard disk for Server02. These virtual hard disks are needed to implement RAID-1 and RAID-5.

1. If necessary, log on to your Host PC with a username of **Student** and a password of **Secret1**.

2. If necessary, to start Microsoft Virtual PC 2007, click **Start**, and then click **Microsoft Virtual PC**.

3. To shut down the Server02 virtual machine, click **Start**, click the arrow next to the Lock button, click **Shut Down**, click the **Option** drop-down list arrow, click **Operating System: Reconfiguration (Planned)**, and then click **OK**.

4. To start the Virtual Disk Wizard, click the **File** menu, click **Virtual Disk Wizard**, and then click **Next** three times.

5. To create the second virtual hard disk, click the **Browse** button, double-click **My Virtual Machines**, type **Second Hard Disk**, click the **Save** button, click **Next** three times, click **Finish**, and then click **Close**.

6. To start the Virtual Disk Wizard, click the **File** menu, click **Virtual Disk Wizard**, and then click **Next** three times.

7. To create the third virtual hard disk, click the **Browse** button, double-click **My Virtual Machines**, type **Third Hard Disk**, click the **Save** button, click **Next** three times, click **Finish**, and then click **Close**.

8. To open the Settings dialog box for Server02, click **Server02**, and then click the **Settings** button.

9. To mount the second hard disk, click **Hard Disk 2**, click the **Virtual hard disk file** option button, click the **Browse** button, click **Second Hard Disk**, and then click **Open**.

10. To mount the third hard disk, click **Hard Disk 3**, click the **Virtual hard disk file** option button, click the **Browse** button, click **Third Hard Disk**, and then click **Open**.

11. To close the Settings dialog box, click **OK**.

12. Leave the computer logged on for the next activity.

Dynamic Disks and Fault Tolerance **189**

Activity 5-9: Converting Basic Hard Drives to Dynamic Drives

Time Required: 20 minutes

Objective: Convert the three basic hard drives to dynamic drives.

Requirements: Completion of Activity 5-8.

Description: In this activity, you will convert three basic hard drives for Server02. This conversion is required to use RAID-1 and RAID5.

1. If necessary, log on to your Host PC with a username of **Student** and a password of **Secret1**.
2. If necessary, to start Microsoft Virtual PC 2007, click **Start**, and then click **Microsoft Virtual PC**.
3. To start the Server02 virtual machine, double-click **Server02** in the Virtual PC Console.
4. Log on to the Server02 virtual machine with a username of **Administrator** and a password of **Secret1**.
5. To open Disk Management, click **Start**, point to **Administrative Tools**, click **Computer Management**, and then click **Disk Management**.
6. To initialize the two new hard disks, ensure the **Disk 1** and the **Disk 2** check boxes are checked, click the **MBR (Master Boot Record)** option button, and then click **OK**.
7. To convert the three hard disks from basic to dynamic, right-click the **Disk 0** button, click **Convert to Dynamic Disk**, check the **Disk 1** check box, check the **Disk 2** check box, click **OK**, review the disks to be converted, click **Convert**, and then click **Yes**.
8. Leave the computer logged on for the next activity.

Activity 5-10: Implementing a RAID-1 Volume

Time Required: 20 minutes

Objective: Implement a RAID-1 mirror.

Requirements: Completion of Activity 5-9.

Description: In this activity, you will implement a disk mirror volume on Disk 1 for Disk 0 for Server02.

1. If necessary, log on to your Host PC with a username of **Student** and a password of **Secret1**.
2. If necessary, to start Microsoft Virtual PC 2007, click **Start**, and then click **Microsoft Virtual PC**.
3. If necessary, to start the Server02 virtual machine, double-click **Server02** in the Virtual PC Console.

4. If necessary, log on to the Server02 virtual machine with a username of **Administrator** and a password of **Secret1**.

5. If necessary, to open Disk Management, click **Start**, point to **Administrative Tools**, click **Computer Management**, and then click **Disk Management**.

6. To allocate the disk mirror, right-click the unallocated area of Disk 1, click **New Mirrored Volume**, click **Next**, click **Disk 2** under Available, click **Add**, type **8000** in the Select the amount of space in MB text box, click **Next** three times, and then click **Finish**.

7. Wait for the volume to format.

8. Leave the computer logged on for the next activity.

Activity 5-11: Implementing a RAID-5 Volume

Time Required: 30 minutes

Objective: Implement a RAID-5 volume.

Requirements: Completion of Activity 5-9.

Description: In this activity, you will implement a RAID-5 volume on Disk 0, Disk 1, and Disk 2 for Server02.

1. If necessary, log on to your Host PC with a username of **Student** and a password of **Secret1**.

2. If necessary, to start Microsoft Virtual PC 2007, click **Start**, and then click **Microsoft Virtual PC**.

3. If necessary, to start the Server02 virtual machine, double-click **Server02** in the Virtual PC Console.

4. If necessary, log on to the Server02 virtual machine with a username of **Administrator** and a password of **Secret1**.

5. If necessary, to open Disk Management, click **Start**, point to **Administrative Tools**, click **Computer Management**, and then click **Disk Management**.

6. If necessary to provide unallocated space in Disk 0, right-click (**C:**), click **Shrink Volume**, type **16000** in the Enter the amount of space to shrink in MB text box, click **Shrink**, and then wait for the shrink to complete.

7. To allocate the RAID-5 volume, right-click the Unallocated area of Disk 0, click **New RAID-5 Volume**, click **Next**, click **Disk 1** under Available, click **Add**, click **Disk 2** under Available, click **Add**, type **8000** in the Select the amount of space in MB text box, click **Next** three times, and then click **Finish**.

8. Wait for the volume to be created, formatted, and a drive letter assigned. The RAID-5 volume should have a status of Healthy.

9. To shut down Server02, click **Start**, click the arrow next to the lock, click **Shut down**, click the **Option** drop-down menu, click **Hardware: Maintenance (Planned)**, and then click **OK**.

Dynamic Disks and Fault Tolerance **191**

NOTE

Normally, Disk Management allocates the RAID-5 volume, formats the volume, and assigns a drive letter. You should see the designation "healthy." However, you might need to assign a drive letter and format the volume. To assign a drive letter, right-click in the light-blue allocated area, click Change Drive Letter and Paths, click the Add button, and then click OK. To format the volume, right-click in the light-blue allocated area, click Format, click the File system drop-down arrow, click NTFS, and then click OK twice.

10. Leave the computer logged on for the next activity.

Activity 5-12: Repairing Fault-Tolerant Volumes

Time Required: 30 minutes

Objective: Repair fault-tolerant volumes.

Requirements: Completion of Activities 5-9 through 5-11.

Description: In this activity, you will take the second hard drive (Disk 1 in Disk Management) out of service, which breaks the fault-tolerant volumes. This will necessitate corrective actions to restore the RAID-1 and RAID-5 volumes.

1. If necessary, log on to your Host PC with a username of **Student** and a password of **Secret1**.

2. If necessary, to start Microsoft Virtual PC 2007, click **Start**, and then click **Microsoft Virtual PC**.

3. If necessary, to Shut down Server02, click **Start**, click the arrow next to the lock, click **Shut Down**, click the **Option** drop-down menu, click **Hardware: Maintenance (Planned)**, and then click **OK**.

4. To take the second hard drive out of service, switch to the Virtual PC Console, click the **Settings** button, click **Hard Disk 2**, click the **None** option button, and then click **OK**.

5. To start the Server02 virtual machine, double-click **Server02** in the Virtual PC Console.

6. Log on to the Server02 virtual machine with a username of **Administrator** and a password of **Secret1**.

7. To open Disk Management, click **Start**, point to **Administrative Tools**, click **Computer Management**, and then click **Disk Management**.

8. Verify that one of the three disks is missing.

9. To shut down Server02, click **Start**, click the arrow next to the lock, click **Shut Down**, click the **Option** drop-down menu, click **Hardware: Maintenance (Planned)**, and then click **OK**.

10. To return the second hard drive to in-service status, switch to the Virtual PC Console, click the **Settings** button, click **Hard Disk 2**, click the **Virtual hard disk file** option button, click **Browse**, click **Second Hard Disk**, click **Open**, and then click **OK**.

11. To start the Server02 virtual machine, double-click **Server02** in the Virtual PC Console.
12. Log on to the Server02 virtual machine with a username of **Administrator** and a password of **Secret1**.
13. To open Disk Management, click **Start**, point to **Administrative Tools**, click **Computer Management**, and then click **Disk Management**.
14. To remove the mirror for the RAID-1 volume, right-click in the **Mirrored Volume** (purple) in Disk 2, click **Remove Mirror**, click the **Remove Mirror** button, and then click **Yes**.
15. To rebuild the RAID-1 volume, right-click the **New Volume** area of Disk 1 (olive), click **Add Mirror**, click **Disk 2** under Disks, and then click **Add Mirror**.

Press the F5 key to refresh the Disk Management pane.

16. Wait for the RAID-1 volume to return to Healthy.
17. To reactivate the RAID-5 volume, right-click in the **RAID-5 volume** (light-blue), click **Reactivate Volume**, and then click **OK**.
18. Wait for the RAID-5 volume to return to Healthy.
19. To save the state of the running virtual machines, click the **Action** menu, click **Close**, and then click **OK**.
20. Repeat Step 22 for any additional open virtual machines.
21. Log off and shut down the host computer.

Troubleshooting Virtual PC Installations

Although most installations of operating systems on Virtual PC 2007 occur without a hitch, the following list describes common problems and their solutions.

- *Response times are slow on a virtual machine*—Install Virtual Machine Additions if the feature is not already installed.
- *Cannot install Virtual Machine Additions*—Log on as Administrator prior to running the installation program.
- *Features of Virtual Machine Additions do not work for cloned virtual hard disks*— When a new virtual machine is created, a new .vmc file is created. The settings for the Virtual Machine Additions are not set. To correct the problem, reinstall Virtual Machine Additions.

- *The virtual machine display appears corrupted when using 24-bit color depth*—Virtual PC 2007 does not support 24-bit color depth. During installation, change settings in the virtual machine operating system to the supported color depth of 16. This is a problem when installing a Linux distribution that defaults to 24-bit color.
- *A shared folder does not appear within the virtual machine operating system*—When the shared folder was set up, it was given a drive letter assignment that conflicts with an existing drive letter assignment in the virtual machine operating system. You must specify a drive letter assignment for the shared folder that is not already used by the virtual machine operating system.
- *The message "The virtual machine could not be restored because an unexpected error occurred." is displayed when a virtual machine is restored on a computer other than the one on which it was saved*—The processor in the computer on which you are restoring the virtual machine does not support certain features included in the processor in the computer on which the virtual machine was saved. If there are incompatibilities between processors, Virtual PC prevents the virtual machine from being restored to avoid damaging the virtual machine. We recommend that you only transfer virtual machines to computers that have the same type of processor.
- *Windows Explorer was used to rename a virtual machine and the new name is not listed in Virtual PC Console*—Virtual PC Console does not detect name changes to virtual machines when you use Windows Explorer or any other file management utility to change the name. Use the New Virtual Machine Wizard to add the virtual machine to Virtual PC Console.
- *Two or more guest operating systems have the same Media Access Control (MAC) address*—If you create an image of a host operating system that includes Virtual PC and virtual machine configuration files (.vmc files) and copy that image to another computer, each virtual machine configuration file included in the image contains a MAC address. The MAC address will not be reset automatically when you place the image on a new physical computer. As a result, the virtual machines that are copied onto the new computer will have the same MAC addresses as the virtual machines on the computer that was used to create the image. Edit the .vmc file to remove the MAC address. Find the following line:

    `<ethernet_card_address type="bytes">0003FFxxxxxx</ethernet_card_address>`

    Remove the number so the line appears as follows:

    `<ethernet_card_address type="bytes"></ethernet_card_address>`

    After you remove the number, Virtual PC will create a new MAC address the next time you start the virtual machine.

- *Windows 95 does not contain the Intel 440BX chipset drivers*—Install the Intel drivers for the 440BX chipset on the Windows 95 guest machine.
- *Dynamically expanding virtual hard disks are slow*—Fixed-size hard disks are significantly faster than dynamically expanding virtual hard disks. Convert the dynamically expanding virtual hard disks to fixed hard disks.
- *Installation from a CD/DVD is slow*—Installation from an ISO image is faster than from the CD/DVD. Capture the .iso file rather than the CD/DVD.
- *Operating system installations are slow*—Set the Virtual PC 2007 Options to run virtual machines at maximum speed. Verify that the RAM setting is adequate.

Chapter Summary

- You should optimize performance to successfully use virtual machines. Performance can be increased by properly allocating CPU time on the host OS and virtual machines. RAM requirements and hard disk settings will also affect the performance of virtual machines.

- You can specify settings for saving changes of the original virtual disk using options for undo disks, or differencing disks. Undo disks allows the removal of changes that are not wanted. The differencing disks method of saving changes involves creating a child disk from an original parent virtual hard disk. The virtual machine will then store changes to the child, or differencing, disk.

- Fault tolerance preserves the integrity of data during a malfunction by enabling the data to be read or created from another hard drive. Dynamic disks can be created by converting the existing basic disks and then initializing them. Conversion to dynamic disks is considered one-way because trying to convert back to basic disks will cause the loss of data.

- Common problems occasionally occur with some Virtual PC 2007 installations and might require troubleshooting. Installation or reinstallation of Virtual Machine Additions does resolve some of the known issues.

Key Terms

basic disk—A physical disk that can be accessed by MS-DOS and all Windows-based operating systems. Basic disks can contain up to four primary partitions, or three primary partitions and an extended partition with multiple logical drives.

dynamic disk—A disk initialized for dynamic storage.

fault tolerance—The ability of a computer or an operating system to respond to a catastrophic event or fault, such as a power outage or hardware failure, in a way that ensures that no data is lost and any work in progress is not corrupted.

mirrored volume—A hard drive or other form of storage media that stores an exact copy of the data from another volume. It is used for fault tolerance, which means a mirrored volume serves as a backup device in case the primary device fails.

parity—A calculated value that can be used to reconstruct data after a failure

PowerShell—A command-line shell designed and developed by Microsoft for system administrators that includes an interactive prompt and a scripting environment.

RAID—(Redundant Array of Independent Disks)—A disk subsystem that is used to increase performance or provide fault tolerance or both.

RAID-1—A storage scheme using disk mirroring, which provides 100 percent duplication of data. Offers highest reliability, but doubles storage cost. RAID-1 is widely used in business applications.

RAID-5—A storage scheme in which data is striped across three or more drives for performance, and parity bits are used for fault tolerance. RAID-5 is widely used in servers.

striped—The spreading out of the blocks of each file across multiple disk drives.

volume—A fixed amount of storage on a disk. The term volume is often used as a synonym for the storage medium itself, but it is possible for a single disk to contain more than one volume or for a volume to span more than one disk.

Review Questions

1. The ability of a computer to preserve the integrity of data during a malfunction is known as _____.
   a. Data backup
   b. Data tolerance
   c. Fault intolerance
   d. Fault tolerance

2. System resources such as CPU processing cycles, memory, and hard disk access _____. (Choose all that apply.)
   a. Do not impact computer system performance
   b. Are critical to performance optimization
   c. Can be ignored by virtual machines
   d. Can be optimized for successful implementation of multiple virtual machines

3. Microsoft recommends using a _____ processor for Virtual PC 2007.
   a. 1-GHz
   b. 10-GHz
   c. 1-MHz
   d. 10-MHz

4. For equal CPU time allocation between virtual machines, the CPU time option should _____.
   a. Allocate all running virtual machines unequal CPU time
   b. Allocate all running virtual machines equal CPU time
   c. Allocate more CPU time to the virtual machine in the active window
   d. Pause virtual machines in inactive windows

5. For there to be no CPU time given to the background virtual machine, the CPU time option should be for _____.
   a. All running virtual machines to get unequal CPU time
   b. All running virtual machines to get equal CPU time
   c. More CPU time to be allocated to the virtual machine in the active window
   d. Pausing virtual machines in inactive windows

6. When all the virtual machines are running in the background, the background option needs to be set to _____ for the host operating system to have background priority.
   a. Give all the running virtual machines equal CPU time
   b. Give processes on the host machine priority
   c. Allow more CPU time to the virtual machine in the active window
   d. Run the virtual machine at maximum speed

7. When all the virtual machines are running in the background, the background option needs to be set to _____ for the guest to have background priority.
   a. Give all the running virtual machines equal CPU time
   b. Give processes on the host machine priority
   c. Allow more CPU time for the virtual machine in the active window
   d. Run the virtual machine at maximum speed

8. The PowerShell _____. (Choose all that apply.)
   a. Is a command-line shell
   b. Includes an interactive prompt
   c. Is used by system administrators to manage servers
   d. Was designed and developed by Microsoft for students

9. RAM _____. (Choose all that apply.)
   a. Can be increased to enhance performance
   b. Needs to be decreased to enhance performance
   c. Has a positive effect on performance when swapped by the OS to disk
   d. Has a negative effect on performance when swapped by the OS to disk

10. When memory requirements are calculated for multiple operating systems, the host and guest overhead requirements are _____.
    a. 256 MB for the host and 128 MB for the guests
    b. 32 MB for the host and 128 MB for the guests
    c. 128 MB for the host and 32 for the guests
    d. 128 MB for the host and 256 MB for the guests
11. The disk images used in Virtual PC 2007 _____. (Choose all that apply).
    a. Are sequentially organized files
    b. Are not sequentially organized files
    c. Resemble files used by databases
    d. Utilize 2-MB blocks that are accessed from an allocation table
12. When the page file is eliminated on a virtual machine, _____. (Choose all that apply.)
    a. The performance of the hard drive is increased
    b. Disk space is saved on the hard drive
    c. You have run Virtual Disk Precompactor
    d. The .vhd files are now stored on a separate physical hard drive
13. When the free space on the virtual disks is zeroed on your virtual machine, _____. (Choose all that apply.)
    a. The performance of the hard drive is increased
    b. Disk space is saved on the hard drive
    c. You have run Virtual Disk Precompactor
    d. The .vhd files are now stored on a separate physical hard drive
14. A virtual hard disk _____. (Choose all that apply.)
    a. File expands and doesn't shrink
    b. Must have the free space zeroed with Virtual Disk Precompactor and then have the hard disk compacted
    c. Uses a large percentage of processor resources when defragmented and compacted
    d. Can easily recover deleted files
15. A differencing virtual hard disk _____. (Choose all that apply.)
    a. Points to the parent virtual hard disk
    b. Is created using the Virtual Disk Wizard
    c. Is created using an existing virtual hard disk
    d. Is also known as a child virtual hard disk

16. Linked disks _____. (Choose all that apply.)
    a. Use an existing physical hard disk
    b. Can use a portion of the hard disk
    c. Must use the entire hard disk
    d. Are read-only by default
17. Basic disks _____. (Choose all that apply.)
    a. Contain basic volumes, such as primary partitions
    b. Have extended partitions with logical drives
    c. Must be used to support fault-tolerant volumes in Windows Server 2008
    d. Allow you to perform disk and volume management without the need to restart Windows
18. Dynamic storage _____. (Choose all that apply.)
    a. Contains basic volumes such as primary partitions
    b. Has extended partitions with logical drives
    c. Must be used to support fault-tolerant volumes in Windows Server 2008
    d. Allows you to perform disk and volume management without the need to restart Windows
19. To implement fault tolerance, _____. (Choose all that apply.)
    a. You must convert basic disk drives to dynamic drives
    b. More than one host operating system is needed
    c. Only one virtual hard disk is required
    d. At least two virtual hard disks are needed
20. A fault-tolerant volume whose data is striped across an array of three or more disks is _____.
    a. RAID-2
    b. RAID-10
    c. RAID-5
    d. RAID-1

Case Projects

Case 5-1: Performance Improvement

You have just been hired as a summer intern at Jordan Products, and the company's virtual machines are performing slower than usual. Table 5-5 lists representative configurations for virtual machines at Jordan Products. All machines have deployed Microsoft Virtual PC. Your supervisor has asked you to come up with a list of ways to improve the performance.

Table 5-5 Representative configurations at Jordan Products

Host operating system	Processor speed	RAM	CPU time priority	Background priority	Virtual machines
Windows XP	1 GHz	2048 GB	Equal CPU time	Host priority	Windows XP—256 GB Windows Vista—512 GB Windows Vista—512 GB
Windows XP	1.6 GHz	2048 GB	More CPU time for foreground	Host priority	Windows XP—256 GB Windows XP—384 GB Windows Vista—512 GB Windows Vista—512 GB
Windows Vista	733 MHz	3072 GB	Equal CPU time	Guest priority	Windows XP—256 GB Windows Vista—512 GB Windows Vista—512 GB Windows Vista—512GB Windows Vista—512 GB
Windows Vista	1 GHz	2048 GB	More CPU time for foreground	Guest priority	Windows XP—256 GB Windows Vista—512 GB Windows Vista—512 GB

Case 5-2: Using Virtual Machines in a Development Environment

You have received a request for multiple desktop computers for use by the training group at your company, an international engineering firm. You have interviewed Yvonne, the manager of the training group, who has outlined the requirements as follows. The computers must be able to:

- Run development software entirely in a virtual machine.
- Test the next version of the development software.
- Run the test clients.

Your manager, Paul, has asked you to prepare a written proposal to meet the training department's needs using virtual machines. Your proposal must meet the requirements described by Yvonne using a single computer for each environment. You should consider implementing differencing disks, cloning, and undo disks.

Case 5-3: Troubleshooting Guide

Develop a troubleshooting guide for your school's student lab virtual machines. The lab currently has a few Windows XP machines, a few machines with Linux, and several machines recently upgraded to Windows Vista.

chapter 6
Implementing Virtual Server

After reading this chapter and completing the exercises, you will be able to:

- Describe the features of Virtual Server
- Install Virtual Server
- Configure Virtual Server
- Implement virtual networks with Virtual Server
- Create a virtual network
- Implement virtual hard disks with Virtual Server
- Implement virtual machines with Virtual Server

In the previous chapters, you learned how to use Microsoft Virtual PC 2007, which is designed with the typical desktop user in mind. Desktop users use Virtual PC to implement multiple virtual machines running desktop operating systems with applications such as Microsoft Office. In this chapter, you will learn how to use Microsoft Virtual Server 2005. Virtual Server gives you an easy way of consolidating multiple servers, operating systems, and applications onto a single computer. Instead of using a dedicated server for every application and service you require, you can run them in virtual machines. This lets you continue to isolate applications and services while making better use of existing hardware.

Virtual PC and Virtual Server differ in terms of how they are used, the types of settings in which they are used, and the types of networks they support. Another key difference lies in the software interface. With Virtual PC, you used a typical windows interface. The Virtual Server administrative interface is browser-based. You access this administrative interface with Microsoft Internet Explorer. Because Virtual Server is designed to manage multiple virtual machines on multiple physical servers in an enterprise environment, a Web-based interface is more appropriate.

As part of mastering Virtual Server, you will learn to link virtual networks, virtual hard disks, virtual machines, and more in this chapter.

Overview of Virtual Server

Whereas Virtual PC runs as an application, Virtual Server runs as a Windows service. A Windows service is a program that starts when the Microsoft Windows operating system is booted and runs in the background as long as Windows is running. By running as a service, Virtual Server is tied into the host operating system's kernel for increased flexibility and performance.

The following sections introduce the key features of Virtual Server and how they compare with Virtual PC.

Virtual Server Architecture

Figure 6-1 illustrates the architecture of Virtual Server's virtual machine technology.

Starting from the bottom of the logical stack, the host operating system (Windows Server 2008) manages the physical computer. Virtual Server consists of a number of software components that run within the confines of the host operating system to provide a virtual environment. These software components are as follows:

- The **Virtual Server service** creates virtual machines and provides all virtual machines with the virtual machine environment's emulated hardware. Also, it provides each virtual machine with its individual 32-bit address space.

- The **Virtual Machine Remote Control (VMRC) server** provides access to the virtual machines.

- The **VMRC protocol** (shown as dashed lines between the VMRC client and each virtual machine) is a presentation and control protocol that allows remote viewing and controlling of virtual machines.

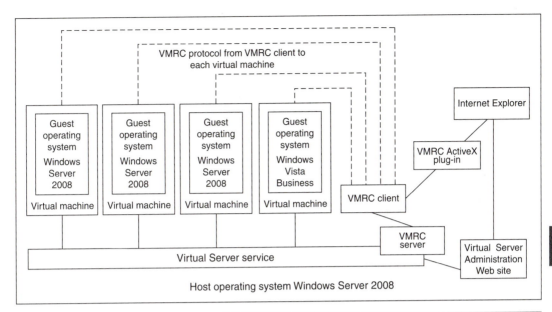

Figure 6-1 Virtual Server architecture

- The **Virtual Machine Remote Control (VMRC) client** allows you to manage the virtual machine and interact with the guest operating system using the VMRC protocol.
- The **VMRC ActiveX plug-in** supports the use of the VMRC client from within Internet Explorer. The first time you use the VMRC client from Internet Explorer, Virtual Server downloads this ActiveX control for the VMRC client to your host computer.
- The **Virtual Server Administration Web site** is a browser-based tool for configuring and managing Virtual Server and its associated virtual machines and virtual networks.

Virtual Machines

As you learned in previous chapters, each virtual machine acts like a stand-alone computer system, with its own video, keyboard, mouse, hard disks, CD/DVD, and network cards. The Virtual Server virtualization software provides virtualized hardware for these components and more. Figure 6-2 on the next page shows the various hardware components that are available in Virtual Server.

"Longhorn" Configuration

General properties	"Longhorn"
When Virtual Server starts:	Never automatically turn on virtual machine
When Virtual Server stops:	Save state
Virtual Machine Additions	Virtual Machine Additions information not available
Memory	128 MB
Hard disks	1 virtual hard disk installed; Undo disks are disabled
Virtual hard disk 1	Attached to primary channel (0)
	Virtual hard disk file "Longhorn.vhd"
	Maximum size is 127 GB; Currently expanded to 256.5 KB
CD / DVD	1 virtual CD / DVD drive installed
Virtual CD / DVD drive 1	Attached to secondary channel (0)
	Host drive "F"
SCSI adapters	No virtual SCSI adapters installed
Network adapters	1 virtual network adapter installed
Virtual network adapter 1	Not connected
	Current Ethernet (MAC) address: 00-03-FF-4F-50-01
Scripts	Scripts disabled
Floppy drive	No media captured
COM ports	2 COM ports installed
COM port 1	Attached to none
COM port 2	Attached to none
LPT ports	1 LPT port installed
LPT port 1	Attached to none

Figure 6-2 Configuration for virtual machine "Longhorn" in Virtual Server

Table 6-1 shows the components that are provided by Virtual Server and emulated by virtual machines.

Table 6-1 Components provided by Virtual Server

Component	Description
Memory	Limited by the amount of physical memory in the physical machine
Hard disk	Access up to three virtual hard disks with a default of 16,384 MB (maximum of 130,577 MB)
CD/DVD	Mount three CD/DVD drives to IDE ports or captured .iso files
SCSI adapters	Access up to four SCSI adapters with seven hard drives per adapter with clustering support
Network adapters	Add up to four network adapters
Scripts	Enable/disable the scripts to be run when conditions are met
Floppy drive	Detected automatically
Communication ports (COM1, COM2)	Map to the physical ports in the host
Printer ports (LPT1)	Map to one printer port

Emulated Hardware

When you are considering the hardware requirements for a given operating system that you want to install in your virtual environment, you should consider the specific hardware that is emulated by Virtual Server. Table 6-2 provides a list of the hardware devices that are emulated by Virtual Server.

Table 6-2 Emulated devices in virtual machines

Component or device	Virtual machine–emulated hardware
BIOS system	AMI BIOS system
Chipset	Intel 440BX
Network adapter	Intel/DEC 21140A 10/100
Video card	S3 Trio 32/64 PCI
SCSI adapter	Adaptec 7870

Supported Operating Systems

Table 6-3, on the next page, enumerates the operating systems supported by Virtual Server. The supported host list is more restrictive than the guest list. Also, it is worth noting that Microsoft supports operating systems from other vendors—Red Hat and SUSE.

Virtual Server can run most x86 operating systems, in addition to the supported operating systems, in a virtual machine environment. For example, Fedora is a Linux operating system that, although not supported by Microsoft, does run within a virtual machine.

You might be wondering whether you can run other Microsoft operating systems in Virtual Server. Yes, you can. You configure the virtual machine properties from the configuration Web page, as shown in Figure 6-2.

Virtual Machine Additions

Just as it does in Virtual PC, the Virtual Machine Additions add-in software delivers increased performance and added features within your virtual machines. You must install VMA in each guest operating system. The advantages of VMA include improved performance, better mouse control within your virtual machines, clock synchronization, and "heartbeat."

Performance Improvements Because drivers for the virtual hard disk controllers and other required virtual hardware are standardized and stable, operations within the virtual machine will usually perform significantly better than the default operating system drivers. These drivers are installed by VMA in the guest operating systems.

Improved Mouse Control Prior to installing Virtual Machine Additions, you must press the right Alt key to free the mouse to move from a window within a virtual machine. After installing Virtual Machine Additions, you can move freely between the host operating system and virtual machine windows. This simplifies switching among virtual machines and the host operating system.

Time Synchronization When Virtual Machine Additions is installed, the virtual machines' system clocks will be synchronized with the host machine's clock. This is important

Table 6-3 Virtual Server–supported operating systems

Host	Guest	Operating system
✔	✔	Microsoft Windows Server 2003, Standard Edition
✔	✔	Microsoft Windows Server 2003, Enterprise Edition
	✔	Microsoft Windows Server 2003, Web Edition
✔	✔	Microsoft Windows Server 2003, Datacenter Edition
	✔	Microsoft Windows 2000 Server
	✔	Microsoft Windows 2000 Advanced Server
	✔	Microsoft Windows NT Server 4.0 with Service Pack 6a (SP6a)
✔	✔	Microsoft Windows XP Professional Service Pack 2 (SP2)
	✔	Red Hat Enterprise Linux 2.1 update 6
	✔	Red Hat Enterprise Linux 3.0 update 6
	✔	Red Hat Enterprise Linux 4.0
	✔	SUSE Linux Enterprise Server 9.0
	✔	Red Hat Linux 7.3
	✔	Red Hat Linux 9.0
	✔	SUSE Linux 9.2
	✔	SUSE Linux 9.3
	✔	SUSE Linux 10.0

because the clock on the virtual machine can tend to drift, especially if the virtual machine is started and stopped frequently.

Virtual Machine Heartbeat The virtual machine sends a regular signal to Virtual Server. The **heartbeat** allows the virtual machine to report to Virtual Server that it is still "alive"—active and functioning.

Activity 6-1: Researching Microsoft Virtual Server

Time Required: 10 minutes

Objective: Research Microsoft Virtual Server on the Web.

Description: In this activity, you will visit the Microsoft Virtual Server Web page and locate information on Microsoft Virtual Server.

1. If necessary, log on to your host PC with a username of **Administrator** and a password of **Secret1**.
2. To launch the Internet Explorer browser, click **Start** and then click **Internet Explorer**.

3. To disable the Internet Explorer Enhanced Security Configuration, click **Start**, point to **Administrative Tools**, click **Server Manager**, click the **Configure IE ESC** link, click the **Off** option under Administrators, click **OK**, and then close the Server Manager window.

4. Type **Microsoft Virtual Server 2005 R2** in the Live Search text box and then press **Enter**.

5. To access the Microsoft Virtual Server Web page, scroll and click the **Microsoft Virtual Server 2005 R2** link. Scroll and click the **Get the Overview** link.

 There are numerous links from which to choose. You want the product overview Web page for Microsoft Virtual Server 2005 R2.

6. Scroll and read each of these items: Introduction, What's New in This Release, and Key Features and Benefits.

7. Close Internet Explorer.

8. Leave the computer logged on for the next activity.

Differences Between Virtual PC and Virtual Server

Because Virtual PC and Virtual Server are designed to serve different purposes, there are crucial differences that you should understand to help you make a more informed decision about which software to use for your situation:

- Virtual PC supports desktop applications—VPC is designed with the typical desktop user in mind and is best used with operating systems such as Microsoft Vista and applications such as Microsoft Word. The configuration options are relatively simple and easy for the average computer user to understand and use.

- Virtual Server runs enterprise server operating systems and applications—Virtual Server provides the configuration and management options required for server management. The user interface, accordingly, is more complex. Consequently, using Virtual Server effectively requires some knowledge of server technologies.

Features Unique to Virtual PC To support the requirements of a desktop environment, Virtual PC provides features that are not available (or typically needed) in Virtual Server:

- Emulated sound card—Only Virtual PC provides an emulated sound card to support the needs and expectations of desktop users.

- Host-guest integration—Virtual PC is designed to provide user convenience in a desktop environment. This allows users to switch between operating systems as easily as they switch between applications by simply clicking on the window that contains the virtual machine. Users also can use the drag-and-drop method to move or copy and paste items from a guest operating system to the host operating system, and vice versa.

- Dynamic resizing—Virtual PC lets you resize the guest operating system desktop when resizing the virtual machine window. Folder sharing between the host operating systems and virtual machines also is supported by Virtual PC.

- Shared networking—Virtual PC offers shared networking through Network Address Translation (NAT). This makes it easy for users to configure a connection to an external network that is shared with the host computer.

Features Unique to Virtual Server To support the requirements of an enterprise environment, Virtual Server provides features that are not available (or typically needed) in Virtual PC:

- Remote management—You can administer Virtual Server remotely using the Web-based Administration Web site. You can also access and administer virtual machines remotely by using VMRC. In addition, you can use Remote Desktop to connect to the virtual machines.
- Scripted management—You can manage Virtual Server and its virtual machines using scripts. For example, scripts written in VBScript can be used to start multiple virtual machines.
- WMI integration—Virtual Server provides Windows Management Instrumentation (WMI) counters to the host operating system. These counters can be queried by scripts to access performance counters for Virtual Server and virtual machines.
- Delegated administration—With Virtual Server, you can delegate administration and provide secure, authenticated guest access.
- System event logging—Virtual Server logs events on the host operating system event log. Logged events can be viewed using Event Viewer. In addition, logged events are viewable on the Virtual Server Administration Web site.
- Flexible memory and CPU allocation—Virtual Server supports flexible memory configuration and dynamic CPU resource allocation for each virtual machine.
- SCSI support—Virtual Server supports virtual SCSI drives up to 2 TB (terabytes) in size. Because each emulated SCSI adapter provides seven virtual hard disks, SCSI is ideal for implementing RAID storage.
- Host multiprocessor support—Virtual Server scales across multiple processors on the host computer—up to 32. Each running virtual machine can take advantage of an allocated CPU. For example, on a 32-processor host computer, you could allocate your CPU capacity so that 31 simultaneously running virtual machines would each use one CPU, leaving a CPU free for the host operating system.
- Multithreading—Virtual Server is a multithreaded application that runs as a system service, with each virtual machine running in its own thread of execution. In contrast, Virtual PC is a single-threaded application in which all simultaneously running virtual machines run on the same processor.
- Large RAM support—Virtual Server supports up to 3.6 GB of RAM per virtual machine. Virtual PC supports up to 3.6 GB total RAM for the host and guest operating systems.
- Support for Secure Sockets Layer (SSL) security—For access to the Administration Web site and the virtual machine VMRC client, Virtual Server supports SSL security, as well as Windows authentication.

- **Configurable user context for virtual machines**—By default, a virtual machine runs under the account of the user who logged on to the host computer. For added security, you can configure each virtual machine to run under a specified user account. Virtual machine scripts can also run under this account. The account must be configured before virtual machine scripts can run.
- **Virtual networking**—With Virtual Server, you can create an unlimited number of virtual networks, each with its own virtual Dynamic Host Configuration Protocol (DHCP) server. You can also configure Domain Name System (DNS) and Windows Internet Naming Service (WINS) server addresses, Internet Protocol (IP) addresses, and IP address lease time.
- **Clustering**—Virtual Server provides simple two-node failover from one virtual machine to another. **Clustering** is a technology that uses two or more computers that function together as a single entity for fault tolerance and load balancing. It can also increase reliability and uptime in a client/server environment. You can use this feature for testing and development only; it is not supported for use in a production environment. In addition, Virtual Server supports creating a Microsoft Cluster Service cluster that uses shared storage on SCSI and includes from two to eight virtual machines.

Installing Virtual Server

Before installing Virtual Server, you need to take care of one important task: Create an Internet-ready networking environment with Internet Connection Sharing (ICS). Although ICS support might not be required in all networking situations, ICS is required for the lab activities in this text.

After completing this task, you will install Virtual Server on your host operating system. In addition, you will take a quick look at Virtual Server and see how to accomplish common tasks.

Activity 6-2: Installing Internet Connection Sharing

Time Required: 10 minutes

Objective: Configure ICS to connect the network adapter in the host computer that runs Windows Server 2008 to the Microsoft Loopback Adapter, which is used by each virtual machine.

Description: In this activity, you will install a Microsoft Loopback Adapter. Next, you will enable ICS. This activity is useful if you want to permit the virtual machines to access the Internet.

1. If necessary, log on to your host PC with a username of **Administrator** and a password of **Secret1**.
2. To open the Add Hardware dialog box, click **Start**, click **Control Panel**, click **Classic View**, and then double-click **Add Hardware**.
3. Click **Next**, click the **Install the hardware that I manually select from a list (Advanced)** option button, and then click **Next**.

4. To select the Network adapters entry, scroll the Common hardware types, click **Network adapters**, and then click **Next**.

5. To select the Microsoft Loopback Adapter, click **Microsoft** under Manufacturer, scroll the Network Adapter list, click **Microsoft Loopback Adapter**, and then click **Next**.

6. To install the Microsoft Loopback Adapter, click **Next**.

7. Wait for the installation to complete, and then click **Finish**.

8. To display the Network and Sharing Center, double-click **Network and Sharing Center**.

9. To display the Local Area Connection Properties dialog box, click the **View status** link for the Local Area Connection entry, and then click **Properties**.

10. To enable ICS, click the **Sharing** tab, check the **Allow other network users to connect through this computer's Internet connection** check box, click **OK**, and then click **Close**.

11. To enable Network discovery, click the **Network discovery** drop-down arrow, click the **Turn on network discovery** option button, click the **Apply** button, and then click **Yes, turn on network discovery for all public networks**.

12. To enable File sharing, click the **File sharing** drop-down list arrow, click the **Turn on file sharing** option button, click the **Apply** button, click **Yes, turn on file sharing for all public networks**, and then close the Network and Sharing Center window.

13. If necessary, minimize the Initial Configuration Tasks window.

14. Leave the computer logged on for the next activity.

Activity 6-3: Installing Microsoft Virtual Server

Time Required: 10 minutes

Objective: Install Microsoft Virtual Server.

Requirements: You will need the server name and share name for the Virtual Server setup program, which will be provided by your instructor.

Description: In this activity, you will install Internet Information Services (IIS), which is required by Virtual Server. Next, you will run the Virtual Server setup program from the provided network server.

1. If necessary, log on to your host PC with a username of **Administrator** and a password of **Secret1**.

2. Maximize the Initial Configuration Tasks window.

3. To install IIS, click the **Add roles** link, click **Server Roles**, and then click the **Web Server (IIS)** check box.

4. When the Add Required Features for Web Server message appears, click the **Add required features** button.

5. Click **Next** three times, and then click the **Install** button.

6. Wait for the installation to complete, and then click **Close**.

7. Minimize the Initial Configuration Tasks window.
8. To access and run the Virtual Server setup program, click **Start**, click **Run**, **\\\\Server\\Share\\setup.exe** (where the server name and share name are provided by your instructor), and then click **OK**.

Obtain the server name and share name from your instructor. Confirm that your institution is a member of the MSDN Academic Alliance and your instructor has registered with Microsoft and downloaded Microsoft Virtual Server 2005 R2 SP1.

9. When the Open File–Security Warning dialog box opens, click the **Run** button.
10. When the Microsoft Virtual Server 2005 R2 SP1 Setup window opens, click the **Install Microsoft Virtual Server 2005 R2 SP1** icon.
11. Click the **I accept the terms in the license agreement** option button, click **Next** five times, and then click the **Install** button.
12. When the Add Required Features message appears, click the **Yes** button, and then click the **Install** button (second time).
13. Wait for the installation to complete, and then click **Finish**.
14. To place a shortcut to Virtual Server on your desktop, click **Start**, click **All Programs**, click **Microsoft Virtual Server**, right-click **Virtual Machine Remote Control Client**, point to **Send To**, click **Desktop (create shortcut)**, right-click **Virtual Server Administration Website**, point to **Send To**, and then click **Desktop (create shortcut)**.
15. To access the Virtual Server Administration Web site, double-click the **Virtual Server Administration Website** shortcut on the desktop.
16. Log on to the Web site with a username of **Administrator** and a password of **Secret1**, click the **Remember my password** check box, and then click **OK**.
17. To establish security for the Web site, click **Tools**, click **Internet Options**, click the **Security** tab, click the **Local intranet** icon, click the **Sites** button, click the **Advanced** button, type **http://host01** in the Add this website to the zone text box, click the **Add** button, click **Yes**, clear the **Require server verification (https:) for all sites in this zone** check box, click **Close**, and then click **OK** twice.
18. Leave the computer logged on for the next activity.

Activity 6-4: Exploring Microsoft Virtual Server Help

Time Required: 15 minutes

Objective: Research information on Microsoft Virtual Server.

Requirements: Completion of Activity 6-3.

Description: In this activity, you will explore Microsoft Virtual Server Help. This activity is useful if you want to locate the answer to a question regarding the use of Microsoft Virtual Server.

1. If necessary, log on to your Host PC with a username of **Administrator** and a password of **Secret1**.
2. To access the Virtual Server Help, click **Start**, click **All Programs**, click **Microsoft Virtual Server**, and then click the **Virtual Server Administrator's Guide**.
3. Expand the **Virtual Server 2005 Administrator's Guide**, expand the **Virtual Server Operations Guide**, expand **How To**, and expand and peruse each topic under How To.
4. Close the Virtual Server 2005 Administrator's Guide window.
5. Leave the computer logged on for the next activity.

Configuring Virtual Server

You access the Virtual Server Administration Web site, as shown in Figure 6-3, by navigating from the Start menu through All Programs and Microsoft Virtual Server to the Virtual Server Administration Website link. The Administration Web site consists of multiple panes. You can use the navigation pane on the left to select an action link. The Master Status pane is the initial pane displayed.

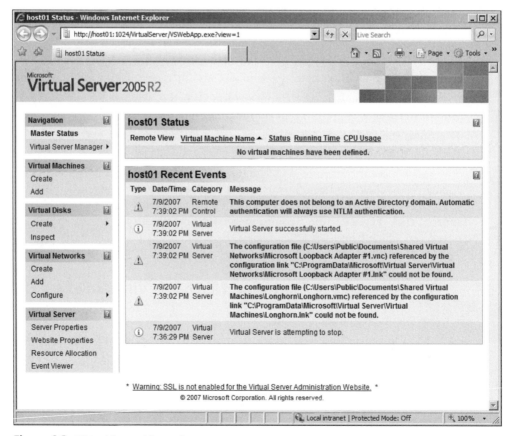

Figure 6-3 Virtual Server Master Status

Server Properties

Figure 6-4 shows the Server Properties pane when accessed from the Server Properties link on the navigation pane of the Administration Web site. Server properties include items such as security for Virtual Server and host (physical) computer settings. You will need to access links in this pane to verify and set server properties.

Virtual Server has a number of global settings that you will need to verify or specify. These include settings for security, remote control, scripts, search paths, and physical computer properties.

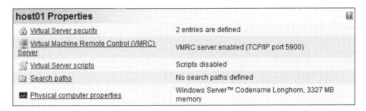

Figure 6-4 Server properties

Virtual Server Security Figure 6-5 shows the pane to manage Virtual Server security. Security settings let you control access to Virtual Server configuration settings. You can add users, and grant or deny users permission to perform specific actions. By default, the local Administrator user account and the members of the Administrators Local Group have full access to the folders where Virtual Server stores the various configuration files.

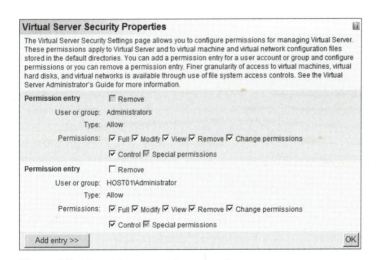

Figure 6-5 Virtual Server security properties

If you need to apply security to individual virtual machines, virtual hard disks, and virtual networks, you can use the NTFS file permissions.

Virtual Machine Remote Control Server Properties Figure 6-6 shows the correctly configured Virtual Machine Remote Control server properties.

Virtual Machine Remote Control (VMRC) Server Properties	
VMRC server	☑ Enable
TCP/IP address:	(All unassigned)
TCP/IP port:	5900
Default screen resolution:	800 x 600
Authentication	Automatic
Disconnect idle connections	☐ Enable
Timeout (in minutes):	15
Multiple VMRC connections	☐ Enable

Figure 6-6 Virtual Machine Remote Control (VMRC) server properties

You must check the Enable check box to use the VMRC server. By default, the VMRC server is disabled. This security precaution prevents unauthorized access to virtual machines using the VMRC client.

Normally, you will not need to change the default TCP/IP address and TCP/IP port. Should you have multiple Web sites on the host server, you could select the IP address of the Virtual Server Web site from the TCP/IP address drop-down list arrow. The default TCP/IP port is 5900. If needed, you could change the port to one in the range of 5900 to 5999.

Ensure that the default screen resolution is less than the screen resolution of the host computer so that the virtual machine is properly displayed within the display of the host computer. For example, the default screen resolution of 800 × 600 works fine with a host resolution of 1024 × 768. If needed, change the default screen resolution.

When you access a virtual machine, you must supply a user ID and a password. VMRC authenticates using Windows authentication. The Kerberos authentication protocol is the default network identity authentication protocol for computers on Active Directory domains. With the default Automatic setting, VMRC can shift to Windows NTLM authentication when Active Directory is not available. The **Windows NT LAN Manager (NTLM) protocol** is used to authenticate logons for stand-alone computers. It is the default for network authentication in the Windows NT 4.0 operating system and is retained for compatibility with down-level clients and servers.

If you are working with a number of virtual machines at the same time, you will want to clear the Disconnect idle connections check box. This will keep the VMRC from dropping a connection to a virtual machine that you have not accessed recently.

Because you are accessing the virtual machines from the host computer on which they are running, there is no need to enable multiple VMRC connections.

If you are running your virtual machines in a production environment, you will want to enable SSL encryption. This topic is beyond the scope of this text.

Virtual Server Scripts To automate the management of Virtual Server, you can use any scripting program that Windows Script Host can execute. For example, you could write a VBScript program to start all of your virtual machines. Because scripting has security implications, scripting is disabled by default. For example, a VBScript could be used to place malware on a VM—malware that can place a significant load on system resources. Instead of affecting just a single VM, these problems are likely to affect other virtualized workloads on the same computer. See Figure 6-7. You must manually enable scripting for Virtual Server or virtual machines.

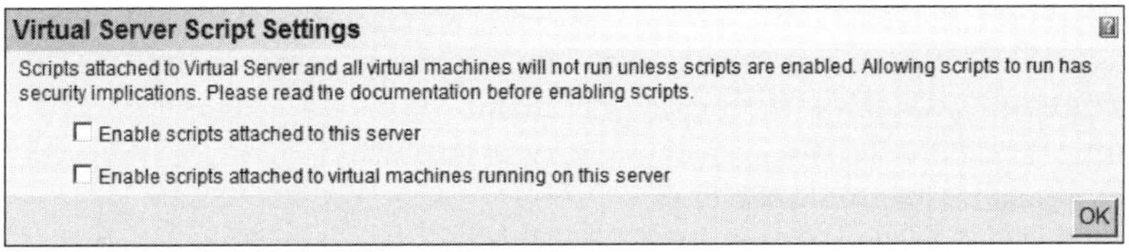

Figure 6-7 Scripts in Virtual Server

Virtual Server Search Paths Virtual Server uses the paths provided in the Virtual Server Paths page, shown in Figure 6-8, to locate the .vmc and .vhd files. In Figure 6-8, the path is shown as C:\Users\Public\Documents\Shared Virtual Machines.

From Windows Explorer, the .vmc files are shown to be at C:\Users\Public\Public Documents\Shared Virtual Machines.

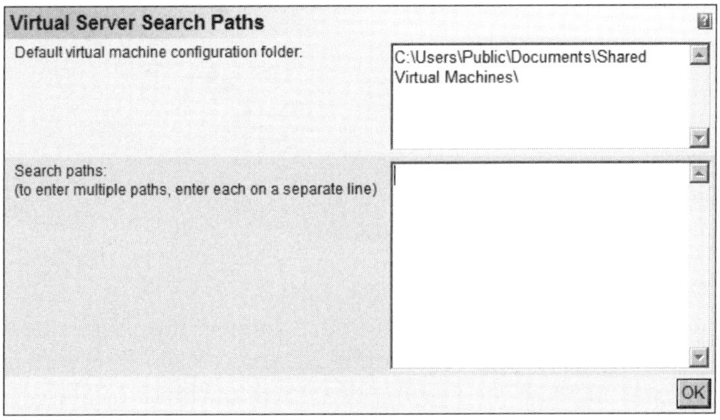

Figure 6-8 Virtual Server search paths

 This path display is just a display trick by Windows. The path is C:\Users\Public\Document, but Windows Explorer displays a name of C:\Users\ Public\Public Documents.

The search paths that you configure are used to populate list boxes in the Administration Web site. Additional search paths are useful when you need to store files by project. For example, you could type in C:\My Virtual Machines in the Search path. Virtual Server provides search paths in place of a Browse button because Web sites do not provide the ability to "browse" through the file system.

Physical Computer Properties The hardware configuration for the host computer is an important factor when determining how many virtual machines can be run. See Figure 6-9. Details on this Web page include the processor, memory, network adapters, and operating system. For example, the Available physical memory specification shows how much memory is available to run additional virtual machines.

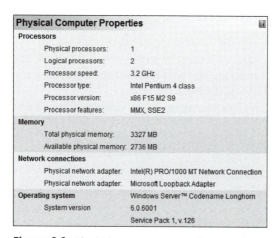

Figure 6-9 Physical computer properties

Administration Web Site Properties

Figure 6-10 shows the page to configure the settings for the Administration Web site where you can control the information that is displayed. For example, if you were working with more than 10 virtual machines, you could increase the number of virtual machines displayed. You can configure the properties listed in Table 6-4.

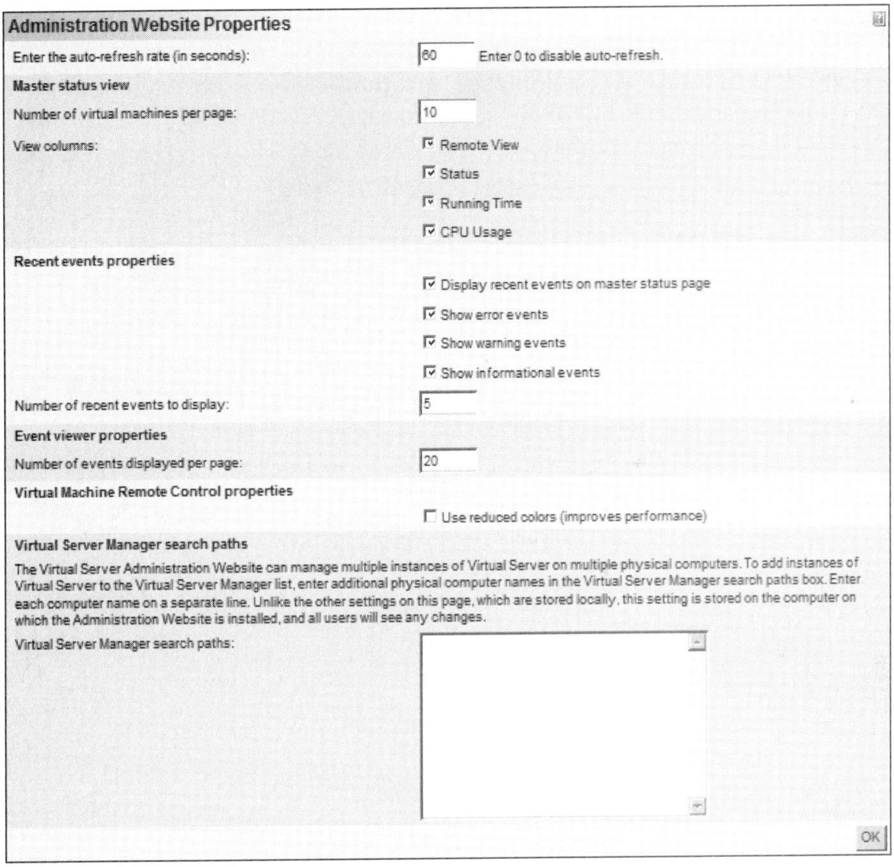

Figure 6-10 Administration Web site properties

Table 6-4 Administration Web site properties

Item	Description
Auto-refresh rate	The interval between Web site refreshes. Default of 60 seconds is appropriate. Too-frequent refreshes might impact performance.
Master status view	The number of virtual machines to display on one page. Also, the items to display for each virtual machine: Remote View icon, Status, Running Time, and CPU Usage.
Recent events properties	The option to display recent Virtual Server events on the Status page and the type (error, warning, or informational).
Event Viewer properties	The number of events to display.
Virtual Machine Remote Control properties	The option to use reduced colors, which improves performance.
Virtual Server Manager search paths	The option to manage additional virtual servers from this host computer. Enter fully qualified domain name or IP address.

CPU Resource Allocation

You use the CPU Resource Allocation page, shown in Figure 6-11, to allocate physical CPU resources to virtual machines. All of the virtual machines currently added to Virtual Server are shown in two lists: Virtual Machines Currently Running and Virtual Machines Not Currently Running.

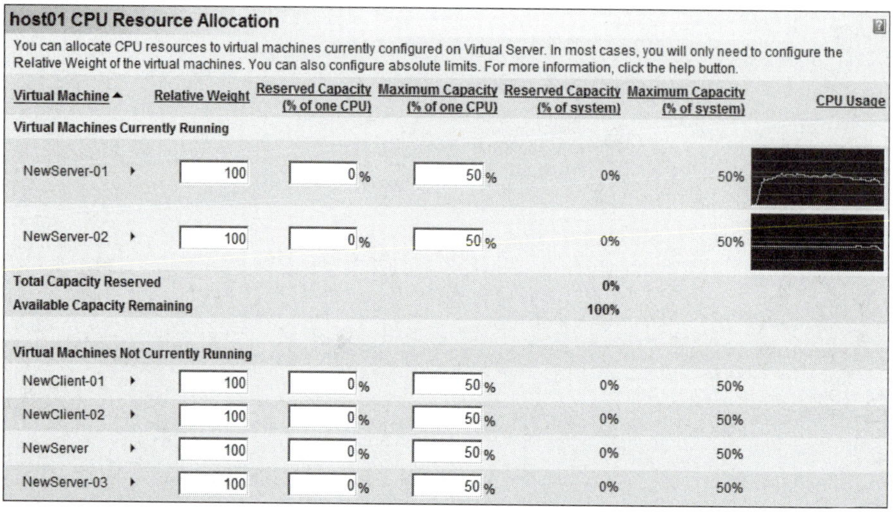

Figure 6-11 CPU resource allocation

Table 6-5 describes the resource allocation information and settings.

Virtual Server runs on physical machines with up to 32 processors. For the settings in Table 6-5, even if the host computer has multiple processors, you must specify the percentage of a single CPU.

You can allocate resources to a machine regardless of whether the virtual machine is running. However, when you allocate resources to a virtual machine that is not running, the allocated resources are not included in the Total Capacity Reserved or Available Capacity Remaining. This means that you could over-allocate and prevent virtual machines from running.

Event Viewer

When you run into problems with your virtual machines or Virtual Server, a good place to find information about the possible source of the problem is the Virtual Server event log. To access the event log, click the Event Viewer link. Figure 6-12 shows a sample Event Viewer log. Events are classified as Errors (red X), Warnings (yellow !), and Information (blue i) in the first column. The date and time appear next on each line. The category of the event is next. The message completes each line.

Table 6-5 CPU Resource Allocation settings

Item	Description
Virtual Machine	The name of the virtual machine.
Relative Weight	The relative weight given to the CPU needs of this virtual machine relative to other virtual machines. The default is 100 so that all virtual machines are equal. In most cases, the relative weight is the only setting that you will need to set. You can assign a relative weight between 1 and 10,000.
Reserved Capacity (% of one CPU)	The capacity of one CPU that is reserved for this virtual machine. The percentage of CPU capacity that is available to the virtual machine will never be less than this percentage.
Maximum Capacity (% of one CPU)	The highest percentage of total resources of a single CPU that can be consumed by this virtual machine at any given time.
Reserved Capacity (% of system)	The percentage of total system CPU capacity that is reserved for this virtual machine.
Maximum Capacity (% of system)	The highest percentage of total system CPU capacity that is reserved for this virtual machine.
CPU Usage	The chart of the CPU usage for this virtual machine over the last minute.
Total Capacity Reserved	The total CPU capacity of the host computer reserved for all currently running virtual machines.
Available Capacity Remaining	The total CPU capacity of the host computer that has not been reserved for currently running virtual machines.

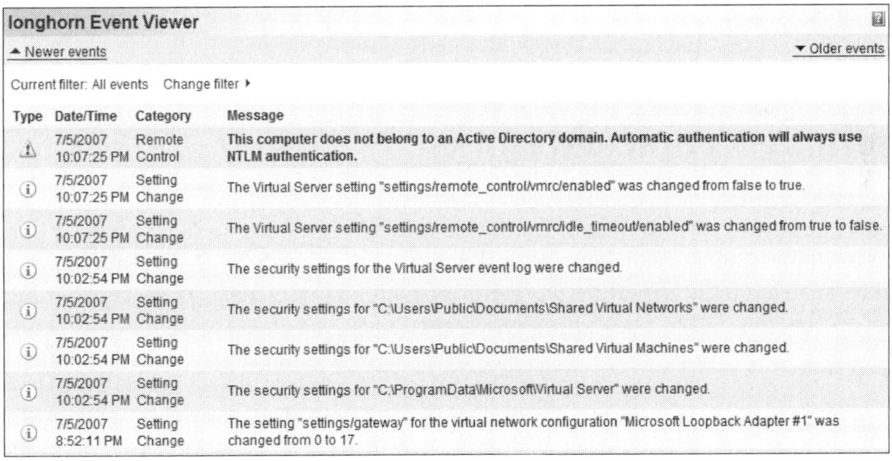

Figure 6-12 Event Viewer

The Change filter link lets you select a filter by which to display events. The filter options are: All events, Virtual Server events, Virtual Disk Operation events, Preference Change events, or Remote Control events. Also, you can filter on the events for a single VM.

Activity 6-5: Configuring Virtual Server

Time Required: 5 minutes

Objective: Configure Microsoft Virtual Server.

Requirements: Completion of Activity 6-3.

Description: In this activity, you will configure Virtual Server. This activity will ensure that Virtual Server and the VMRC server are properly configured for your use.

1. If necessary, log on to your Host PC with a username of **Administrator** and a password of **Secret1**.

2. If necessary, to access the Virtual Server Administration Web site, double-click the **Virtual Server Administration Website** shortcut on the desktop.

3. To open the Server Properties page, click the **Server Properties** link in the navigation pane.

4. To verify the Virtual Server Security Properties, click the **Virtual Server security** link, verify that the Administrators group and the Administrator have full access (if they do not, contact your instructor), and then click the **Server Properties** link in the navigation pane.

5. To enable the VMRC server, click the **Virtual Machine Remote Control (VMRC) Server** link, check the **Enable** check box next to the VMRC server, clear the **Enable** check box next to Disconnect idle connections, and then scroll and click **OK**.

6. Leave the computer logged on for the next activity.

Implementing Virtual Networks

Virtual networking gives you more secure, flexible networking with guest-to-guest, guest-to-host, and guest-to-external network connectivity. A virtual network consists of one or more virtual machines configured to access local or external resources with one or more other virtual machines. Setting up a virtual network can provide many distinct advantages in testing configuration changes and application deployments.

Virtual Server includes several options for the creation and use of virtual networks, including internal networks, the network adapter on the host computer, and the Microsoft Loopback Adapter. Also, you can implement Internet Connection Sharing on the host computer to provide access to the Internet. Virtual Server supports an unlimited number of virtual networks, and an unlimited number of virtual machines can be connected to a virtual network.

Internal Network

The local option for virtual networks lets all of the virtual machines communicate over a local "internal" network. The virtual machines do not have access to network resources on the host computer system.

Network Adapter on the Physical Computer

With the network adapter on the physical computer option, the virtual machine is connected directly to the network served by the physical adapter of the host computer system. See Figure 6-13. The virtual machine will appear as if it were physically connected to the physical network with addresses on the same network as the physical network. If the physical network uses DHCP, the virtual machine will receive an IP address configuration from the physical network's DHCP server.

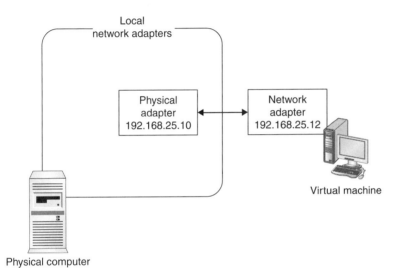

Figure 6-13 Network adapter on physical computer

Microsoft Loopback Adapter

You can use the Microsoft Loopback Adapter as a network interface driver. Included with Windows Server 2008, Microsoft Loopback Adapter must be installed in the host computer, as shown in Figure 6-14 on the next page. Then, you configure the virtual machines to access the virtual network supported by each Microsoft Loopback Adapter. You will need to assign network IP addresses to the machines on each virtual network.

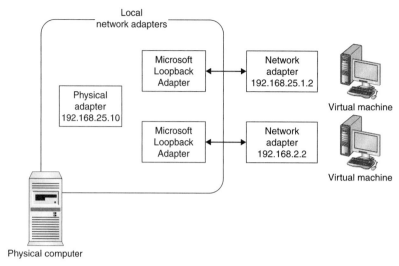

Figure 6-14 Microsoft Loopback Adapters

Internet Connection Sharing

You will likely want your virtual machines to have access to the Internet for operating system updates. With Internet Connection Sharing (ICS), which is included in Microsoft Server 2008 and which you installed in Activity 6-2, you can connect one or more virtual machines to the Internet using the Internet connection provided by the host computer. See Figure 6-15.

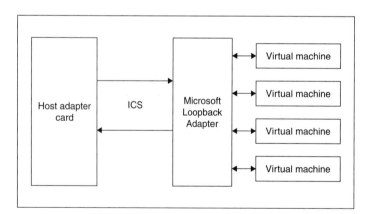

Figure 6-15 Internet Connection Sharing

The host computer needs two network connections:

- The local area network connection, automatically created by installing a network adapter in the host computer, connects to the computers on the main network.
- The other network adapter is provided by the Microsoft Loopback Adapter.

ICS provides the services required by your virtual machines to access both the main network and virtual network shared by the virtual machines. These services are as follows:

- Network Address Translation (NAT)—Translates an IP address used within one network (in this case, the virtual network) to an IP address known within another network (in this case, the main network)
- IP addressing—Provides the IP address, subnet mask, and gateway address for each VM
- Name resolution services—Enables host names to be resolved to IP addresses

Virtual Machine Network Services Driver

Virtual Server loads the Virtual Machine Network Services Driver on your host operating system and binds it to each adapter in use. The purpose of the Virtual Machine Network Services Driver is to route Ethernet panes between virtual machines and (optionally) the network to which the host computer is connected. All Ethernet panes are intercepted by the Virtual Machine Network Services Driver. Based on the network configuration, the Ethernet panes are routed between the virtual machines or to the host's physical adapter.

DHCP Server

Most likely, the physical network to which your host computer is connected receives its IP configuration from a DHCP server. Administrators use DHCP servers because a DHCP server simplifies IP address management.

By default, Virtual Server enables a DHCP server on each virtual network. This DHCP server provides IP configurations to virtual machines only.

Creating a Virtual Network

To create a virtual network using Virtual Server, click the Create link under Virtual Networks in the navigation pane. The link brings up the Network Properties page, as shown in Figure 6-16.

You must name the virtual network that you are creating by typing over the New Virtual Network text in the Virtual network name text box.

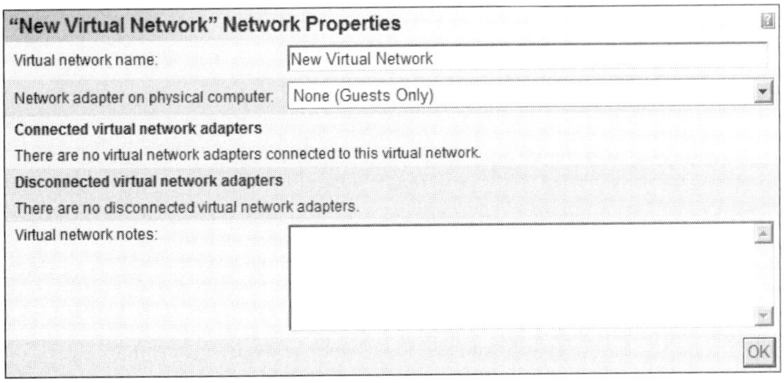

Figure 6-16 Network properties

By clicking on the Network adapter on physical computer drop-down list arrow, you select the adapter to use for the virtual network. The choices for the physical adapter in the list are as follows:

- *None (Guests Only)*—Internal network for virtual network use
- *Physical adapter in the host computer*—Name of external network adapter on the physical computer
- *Microsoft Loopback Adapter*—External network installed in the host computer to support a virtual network

To see the notes for the available network adapters, point to Configure under Virtual Networks in the navigation pane and click View All. Figure 6-17 shows notes relevant to the virtual network connections. You should refer to these notes when deciding which adapter to select for a particular network.

Virtual Networks	
Name ▲	Notes
External Network (Intel(R) PRO_1000 MT Network Connection) ▶	This virtual network is connected to the "Intel(R) PRO/1000 MT Network Connection" physical network adapter. Virtual machines attached to this virtual network can access the physical computer, the external network and other virtual machines also attached to this virtual network.
External Network (Microsoft Loopback Adapter) ▶	This virtual network is connected to the "Microsoft Loopback Adapter" physical network adapter. Virtual machines attached to this virtual network can access the physical computer, the external network and other virtual machines also attached to this virtual network.
Internal Network ▶	This is the internal virtual network. Virtual machines connected to this virtual network can only see other virtual machines.

Figure 6-17 Virtual networks details

To view the properties of an existing virtual network, point to Configure under Virtual Networks in the navigation pane and click the desired virtual network. The "Internal Network" properties are shown in Figure 6-18.

"Internal Network" Virtual Network Properties	
Physical network adapter	None (Guests Only)
Notes	This is the internal virtual network. Virtual machines connected to this virtual network can only see other virtual machines.
.vnc file	C:\Users\Public\Documents\Shared Virtual Networks\Internal Network.vnc
"Internal Network" Virtual Network Properties	
ⓘ Network Settings	"Internal Network"
DHCP server	The virtual DHCP server is enabled.

Figure 6-18 "Internal Network" virtual network properties

To view the network settings, click the Network Settings link. Figure 6-19 shows the network properties for the internal network. When virtual machines are created and virtual networks are connected, entries will appear in the Connected and Disconnected virtual network adapters lists. These two lists are handy when you need to know which virtual machines are (or are not) connected to a virtual network.

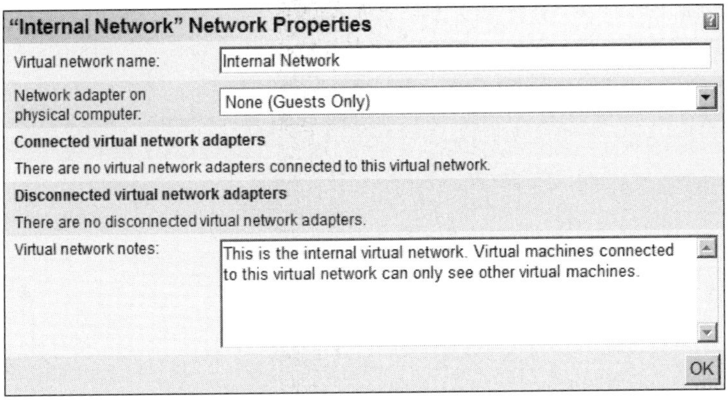

Figure 6-19 "Internal Network" network properties

To view the DHCP server properties, click the network's DHCP server link (refer to Figure 6-18). Figure 6-20 shows the DHCP server properties for the internal network. By default, networks for the DHCP server start at 10.237.0.0. The next network would be 10.238.0.0, and so on. The network mask of 255.255.0.0 provides 65,000 hosts per network. The virtual DHCP server reserves the first 16 IP addresses from the start of the specified IP address range. These 16 IP addresses are never assigned.

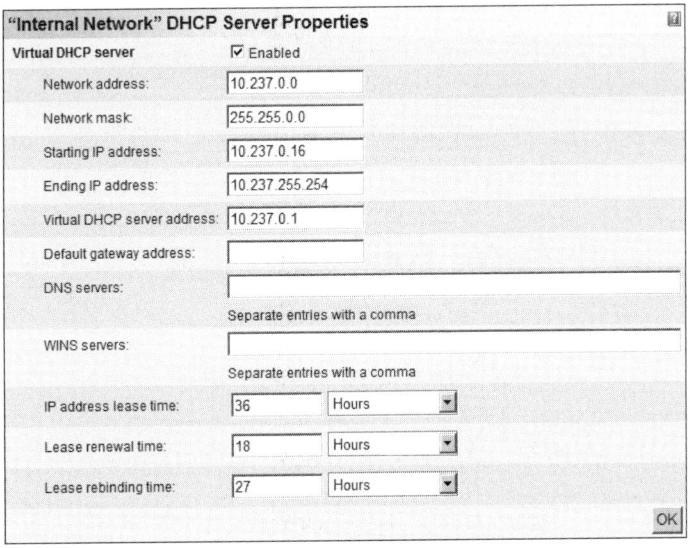

Figure 6-20 "Internal Network" DHCP server properties

When the DHCP server is enabled, you can configure the options described in Table 6-6.

Table 6-6 DHCP server options

DHCP option	Description
Network address	IP address of this virtual network.
Network mask	Subnet mask for this virtual network.
Starting IP address	First IP address in the range maintained for assignment to clients.
Ending IP address	Last IP address in the range maintained for assignment to clients.
Virtual DHCP server address	IP address of this virtual DHCP server.
Default gateway address	IP address of a local IP router (gateway) that forwards traffic beyond this virtual network.
DNS servers	IP addresses for DNS servers that DHCP clients can contact and use to resolve a domain host name query.
WINS servers	IP addresses of primary and secondary WINS servers for the DHCP client to use for NetBIOS name queries.
IP address lease time	Duration of the IP address lease offered by the server. This option defines the length of time during which the client can use the assigned IP address. The minimum value allowed is 60 seconds.
Lease renewal time	Time interval from IP address assignment until the client starts IP address renewal. The minimum value allowed is 30 seconds.
Lease rebinding time	Time interval from IP address assignment until the client starts IP address rebinding. The minimum value allowed is 45 seconds.

Activity 6-6: Creating a Virtual Network

Time Required: 5 minutes

Objective: Create a virtual network for Internet access.

Requirements: Completion of Activity 6-3.

Description: In this activity, you will create a virtual network to access the Microsoft Loopback Adapter installed in the host computer. This activity is useful to access the Internet.

1. If necessary, log on to your Host PC with a username of **Administrator** and a password of **Secret1**.

2. If necessary, to access the Virtual Server Administration Web site, click the **Virtual Server Administration Website** shortcut on the desktop.

3. To open the Create Virtual Networks page, click the **Create** link under Virtual Networks.

4. To name the Virtual Network, type **Internet** over New Virtual Network in the Virtual network name text box.

5. To specify the Microsoft Loopback Adapter on the host computer, click the **Network adapter on physical computer** drop-down list arrow, click **Microsoft Loopback Adapter**, and then click **OK**.

6. Leave the computer logged on for the next activity.

Virtual Disks in Virtual Server

Each virtual machine in Virtual Server is provided with up to three virtual hard disks on a single IDE controller. In addition, up to four SCSI adapters can each support seven hard drives per adapter.

Recall that virtual hard disks are files stored on the hard disk of the physical computer. To the virtual machine, the virtual hard disk looks and acts like an entire hard disk separate from that of the host. Any operation that the guest operating system performs is mapped back to the data stored within the .vhd file extension (recall that the .vhd extension stands for virtual hard disk).

When accessing a .vhd file, a guest operating system running within a virtual machine cannot access any area of the host's physical disk outside of the .vhd file. This is true even for low-level operations, including partitioning and formatting of the virtual hard drive.

Virtual Server includes five options for the creation and use of virtual hard disks: dynamically expanding, fixed size, linked to a hard disk, differencing, and undo disk.

Dynamically Expanding

You learned about dynamically expanding virtual hard disks in previous chapters. See Figure 6-21 on the next page. The size of the virtual hard disk expands as data is written to the .vhd file. The .vhd file starts at about 135 KB in size and grows from there until it reaches the limit that you specified. The dynamically expanding option is the recommended (and default) option that is suitable for most operating system installations. When you use this option, the space required for the .vhd file will be only as large as required by the guest operating system. This results in more effective hard disk utilization for the host operating system.

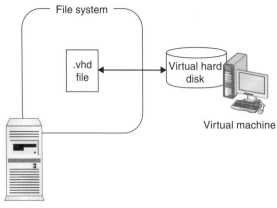

Figure 6-21 Dynamically expanding hard disk

Fixed Size

The fixed size option limits the .vhd file to the size that you specify. Fixed size virtual hard disks work the same in Virtual Server as in Virtual PC. When the .vhd file is created, the file is allocated to the specified limit. For example, if you create a 50-GB, fixed-size .vhd, the space allocated for the .vhd file will be 50 GB. This option might yield higher performance than the others, but it uses more hard disk space on your host computer.

If the space needed is known, then the fixed size option will work because the space is allocated when the disk is defined. However, if there is any chance there will be more space required at a later time, the dynamically expanding Virtual Hard Disk option is the better choice because it will allocate more space as needed.

Linked to a Hard Disk

Use the linked to a hard disk option if you want your virtual machine to use an existing physical hard disk. Virtual Server uses linked disks the same way as Virtual PC does. You configure the virtual machine to point to the existing physical hard disk. You must use the entire hard disk. You cannot link to a volume on the disk. When using this option, the virtual machine operates at the physical hard disk level—not at the logical volume level.

Differencing

The use of differencing disks in Virtual Server is the same as in Virtual PC. When you create a differencing virtual hard disk, you are asked to specify an existing virtual hard disk, called the parent virtual hard disk, to which the differencing virtual hard disk points. When the virtual machine uses this differencing (or child) virtual hard disk, the changes are stored in the differencing hard disk. See Figure 6-22. The virtual machine will boot from the parent hard disk and store the changes in the child hard disk.

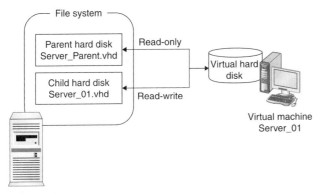

Figure 6-22 Differencing disks

The main benefit of differencing disks is speed. Differencing disks can speed up the creation of multiple virtual machines. In Chapter 8, you will use these techniques to create three virtual machines from one parent. You will install Windows Server 2008 on the parent virtual machine and use differencing disks for the three servers. Recall that operating system installation is time consuming. You will need to install the Windows Server 2008 only once for the parent, cutting the time to install the servers to one-third.

Enable Undo Disks

Like Virtual PC, Virtual Server has an Enable undo disks option that saves changes to an undo disk (temporary file with a .vud extension). See Figure 6-23. When the virtual machine is shut down, you will have the option to delete the changes, commit the changes to the .vhd file, or save the changes for another time. Deleting the changes removes the .vud file. The Enable undo disks option can only be selected when the virtual machine is not running. The Enable undo disks option pertains to all of the virtual hard disks used by the virtual machine—you cannot enable only one when the virtual machine is using multiple virtual hard disks.

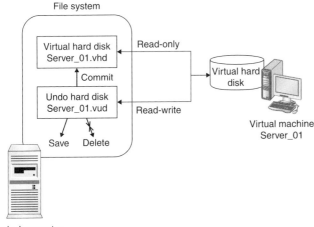

Figure 6-23 Undo disks

This option is useful in situations where you want to start with a pristine operating system configuration. After changes are made to the configuration, the changes are deleted; this approach is especially useful in program testing. Likewise, this option can be used in training classes where multiple students complete the same training activity.

Virtual Floppy Disk

Virtual floppy disks have the full functionality of a real floppy disk. For example, you can transfer files and read data from the virtual floppy disk by using the standard operating system interface of the virtual machine. Virtual floppy drives are initially empty after you create them.

Virtual floppy disks are saved as .vfd files. One use of .vfd files is to provide boot images to start DOS-based operating systems.

Creating a Virtual Disk

You create a virtual disk by pointing to the Create link under Virtual Disks and selecting from these options:

- Dynamically Expanding Virtual Hard Disk—Disk space allocated as needed
- Fixed Size Virtual Hard Disk—Space allocated at definition
- Differencing Virtual Hard Disk—Child disk that stores changes from parent disk
- Linked Virtual Hard Disk—Pointer to actual physical hard disk on host computer
- Virtual Floppy Disk—File-based version of a physical floppy disk

To create any of these disk types, you select the desired type from the Administration Web site by clicking Create under Virtual Disks in the navigation pane and selecting the desired disk type. For example, to create a dynamically expanding virtual hard disk, select Dynamically Expanding Virtual Hard Disk. Figure 6-24 shows the pane for this task. The Location drop-down list arrow lists the known locations. Select a known location from the list and type the virtual hard disk file name. If you select None, you will need to type the fully qualified path, for example, C:\My Virtual Machines\Server01.vhd. The maximum size can be specified in megabytes or gigabytes. Type the maximum size in the Size text box and then select the units. When you have completed the entries, click the Create button.

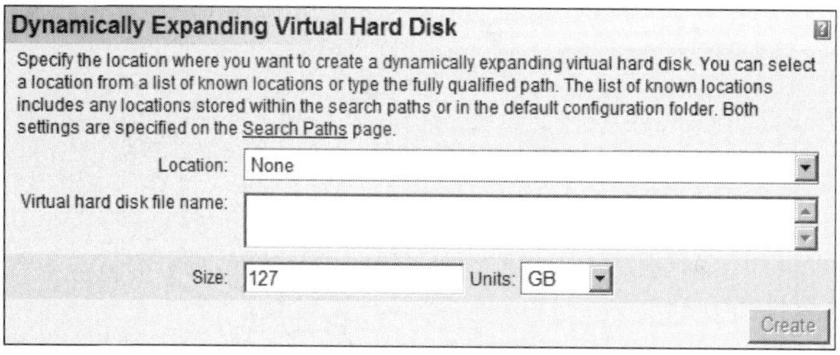

Figure 6-24 Dynamically expanding virtual hard disk

TIP Press the F5 key to refresh the Web page.

The text boxes and steps for fixed size virtual hard disk are essentially the same as for the dynamically expanding virtual hard disk.

The pane to select a differencing virtual hard disk is shown in Figure 6-25. There are two sets of Location and Virtual hard disk file name text boxes. The top set is for the specification for the child virtual hard disk. The bottom set is for the parent virtual hard disk. Normally, the parent virtual hard disk contains the virtual machine selected from known .vhd files.

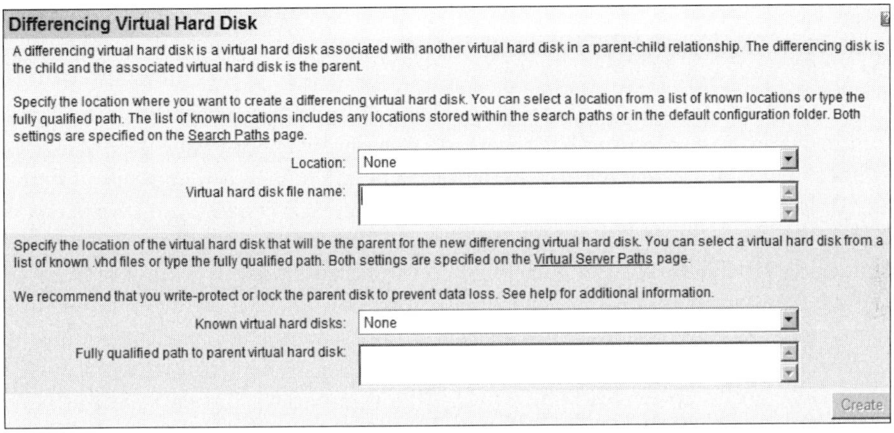

Figure 6-25 Differencing virtual hard disk

Figure 6-26 shows the Web page for creating a linked virtual hard disk. After specifying a virtual hard disk to mount the physical hard disk, you select the Physical computer drive.

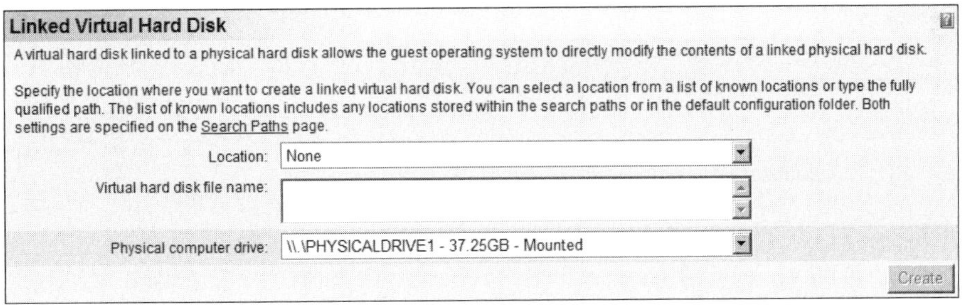

Figure 6-26 Linked virtual hard disk

The pane for creating a virtual floppy disk is shown in Figure 6-27. You specify the location of the .vfd file as shown in the figure.

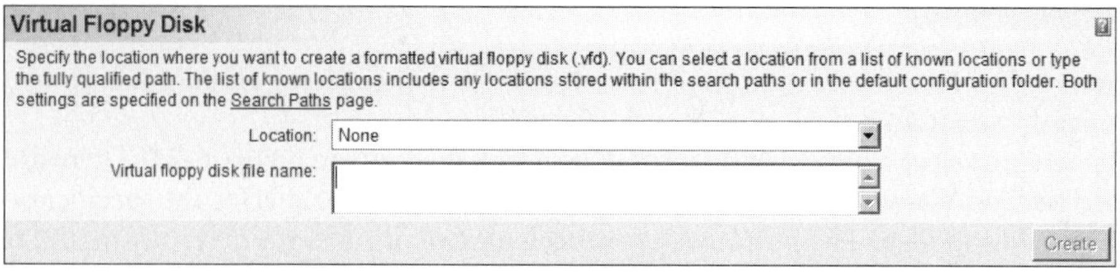

Figure 6-27 Virtual floppy disk

Virtual Hard Disks on SCSI Adapters

Virtual Server provides four SCSI adapters and each SCSI adapter can have up to seven virtual hard disks. This is an impressive amount of storage. The virtual machines can access any or all hard drives available to the host computer. For example, if the host computer has access to a storage area network, these drives are available to the virtual machines. A **storage area network (SAN)** is a high-speed network of shared storage devices. In large enterprises, a SAN connects multiple servers to a centralized pool of disk storage.

When using virtual hard disks with SCSI adapters, you must first add the SCSI adapter by clicking the Configuration link under Virtual Machines in the navigation pane, selecting the virtual machine to configure, and clicking the SCSI Adapters link from the configuration pane for the virtual machine. Next, click the Add SCSI Adapter button to work with the SCSI adapter properties, as shown in Figure 6-28. If you intend to share a SCSI bus between two virtual machines, click the Share SCSI bus for clustering check box. Click OK to add the adapter.

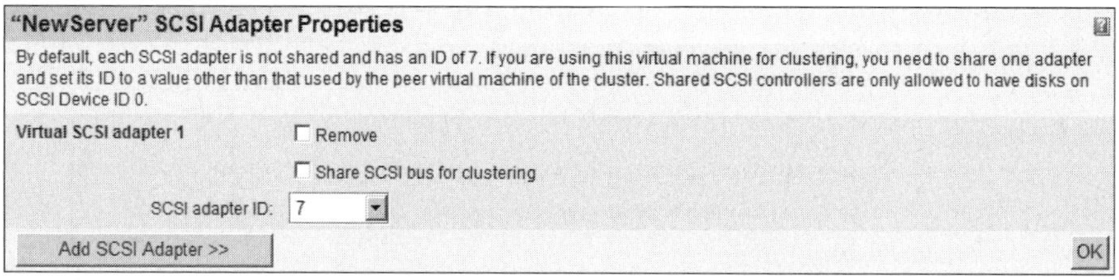

Figure 6-28 SCSI adapter properties

You learned about RAID-5 storage in Chapter 5. With the potential for attaching up to seven virtual hard disks to a SCSI adapter, Virtual Server supports the creation of larger RAID-5 storage arrays. These virtual hard disks are created as in Virtual PC, but they are attached to the SCSI adapter, as shown in Figure 6-29. The SCSI 0 ID 0 is the first emulated hard drive on the first SCSI adapter previously created.

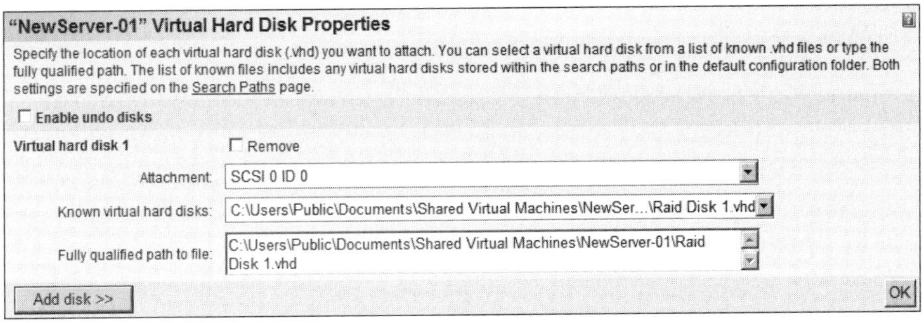

Virtual Disks in Virtual Server   **233**

Figure 6-29 Emulated SCSI hard disk

To create additional virtual hard drives, create virtual hard disks and attach to the next SCSI drive, SCSI 0 ID 1, SCSI 0 ID 2, and so on through SCSI 0 ID 6. ID 7 is used by the SCSI adapter.

When the virtual hard disks are available, you create the RAID-5 array within the virtual machine. To do this, click Start, point to Administrative Tools, click Computer Management, and then click Disk Management. Convert the Basic Disk to a dynamic disk by right-clicking the disk icon and clicking Convert to Dynamic Disk. Select the remaining hard disks for the RAID-5 array and then click OK. As you did in Chapter 5, point to the unallocated area in the first disk for the RAID array, right-click and select New RAID-5 Volume. Add the remaining hard disks for the RAID array, and then accept the default selections in the remaining dialog boxes.

Activity 6-7: Creating a Virtual Hard Disk

Time Required: 5 minutes

Objective: Create a virtual hard disk.

Requirements: Completion of Activity 6-3.

Description: In this activity, you will create a dynamically expanding virtual hard disk.

1. If necessary, log on to your Host PC with a username of **Administrator** and a password of **Secret1**.
2. If necessary, to access the Virtual Server Administration Web site, click the **Virtual Server Administration Website** shortcut on the desktop.
3. To open the Create Virtual disks page, point to the **Create** link under Virtual Disks.
4. To create a dynamically expanding virtual hard disk, click **Dynamically Expanding Virtual Hard Disk**, click the **Location** drop-down list arrow, click C:\Users\Public\Documents\Shared Virtual Machines\, type **Server01** at the end of C:\Users\Public\Document\Shared Virtual Machines\ in the Virtual hard disk file name text box, type **32** in the Size text box, and then click **Create**.
5. Leave the computer logged on for the next activity.

Implementing Virtual Machines

Unlike Virtual PC, Virtual Server does not have a New Virtual Machine Wizard. You will need to enter the configuration for each virtual machine. As shown in Figure 6-30, you need to create these three objects:

- Virtual machine configuration file (.vmc)—Specifies disk, memory, and other settings for the virtual machine. This file is XML-based.
- Virtualized network adapter file (.vnc)—Stores details related to the configuration of a virtual network, including if it is connected to a physical adapter or a Microsoft Loopback Adapter. This file was created when you created each virtual network.
- Virtual hard disk file (.vhd)—Includes dynamically expanding hard disks, fixed-size hard disks, and differencing disks. You created these when you created each virtual hard disk.

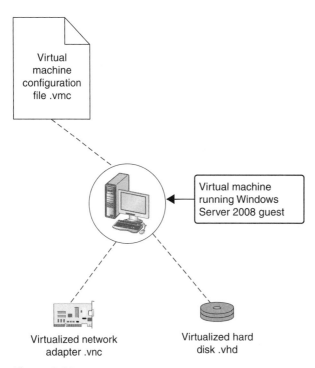

Figure 6-30 Virtual Server objects

Creating a Virtual Machine

When you define a virtual machine in Virtual Server, you combine the virtual network and virtual hard disk objects. Figure 6-31 shows the pane to create a virtual machine.

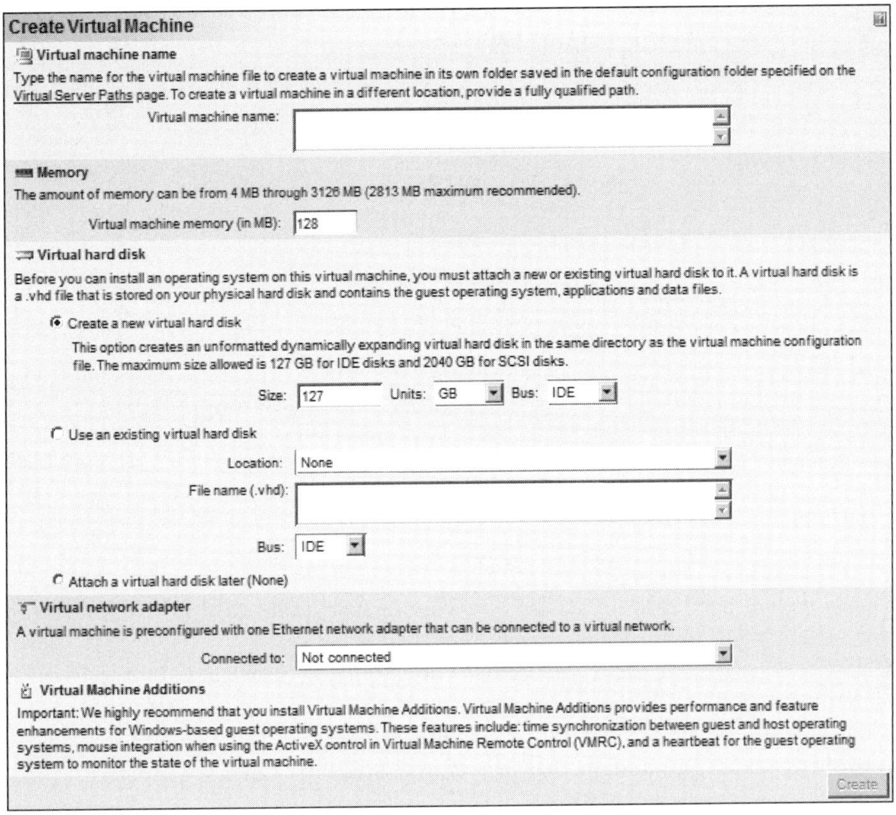

Figure 6-31 Create a virtual machine

You start with the name of the virtual machine, which is typed in the Virtual machine name text box. This becomes the name for the .vmc file. By default, this entry creates a folder subordinate to a default configuration folder. For example, a name of Server01 creates a folder with this path: C:\Users\Public\Public Documents\Shared Virtual Machines\Server01. Within this folder, the Server01.vmc is created. Next, you specify the memory to be allocated to the virtual machine. Be sure to allocate enough memory for the operating system and applications. Use Table 6-7, found on the next page, as a guide.

When associating a virtual hard disk with the new virtual machine, you have three choices for the virtual hard disk:

- Create a new dynamically expanding virtual hard disk, specifying the size and type of bus (IDE or SCSI). If the IDE bus is selected, the filename will be Server01.vhd because this was the name previously specified. The file will be placed in the same folder as the Serv01.vmc file.

- Use an existing virtual hard disk, which allows you to provide the location and name for an existing virtual hard disk. You would use this option for a differencing or fixed virtual hard disk.

- Attach a virtual hard disk later (None), which allows you to make the decision at a later date and time.

Table 6-7 Required memory and virtual disk space

Operating system	Memory required	Virtual disk space required
Windows 98	64 MB	16,384 MB
Windows NT Workstation, Windows NT Server	64 MB	8,192 MB
Window 2000, Windows XP	128 MB	16,384 MB
IBM OS/2	64 MB	2,048 MB
Windows Vista	512 MB	65,536 MB
Windows 2000 Server	256 MB	16,384 MB
Windows Server 2003	256 MB	65,536 MB
Windows Server 2008	512 MB	65,536 MB
Other	128 MB	16,384 MB

To use a virtual hard disk on a SCSI bus, you must first add the SCSI adapter to the virtual machine. Then, you can specify a virtual hard disk.

The last task is to provide a virtual network adapter. Select a virtual network from the Connected to drop-down list.

Virtual Machine Additions can only be added after the operating system is installed. Be sure to return to this page and to add Virtual Machine Additions.

Running a Virtual Machine in Virtual Server

Whereas Virtual PC displays virtual machines in windows, Virtual Server requires one of the following three client programs to access the running virtual machine:

- Virtual Machine Remote Control (VMRC) client—The VMRC client is a client application for remote control of a virtual machine. This program is installed with Virtual Server.
- VMRCplus—**VMRCplus** is a tool for creation and configuration of Virtual Server and remote control of virtual machines. You will learn about this client program in Chapter 7.
- Remote Desktop—**Remote Desktop** is a client application for access to a virtual machine session that is running on your computer. The client is provided by various Windows operating systems starting with Windows XP and Server 2003.

Master Status Pane The Master Status pane is the Virtual Machine Remote Control client starting point. The Master Status pane, shown in Figure 6-32, displays the list of virtual machines currently configured on Virtual Server along with the status of each one.

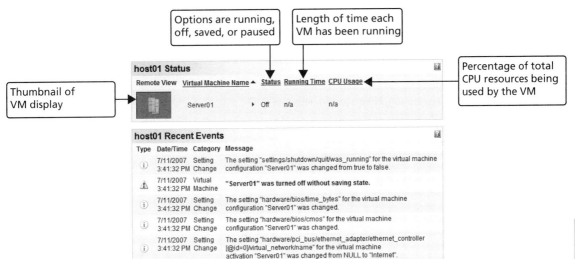

Figure 6-32 Master Status pane

You can sort the status list by clicking the column headings. For example, to sort by running time, click the Running Time label. By right-clicking the virtual machine name, you can edit the virtual machine configuration, change the status, or remove a virtual machine.

You can perform the following tasks from the Master Status pane:

- Reorder the list of virtual machines by name, status, running time, or CPU usage, by clicking the appropriate heading.
- Quickly turn on a virtual machine or go to Remote Control view for a virtual machine that is running by clicking its Remote View image.
- Gain access to VM configuration and control features by pointing to the virtual machine name and clicking the appropriate option.
- Quickly change CPU resource allocation settings for a running virtual machine by clicking its CPU Usage image.

Virtual Machine Remote Control Client To use the Virtual Machine Remote Control (VMRC) client, click the Remote View icon for the desired virtual machine on the Master Status pane. The first time you run VMRC, Virtual Server attempts to download the ActiveX control for the VMRC client to your computer.

You can access a single virtual machine from a single VMRC session. You will need to start a VMRC session for each virtual machine that you want to access. Figure 6-33 on the next page shows the VMRC interface.

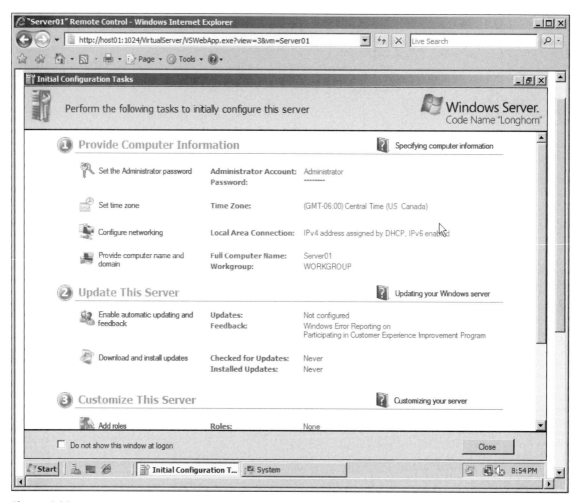

Figure 6-33 VMRC session

 For training and lab scenarios, multiple users can access the guest operating system without the knowledge of the other users. This is handy when one user wants to demonstrate a task to other users who are connected to the same remote session.

Remote Desktop Remote Desktop, which is included in Microsoft Windows Server 2008 and other operating systems, provides the Windows graphical user interface to remote devices over local area network (LAN), wide area network (WAN), or Internet connections. The Remote Desktop exchanges only keystrokes and screen changes. You can use any Windows laptop or desktop machine from a remote location to run your Windows Server 2008 machine as if you were sitting in front of it. Remote Desktop provides an alternative method to gain access to a running virtual machine. Figure 6-34 shows the Remote Desktop Connection dialog box.

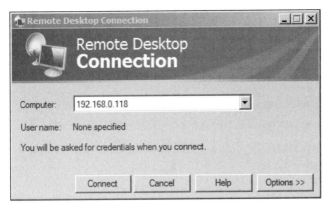

Figure 6-34 Remote Desktop Connection

You will learn to use the Remote Desktop in Activity 6-11.

Activity 6-8: Creating a Virtual Machine

Time Required: 5 minutes

Objective: Create a virtual machine.

Requirements: Completion of Activities 6-6 and 6-7.

Description: In this activity, you will create the Server01 virtual machine.

1. If necessary, log on to your Host PC with a username of **Administrator** and a password of **Secret1**.
2. If necessary, to access the Virtual Server Administration Web site, click the **Virtual Server Administration Website** shortcut on the desktop.
3. To open the Create Machines disks page, click the **Create** link under Virtual Machines.
4. To name the virtual machine, type **Server01** in the Virtual machine name text box.
5. To specify the amount of memory, type **640** in the Virtual machine memory (in MB) text box.
6. To specify the virtual hard disk, scroll and click the **Use an existing virtual hard disk** option button, click the **Location** drop-down list arrow, and then click **C:\Users\Public\Documents\Shared Virtual Machines\Server01.vhd**.
7. To specify the virtual network adapter, scroll and click the **Connected to** drop-down list arrow, and then click **Internet**.
8. Review the configuration and then click **Create**.
9. Close the Virtual Server Administration Web site.

Activity 6-9: Installing an Operating System

Time Required: 90 minutes

Objective: Install Microsoft Server 2008.

Requirements: Completion of Activities 6-6 through 6-8 and the Microsoft Server 2008 DVD.

Description: In this activity, you will install Microsoft Server 2008 on the Server01 virtual machine.

1. If necessary, log on to your Host PC with a username of **Administrator** and a password of **Secret1**.
2. To start Internet Explorer, click **Start**, and then click **Internet Explorer**.
3. To remove the status bar, click the **Tools** menu, point to **Toolbars**, and then click **Status Bar**.
4. To remove the Tab bar, click the **Tools** menu, click **Internet Options**, click the **Settings** button in the Tabs section, clear the **Enable Tabbed Browsing (requires restarting Internet Explorer)** check box, click **OK** twice, and then close Internet Explorer.
5. To access the Virtual Server Administration Web site, double-click the **Virtual Server Administration Website** shortcut on the desktop.
6. If necessary, click the **Master Status** link.
7. Insert the Microsoft Windows Server 2008 DVD into the CD/DVD drive.
8. To start the Server01 virtual machine, click the **Server01** Remote View. When the AutoPlay window for Host01 appears, close the window.
9. To start VMRC, click the **Server01** Remote View.
10. If the Internet Explorer - Security Warning dialog box appears, click the **Install** button.
11. If the Unencrypted Connection dialog box appears, click the **Don't ask me again** check box, and then click **Yes**.
12. If the NTLM Authentication dialog box opens, click the **Don't ask me again** check box, and then click **Yes**.
13. Wait for Windows to load files.

To improve accessibility to the virtual machine, resize the Remote Control window and scroll the remote window until the virtual machine display is fully visible.

14. To activate the virtual machine window, click in the Server01 virtual machine window.
15. When the regional settings dialog box opens, verify the language, time and currency, and keyboard. Make corrections as needed, and then click **Next**.
16. Click the **Install now** link.
17. To indicate that this virtual machine is using an evaluation copy, wait for the Type your product key for activation dialog box to open, clear the **Automatically activate Windows when I'm online** check box, click **Next**, and then click **No**.

18. To indicate which version to install, click **Windows Server 2008 Standard (Full Installation)**, check the **I have selected the edition of Windows that I purchased** check box, and then click **Next**.

19. When the Please read the license terms dialog box opens, check the **I accept the license terms** check box, and then click **Next**.

20. Click the **Custom (advanced)** icon.

21. Review the disk space allocation, and then click **Next**.

22. Wait for Windows to copy and expand files, install features and updates, and restart to complete the installation.

23. Ignore the Press any key to boot from CD or DVD message.

24. Wait while Windows prepares to start for the first time and to complete the installation.

25. When the user's password must be changed before logging on the first time message appears, click **OK**. Type **Secret1** in the New password text box, press **Tab**, type **Secret1** in the Confirm password text box, press **Enter**, and then click **OK**.

26. To set the time zone, click the **Set time zone** link, review the date and time and change if needed, click the **Change time zone** button, click the appropriate time zone, and then click **OK** twice.

27. To provide a computer name, click the **Provide computer name and domain** link, click the **Change** button, type **Server01** in the Computer name text box, click **OK** twice, click **Close**, and then click the **Restart Now** button.

28. Wait for the virtual machine to restart.

29. Ignore the Press any key to boot from CD or DVD message.

30. Press right **Alt+Delete** and log on to your Server01 virtual machine with a username of **Administrator** and a password of **Secret1**.

31. To enable network discovery and file sharing, click **Start**, right-click **Network**, click **Properties**, click the **Network discovery** drop-down list arrow, click the **Turn on network discovery** option button, click the **Apply** button, click the **No, make the network that I am connected to a private network** link, click the **File sharing** drop-down list arrow, click the **Turn on file sharing** option button, click the **Apply** button, and then close the Network and Sharing Center window.

32. Remove the Windows Server 2008 DVD from the drive.

33. Leave the computer logged on for the next activity.

Activity 6-10: Installing Virtual Machine Additions

Time Required: 10 minutes

Objective: Install Virtual Machine Additions into the Server01 virtual machine.

Requirements: Completion of Activities 6-6 through 6-9.

Description: In this activity, you will install Virtual Machine Additions into the guest virtual machine.

1. If necessary, log on to your Host PC with a username of **Administrator** and a password of **Secret1**.
2. If necessary, to access the Virtual Server Administration Web site, double-click the **Virtual Server Administration Website** shortcut on the desktop.
3. If necessary, to start the Server01 virtual machine, click the **Server01** Remote View.
4. If necessary, to start VMRC, click the **Server01** Remote View.
5. If necessary, log on with a username of **Administrator** and a password of **Secret1**.
6. To install Virtual Machines Additions in a guest operating system, press the right **Alt** key, switch to the Virtual Server Administration Website, click **Configure** under Virtual Machines, click **Server01**, click the **Install Virtual Machine Additions** link, click the **Install Virtual Machine Additions** check box, and then click **OK**.
7. Click in the Server01 virtual machine window.
8. Click **Run setup.exe**.
9. Click **Next**, wait for the installation to complete, and then click **Finish**.
10. When requested to restart your system, click **Yes**.
11. Wait for Server01 to restart.
12. Log on to your virtual machine with a username of **Administrator** and a password of **Secret1**.
13. Leave the computer logged on for the next activity.

Activity 6-11: Using Remote Desktop

Time Required: 10 minutes

Objective: Configure Server01 for Remote Desktop program access.

Requirements: Completion of Activities 6-6 through 6-10.

Description: In this activity, you will configure the guest computer to use Remote Desktop. Next, you will use Remote Desktop to connect to a virtual machine.

1. If necessary, log on to your Host PC with a username of **Administrator** and a password of **Secret1**.
2. If necessary, to access the Virtual Server Administration Web site, double-click the **Virtual Server Administration Website** shortcut on the desktop.
3. If necessary, to start the Server01 virtual machine, click the **Server01** Remote View.
4. If necessary, to start VMRC, click the click the **Server01** Remote View.
5. If necessary, log on to Server01 with a username of **Administrator** and a password of **Secret1**.
6. To set Remote Desktop security on Server01, click **Start**, right-click **Computer**, click **Properties**, click the **Remote settings** link, click the **Allow connections from computers running any version of Remote Desktop (less secure)** option button, and then click **OK** twice.

7. To determine the IP address for Server01, click **Start**, click **Run**, type **cmd** in the Open text box, and then click **OK**.
8. To see the IP address, type **ipconfig**, press **Enter**, record the IP address, and then close the command prompt window.
9. Close the VMRC window.
10. To launch Remote Desktop on the host computer, click **Start**, click **All Programs**, click the **Accessories** folder, and then click **Remote Desktop Connection**.
11. Type the IP address recorded in Step 8 in the Computer text box, and then click the **Connect** button.
12. When the Windows Security dialog box opens, log on to Server01 with a username of **Administrator** and a password of **Secret1**.
13. Wait for the Remote Desktop to appear.
14. To gain access to the host computer, minimize the yellow taskbar.
15. To return to Server01, restore the remote desktop from the status bar.
16. To shut down Server01, click in the virtual machine window, click **Start**, click the arrow next to the Lock button, click **Shut Down**, click the **Option** drop-down list arrow, click **Operating System: Reconfiguration (Planned)**, click **OK**, and then click **Yes**.
17. To shut down Host01, click **Start**, click the arrow next to the Lock button, click **Shut Down**, click the **Option** drop-down list arrow, click **Operating System: Reconfiguration (Planned)**, and then click **OK**.

Chapter Summary

- Virtual Server is a service that ties into the operating system's kernel for increased flexibility and performance for virtual machines. The configuration and management options it provides are required for server management. The features of Virtual Server differ from those of Virtual PC and include but are not limited to remote management, large RAM support, virtual networking, system event logging and delegated administration.

- Installation of Virtual Server is not as user-friendly as Virtual PC because it does not support desktop applications. Before Virtual Server is installed, you should search the Microsoft Virtual Server Web Page for up-to-the-minute information related to Virtual Server's installation and features. Your host PC must already have an Internet-ready networking environment created with Internet Connection Sharing enabled.

- Virtual Server needs to have the options configured correctly. You must enable features such as Virtual Machine Remote Control. You also must enable scripting to use scripts.

- Implementations of virtual networks connect one virtual machine to another virtual machine. The Virtual Server navigation pane has a link under Virtual Networks that opens a Network Properties page. Review the DHCP server options to verify your network is set up correctly for your virtual machines.

- You have five options from which to choose when implementing a virtual hard disk: dynamically expanding, fixed, differencing, linked, and floppy.
- The implementation of virtual machines does not use a wizard. You must configure each virtual machine separately. To create a virtual machine in Virtual Server, you need the virtual machine configuration file (.vmc), a virtual network (.vnc), and a virtual hard disk (.vhd). You must name the virtual machine, create sufficient memory for the operating system, choose the desired virtual hard disk choice, and select a virtual network adapter. Virtual Machine Additions can be added only after the operating system is installed.

Key Terms

clustering—Linking two or more computer systems (generally, servers) that work together to handle variable workloads or to provide continued operation in case one fails.

heartbeat—A regular signal sent to Virtual Server that allows the virtual machine to report that it is still functioning.

Kerberos authentication protocol—A computer network identity authentication protocol; the default protocol for computers in Active Directory domains.

Remote Desktop—A Windows feature that allows a machine to be run remotely from another Windows machine.

storage area network (SAN)—A high-speed subnetwork of shared storage devices.

Virtual Machine Remote Control (VMRC) client—A Virtual Server client application that allows a running virtual machine to be managed remotely.

Virtual Machine Remote Control (VMRC) server—A Virtual Server server application that manages virtual machines by using a Virtual Machine Remote Control protocol to interact with the machines using the keyboard and mouse.

Virtual Server Administration Web site—A Web site created with the installation of Virtual Server that administrators use to run virtual machines, virtual networks, and virtual hard disks.

Virtual Server service—A service that creates the virtual machines and provides all virtual machine functionality.

VMRC ActiveX plug-in—A plug-in that supports the use of the VMRC client from within Internet Explorer.

VMRC protocol—A remote presentation and control protocol that administrators use to view and control virtual machines across networked environments.

VMRCplus—A client application for creation and configuration management of Virtual Server and remote control of virtual machines.

Windows NT LAN Manager (NTLM) protocol—A protocol used to authenticate logons to stand-alone computers. The default for network authentication in the Windows NT 4.0 operating system, it is retained for compatibility with down-level clients and servers.

Windows service—A program that starts when the Microsoft Windows operating system is booted and runs in the background as long as Windows is running.

Review Questions

1. The software component Virtual Server uses to provide a virtual environment is _____. (Choose all that apply.)
   a. Virtual Server service
   b. Virtual Machine Remote Control server
   c. Virtual Machine Remote Control client
   d. Virtual PC

2. Virtual Server service _____. (Choose all that apply.)
   a. Creates virtual machines
   b. Provides each virtual machine with individual 32-bit address space
   c. Uses the Virtual Machine Remote Control protocol
   d. Manages the CPU and hardware during virtual machine operations

3. Virtual Machine Remote Control server _____.
   a. Creates virtual machines
   b. Provides each virtual machine with individual 32-bit address space
   c. Uses the Virtual Machine Remote Control protocol
   d. Manages the CPU and hardware during virtual machine operations

4. VMRCplus _____.
   a. Creates virtual machines
   b. Configures virtual machines
   c. Requires Internet Information Services (IIS)
   d. Manages user authentication during virtual machine operations

5. In Virtual Server, each virtual machine is provided with up to _____ virtual hard disks on an IDE controller.
   a. Two
   b. Three
   c. Five
   d. Seven

6. The size of the virtual hard disk _____ as data is written to the .vhd file.
   a. Stays at 135 KB
   b. Stays at 256 KB
   c. Expands
   d. Shrinks

7. The benefit of a differencing disk is its _____.
    a. Volume
    b. Convenience for performing backups
    c. Speed
    d. Accuracy
8. Virtual floppy disks _____. (Choose all that apply.)
    a. Are saved as .vhd files
    b. Are saved as .vfd files
    c. Provide boot images to start DOS-based operating systems
    d. Are initially empty after you create them
9. The heartbeat is _____.
    a. A signal from the virtual machine indicating a system failure
    b. A signal from the host operating system indicating it is shutting down
    c. A signal from the virtual machine indicating to Virtual Server that it is alive
    d. A host operating system failure report
10. Virtual Server _____. (Choose all that apply.)
    a. Supports desktop applications
    b. Was designed for the typical desktop user
    c. Runs enterprise server operating systems and applications
    d. Has a more complex user interface than Virtual PC
11. Features common to both Virtual Server and Virtual PC include _____. (Choose all that apply.)
    a. An emulated sound card
    b. Integration with the computer's mouse and keyboard
    c. Simple and easy-to-use configuration options
    d. Support for Virtual Machine Additions installation
12. Features unique to Virtual Server include _____. (Choose all that apply.)
    a. WMI integration
    b. Large RAM support
    c. Virtual networking
    d. Sharing of folders between the host operating systems and virtual machines

13. Virtual Server _____. (Choose all that apply.)
    a. Is a multithreaded process that runs as a system service
    b. Has each virtual machine running its own thread of execution when multithreading
    c. Is a single-threaded application
    d. Has all simultaneously running virtual machines running on the same processor
14. By default, the local Administrator user account and the members of the Administrators Local Group have _____ access to the folders where Virtual Server stores the various configuration files.
    a. No
    b. Read-only
    c. Timed
    d. Full
15. Remote Desktop _____. (Choose all that apply.)
    a. Uses a graphical user interface to remote devices over LANs, WANs, or Internet connections
    b. Is a feature of Microsoft Windows Server 2008
    c. Is an alternative method to access a running virtual machine
    d. Only works with desktop clients that are off-site
16. By default, the VMRC client _____.
    a. Is enabled
    b. Is not installed
    c. Is disabled
    d. Is disabled after each use
17. Scripting is disabled by default because _____.
    a. Scripting has security implications
    b. Scripting must be written in VBScript
    c. Scripting slows down the host system
    d. Using scripting can often lead to unintended configuration errors
18. When problems occur with your virtual machines, you should first seek troubleshooting information _____.
    a. On the Internet
    b. In the Virtual Server event log
    c. In Virtual Server online help
    d. From your instructor

19. A hard disk that has all of the disk space allocated at creation is known as a _____.
    a. Virtual floppy disk
    b. Linked virtual hard disk
    c. Differencing virtual hard disk
    d. Fixed size virtual hard disk

20. To create a virtual machine with Virtual Server, the objects needed are _____. (Choose all that apply.)
    a. Virtual configuration file (.vmc)
    b. Virtual network file (.vnc)
    c. Virtual PC
    d. Virtual hard disk file (.vhd)

Case Projects

Case 6-1: Diagramming Virtual Server Architecture

Administrators at your school are considering using Virtual Server in the student lab. John, the lab supervisor, has asked you to provide diagrams that would illustrate possible architecture layouts for the proposal he is considering presenting to the department chair. The operating systems currently being used in the lab are Microsoft Windows 2000 Server, Microsoft Windows XP Professional Server Pack 2 (SP2), Red Hat Enterprise Linux 4.0, SUSE Linux 9.3, Microsoft Windows Server 2003, Enterprise Edition, and Microsoft Window Server 2003, Web Edition. The lab consists of 24 personal computers with 2 GB of memory and 250-GB hard drives.

Case 6-2: Specifying Virtual Server Settings

You work for a large energy corporation. Your supervisor is considering using Virtual Server for consolidation of servers at remote sites and needs more details on this possible implementation. Each remote site has from two to five servers running Windows operating systems—Windows 2000 Server and Windows Server 2003. The corporate specifications for the computers at a remote site are 2 GB of memory and 500-GB hard disks. Each remote site has a computer dedicated to running Active Directory and DNS. DHCP services are provided on the first file server. Additional file servers are installed as needed to store user files. Your job is to provide the details for the virtual machines, virtual hard disks, and virtual networks for a single computer to run the existing operating systems and applications.

Case 6-3: Using Virtual Machines

Remote Desktop allows you to access running virtual machines. Provide two or three examples of how this program can be put to practical use in real-life situations.

chapter 7

Using Microsoft VMRCplus

After reading this chapter and completing the exercises, you will be able to:

- Describe the features of VMRCplus
- Install and configure VMRCplus
- Create and run a virtual machine
- Use the VMRCplus managers

Developed by Microsoft as an alternative to the Virtual Server Administration Web site and the Virtual Machine Remote Control client, **VMRCplus** does not replace every function of the Web site, but it does provide useful features that the Web site does not have. For example, VMRCplus can generate the configurations for multiple child virtual machines from a parent virtual machine.

VMRCplus also provides a Windows GUI that is easier to use than the Virtual Server Administration Web site for configuring and managing virtual machines. The virtual machines are displayed in a tabbed window, which makes it easy to jump from virtual machine to virtual machine when working with multiple running virtual machines.

You will discover that creating a virtual machine is easy and intuitive using VMRCplus. Although VMRCplus does not have wizards like those in Virtual PC, the creation of a virtual machine follows the logic of the Virtual PC New Virtual Machine Wizard.

Although all of the VMRCplus control occurs without the use of the Virtual Server Web-based administration console, you will need to install Virtual Server to use VMRCplus.

Overview of VMRCplus

The VMRCplus application was developed by the Virtual Server development group at Microsoft. VMRCplus is considered a resource kit tool. The tools in a Microsoft resource kit help you perform administrative tasks when working with Microsoft products; resource kit tools are not supported by Microsoft Support Services. This means that VMRCplus is not supported under any Microsoft standard support program or service; nonetheless, you can download and install VMRCplus on your computer for free.

Figure 7-1 shows the VMRCplus Virtual Machine Manager window. The Virtual Machine Manager consolidates the functions of working with virtual machines and is the starting point for these operations. At first glance, VMRCplus might appear a bit different from other windows applications; however, as you work with it, you will appreciate its power and ease of use.

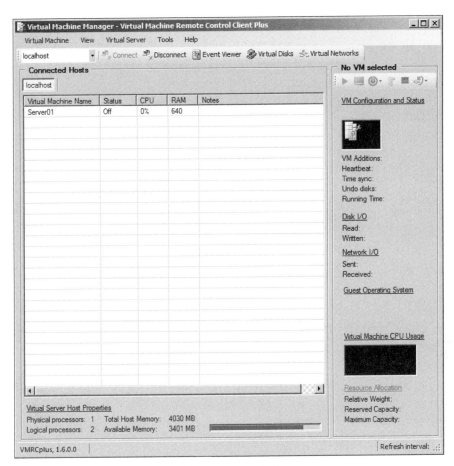

Figure 7-1 VMRCplus Virtual Machine Manager window

You access your running virtual machines from within the VMRCplus Console Manager window. Figure 7-2, on the next page, shows a familiar window format—a virtual machine running in a window.

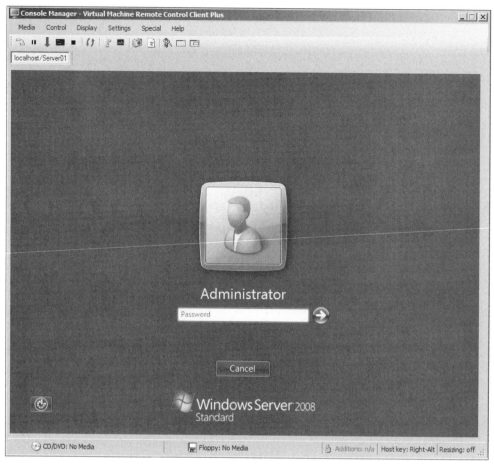

Figure 7-2 The Longhorn virtual machine running in a VMRCplus window

Key Features

VMRCplus provides many key features that can make your use of virtual machines easier. The following is an abbreviated list of the key features listed by the developers:

- Direct control of the local Virtual Server service; the Microsoft Internet Explorer browser is no longer required
- Automatic reconnect to a designated Virtual Server host
- Virtual Networks Manager and Virtual Disks Manager, which cover all features
- Browse button navigation for media, hard disk images, ISO images, .vmc files, and so on
- Ability to create a virtual machine (or multiple virtual machines) from a parent
- Toolbars in both Virtual Machine Manager and Console Manager for quick access
- Automatic detection of Virtual Machine Additions and notification

- Resizable desktop support for guests running Virtual Machine Additions
- Reusable saved states; this feature allows users to preserve a particular saved state and return to that state at any time
- Multiple virtual machine selection supported for startup/shutdown/save/display

Installing and Configuring VMRCplus

Installing VMRCplus is just like installing any Windows application. Simply download VMRCplus from the Microsoft Web site and run the setup procedure to install VMRCplus from the Windows Explorer window.

Follow the steps within the wizard to complete the installation. You will learn how to install VMRCplus on your computer in Activity 7-1.

To review and change the VMRC Server settings, you click the Virtual Server menu, and then click VMRC Server. Figure 7-3 shows the VMRC Server settings window. By default, the Disconnect Idle Connections check box is unchecked to prevent the VMRC Server from dropping a connection to a virtual machine that you have not visited in over 15 minutes; however, disabling this setting presents your system with a greater security risk because connections will be left open indefinitely.

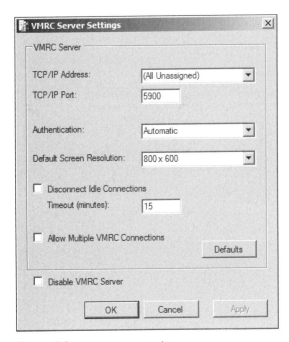

Figure 7-3 VMRC Server settings

If you are working on a project, you might want to change the location of your virtual machines, virtual hard disks, and virtual machine configurations. This can be done by clicking the Virtual Server menu in the Virtual Machine Manager window, clicking Default VM Location, and browsing using the Select Location button to indicate the folder for your virtual machines. See Figure 7-4.

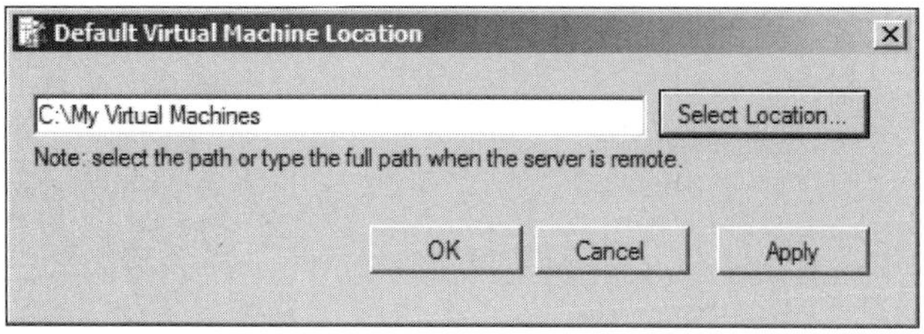

Figure 7-4 Setting the default virtual machine location

To review or update the security settings for VMRC Server, you click the Virtual Server menu in the Virtual Machine Manager window, and then click Security. Figure 7-5 shows the Virtual Server Security Settings window. Although the default security settings are usually sufficient, you might need to add an additional user account to permit another user to run a virtual machine. To do this, click the Add button and complete the security permissions.

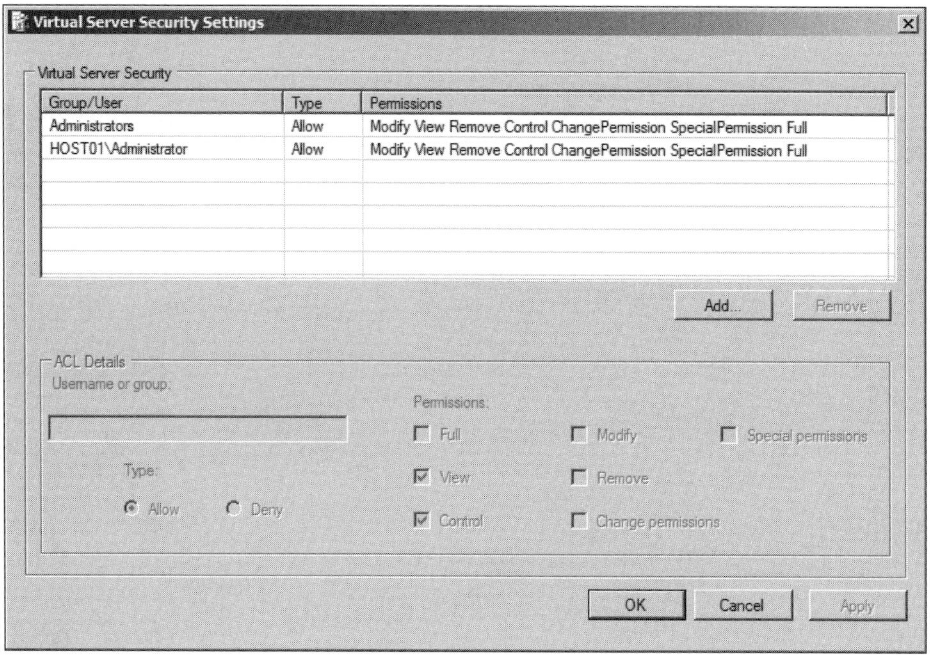

Figure 7-5 Virtual Server Security Settings window

To view useful virtual server properties, click the Virtual Server menu in the Virtual Machine Manager window, and then click Properties. Figure 7-6 shows the Virtual Server Properties window. From this window, you can review the Virtual Server Service and Physical Computer properties. This information is useful when working on an unfamiliar computer.

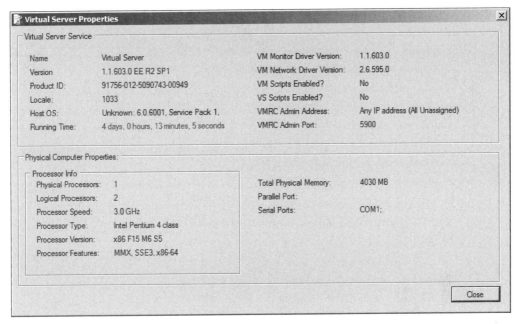

Figure 7-6 Virtual Server Properties window

Another convenient option is to have VMRCplus connect to your Virtual Server at start-up. This is done by right-clicking localhost under Connected Hosts in the Virtual Machine Manager window, and then clicking Reconnect to this host on startup.

Activity 7-1: Installing VMRCplus

Time Required: 15 minutes

Objective: Install VMRCplus.

Description: In this activity, you will download and install VMRCplus.

1. If necessary, log on to your Host PC with a username of **Administrator** and a password of **Secret1**.
2. To launch Internet Explorer, click **Start**, point to **All Programs**, and then click **Internet Explorer**.
3. To search for VMRC, type **vmrcplus download** in the Live Search text box and then press **Enter**.
4. To open the download Web page, scroll and click the link for the VMRCplus download.

Your search will return many hits for VMRCplus. Be sure you select a link that leads to the VMRCplus downloadable file from the Microsoft Web site.

5. Scroll and click the link for the correct version for your host machine (X64 is for 64-bit processors and x86 is for 32-bit processors).
6. When the File Download dialog box opens, click **Open**.
7. When the VMRCplus window opens, double-click the **setup** executable, click the **Run** button, and then click **Next**.
8. Check the **I accept the terms in the License Agreement** check box, click **Next** twice, and then click the **Install** button.
9. Wait for the installation to complete, and then click **Finish**.
10. To place a shortcut for VMRCplus on the desktop, click **Start**, point to **All Programs**, right-click the **VMRCplus** icon, point to **Send To**, and then click **Desktop (create shortcut)**.
11. Close the open windows.
12. Leave the computer logged on for the next activity.

Activity 7-2: Configuring VMRCplus

Time Required: 5 minutes

Objective: Configure VMRCplus.

Requirements: Completion of Activity 7-1.

Description: In this activity, you will configure the VMRCplus program to connect to Host01 to manage Virtual Server. Also, you will verify that the Disconnect Idle Connections check box is cleared.

1. If necessary, log on to your Host PC with a username of **Administrator** and a password of **Secret1**.
2. To launch VMRCplus, double-click the **VMRCplus** icon on the desktop.
3. To connect to the Host01 computer, click the **Connect** button.
4. If the VMRC server request message appears, click **Yes**.
5. To configure VMRCplus to connect to the host computer each time, right-click **localhost** under Connected Hosts, and then click **Reconnect to this host on startup**.
6. To review and change the VMRC Server settings, click the **Virtual Server** menu, click **VMRC Server**, clear the **Disconnect Idle Connections** check box, if needed, and then click **OK**.
7. Leave the computer logged on for the next activity.

Activity 7-3: Exploring VMRCplus Help

Time Required: 15 minutes

Objective: Research information on VMRCplus.

Requirements: Completion of Activity 7-1.

Description: In this activity, you will explore VMRCplus Help. This activity is useful if you want to locate the answer to a question regarding the use of VMRCplus.

1. If necessary, log on to your Host PC with a username of **Administrator** and a password of **Secret1**.
2. If necessary, to launch VMRCplus, double-click the **VMRCplus** icon on the desktop.
3. To access VMRCplus Help, click the **Help** menu and then click **Contents**.
4. Click the **Contents** tab.
5. Expand **Using VMRCplus**, and then peruse each topic under Using VMRCplus.
6. Expand **How To**, and then expand and peruse each topic under How To.
7. Close the VMRCplus Help window.
8. Leave the computer logged on for the next activity.

You have installed VMRCplus, configured some useful options, perused Help, and are ready to start using VMRCplus.

Creating and Running Virtual Machines

The real power of VMRCplus is best demonstrated by creating and running a virtual machine. The details of the various managers are covered later in this chapter. In this part of the chapter, only the incidentals to create and run a virtual machine are covered.

Creating the First Virtual Machine

When you launch VMRCplus, the first window you see is the Virtual Machine Manager, as shown previously in Figure 7-1. From this window, you can create virtual machines. To do this, you click the Virtual Machine menu and select Create, which displays the Create New Virtual Machine window.

From the Create New Virtual Machine window, you fill in the details that define your virtual machine. Figure 7-7 on the next page shows a partially completed Create New Virtual Machine window.

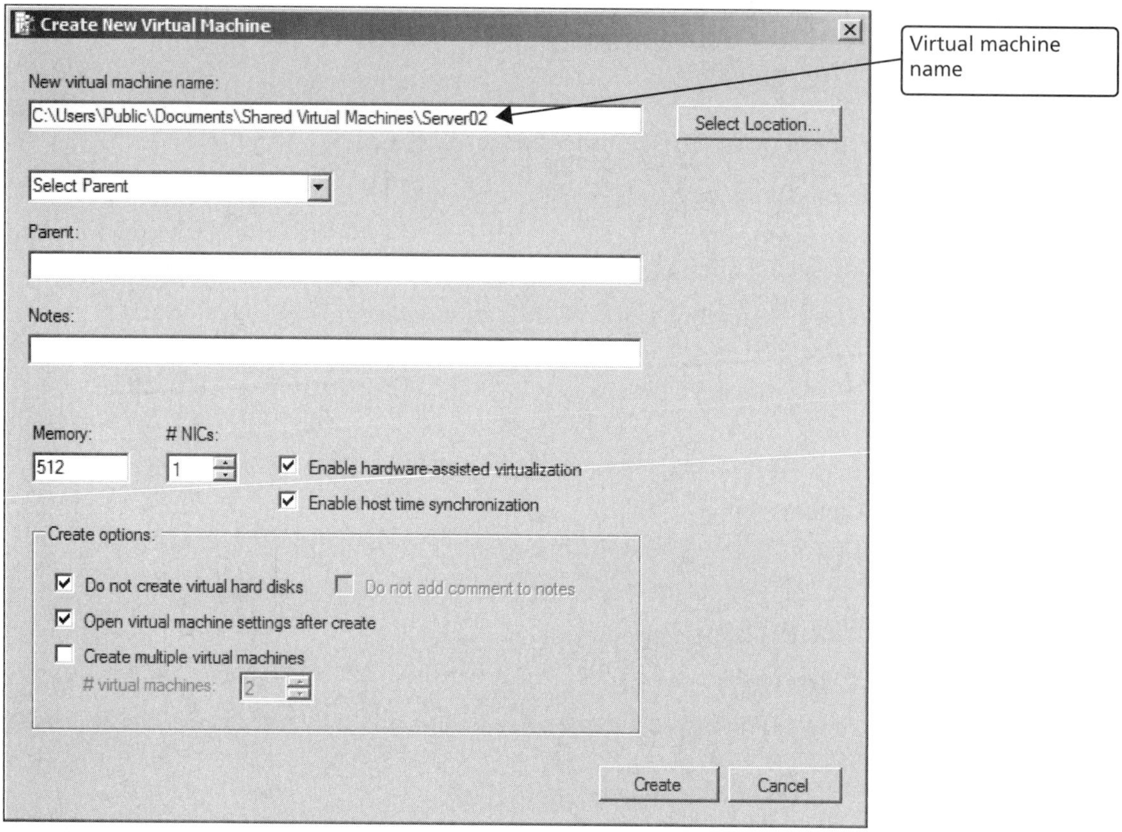

Figure 7-7 Partially completed Create New Virtual Machine window

To create the entries, you enter the information for the virtual machine, as shown in Figure 7-7. Type the virtual machine name at the end of the path for the New virtual machine name text box. Type the use for the virtual machine (or other useful information) in the Notes text box. Type the amount of RAM to be used by the virtual machine in the Memory text box. If the virtual machine will be using more than one network adapter, adjust the # NICs spin box to reflect the number of network adapters. If the host computer does not have hardware virtualization, clear the Enable hardware-assisted virtualization check box. Check the Do not create virtual harddisks check box. Clicking the Create button creates the virtual machine.

Because the Open virtual machine settings after create check box was checked (this is the default setting), the Settings window appears next.

At this point, there are two tasks remaining: Create a virtual hard disk and connect the network adapter to a virtual network. Both of these can be done from the window shown in Figure 7-8.

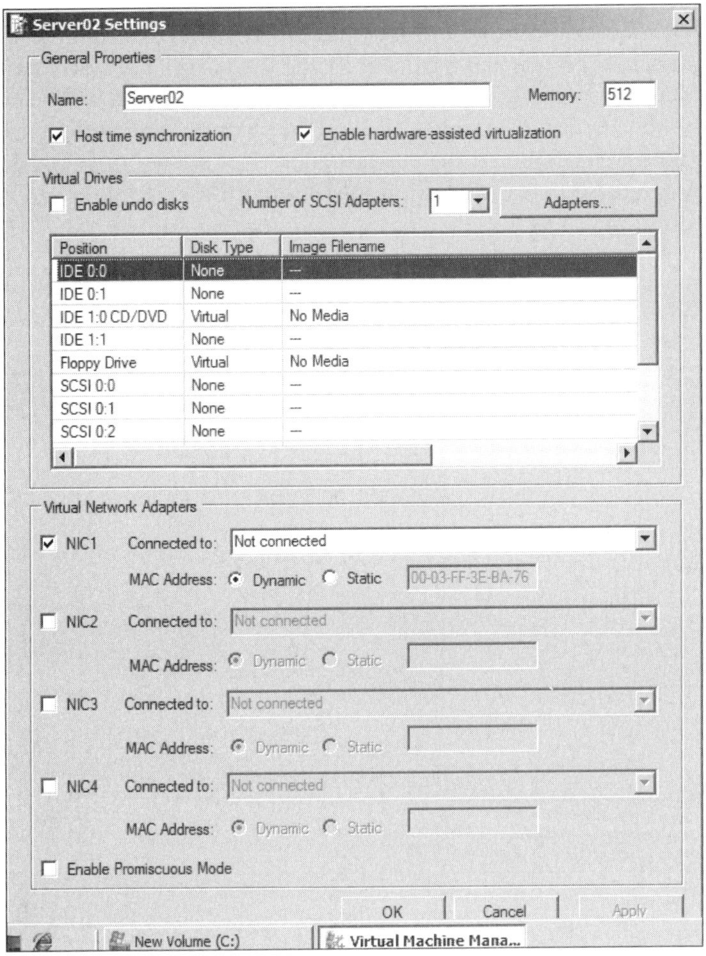

Figure 7-8 Server02 settings

Because the virtual machine is using IDE drives (IDE drives were used when virtual hard disks were created in Chapter 6), click the Number of SCSI Adapters drop-down list arrow and click 0. To access the Virtual Disks Manager to create a virtual hard disk, right-click the IDE0:0 line and select Create a New Disk Here.

Create the virtual hard disk for the virtual machine using the Virtual Disks window. Figure 7-9 shows the completed entries for the virtual hard disk. Type the virtual hard disk name at the end of the path for the New dynamically expanding virtual hard disk text box. The maximum size for the disk must be specified in megabytes. Type the maximum size in the Disk size (in MB) text box. When you have completed the entries, click the Create button. Wait for the virtual hard disk to be created. Review the creation message in the message box and then click Close to close the window.

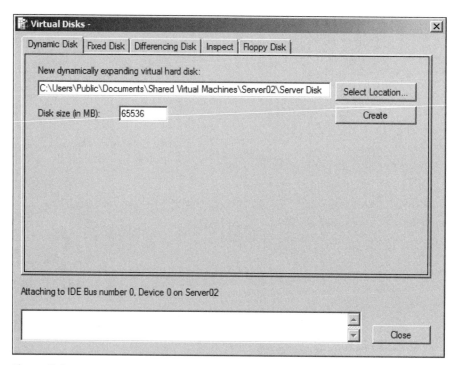

Figure 7-9 Completed dynamically expanding virtual hard disk entries

NOTE When you are typing the name for the virtual hard disk, the typed characters might exceed the length of the New dynamically expanding virtual hard disk text box. When this occurs, the previous characters are no longer displayed. This is a minor glitch; just keep typing.

To connect to the virtual network, click the Virtual Network Adapter for NIC 1 drop-down list arrow and select the proper virtual adapter for this virtual machine. The completed hardware settings are shown in Figure 7-10.

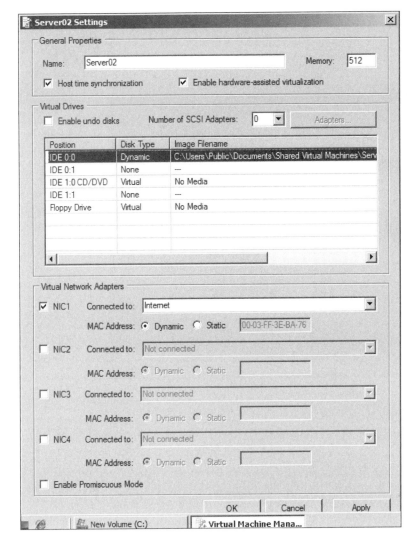

Figure 7-10 Completed settings for Server02

Installing an Operating System for the First Virtual Machine

Start by inserting the installation CD/DVD for the operating system in the CD/DVD drive. To start a virtual machine and install an operating system, double-click the virtual machine name in the Virtual Machine Manager window. To view the display for the virtual machine, click the thumbnail to the right. Figure 7-11 on the next page shows the Console Manager window from which you access and control virtual machines.

You will need a work-around to use the DVD to install an operating system. To mount the DVD in the CD/DVD drive, click the Media menu and select the Mount Host CD/DVD Drive option. To reboot the system and access the DVD, click the Control menu, select Reset, and then click Yes. From this point, you complete the OS installation as you have done in previous chapters.

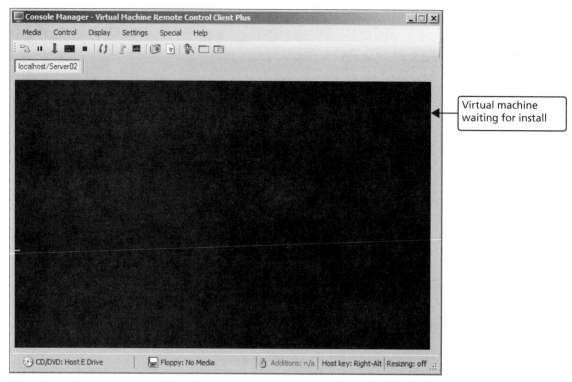

Figure 7-11 Console Manager window

Installing Virtual Machine Additions for the First Virtual Machine

Virtual Machine Additions can only be added after the operating system is installed. If the Windows Server 2008 DVD is in the CD/DVD drive, click Media and select Eject CD/DVD Media. To mount the Virtual Machine Additions, click the Media menu, press right Alt, click the Media menu, click Load ISO Image, double-click Computer, double-click New Volume (C:), double-click Program Files, double-click Microsoft Virtual Server, double-click Virtual Machine Additions, click VMAdditions.iso, and then click Open. Wait for the Autoplay window to open, and click Run setup.exe. Click Next, wait for the installation to complete, and then click Finish. When requested to restart your system, click Yes.

Activity 7-4: Creating the First Virtual Machine

Time Required: 5 minutes

Objective: Create the first virtual machine.

Requirements: Completion of Activities 7-1 and 7-2.

Description: In this activity, you will use the Virtual Machine Manager and the Virtual Disks Manager to create the first virtual machine. This activity is useful if you want to create a virtual machine using the most direct approach.

1. If necessary, log on to your Host PC with a username of **Administrator** and a password of **Secret1**.
2. If necessary, to launch VMRCplus, double-click the **VMRCplus** icon on the desktop.
3. To open the Create New Virtual Machine window, click the **Virtual Machine** menu and then click **Create**.
4. To name the virtual machine, type **Server02** at the end of the path for the New virtual machine name text box.
5. To provide notes for this virtual machine, type the use for the virtual machine (or other useful information) in the Notes text box.
6. To specify the amount of RAM, type **512** in the Memory text box.
7. If the host computer does not have hardware virtualization, clear the **Enable hardware-assisted virtualization** check box.
8. To avoid creating two SCSI virtual hard disks by default, check the **Do Not create virtual hard disks** check box.
9. To create the virtual machine, click the **Create** button.
10. Wait for the Server02 Settings window to open.
11. Because you will not be using the SCSI adapters, if necessary, remove them by clicking the **Number of SCSI Adapters** drop-down list arrow and setting it to 0.
12. To access the Virtual Disks Manager to create a virtual hard disk, right-click the **IDE0:0** line and select **Create a New Disk Here**.
13. Wait for the Virtual Disks window to open.
14. To name the virtual hard disk, type **Server02** at the end of the path for the New dynamically expanding virtual hard disk text box.
15. Type **65536 in** the Disk size (in MB) text box.

The maximum size for the virtual hard disk must be specified in megabytes.

To create an evenly sized disk, remember that every 1 GB equals 1024 MB.

16. Click the **Create** button.
17. Wait for the virtual hard disk to be created.
18. Review the creation message in the message box and then click **Close**.
19. To connect to the virtual network, click the **Virtual Network Adapter for NIC 1** drop-down list arrow and select **Internet**.

20. Review the settings and click **OK**.
21. Leave the computer logged on for the next activity.

Activity 7-5: Installing an Operating System in the First Virtual Machine

Time Required: 90 minutes

Objective: Install an OS in the first virtual machine.

Requirements: Completion of Activities 7-1, 7-2, and 7-4.

Description: In this activity, you will use the Virtual Machine Manager and the Console Manager to install the operating system in the first virtual machine. For the purposes of this activity, you will install Windows Server 2008 in a virtual machine.

1. If necessary, log on to your Host PC with a username of **Administrator** and a password of **Secret1**.
2. If necessary, to launch VMRCplus, double-click the **VMRCplus** icon on the desktop.
3. Insert the Microsoft Windows Server 2008 DVD into the CD/DVD drive.
4. To start a virtual machine and install an operating system, double-click **Server02** in the Virtual Machine Manager window.
5. To view the display for the virtual machine, click the **Server02** thumbnail to the right.
6. Wait for the Console Manager window to open.
7. To mount the DVD in the CD/DVD drive, click the **Media** menu and select the **Mount Host CD/DVD Drive** option.
8. To reboot the virtual machine, click the **Control** menu, select **Reset**, and then click **Yes**.
9. Wait for Windows to load files.
10. To activate the virtual machine window, click in the **Server02** console window.
11. When the regional settings dialog box opens, verify the language, time and currency, and keyboard. Correct as needed, and then click **Next**.
12. Click the **Install now** link.
13. To indicate that this virtual machine is using an evaluation copy, wait for the Type your product key for activation dialog box to open, clear the **Automatically activate Windows when I'm online** check box, click **Next**, and then click **No**.
14. To indicate which version to install, click **Windows Server 2008 Enterprise (Full Installation)**, check the **I have selected the edition of Windows that I purchased** check box, and then click **Next**.
15. When the Please read the license terms dialog box opens, check the **I accept the license terms** check box, and then click **Next**.
16. Click the **Custom (advanced)** icon.
17. Review the disk space allocation and then click **Next**.

18. Wait for Windows to copy and expand files, install features and updates, and restart to complete the installation.
19. Ignore the Press any key to boot from CD or DVD message.
20. Wait while Windows prepares to start for the first time and to complete the installation.
21. When the user's password must be changed before logging on the first time message appears, click **OK**. Type **Secret1** in the New password text box, press **Tab**, type **Secret1** in the Confirm password text box, press **Enter**, and then click **OK**.
22. To set the time zone, click the **Set time zone** link, click the **Change time zone** button, click the appropriate time zone, click **OK**, review the date and time and change if needed, and then click **OK**.
23. To provide a computer name, click the **Provide computer name and domain** link, click the **Change** button, type **Server02** in the Computer name text box, click **OK** twice, click **Close**, and then click the **Restart Now** button.
24. Wait for the virtual machine to restart.
25. Ignore the Press any key to boot from CD or DVD message.
26. Press right **Alt+Delete** and log on to your Server02 virtual machine with a username of **Administrator** and a password of **Secret1**.
27. To enable network discovery and file sharing, click **Start**, right-click **Network**, click **Properties**, click the Network discovery drop-down list arrow, click the **Turn on network discovery** option button, click the **Apply** button, click the **No, make the network that I am connected to a private network** link, click the **File sharing** drop-down list arrow, click the **Turn on file sharing** option button, click the **Apply** button, and then close the Network and Sharing window.
28. Leave the computer logged on for the next activity.

Activity 7-6: Installing Virtual Machine Additions in the First Virtual Machine

Time Required: 10 minutes

Objective: Install Virtual Machine Additions into the Server02 virtual machine.

Requirements: Completion of Activities 7-1, 7-2, 7-4, and 7-5.

Description: In this activity, you will install Virtual Machine Additions into the virtual machine. This activity is useful if you want to use the features of Virtual Machine Additions.

1. If necessary, log on to your Host PC with a username of **Administrator** and a password of **Secret1**.
2. If necessary, to launch VMRCplus, double-click the **VMRCplus** icon on the desktop.
3. If necessary, to start the Server02 virtual machine, double-click the **Server02 virtual machine**.

4. If necessary, log on with a username of **Administrator** and a password of **Secret1**.

5. To mount the Virtual Machine Additions, click the **Media** menu, press right **Alt**, click the **Media** menu, click **Load ISO Image**, double-click **Computer**, double-click **New Volume (C:)**, double-click **Program Files**, double-click **Microsoft Virtual Server**, double-click **Virtual Machine Additions**, click **VMAdditions.iso**, and then click **Open**.

6. Wait for the Autoplay window to open, click in the Server01 virtual machine window, and then click **Run setup.exe**.

7. Click **Next**, wait for the installation to complete, and then click **Finish**.

8. When requested to restart your system, click **Yes**.

9. Wait for Server02 to restart.

10. Log on to your virtual machine with a username of **Administrator** and a password of **Secret1**.

11. Leave the computer logged on for the next activity.

VMRCplus Managers

You access the features of VMRCplus using the various managers, which are control tools included in the software. You used the Virtual Machine Manager to create a virtual machine. From the Console Manager, you accessed a running virtual machine. VMRCplus includes two additional managers—the Virtual Disks Manager and the Virtual Networks Manager.

The starting point for accessing the VMRCplus managers is the Virtual Machine Manager, which is the default window when VMRCplus starts.

These VMRCplus managers are explained in detail in the following sections.

The Virtual Machine Manager

The Virtual Machine Manager is the main application window of VMRCplus. See Figure 7-12. You already have used this window as the starting point for your VMRCplus operations.

Menu options within the Virtual Machine Manager are as follows:

- Virtual Machine—Create, add, remove (unregister), or delete (unregister and delete folder) a virtual machine.

- View—Change the refresh interval for the virtual machine list, force a refresh of the virtual machine list, and add/remove the toolbars in the Virtual Machine Manager window.

- Virtual Server—Review and modify the VMRC Server settings, set the default location for the VM folder, review and modify the security settings, and display the Virtual Server and physical computer properties.

- Tools—Launch the Virtual Disks Manager, Virtual Networks Manager, Event Viewer, and set VMRCplus behavior options.

- Help—Launch VMRCplus Help.

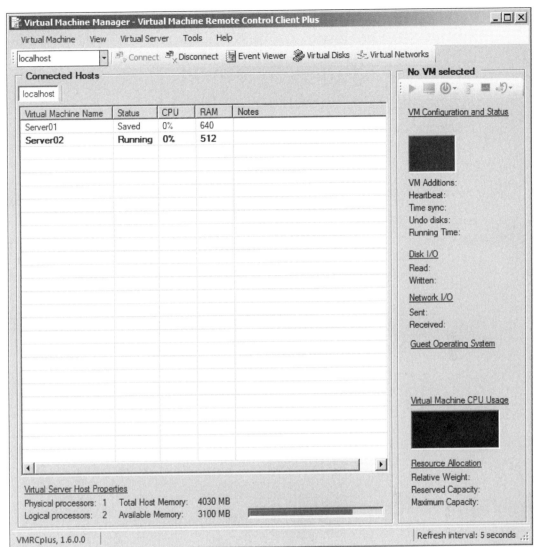

Figure 7-12 Virtual Server Manager window showing created guests

For a virtual machine to appear in the Virtual Machine Manager list, it must be registered—the Virtual Machine, Create and Virtual Machine, Add options perform this registration task. To remove a virtual machine, you would use the Virtual Machine, Remove or Virtual Machine, Delete options. All of these options are available from the Virtual Machine menu in Virtual Machine Manager.

Information on these menu options is presented in the following sections.

The Virtual Machine Menu From the Virtual Machine menu in the Virtual Machine Manager window, you have these options:

- Create—Create a new virtual machine.
- Add—Register an existing .vmc file. You would do this if you were importing an existing virtual machine from another server.

- Remove—Unregister an existing .vmc file and hide the virtual machine within the Virtual Machine Manager. You would do this to prevent a virtual machine from running without deleting its .vmc and .vhd files.
- Delete—Unregister an existing .vmc file and delete the .vmc and .vhd files.

Creating Virtual Machines You learned how to create a single virtual machine in Activity 7-4.

VMRCplus can create multiple virtual machines based upon a parent configuration. A **parent-child relationship** exists with differencing virtual hard disks created for the children.

To start the process, create a parent virtual machine using the steps to create a virtual machine. When you have completed these steps, you will have a parent virtual machine similar to the one shown in Figure 7-13. You can use virtual machine names other than *Parent*. Note that the disk type for the Parent virtual machine is Dynamic.

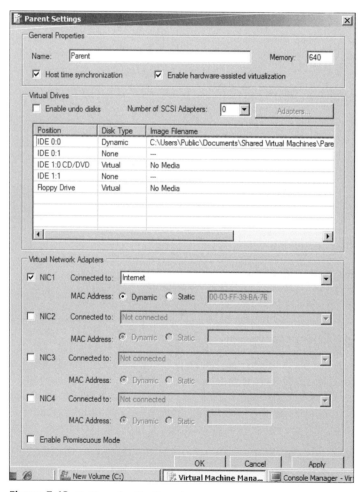

Figure 7-13 Settings for the Parent

The next task is to create the multiple child virtual machines (children) using the Parent as a template. Figure 7-14 shows the window used to create the four children. You must enter the name for the children after the path in the New virtual machine name text box. You can use virtual machine names other than *Child*. To specify the parent to use, click the Select Parent drop-down list arrow and select the Parent that was previously created. Click the Create multiple virtual machines check box and adjust the # guests spin box to indicate the number of virtual machines to create. You must create at least two. Clicking the Create button completes the process.

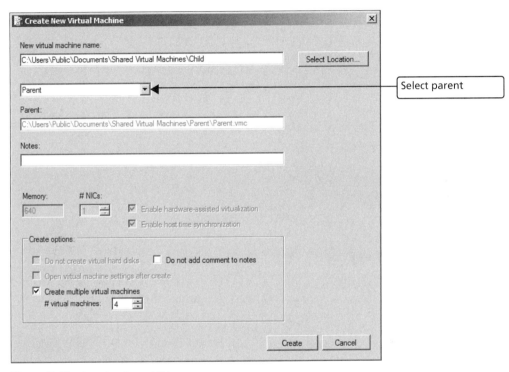

Figure 7-14 Creating four children

After the children are created, they appear in the Virtual Machine Manager virtual machine list, as shown in Figure 7-15. Notice that VMRCplus added sequence numbers as a suffix to each child virtual machine.

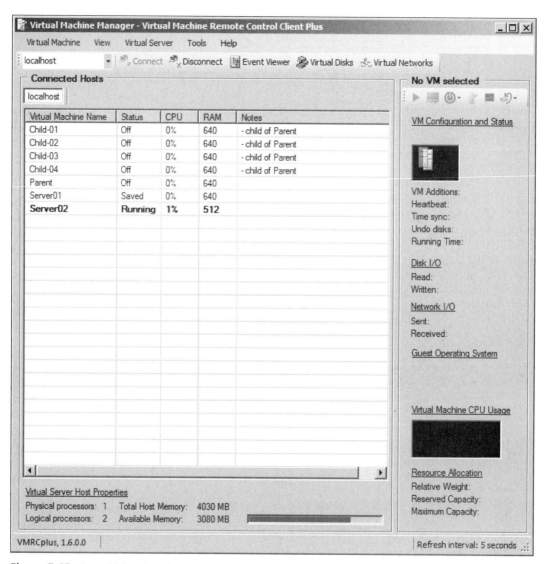

Figure 7-15 Four children based on parent

Figure 7-16 shows the hardware properties for the Child-01 virtual machine. Note that the disk type is differencing, which is used with children in a parent-child relationship. When using differencing disks, the Child-01 virtual machine is started from the Parent virtual hard disk with changes written to the Child-01 virtual hard disk. The Parent is used to start the remaining children with the changes written to their respective virtual hard disks. The advantage of this arrangement is that only one installation of the operating system—the Parent's—is required.

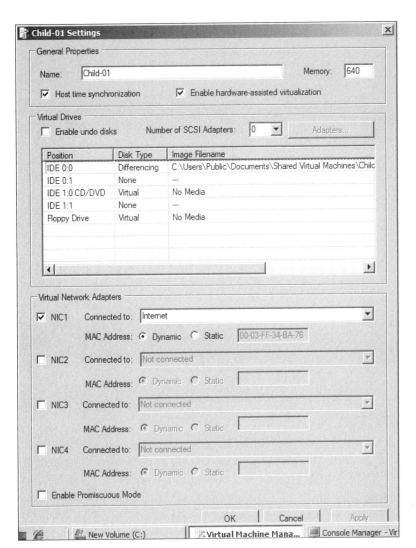

Figure 7-16 Settings for Child-01

Adding a Virtual Machine To add a virtual machine that was previously removed (see the "Removing a Virtual Machine" section on the next page), select Add from the Virtual Machine menu, which launches the Open dialog box, as shown in Figure 7-17 on the next page. Navigate to the folder for the virtual machine. Double-click on this folder, click the virtual machine file, and then click Open.

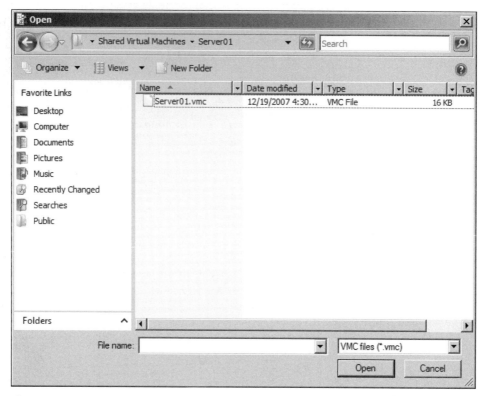

Figure 7-17 Open dialog box

To add a virtual machine, you must register its .vmc file with the Virtual Machine Manager. You would need to perform this step if you previously had removed a virtual machine or imported a virtual machine from another server.

Removing a Virtual Machine To remove a virtual machine, click the virtual machine in the Virtual Machine Manager list and select Remove from the Virtual Machine menu. You will be asked to confirm your decision. This step unregisters the virtual machine. The folder and the files for the virtual machine are not removed from the host computer. Removing a virtual machine hides it from the Virtual Machine Manager, preventing it from running. For example, to protect the parent in a parent-child relationship, you will want to remove the parent in the Virtual Machine Manager.

Deleting a Virtual Machine To delete a virtual machine, click the virtual machine in the Virtual Machine Manager list and select Delete from the Virtual Machine menu. You will be asked to confirm your decision. As with removing virtual machines, deleting a virtual machine unregisters it. However, the folder and files for the virtual machine are deleted and moved to the Recycle Bin.

The View Menu From the View menu, you can complete these tasks:

- Refresh Interval—Set the refresh interval for the active virtual machine list to one of these settings: Never, 5 seconds (the default), 30 seconds, 1 Minute, 5 Minutes, or 15 Minutes.
- Refresh VM List—Force a refresh of the virtual machine list or press the F5 key. You might want to do this if you have started or stopped a virtual machine.

- Toolbar—Turn off or on these toolbars: Show Screen Tips and Show Image and Text. This controls the appearance of the toolbar under the Virtual Machine Manager menu bar.

The Virtual Server Menu From the Virtual Server menu, you can display and modify the VMRC Server settings, set the default virtual machine location, set the security settings, and view the Virtual Server settings.

The Tools Menu From the Tools menu, you can access the Virtual Disks Manager and Virtual Networks Manager. Information on these two managers is presented in detail in the "Using the Virtual Disks Manager" and "Implementing Virtual Networks" sections later in this chapter.

When you run into problems with your guests or with Virtual Server, you can use the Event Viewer to find information about the possible source of the problem. From the Tools menu, select Event Viewer. Figure 7-18 shows a sample Event Viewer log. The first column, Type, classifies an event as Error, Warning, or Info. The date and time the problem occurred appear next on each line. The message that completes each line provides helpful information to resolve the problem.

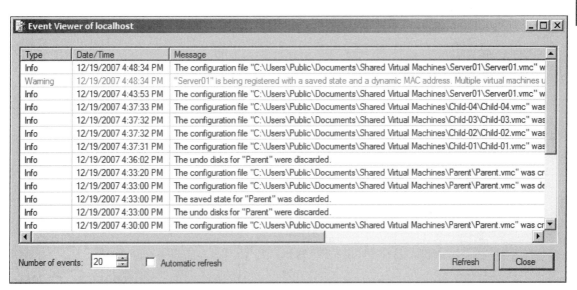

Figure 7-18 Event Viewer of localhost

Options is the last item on the Tools menu. From this menu, you can set the default location for your .iso files. Choose between minimizing to the system tray or taskbar. Because the installed version of Virtual Server is Virtual Server 2005 SP1, the SP1 check permits the additional features of Service Pack 1 to be used.

Working with Selected Virtual Machines

To view a virtual machine's properties, you select it from the list of virtual machines within the Virtual Machine Manager, as shown in Figure 7-19 on the next page. This information is useful as you work with your virtual machines.

Table 7-1, on the next page, summarizes the data shown in the figure.

274 Chapter 7 Using Microsoft VMRCplus

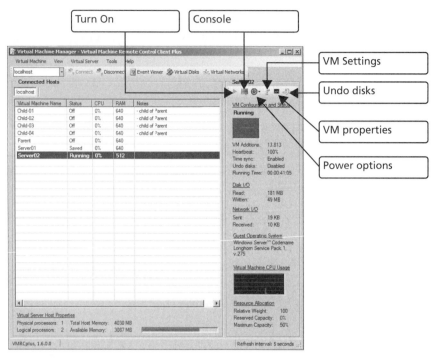

Figure 7-19 Virtual Machine Manager with properties for selected virtual machine and action icons

Table 7-1 Virtual machine data

Item	Description
Status	State of the virtual machine: Powering up, Running, Off
Thumbnail	Image of the desktop for the virtual machine
VM Additions	Version number of Virtual Machine Additions after the virtual machine has been logged onto; shows n/a if not installed
Heartbeat	Percentage heartbeats received from virtual machine
Time sync	Indication that date/time are synchronized between physical computer and virtual machine
Undo disks	Indication that undo disks are being used by virtual machine
Running Time	Uptime for virtual machine
Virtual Machine Operating System	Name and version of operating system, service pack level
Load and Resource Allocation	Percentage CPU utilization for virtual machine
Disk I/O Read	Megabytes read by virtual hard disk(s)
Disk I/O Written	Megabytes written by virtual hard disk(s)
Network I/O Sent	Kilobytes sent by virtual network adapter(s)
Network I/O Received	Kilobytes received by virtual network adapter(s)

You can use the small icons, called action icons, above the Virtual Machine Properties and Status section to control the selected virtual machine.

When a virtual machine is selected, the Virtual Machine Manager action icons perform the tasks listed in Table 7-2. Further information on each of the icons is presented in the following sections.

Table 7-2 Actions for virtual machines

Icon function	Description
Turn On	Start the virtual machine
VM Console	Open the console window for the virtual machine
Power Options	Power down options: Pause/Resume, Reset, Save State, Shutdown, and Turn Off
VM Settings	Virtual machine configuration
Vm Properties	Tabbed properties pages for virtual machine Info, COM/LPT ports, Resource Settings, Startup/Shutdown, Notes and Scripts
Undo Disks Options	Disposition when undo disks are used

Turn On Icon You start a virtual machine by clicking the Turn On icon. You might see the words "Starting VMRC" above the icons. If so, you will need to wait until the VMRC Server has connected to the running virtual machine. It is best to wait until the virtual machine thumbnail displays a screen from the virtual machine operating system.

You can start multiple virtual machines by selecting the virtual machines using the techniques used to select multiple files in a folder and then clicking the Turn On icon.

VM Console Icon To display the desktop of a running virtual machine, click the Console icon or click the thumbnail for the virtual machine. Figure 7-20 on the next page shows a running virtual machine displayed in the Console Manager window. You will learn about the Console Manager later in this chapter.

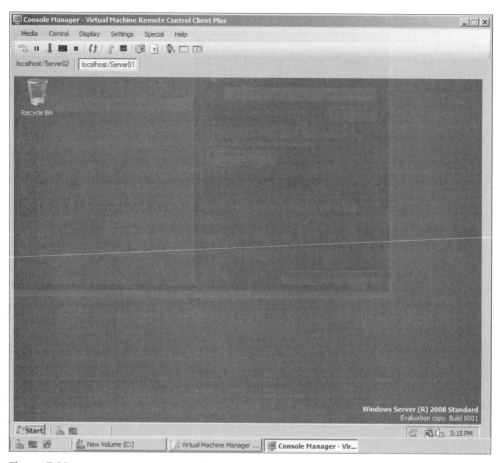

Figure 7-20 Console for running virtual machine

Power Options Icon Clicking the Power Options icon opens a drop-down list of the options available for powering down virtual machines. Table 7-3 explains these Power options.

Table 7-3 Power down options

Option	Explanation
Pause/Resume	Pause prevents the virtual machine from performing any further operations. Resume changes the virtual machine from the Pause state and is good for temporarily stopping a virtual machine to provide resources to other virtual machines.
Reset	Action similar to power-cycling a computer. Most useful when an OS crashes or becomes unresponsive. The OS will not be shut down cleanly.
Save State	Contents of memory are dumped to a disk file. A very quick way of stopping a virtual machine without losing changes. The virtual machine can be restarted from the saved state file.
Shutdown	Equivalent of issuing a shutdown command within the virtual machine's operating system. Requires Virtual Machine Additions.
Turn Off	Same as cutting off power to the virtual machine or "Pulling the plug."

VM Settings Icon You can view the settings for a selected virtual machine by clicking the VM Settings icon to open the virtual machine's Settings dialog box. You can update the fields in this dialog box when the virtual machine is not running. This is a quick way to review and make changes to a virtual machine. Figure 7-21 shows the settings for the Server01 virtual machine. For running virtual machines, you can change the virtual adapters on the fly. This is useful if you need to change a running virtual machine's adapter to another virtual network.

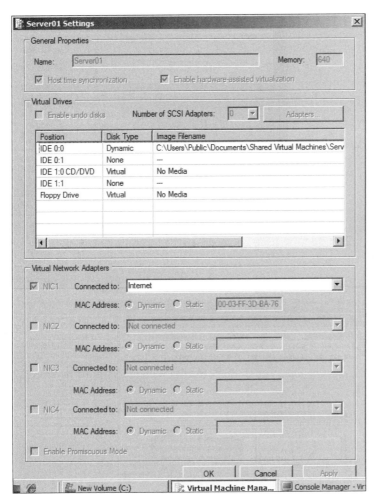

Figure 7-21 Settings for Server01 virtual machine

VM Properties Icon Clicking the VM Properties icon displays a window with tabs for Virtual Machine Info, COM/LPT ports, Resource Settings, Startup/Shutdown, Notes, and Scripts, as shown in Figure 7-22. The Virtual Machine Info tab provides useful information such as the configuration file for the virtual machine.

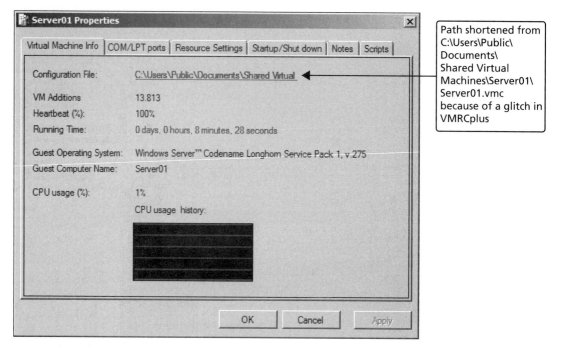

Figure 7-22 VM Properties, Virtual Machine Info tab

The COM/LPT ports tab provides settings for the physical serial (or COM, which stands for communications) ports, or physical printer ports (or LPT1, which stands for line printer). See Figure 7-23.

You use the VM Properties Resource Settings tab, shown in Figure 7-24, to allocate physical CPU resources to virtual machines. For each virtual machine, you allocate CPU resources as follows:

- Maximum CPU usage—The highest percentage of total resources of a single CPU that can be used by this virtual machine at any given time.

- Minimum CPU reserve—The capacity of one CPU that is reserved for this virtual machine. The percentage of CPU capacity that is available to the virtual machine will never be less than this percentage.

- Relative Weight—The relative weight given to the CPU needs of this virtual machine relative to other virtual machines. The default is 100 so that all virtual machines are equal. In most cases, the relative weight is the only setting that you will need to set. You can assign a relative weight between 1 and 10,000.

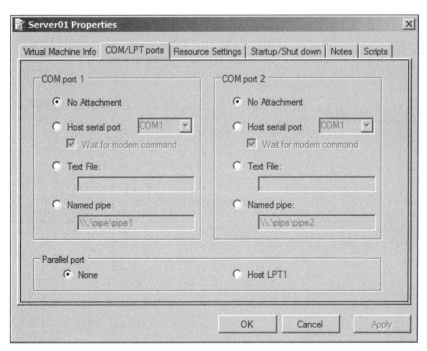

Figure 7-23 VM Properties, COM/LPT ports tab

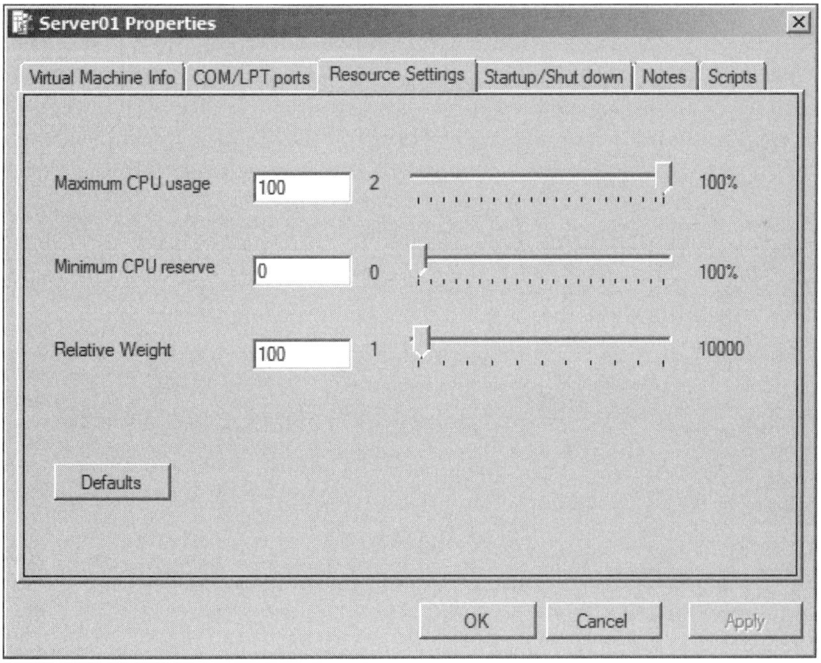

Figure 7-24 VM Properties, Resource Settings tab

You can control the action that you want when the virtual machine is still running and Virtual Server stops. This could occur if you shut down your physical (host) computer, computer with virtual machine running. For each virtual machine, you specify that you want to take one of these actions—Save State, Turn Off Virtual Machine, Shut Down Guest OS—when Virtual Server stops. See Figure 7-25.

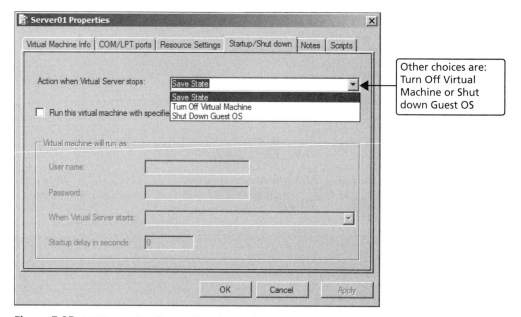

Figure 7-25 VM Properties, Startup/Shutdown tab

Within the Startup/Shutdown tab, you can choose to run the virtual machine using some user account other than the Administrator account. You might want to do this to allow the virtual machine to be run by a person without administrator rights.

If you specify a user account, you can delay the start-up of this virtual machine by a number of seconds. This is useful if you start a number of virtual machines simultaneously and need to stage the start-ups.

The contents of the Scripts tab is beyond the scope of this text.

Undo Disk Options Icon If you are running undo disks, you can use the Undo Disk Options icon to perform the following actions:

- Commit Changes—Merge the undo disk(s) into the virtual hard disk(s).
- Discard Undo Disks—Delete the undo disks.
- Keep Undo Disks—Retain the undo disks.

Using the Console Manager

When you double-click a virtual machine in the Virtual Machine Manager, the Console Manager window shows the desktop for the running virtual machine. Refer back to Figure 7-20. The Console Manager window also opens when you click the VM Console button or right-click the virtual machine and select the VM Console.

Console Manager Menu The Console Manager contains a menu and toolbar and also displays a status bar. The toolbar contains the most frequently used commands from the menu. The status bar shows a CD/DVD or floppy drive has been mounted, indicates whether Virtual Machine Additions has been installed, and displays the current "host key."

Media Menu The Media menu maps CD/DVD and floppy drives for use by the virtual machine. In addition, you can access the equivalent CD/DVD and floppy drive files—.iso and .vfd image files. From the Media menu, you have these options:

- Mount Host CD/DVD Drive—Capture the media in the host CD/DVD drive for use by this virtual machine.
- Mount Host Floppy Drive—Capture the disk in the host floppy drive for use by this virtual machine.
- Load a Floppy Disk Image—Navigate to the location of a .vfd file and use the contents.
- Eject Floppy Media—Release the floppy drive or floppy disk image.
- Load ISO Image—Access the .iso image files.
- Eject CD/DVD Media—Release the CD/DVD drive or .iso image.
- Install Current VM Additions—Install Virtual Machine Additions.

Control Menu The options for controlling power and undo disks settings are located in the Control menu:

- Pause/Resume—Pause prevents the virtual machine from performing any further operations. Resume changes the virtual machine from the Pause state. Pause is useful for temporarily stopping a virtual machine to provide resources to other virtual machines.
- Save State Options—Contents of memory are dumped to a disk file. A very quick way of stopping a virtual machine without losing changes. The virtual machine can be restarted from the saved state file. When undo disks are used, this setting supports the undo disks options.
- Shut Down—Equivalent to issuing a shutdown command within the virtual machine operating system. Requires Virtual Machine Additions.
- Reset—Equivalent to power-off/power-on for the virtual machine.
- Turn off—Same as cutting off power to the virtual machine, or "pulling the plug."

Display Menu From the Display menu, you can turn on the Allow Arbitrary Screen Resize and Refresh the VMRC option. When the Allow Arbitrary Screen Resize is on, you can resize the console display by dragging the lower-right corner. The virtual machine will be resized to fill the console window.

Settings Menu The Settings menu gives you access to options for controlling the host key, connections, and hardware properties:

- Host Key—Change the host key from its default (the right Alt key) to one of seven alternatives: Application key, left Alt key, left Ctrl key, left Shift key, right Alt key, right Ctrl key, right Shift key.
- Connection Properties—Review the properties being used by the session with the VMRC Server.
- Virtual Machine Settings—Same as VM Settings as displayed within Virtual Machine Manager.
- Virtual Machine Properties—Same as VM Properties as displayed within Virtual Machine Manager.

Special Menu The Special menu allows you to use common key combination actions within virtual machine sessions. For example, you use Ctrl+Alt+Del within the virtual machine. Also, you can send the PrintScrn and Alt+PrintScrn functions to the virtual machine. If you need a snapshot of the virtual machine's display, you can save a .jpg file containing the screen image. Capturing the display is useful if you need to keep a picture of an error. The last option within the Special menu "types" a series of keystrokes to the virtual machine. Similar to creating a macro, the keystroke option can automate routine functions by cutting and pasting character strings from a reference document.

Help Menu From the Help menu, you can access the VMRCplus Help from the Contents node and the Virtual Machine Manager nodes. This approach saves time because you do not need to return to the Virtual Machine Manager to access Help.

Console Manager Toolbar The Console Manager makes the most frequently used menu items available on the toolbar, as shown in Figure 7-26. Table 7-4 describes these toolbar items.

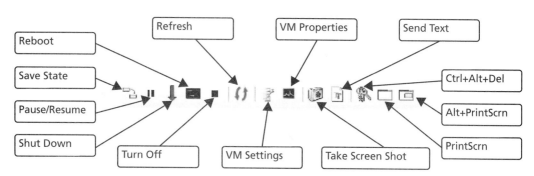

Figure 7-26 Console Manager toolbar

Table 7-4 Descriptions of toolbar items

Icon	Description
Save State	Quickly stops a virtual machine without losing changes. The virtual machine can be restarted from the saved state file.
Pause/Resume	Prevents the virtual machine from performing any further operations. Resume restores the virtual machine from the Pause state. This combination of actions is good for temporarily stopping a virtual machine to provide resources to other virtual machines.
Shut Down	Equivalent to issuing a shutdown command within the virtual machine's operating system. Requires Virtual Machine Additions.
Reboot	Equivalent to power-off/power-on for the virtual machine.
Turn Off	Same as cutting off power to the virtual machine, or "pulling the plug."
Refresh	Refreshes the VMRC Server connection.
VM Settings	Same as virtual machine configuration as displayed within Virtual Machine Manager.
VM Properties	Same as VM Properties as displayed within Virtual Machine Manager.
Take Screen Shot	Saves a .jpg file containing the screen image.
Send Text	"Types" a series of keystrokes to the virtual machine.
Ctrl+Alt+Del	Issues the secure logon request.
PrintScrn	Copies the entire screen to the Clipboard.
Alt+PrintScrn	Copies only an active window to the Clipboard.

Console Manager Status Bar The status bar shows mounted DVD and floppy drive or image status. The status bar also displays the Virtual Machine Additions version (the version number for VMA) being used by the virtual machine, the current host-key combination, and the setting of arbitrary screen resizing.

Using the Virtual Disks Manager

You use the Virtual Disks Manager to create and manage virtual disks. To launch the Virtual Disks Manager, click the Disks icon in the Virtual Machine Manager window. Figure 7-27 on the next page shows the tabs in the Virtual Disks Manager window.

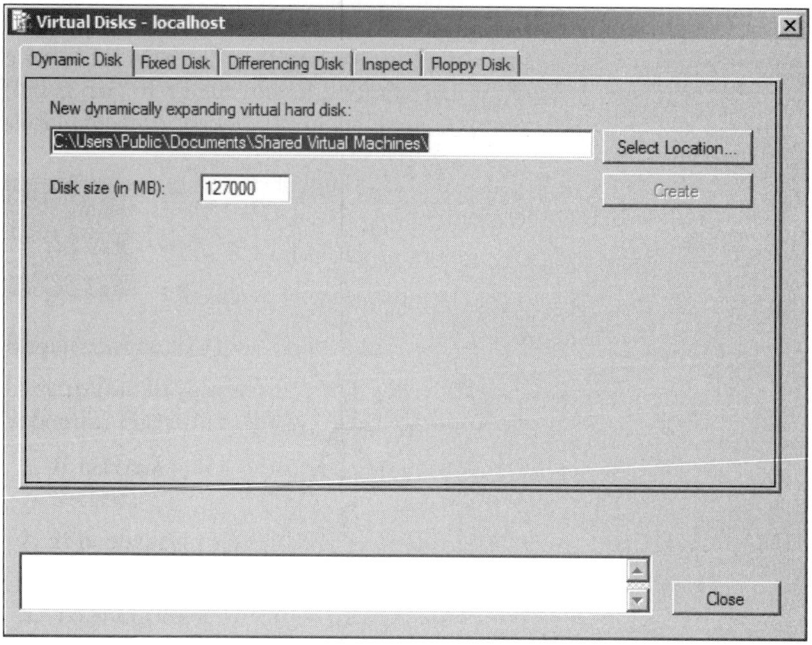

Figure 7-27 Virtual Disks Manager tabs

The Virtual Disks Manager window provides tabs for creating the four various types of virtual hard disks: dynamically expanding, fixed size, differencing, and floppy. The Inspect tab is used to inspect a virtual hard disk. Inspecting a virtual hard disk displays a page that lists information about the virtual hard disk and all the modifications that you can make.

For example, to create a dynamically expanding virtual hard disk, select the Dynamic Disk tab. Clicking the Select Location button opens a dialog box from which you can select the location for the new dynamic disk. See Figure 7-28. If you are creating a virtual hard disk for a virtual machine, you might want to create a folder for the files for this virtual machine. To do this, click the Make New Folder button.

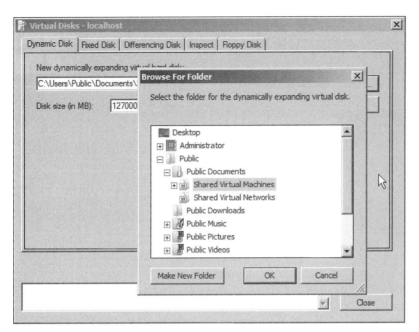

Figure 7-28 Specifying a location for the virtual hard disk

Type the name for the virtual hard disk in the New dynamically expanding hard disk text box following the path. The maximum size must be specified in megabytes. Type the maximum size in the Disk size (in MB) text box. When you have completed the entries, click the Create button. Figure 7-29 on the next page shows the completed virtual hard disk configuration.

To create a fixed-size virtual hard disk, select the Fixed Disk tab. The text boxes and steps are similar to the steps for the dynamic disk.

To create a differencing virtual hard disk, select the Differencing Disk tab. The completed settings are shown in Figure 7-30 on the next page. There are two sets of location and virtual hard disk pathname boxes; the top set is for the specification for the child virtual hard disk and the bottom is for the parent virtual hard disk. The parent virtual hard disk contains a virtual machine operating system that will be used with one or more children.

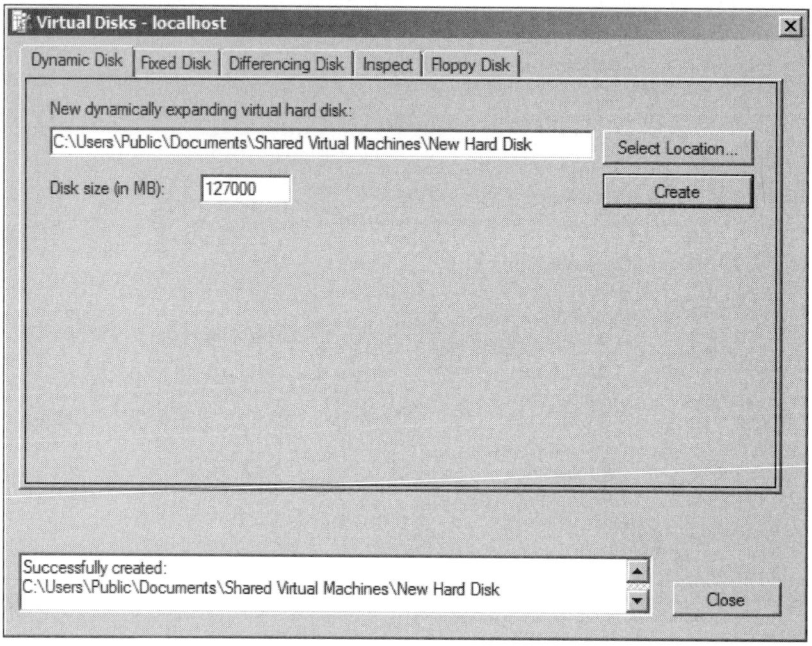

Figure 7-29 Entries for a dynamic disk

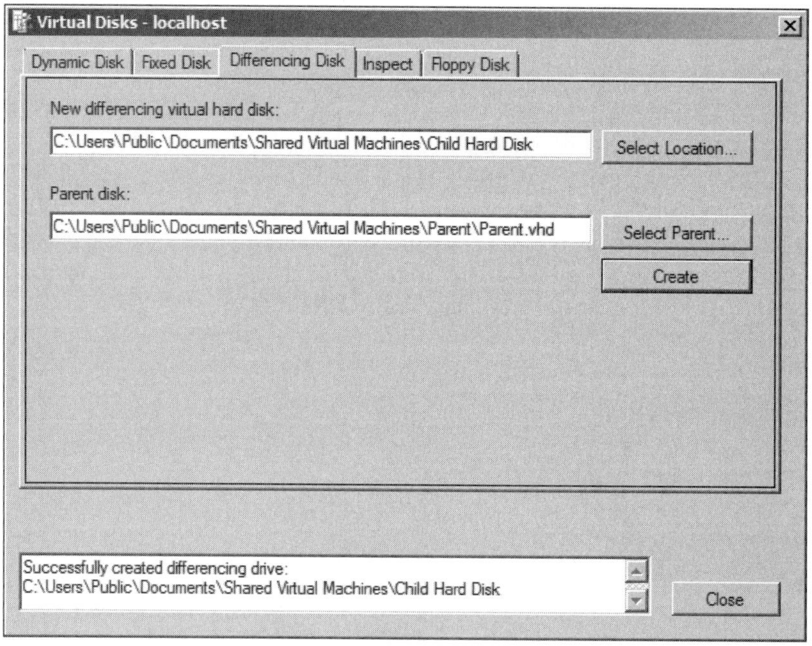

Figure 7-30 Differencing virtual hard disk

To create a link to a virtual floppy disk, select the Floppy Disk tab. You specify the location of the .vfd file, as shown in Figure 7-31.

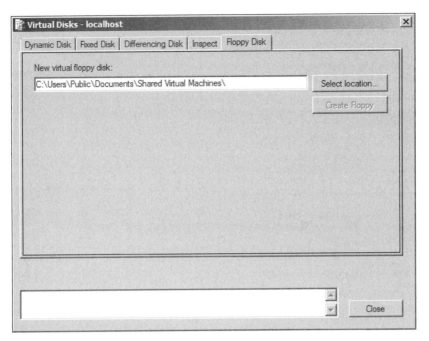

Figure 7-31 Virtual floppy disk

There is no remove feature exclusively for virtual hard disks in VMRCplus. You must use Windows Explorer to delete the virtual hard disk. First navigate to the C:\Users\Public\Public Documents\Shared Virtual Machines\ folder, then navigate to the folder for the virtual machine and delete the virtual hard disk.

Activity 7-7: Creating Four Child Virtual Machines

Time Required: 10 minutes

Objective: Create the four children.

Requirements: Completion of Activities 7-1, 7-2, 7-5, and 7-6.

Description: In this activity, you will use the Virtual Manager and the Virtual Disks Manager to create a parent virtual machine. Then, you will create four child virtual machines from the parent. This activity is useful if you need to create four child virtual machines that use differencing virtual hard disks from the parent.

1. If necessary, log on to your Host PC with a username of **Administrator** and a password of **Secret1**.
2. If necessary, to launch VMRCplus, double-click the **VMRCplus** icon on the desktop.
3. To open the Create New Virtual Machine window, click the **Virtual Machine** menu and then click **Create**.
4. To name the virtual machine, type **Parent** at the end of the path for the New virtual machine name text box.
5. To specify the amount of RAM, type **512** in the Memory text box.

6. If the host computer does not have hardware virtualization, clear the **Enable hardware-assisted virtualization** check box.

7. To avoid creating the two default SCSI virtual hard disks, check the **Do Not create virtual hard disks** check box.

8. To create the virtual machine, click the **Create** button.

9. Wait for the Parent Settings window to open.

10. To remove the SCSI adapters, click the **Number of SCSI Adapters** drop-down list arrow and click on **0**.

11. To access the Virtual Disks Manager to create a virtual hard disk, right-click the **IDE0:0** line and select **Create a New Disk Here**.

12. Wait for the Virtual Disks Manager window to open.

13. To name the virtual hard disk, type **Parent** at the end of the path for the New dynamic disk text box.

14. Type **65536** in the Disk size (in MB) text box.

15. Click the **Create** button.

16. Wait for the virtual hard disk to be created, click **Close**, and then click **OK**.

17. To open the Create New Virtual Machine window, click the **Virtual Machine** menu, and then click **Create**.

18. To name the virtual machine, type **Child** at the end of the path for the New virtual machine name text box.

19. To indicate the parent, click the **Select Parent** drop-down list arrow, and then click **Parent**.

20. Click the **Create multiple virtual machines** check box, click the spin-box until **4** appears, and then click the **Create** button.

21. Wait for the four child virtual machines to be created.

22. Review the entries in the Virtual Machine Manager list.

23. Leave the computer logged on for the next activity.

Activity 7-8: Creating a Dynamically Expanding Virtual Hard Disk

Time Required: 5 minutes

Objective: Create a dynamically expanding virtual hard disk.

Requirements: Completion of Activity 7-4.

Description: In this activity, you will practice creating a dynamically expanding virtual hard disk to be used for a parent for future differencing virtual hard disks.

1. If necessary, log on to your Host PC with a username of **Administrator** and a password of **Secret1**.

2. If necessary, to launch VMRCplus, double-click the **VMRCplus** icon on the desktop.

3. To open the Virtual Disks Manager, click the **Disks** icon in the Virtual Machine Manager window.
4. To create a dynamically expanding virtual hard disk, click the **Dynamic Disk** tab, click the **Select Location** button, navigate to the **C:\Users\Public\Public Documents\Shared Virtual Machines** folder, click the **Make New Folder** button, type **Father** over New Folder, click **OK**, type **Father** at the end of the path in the New dynamic disk text box, type **65536** in the Disk size (in MB) text box, and then click the **Create** button.
5. Verify that the dynamic disk was created in the message box, and then click **Close**.
6. Leave the computer logged on for the next activity.

Activity 7-9: Creating a Differencing Virtual Hard Disk

Time Required: 5 minutes

Objective: Create a differencing virtual hard disk.

Requirements: Completion of Activities 7-5 and 7-8.

Description: In this activity, you will create a differencing virtual hard disk (the child) to be connected to a parent virtual hard disk.

1. If necessary, log on to your Host PC with a username of **Administrator** and a password of **Secret1**.
2. If necessary, to launch VMRCplus, double-click the **VMRCplus** icon on the desktop.
3. To open the Virtual Disks Manager, click the **Disks** icon in the Virtual Machine Manager window.
4. To create a differencing virtual hard disk, click the **Differencing Disk** tab, click the **Select Location** button, navigate to the **C:\Users\Public\Public Documents\Shared Virtual Machines** folder, click the **Make New Folder** button, type **Son** over New Folder, click **OK**, and then type **Son** at the end of the path in the New differencing virtual hard disk text box.
5. To link to the parent virtual hard disk, click the **Select Parent** button, click **Shared Virtual Machines** in the Address bar, double-click the **Father** folder, click **Father.vhd**, click **Open**, and then click the **Create** button.
6. Verify that the differencing disk was created in the message box, and then click **Close**.
7. Leave the computer logged on for the next activity.

Implementing Virtual Networks

With virtual networking, you can connect a virtual machine to another virtual machine to share files, surf the Internet, and more. It is important to know how to use virtual networking so that you can make the best choices for a given situation.

You use the Virtual Networks Manager to create and manage virtual networks. To view the existing virtual networks, click the Virtual Networks icon in the Virtual Machine. Figure 7-32, on the next page, shows the existing virtual networks.

To review and change the settings for a virtual network, click the network and view the settings, as shown in Figure 7-33 on the next page.

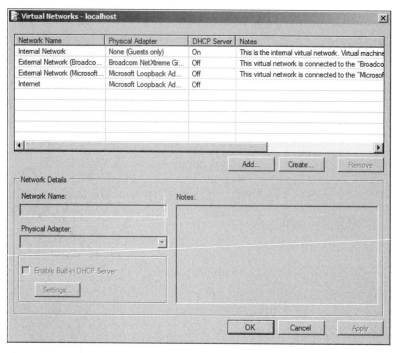

Figure 7-32 Virtual Networks Manager

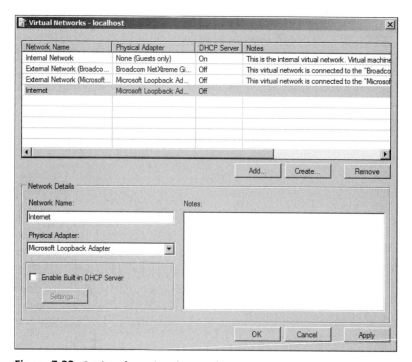

Figure 7-33 Settings for a virtual network

With the Add button, you can register an existing .vnc file. You might need to do this if you were importing a virtual network from another server. The Create button creates a new virtual network. The Remove button unregisters the virtual network and deletes the .vnc file.

To create a new virtual network, click the Create button and complete the entries, as shown in Figure 7-34.

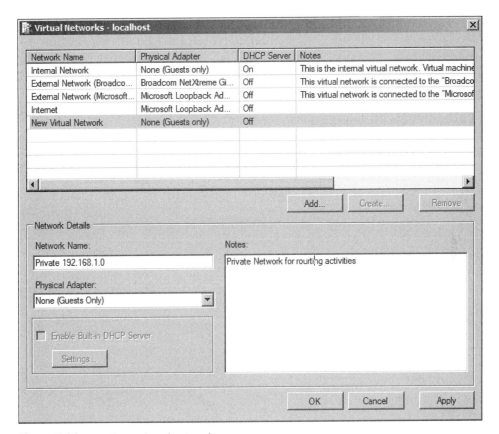

Figure 7-34 Creating a virtual network

By clicking the Physical Adapter drop-down list arrow, you select the adapter to be used by the virtual network. The choices from the Physical Adapter drop-down list are as follows:

- None (Virtual Machines Only)—Internal network for virtual network use.
- Physical adapter in the host computer—Name of external network adapter on the physical computer.
- Microsoft Loopback Adapter—External network installed in the host computer to support a virtual network.

Until you click the Apply button, the DHCP server option is not available. You can turn on the DHCP server by clicking the Enable Built-in DHCP Server check box. You can review and configure the DHCP server settings by clicking the Settings button. Figure 7-35 shows the settings for the private 192.168.1.0 network.

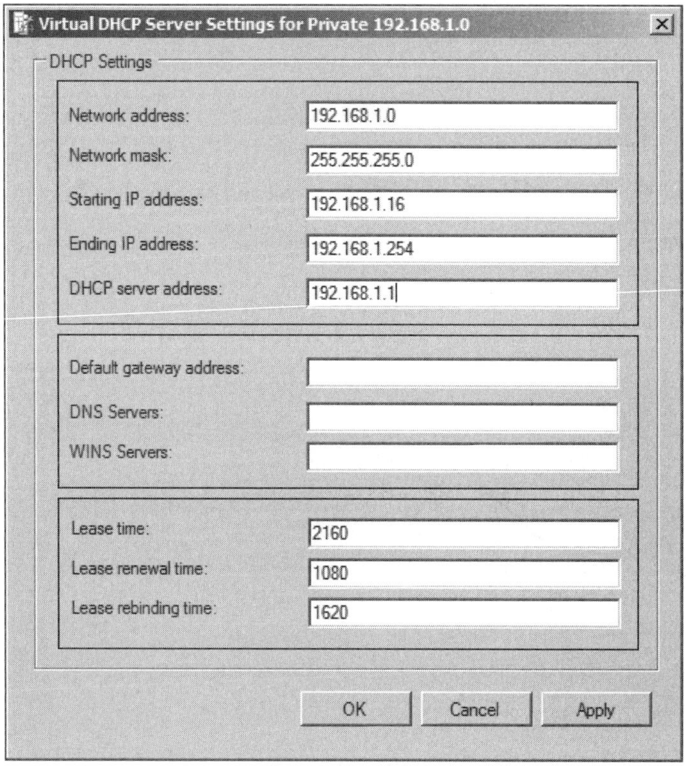

Figure 7-35 Settings for private 192.168.1.0 network

Following the IP addressing conventions of Virtual Server, the first 16 IP addresses were reserved for static IP addresses. These static IP addresses will be used by servers on the private network.

When the DHCP server is enabled, the options in Table 7-5 can be configured for the DHCP server.

Table 7-5 DHCP server settings

DHCP Option	Description
Network address	IP address of this virtual network.
Network mask	Subnet mask for this virtual network.
Starting IP address	First IP address in the range maintained for assignment to clients.
Ending IP address	Last IP address in the range maintained for assignment to clients.
Virtual DHCP server address	IP address of this virtual DHCP server.
Default gateway address	IP address of a local IP router (gateway) that forwards traffic beyond this virtual network.
DNS Servers	IP addresses for DNS servers to which DHCP clients can contact and that they can use to resolve a domain host name query.
WINS Servers	IP addresses of primary and secondary WINS servers for the DHCP client to use for NetBIOS name queries.
IP address lease time	Duration of the IP address lease offered by the server. This defines the length of time during which the client can use the assigned IP address. The minimum value allowed is 60 seconds.
Lease renewal time	Time interval from IP address assignment until the client starts IP address renewal. The minimum value allowed is 30 seconds.
Lease rebinding time	Time interval from IP address assignment until the client starts IP address rebinding. The minimum value allowed is 45 seconds.

Activity 7-10: Creating a Virtual Network

Time Required: 5 minutes

Objective: Create a virtual network for a private network.

Requirements: Completion of Activities 7-1 through 7-2.

Description: In this activity, you will create a private virtual network. This activity is useful to set up a private network for future activities.

1. If necessary, log on to your Host PC with a username of **Administrator** and a password of **Secret1**.
2. If necessary, to launch VMRCplus, double-click the **VMRCplus** icon on the desktop.
3. To open the Virtual Networks Manager, click the **Networks** icon in the Virtual Machine Manager window.
4. To create a new virtual network, click the **Create** button.
5. To name the virtual network, type **Private Network 192.168.1.0** over New Virtual Network in the Network Name text box.
6. To practice specifying the physical network, click the **Physical Adapter** drop-down list arrow, and then click **None** (**Virtual Machines Only**).

7. To enter a note about the network, type **Private network for routing activities** in the Notes text box and then click the **Apply** button.
8. To enable the DHCP server, click the **Enable Built-in DHCP Server** check box.
9. To access the Virtual DHCP Server Settings window, click the **Settings** button.
10. To enter the virtual DHCP server settings, type **172.16.0.0** in the Network address text box, type **172.16.0.16** in the Starting IP address text box, type **172.16.255.254** in the Ending IP address text box, type **172.16.0.1** in the DHCP Server text box, and then click **OK** twice.
11. Leave the computer logged on for the next activity.

Activity 7-11: Removing Virtual Machines from the Virtual Machine Manager

Time Required: 5 minutes

Objective: Remove virtual machines from the Virtual Machines Manager.

Requirements: Completion of Activities 7-1 through 7-9.

Description: In this activity, you will remove the registered virtual machine from the Virtual Machines Manager list. This activity is useful to practice multiple activities from the Virtual Machine Manager. Also, this activity will provide a clean Virtual Machine Manager list for the next chapter.

1. If necessary, log on to your Host PC with a username of **Administrator** and a password of **Secret1**.
2. If necessary, to launch VMRCplus, double-click the **VMRCplus** icon on the desktop.
3. Verify that all of the virtual machines are either Off or Saved. If any virtual machines are running, right-click on the running virtual machine, and then click **Save State**.
4. Wait for the virtual machine state to indicate Saved.
5. To remove the virtual machines, right-click the first virtual machine name, click **Remove**, and then click **Yes**.
6. Repeat Step 5 for the remaining virtual machines.
7. Close the Virtual Machine Manager window.
8. Close any open windows.
9. To shut down Host01, click **Start**, click the arrow next to the Lock button, click **Shut Down**, click the **Option** drop-down list arrow click **Operating System: Reconfiguration (Planned)**, and then click **OK**.

Chapter Summary

- VMRCplus is a Microsoft product that was originally created for use by a tester, and that has proven to be useful in working with virtual machines. The Virtual Machine and Console Managers allow for quick access to manage the virtual machines.

Multiple virtual machines are also easily created from parents and they can be managed through the toolbars that are found in the managers.

- The installation of VMRCplus is similar to other software products from Microsoft. You must download VMRCplus from the Microsoft Web site.
- To create a virtual machine in VMRCplus, you need to use the menu option Virtual Machine in the Virtual Machine Manager window. You must specify several options, including virtual machine name, RAM, and hardware virtualization. You also must create a virtual hard disk and connect the network adapter to a virtual network. Also, the operating system and Virtual Machine Additions must be installed.
- The VMRCplus managers are accessed through the Virtual Machine Manager, which is the main application. The other managers are the Virtual Disks Manager and the Virtual Networks Manager.

Key Terms

parent-child relationship—A differencing virtual hard disk is a virtual hard disk associated with another virtual hard disk in a parent-child relationship. The differencing disk is the child and the associated virtual disk is the parent.

VMRCplus—A free tool developed by Microsoft that allows you to use Virtual Server without using the Virtual Server Administration Web site.

Review Questions

1. When working with parent-child relationships, the parent _____. (Choose all that apply.)
   a. Can only be copied a limited number of times
   b. Is a template for the development of child virtual machines
   c. Is used to install the initial virtual machine operating system
   d. Is still in development

2. The event viewer log provided by VMRCplus _____. (Choose all that apply.)
   a. Outlines the possible source of a problem
   b. Classifies the event viewer as Error, Info, or Warning
   c. Provides the date and time for the event
   d. Links to the Microsoft Web site for additional information

3. VMRCplus is _____. (Choose all that apply.)
   a. An alternative to the Virtual Server Administration Web site
   b. Not supported by Microsoft Support Services
   c. Available through download for free
   d. Only accessible using Internet Explorer

4. Using the Virtual Disks Manager within VMRCplus, you can _____. (Choose all that apply.)
   a. Create a dynamically expanding hard disk
   b. Link a differencing disk to a parent hard disk
   c. Create a floppy disk
   d. Create a fixed-size disk

5. From the Virtual Networks Manager, you _____. (Choose all that apply.)
   a. Use a physical adapter used by the host computer
   b. Configure DHCP settings for a virtual machine-only network
   c. Remove a .vnc file
   d. Use a Microsoft Loopback Adapter

6. Clearing the Disconnect Idle Connections check box _____.
   a. Prevents VMRC Server from dropping a connection to a virtual machine that you have not visited in over 15 minutes
   b. Keeps computers from outside of your network from accessing your virtual machine
   c. Keeps your host operating system from turning off
   d. Should never be done

7. The main application window of VMRCplus is the _____.
   a. Create New Virtual Machine window
   b. Service menu
   c. Virtual Server Administration Web site
   d. Virtual Machine Manager

8. The Tools menu option of Virtual Machine Manager is used to _____.
   a. Delete a virtual machine
   b. Set the VMRCplus behavior options
   c. Review and modify the VMRC settings
   d. Launch VMRCplus Help

9. The Virtual Server menu option of Virtual Machine Manager is used to _____.
   a. Review and modify the security settings
   b. Delete a virtual machine
   c. Launch VMRCplus Help
   d. Review and modify the VMRC settings

10. VMRCplus can _____. (Choose all that apply.)
    a. Only create one virtual machine account at a time
    b. Create multiple virtual machines based upon a parent configuration that uses differencing virtual hard disks for the children
    c. Only use the original virtual machine names provided
    d. Use virtual machine names other than *parent* or *child* when creating multiple guests
11. When a virtual machine is removed by selecting Remove from the Virtual Machine menu, _____. (Choose all that apply.)
    a. You are asked to confirm your decision
    b. The virtual machine is unregistered
    c. The folders and files are deleted and moved to the Recycle Bin
    d. The virtual machine is hidden to keep it from running; the files and folders are not removed from the host computer
12. When a virtual machine is deleted by selecting Delete from the Virtual Machine menu, _____. (Choose all that apply.)
    a. You are asked to confirm your decision
    b. The virtual machine is unregistered
    c. The folders and files are deleted and moved to the Recycle Bin
    d. The virtual machine is hidden to keep it from running; the files and folders are not removed from the host computer
13. You can _____ from the View menu in Virtual Machine Manager.
    a. Review and modify VMRC settings
    b. Launch the Virtual Disks Manager
    c. Display the Virtual Server and host computer properties
    d. Refresh the virtual machine list
14. From the Virtual Server menu in Virtual Server Manager, you can select the task to _____.
    a. Create a virtual machine
    b. Launch the Virtual Disks Manager
    c. Display the Virtual Server and host computer properties
    d. Refresh the virtual machine list
15. A quick way to stop a virtual machine without losing changes is to choose _____ from the Power option drop-down menu.
    a. Save State
    b. Pause/Resume
    c. Reset
    d. Turn Off

16. When allocating CPU resources for virtual machines, you can set a relative weight _____.

    a. Between 1 and 100
    b. Of 100
    c. Between 1 and 10,000
    d. Between 10,000 and 100,000

17. Files with extensions of .iso and .vhd are _____.

    a. Corrupted files
    b. Media files
    c. Only used for temporary data
    d. Read only

18. The toolbar icon that will issue a secure logon request is _____.

    a. Send Text
    b. Advanced Properties
    c. Hardware Properties
    d. Ctrl+Alt+Del

19. To remove a virtual hard disk in VMRCplus, _____.

    a. Select the Remove icon from the Console Manager
    b. Select the Tools option from the Virtual Machine menu
    c. Use Windows Explorer to delete the virtual hard disk
    d. Reboot your system

20. Virtual networks _____. (Choose all that apply.)

    a. Require Virtual PC
    b. Are managed by the Virtual Networks Manager
    c. Follow the IP addressing conventions of Virtual Server
    d. Can be used to access the Internet.

Case Projects

Case 7-1: Comparing VMRCplus and Virtual Server
Your lab supervisor, Ted, has been reading about VMRCplus and is considering having it installed in the new student lab. Now that you have worked with both Virtual Server and VMRCplus, he has asked you to prepare a comparison between VMRCplus and the Virtual Server Web Administration Web site. He wants to know how the two products differ in terms of their ease of use when creating and managing virtual machines.

Case 7-2: Building Parent-Child Relationships
VMRCplus can assist in the building of parent-child virtual machine relationships. Prepare a procedure to produce virtual machines for two or more children. Include steps to load the operating system(s).

Case 7-3: Documenting Errors
A screen capture can be invaluable when an error occurs in your virtual networks. Develop a procedure to save a virtual machine screen display within VMRCplus. Include the steps to send the screen shot to another networked computer.

chapter 8

Implementing the Classroom.local Virtual Network

After reading this chapter and completing the exercises, you will be able to:

- Describe the Classroom.local network
- Implement a local network for Classroom.local
- Implement directory services for Classroom.local
- Configure domain name system services for Classroom.local

In the previous three chapters, you learned a great deal about Virtual Server and related software tools, such as VMRCplus. In this chapter, you will put this information to work as you build a virtual demonstration network for the fictitious Classroom environment.

The first task is to describe the local network for Classroom.local. You must define the roles for the five virtual machines with their operating system requirements. You must also define the IP addressing scheme to ensure proper communications among the virtual machines.

After defining the five virtual machines, you will install and configure them. To ensure that the virtual machines can communicate in a network, you will test using communication utilities.

The last task implements Active Directory Domain Services (AD DS) and Domain Name System (DNS) services to provide centralized security management of the virtual machines and other network objects. You will take steps to bring the five virtual machines into a cohesive network. You will configure DNS services to support a second DNS server to provide redundancy.

Describing the Classroom.local Virtual Network

Classroom is a fictitious company headquartered in Dallas. As the IT manager for Classroom, you will be managing and expanding the Classroom.local network. Classroom uses Microsoft products and builds its network around Microsoft Windows Server.

Classroom is a learning environment that enables students to experiment with the various roles of virtual machines that they will encounter in the real world. Virtual Server is commonly deployed in these environments:

- Server consolidation—Many enterprises today have numerous departmental or branch office servers dedicated to running applications that only partially use the servers' available resources. This costly situation can be addressed by deploying Virtual Server to consolidate such applications onto a single physical server.

- Application migration—Many enterprises run line-of-business applications that require older, often obsolete operating systems. Virtual Server allows you to move applications running on older hardware and operating systems, such as Microsoft Windows 2000 Server, onto virtual machines on newer systems running Windows Server 2008 operating systems, without rewriting the application.

- Application development—Enterprises are looking for ways to accelerate application development, while at the same time reducing costs and maintaining a high level of quality. However, test coverage for high-quality applications requires replicating production environments in isolated test environments, straining budgets and schedules. Virtual Server can be used in situations that require rapid and frequent server reconfiguration, as required with development and testing, product demonstrations, and training.

Although there are a number of ways to implement a virtual network, the initial network design Classroom has chosen focuses on the roles found in all networks. The initial network diagram is shown in Figure 8-1. These virtual machines will communicate with one another over a local virtual network.

The three servers (Server-01, Server-02, and Server-03) are virtual machines running Windows Server 2008. The virtual machines, Client-01 and Client-02, are desktop computers running

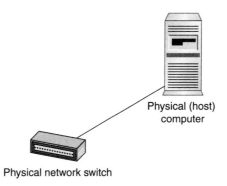
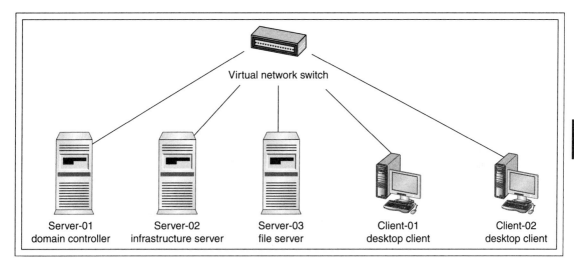

Figure 8-1 Initial network diagram for Classroom.local

Microsoft Windows Vista Business. These five virtual machines share a virtual network; the physical (host) computer is running Windows Server 2008 and Virtual Server 2005 SP1. To create and manage these virtual machines, Classroom deploys VMRCplus.

Begin by discovering the role of these computers and operating system requirements in the Classroom.local network.

Server-01 Role—Domain Controller

Server-01 is the virtual machine that manages the Classroom.local domain. You learned in Chapter 4 that a domain is a logical group of computers that shares access to network resources with centralized administration and security policies. Also, you learned that the domain controller is the server that responds to security authentication requests. A directory service is a software application that stores and organizes information about a computer network's users and network resources, and that allows network administrators to manage users' access to the resources. Active Directory Domain Services is the native directory service included with Windows Server 2008. You will implement the domain controller role by promoting Server-01 to function as a domain controller.

In Chapter 4, you learned about the Domain Name System (DNS). DNS lets computers locate other computers and services using user-friendly names by translating the common names that people readily understand (for example, *www.microsoft.com*) to the IP addresses that computers understand (for example, 207.46.193.254). Active Directory Domain Services uses DNS to maintain domain-naming structures and to locate network resources. DNS maintains databases of IP addresses for host names. Active Directory Domain Services is designed to take advantage of DNS's powerful capabilities, so AD DS names must follow standard DNS naming conventions. You will implement the DNS role on Server-01 for the Classroom.local domain as part of establishing Server-01 as a domain controller (installing the AD DS service).

Server-02 Role—Infrastructure Server

Server-02 is an **infrastructure server**—a server that provides network services like DNS and DHCP. Recall that Dynamic Host Configuration Protocol (DHCP) is a protocol for assigning dynamic IP addresses for computers on a network. You will learn more about DHCP in Chapter 9. On Server-02, you will implement a backup for the DNS service installed with AD DS on Server-01.

Server-03 Role—File Server

Server-03 serves as a file server—a server that is responsible for the central storage and management of data files so that other computers on the Classroom.local network can access these files. So that it can participate in AD DS security, you must join Server-03 to the Classroom.local domain. As a domain member, Server03 coordinates the security access of its files with AD DS.

Client-01 Role—Desktop Client

Client-01 is a desktop client that will be running software applications such as Microsoft Office. These software applications will need to access shared folders and files on the network file server. The desktop client relies on the servers located on the Classroom.local domain. Server-01, with Active Directory Domain Services and DNS, helps locate network resources and controls security access to these network resources. Server-02 provides the IP address configurations. Server-03 holds the data files that Client-01's applications require.

Client-02 Role—Desktop Client

Client-02's role is the same as Client-01. Client-02 relies on the Windows Server 2008 virtual servers for the same services as Client-01. You will use Client-02 in Chapter 9.

Operating System Requirements

When sizing RAM and hard disk space, you need to take into consideration the roles that the particular virtual machines will be playing in your network. Table 8-1 presents a summarization of these two critical variables for the virtual machines in the Classroom.local network.

You will use the information in Table 8-1 to complete Activity 8-2, where you create these virtual machines.

Table 8-1 Operating system requirements

Virtual machine	Role	Operating system	RAM requirement	Operating system hard disk requirement
Server-01	Domain controller	Windows Server 2008	640 MB	65,536 MB
Server-02	Infrastructure server	Windows Server 2008	640 MB	65,536 MB
Server-03	File server	Windows Server 2008	512 MB	65,536 MB
Client-01	Desktop client	Windows Vista Business	512 MB	65,536 MB
Client-02	Desktop client	Windows Vista Business	512 MB	65,536 MB

Activity 8-1: Creating the Virtual Machines for the Servers

Time Required: 15 minutes

Objective: Create the three virtual machines for the three virtual servers.

Requirements: Completion of Activities 7-1, 7-2, and 7-3 where you learned to use VMRCplus.

Description: In this activity, you will create the three virtual machines (Server-01, Server-02, and Server-03) for Classroom.local. You will create a parent virtual machine, called Server, and use it as the basis for the three child virtual machines.

1. If necessary, log on to your host PC with a username of **Administrator** and a password of **Secret1**.
2. To launch VMRCplus, double-click the **VMRCplus** icon on the desktop.

Creating the Parent Virtual Machine

3. To open the Create New Virtual Machine window, click the **Virtual Machine** menu, and then click **Create**.
4. To name the virtual machine, type **Server** at the end of the path for the New virtual machine name text box. To provide notes for this virtual machine, type the use for the virtual machine (or other useful information) in the Notes text box.
5. To specify the amount of RAM, type **640** in the Memory text box.
6. If the physical computer does not have hardware virtualization, clear the **Enable hardware-assisted virtualization** check box.
7. To avoid creating the two default SCSI virtual hard disks, check the **Do not create virtual hard disks** check box.
8. To create the virtual machine, click the **Create** button.
9. Wait for the Server Settings window to open.
10. To remove the SCSI adapters, click the **Number of SCSI Adapters** drop-down list arrow, and click 0.
11. To access the Virtual Disks Manager to create a virtual hard disk, right-click the **IDE0:0** line, and select **Create a New Disk Here**.

12. Wait for the Virtual Disks Manager window to open.
13. To name the virtual hard disk, type **Server** at the end of the path for the New dynamically expanding virtual hard disk text box.
14. Type **65536** in the Disk size (in MB) text box.
15. Click the **Create** button.
16. Wait for the virtual hard disk to be created.
17. Review the creation message in the message box, and then click **Close**.
18. To connect to the virtual network, click the **Virtual Network Adapter for NIC 1** drop-down list arrow, and select **External Network (Microsoft Loopback Adapter)** for this virtual machine.
19. Review the settings, and click **OK**.

Creating the Three Child Virtual Machines

20. To open the Create New Virtual Machine window, click the **Virtual Machine** menu, and then click **Create**.
21. To name the virtual machine, type **Server** at the end of the path for the New virtual machine name text box.
22. To specify the parent on which to base the child, click the **Select Parent** drop-down list arrow, and then click **Server**.
23. Click the **Create multiple virtual machines** check box, click the spin box until **3** appears, and then click the **Create** button.
24. Wait for the three child virtual machines to be created.
25. Review the entries in the Virtual Machine Manager list.
26. Leave the computer logged on for the next activity.

Activity 8-2: Creating the Virtual Machines for Desktop Clients

Time Required: 15 minutes

Objective: Create the two child desktop clients.

Requirements: Completion of Activities 7-1, 7-2, 7-3, and 8-1.

Description: In this activity, you will create the two client virtual machines (Client-01 and Client-02) for Classroom.local. You will create a parent, called Client, and then create the two child virtual machines based on the Client parent.

1. If necessary, log on to your host PC with a username of **Administrator** and a password of **Secret1**.
2. If necessary, to launch VMRCplus, double-click the **VMRCplus** icon on the desktop.

Describing the Classroom.local Virtual Network   **307**

Creating the Parent Virtual Machine

3. To open the Create New Virtual Machine window, click the **Virtual Machine** menu, and then click **Create**.
4. To name the virtual machine, type **Client** at the end of the path for the New virtual machine name text box.
5. To provide notes for this virtual machine, type the use for the virtual machine (or other useful information) in the Notes text box.
6. To specify the amount of RAM, type **512** in the Memory text box.
7. If the physical computer does not have hardware virtualization, clear the **Enable hardware-assisted virtualization** check box.
8. To avoid creating the two default SCSI virtual hard disks, check the **Do not create virtual hard disks** check box.
9. To create the virtual machine, click the **Create** button.
10. Wait for the Client Settings window to open.
11. To remove the SCSI adapters, click the **Number of SCSI Adapters** drop-down list arrow, and click 0.
12. To access the Virtual Disks Manager to create a virtual hard disk, right-click the **IDE0:0** line, and select **Create a New Disk Here**.
13. Wait for the Virtual Disks Manager window to open.
14. To name the virtual hard disk, type **Client** at the end of the path for the New dynamically expanding virtual hard disk text box.
15. Type **65536** in the Disk size (in MB) text box.
16. Click the **Create** button.
17. Wait for the virtual hard disk to be created.
18. Review the creation message in the message box, and then click **Close**.
19. To connect to the virtual network, click the **Virtual Network Adapter for NIC 1** drop-down list arrow, and select **External Network (Microsoft Loopback Adapter)** for this virtual machine.
20. Review the settings, and click **OK**.

Creating the Two Child Virtual Machines

21. To open the Create New Virtual Machine window, click the **Virtual Machine** menu, and then click **Create**.
22. To name the virtual machine, type **Client** at the end of the path for the New virtual machine name text box.
23. To indicate the parent, click the **Select Parent** drop-down list arrow, and then click **Client**.
24. Click the **Create multiple virtual machines** check box, and then click the **Create** button.
25. Wait for the two child virtual machines to be created.

26. Review the entries in the Virtual Machine Manager list.
27. Leave the computer logged on for the next activity.

Implementing the Classroom.local Network

In a later activity, you will be installing the two operating systems for the Classroom.local network. Before you can begin these installations, you must define the communications scheme.

Classroom.local Network Diagram

Figure 8-2 shows devices for the network. Locate the virtual network switch in the middle of the diagram. The five virtual machines, Server-01, Server-02, Server-03, Client-01, and Client02, access the Classroom.local network through this virtual switch. The host computer, Host01, contains a Microsoft Loopback Adapter. This Microsoft Loopback Adapter also participates as a member of the virtual network.

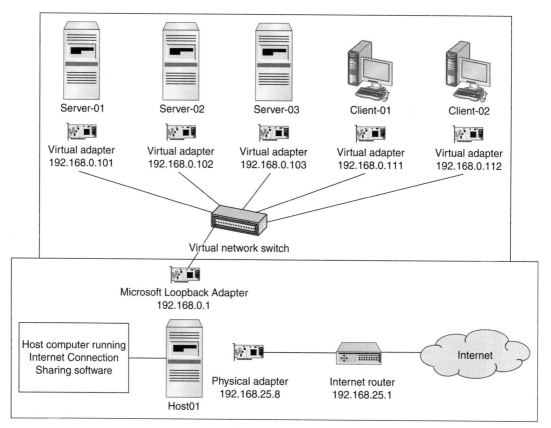

Figure 8-2 Detailed network diagram for Classroom.local

The host computer runs the Internet Connection Sharing (ICS) software (recall that you learned about ICS and installed it in Chapter 6). With ICS, you can connect the three virtual machines to the Internet using the Internet connection provided by the host computer. ICS routes packets between the two network adapters on the host—the physical network adapter and the Microsoft Loopback Adapter. In addition, ICS supports DNS name resolution, which is used to resolve the computers on the Internet to IP addresses.

To begin, remember that servers should always use static IP addressing to ensure they can be reached by other machines at all times (even in the event of a DHCP failure). To further ensure and simplify communication between the virtual machines, the remaining virtual machines should also use static IP addressing. By using static IP addresses, you will always know the IP address configurations for the virtual machines. This simplifies the configuration and testing of your virtual machines. Table 8-2 shows the initial IP address configurations for the five virtual machines and the host computer.

Table 8-2 Summary of IP addressing

Virtual machine/ Computer	Adapter type	Assigned IP address	Subnetmask	Gateway address	DNS address
Server-01	Virtual adapter	192.168.0.101	255.255.255.0	192.168.0.1	192.168.0.101
Server-02	Virtual adapter	192.168.0.102	255.255.255.0	192.168.0.1	192.168.0.101
Server-03	Virtual adapter	192.168.0.103	255.255.255.0	192.168.0.1	192.168.0.101
Client-01	Virtual adapter	192.168.0.111	255.255.255.0	192.168.0.1	192.168.0.101
Client-02	Virtual adapter	192.168.0.112	255.255.255.0	192.168.0.1	192.168.0.101
Host01	Microsoft Loopback Adapter	192.168.0.1	255.255.255.0	Provided by ICS	Provided by ICS
Host01	Physical adapter	192.168.25.4 Provided by Internet router	255.255.255.0	192.168.25.1 Provided by Internet router	192.168.25.1 Provided by Internet router

Each virtual machine is assigned a unique static IP address, for example, Server-01 has 192.168.0.101. All Internet-bound traffic travels through the gateway at IP address 192.168.0.1. As all of the virtual machines will access the future DNS service on Server-01, the DNS address for the five virtual machines is 192.168.0.101.

Installing Operating Systems

In the activities that follow, you will install the operating systems for the two "parent" virtual machines—Server and Client. Although you have previously installed these operating systems in the activities in earlier chapters, pay special attention to the configurations in these activities. Failure to do so might make future activities difficult or impossible to complete.

Configuring the Child Servers

When you create a differencing virtual hard disk, you are asked to specify an existing virtual hard disk, called the parent virtual hard disk, to which the differencing virtual hard disk points. When the virtual machine uses this differencing (or child) virtual hard disk, the changes are stored in the differencing hard disk.

Consider a situation where you configure parent and child disks for the Server-01, Server-02, and Server-03 virtual machines, as shown in Figure 8-3. Each child will boot from the parent disk. As changes occur, the changes are written to the appropriate child disk.

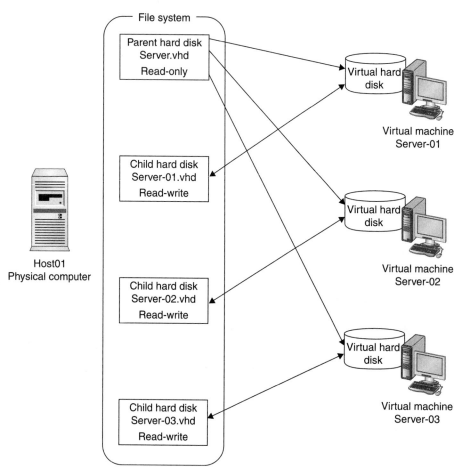

Figure 8-3 Virtual hard disks for parent and child servers

The main benefit of using differencing disks is faster creation of multiple virtual machines. You will use these techniques to create three virtual machines from one parent. You will install Windows Server 2008 on the parent virtual machine and use differencing disks for the three servers. Recall that OS installation is time consuming. Installing Windows Server 2008 only once for the parent reduces the time to install the servers' operating systems to one-third of the time.

Using Sysprep As you learned in Chapter 3, the System Preparation (Sysprep) tool prepares an installation of Windows for duplication. When you use differencing virtual hard disks, you are duplicating the parent virtual hard disk. The Sysprep program was copied to the virtual hard disk during the installation of Windows Server 2008. Sysprep removes all system-specific information from an installed Windows image, including the computer security identifier (SID). Figure 8-4 shows the Sysprep command.

Figure 8-4 Running Sysprep

Out-of-Box Experience When you first start a virtual machine that has been Sysprepped, you duplicate the out-of-box experience that occurs when a user first turns on a new computer with a Windows operating system installed (recall that the /oobe switch included in the Sysprep command causes Windows Welcome to run the next time the computer boots). The user typically must follow steps to set up the new computer.

Although Sysprep enables you to skip the file copies and other time-consuming activities related to installing a new virtual machine, you will need to repeat these tasks for each differenced installation:

- Complete the region setup.
- Provide a product key.
- Accept the license terms.
- Name the computer.
- Verify the time zone, date, and time.

This abbreviated task list is easier to complete than the many steps required when starting from scratch with the Windows Server 2008 installation DVD.

Saved State Rather than shutting down a virtual machine at the end of a session, you can save valuable time by using the Saved State option. To save the state of a running virtual machine, click the Control menu on the Console Manager window, click Save State Options, and then click Save State. Another way to do this is to click the Power Options icon for the running virtual machine and then click Save State. With the Saved State, you save the current state of the virtual machine and stop the virtual machine from running. This creates a temporary file in the same location as the virtual machine configuration files with a **.vsv** extension that contains state information. When the virtual machine is restored from the saved state, it returns to the condition that it was in when its state was saved. Note that Pause/Resume does not save the state of the running virtual machine. You will want to use the Saved State option because it is faster than using Shutdown/Restart.

Do not use saved states on a virtual machine configured as a domain controller. Problems might occur with replication because you can revert the virtual machine to an earlier state.

Activity 8-3: Installing Windows Server 2008 in a Virtual Machine

Time Required: 60–90 minutes

Objective: Install Windows Server 2008 in the parent virtual machine Server.

Requirements: Completion of Activities 8-1 and 8-2 and the Windows Server 2008 DVD.

Description: In this activity, you will install Windows Server 2008 for the parent virtual machine server.

1. If necessary, log on to your Host PC with a username of **Administrator** and a password of **Secret1**.
2. To launch VMRCplus, double-click the **VMRCplus** icon on the desktop.
3. To start the server virtual machine, click **Server**, and then click the **Turn On** icon.
4. To view the display for the virtual machine, click the **Server** thumbnail to the right.
5. Wait for the Console Manager to open.
6. Insert the Microsoft Windows Server 2008 DVD into the CD/DVD drive.
7. To mount the DVD and start the installation, click the **Media** menu, click **Mount Host CD/DVD Drive**, click the **Control** menu, click **Reset**, and then click **Yes**.
8. Wait for Windows to load files.
9. To activate the virtual machine, click in the Server virtual machine window.

At some time during this installation, the Virtual Machine Additions is not installed on this virtual machine dialog box might appear. If this occurs, check the Don't show this message again check box, and then click OK.

10. When the regional settings dialog box opens, verify the language, time and currency, and keyboard. Correct as needed, and then click **Next**.
11. Click the **Install now** link.
12. To indicate that this virtual machine is using an evaluation copy, wait for the Type your product key for activation dialog box, clear the **Automatically activate Windows when I'm online** check box, click **Next**, and then click **No**.
13. To indicate the version to install, click **Windows Server 2008 Enterprise (Full Installation)**, check the **I have selected the edition of Windows that I purchased** check box, and then click **Next**.
14. When the Please read the license terms dialog box opens, check the **I accept the license terms** check box, and then click **Next**.

15. To start the installation, click **Custom (advanced)**.
16. When the Where do you want to install Windows? message appears, click **Next**.
17. Wait for Windows to copy and expand files, install features and updates, and restart to complete the installation.
18. Ignore the Press any key to boot from CD or DVD message.
19. Wait while Windows prepares to start for the first time and to complete the installation.
20. To activate the virtual machine, click in the Server virtual machine.
21. When the user's password must be changed before logging on the first time message appears, click **OK**. Type **Secret1** in the New password text box, press **Tab**, type **Secret1** in the Confirm password text box, press **Enter**, and then click **OK**.
22. To set the time zone, click the **Set time zone** link, click the **Change time zone** button, click the appropriate time zone, click **OK**, review the date and time and change if needed, and then click **OK**.
23. To provide an IP configuration, click the **Configure networking** link, right-click **Local Area Connection**, click **Properties**, clear the **Internet Protocol Version 6 (TCP/IPv6)** check box, click **OK**, and then close the Network Connections window.
24. To provide a computer name, click the **Provide computer name and domain** link, click the **Change** button, type **Server** in the Computer name text box, click **OK** twice, click **Close**, and then click the **Restart Now** button.
25. Wait for the virtual machine to restart.
26. Ignore the Press any key to boot from CD or DVD message.
27. Press right **Alt+delete** and log on to your Server virtual machine with a username of **Administrator** and a password of **Secret1**.
28. To enable network discovery and file sharing, click **Start**, right-click **Network**, click **Properties**, click the **Network discovery** drop-down list arrow, click the **Turn on network discovery** option button, click the **Apply** button, click the **No, make the network that I am connected to a private network** link, click the **File sharing** drop-down list arrow, click the **Turn on file sharing** option button, click the **Apply** button, and then close the Network and Sharing Center window.
29. Click the **Do not show this window at logon** check box, and close the Initial Configuration Tasks window.
30. To open a command prompt window, click **Start**, and then click **Command Prompt**.
31. To launch the Sysprep program, type **cd \windows\system32\sysprep**, press **Enter**, type **sysprep /oobe /generalize**, and then press **Enter**.
32. Wait for Sysprep to finish running and the Server virtual machine to shut down.
33. To protect the virtual hard disk by setting file attributes to read-only, click **Start**, click **Computer**, click the **Public** folder, double-click the **Public Documents** folder, double-click the **Shared Virtual Machines** folder, double-click the **Server** folder, right-click the **Server** file (the .vhd file), click the **Properties** button, click the **Read-only** check box, click **OK**, and then close the **Server** window.
34. Leave the computer logged on for the next activity.

Activity 8-4: Configuring the Child Servers

Time Required: 60–90 minutes

Objective: Start and configure the child servers (Server-01, Server-02, and Server-03).

Requirements: Completion of Activities 8-1 and 8-3.

Description: In this activity, you will start each of the child servers and complete the configuration for each child virtual machine, which will run Windows Server 2008.

1. If necessary, log on to your Host PC with a username of **Administrator** and a password of **Secret1**.
2. To launch VMRCplus, double-click the **VMRCplus** icon on the desktop.

Do not start the Server parent. To do so will corrupt all of the child servers. If you do start the parent, you will see the message "The parent hard disk appears to have been modified without using the differencing virtual hard disk" in the event log.

Configuring Server-01

3. To start the Server-01 virtual machine, click **Server-01**, and then click the **Turn On** icon.
4. To view the display for the virtual machine, click the **VM Console** icon.
5. Wait for the Console Manager to open.

Several black screens will appear between the initial steps. Do not panic!

6. Wait for Windows to run for the first time.
7. When the splash screen appears with the Please wait message, wait for Windows to start configuration.
8. Wait for Windows to restart.
9. Ignore the Press any key to boot from CD or DVD message.
10. Wait for Windows to complete configuration.
11. Click in the **Server-01** virtual machine.
12. When the regional settings dialog box opens, verify the language, time and currency, and keyboard. Correct as needed, and then click **Next**.
13. To indicate that this virtual machine is using an evaluation copy, wait for the Type your product key for activation dialog box, clear the **Automatically activate Windows when I'm online** check box, and then click **Next**.

14. When the Please read the license terms dialog box opens, check the **I accept the license terms** check box, type **Server-01** in the Type a computer name (for example, Office-PC) text box, and then click **Start**.

15. When the user's password must be changed before logging on the first time message appears, click **OK**. Type **Secret1** in the New password text box, press **Tab**, type **Secret1** in the Confirm password text box, press **Enter**, and then click **OK**.

16. Wait for the Server Manager window to appear.

17. To open the Local Area Connection properties dialog box, click the **View Network Connections** link, right click **Local Area Connection**, and then click **Properties**.

18. To provide an IP configuration, clear the **Internet Protocol Version 6 (TCP/IPv6)** check box, click **Internet Protocol Version 4 (TCP/IPv4)**, click the **Properties** button, click the **Use the following IP address** option button, type **192.168.0.101** in the IP address text box, press **Tab** twice, type **192.168.0.1** in the Default gateway text box, press **Tab** twice, type **192.168.0.101** in the Preferred DNS server text box, click **OK**, click **Close**, and then close the Network Connections window.

19. Click the **Restart** link (located after the Console cannot refresh until computer is restarted message) and then click **Yes**.

20. Press right **Alt+delete** and log on to the Server-01 virtual machine with a username of **Administrator** and a password of **Secret1**.

21. Wait for the desktop to be displayed.

22. To save the current state of the server, press right **Alt**, click the **Save State** icon (first icon on the Console Manager tool bar).

Configure Server-02

23. Repeat Steps 3 through 16 using Server-02 in place of Server-01.

24. To open the Local Area Connection properties dialog box, click the **View Network Connections** link, right-click **Local Area Connection**, and then click **Properties**.

25. To provide an IP configuration, clear the **Internet Protocol Version 6 (TCP/IPv6)** check box, click **Internet Protocol Version 4 (TCP/IPv4)**, click the **Properties** button, click the **Use the following IP address** option button, type **192.168.0.102** in the IP address text box, press **Tab** twice, type **192.168.0.1** in the Default gateway text box, press **Tab** twice, type **192.168.0.101** in the Preferred DNS server text box, click **OK**, click **Close**, and then close the Network Connections window.

26. Repeat Steps 19 through 22 using Server-02 in place of Server-01.

Configuring Server-03

27. Repeat Steps 3 through 16 using Server-03 in place of Server-01.

28. To open the Local Area Connection properties dialog box, click the **View Network Connections** link, right-click **Local Area Connection**, and then click **Properties**.

29. To provide an IP configuration, clear the **Internet Protocol Version 6 (TCP/IPv6)** check box, click **Internet Protocol Version 4 (TCP/IPv4)**, click the **Properties** button, click

the **Use the following IP address** option button, type **192.168.0.103** in the IP address text box, press **Tab** twice, type **192.168.0.1** in the Default gateway text box, press **Tab** twice, type **192.168.0.101** in the Preferred DNS server text box, click **OK**, click **Close**, and then close the Network Connections window.

30. Repeat Steps 19 through 22 using Server-03 in place of Server-01.
31. Leave the computer logged on for the next activity.

Activity 8-5: Installing Windows Vista Business

Time Required: 60–90 minutes

Objective: Install Windows Vista Business in the parent virtual machine client.

Requirements: Completion of Activities 8-1 and 8-2 and the Windows Vista Business DVD.

Description: In this activity, you will install Microsoft Vista Business for the parent virtual machine Client.

1. If necessary, log on to your Host PC with a username of **Administrator** and a password of **Secret1**.
2. To launch VMRCplus, double-click the **VMRCplus** icon on the desktop.
3. To start the client virtual machine, click **Client**, and then click the **Turn On** icon.
4. To view the display for the virtual machine, click on the **VM Console** icon.
5. Insert the Windows Vista Business DVD into the DVD drive.
6. If the Autoplay window opens, close the window.
7. To mount the DVD and start the installation, click the **Media** menu, click **Mount Host CD/DVD Drive**, click the **Control** menu, click **Reset**, and then click **Yes**.
8. Wait for Windows Vista to load files.
9. When the splash screen is displayed, click the mouse in the virtual machine window.
10. When the regional settings dialog box opens, verify the language, time and currency, and keyboard. Correct as needed, and then click **Next**.
11. To start the installation, click the **Install now** link.
12. Wait for Windows Vista to load files.

At some time during this installation, the Virtual Machine Additions is not installed on this virtual machine dialog box might appear. If this occurs, check the Don't show this message again check box, and then click OK.

13. To indicate that you want to install an evaluation copy of Windows Vista and when the Type your product key for activation dialog box opens, clear the **Automatically activate Windows when I'm online** check box, click **Next**, and then click **No**.
14. When the Select the edition of Windows that you purchased dialog box opens, click **Windows Vista Business**, check the **I have selected the edition of Windows that I purchased** check box, and then click **Next**.

15. When the Please read the license terms dialog box opens, check the **I accept the license terms** check box, and then click **Next**.
16. When the Which type of installation do you want? dialog box opens, click **Custom (advanced)**.
17. When the Where do you want to install Windows? dialog box opens, click **Next**.
18. Wait for Windows to copy and expand files, install features and updates, and then restart to complete the installation.
19. Ignore the Press any key to boot from CD or DVD message.
20. Wait while Windows prepares to start for the first time and complete installation.
21. When the Choose a user name and picture dialog box opens, type **Student** in the Type a user name (for example, John) text box, press **Tab**, type **Secret1** in the Type a password (recommended) text box, press **Tab**, type **Secret1** in the Retype your password text box, and then click **Next**.
22. When the Type a computer name and choose a desktop background dialog box opens, type **Client** in the Type a computer name (for example, Office-PC) text box, and then click **Next**.
23. When the Help protect Windows automatically dialog box opens, click **Install important updates only**.
24. To set the time zone, click the **Time zone** drop-down list arrow, click the appropriate time zone, review the date and time and correct as needed, and then click **Next**.
25. When the Select your computer's current location dialog box opens, click **Work**, and then click **Start**.
26. Wait for the Password screen, type **Secret1**, and then press **Enter**.
27. Wait for Windows Vista to prepare your desktop and set personalized settings.
28. Wait for Windows Vista to complete configuration and to download and install updates.
29. If the Welcome Center window opens, close the Welcome Center window.
30. Click **Start**, click **Control Panel**, and then click the **View network status and tasks** link under Network and Internet.
31. To enable file sharing, click the **File sharing** drop-down list arrow, click the **Turn on file sharing** option button, and then click the **Apply** button.
32. When the User Account Control dialog box opens, click the **Continue** button.
33. Wait for the File sharing setup to complete and then close the Network and Sharing Center window.
34. To open a command prompt window, click **Start**, type **cmd** in the Start Search text box, and then press **Enter**.
35. To launch the Sysprep program, type **cd\windows\system32\sysprep**, press **Enter**, type **sysprep /oobe /generalize**, and then press **Enter**.
36. When the User Account Control dialog box opens, click the **Continue** button.
37. Wait for Sysprep to complete and the client virtual machine to shut down.

38. To protect the virtual hard disk by setting file attributes to read-only, click **Start,** click **Computer,** click the **Public** folder, double-click the **Public Documents** folder, double-click the **Shared Virtual Machines** folder, double-click the **Client** folder, right-click the **Client.vhd** file, click **Properties,** click the **Read-only** check box, click **OK,** and then close the Client window.

39. Leave the computer logged on for the next activity.

Activity 8-6: Configuring the Child Clients

Time Required: 60–90 minutes

Objective: Start and configure the child clients (Client-01 and Client-02).

Requirements: Completion of Activities 8-1, 8-2, and 8-5.

Description: In this activity, you will start each of the child clients and complete the configuration for each child virtual machine, which will run Windows Vista Business.

1. If necessary, log on to your host PC with a username of **Administrator** and a password of **Secret1**.
2. To launch VMRCplus, double-click the **VMRCplus** icon on the desktop.

Do not start the Client parent. To do so will corrupt all of the child clients.

Configuring Client-01

3. To start the client virtual machine, click **Client-01,** and then click the **Turn On** icon.
4. To view the display for the virtual machine, click on the **VM Console** icon.
5. Wait for the Console Manager to open.
6. Click in the **Client-01** virtual machine.
7. Wait for Windows to run for the first time.
8. When the splash appears with Please wait, wait for Windows to start configuration.
9. Wait for Windows to restart.
10. Ignore the Press any key to boot from CD or DVD message.
11. Wait for Windows to complete configuration.
12. Click in the **Client-01** virtual machine.
13. When the regional settings dialog box opens, verify the language, time and currency, and keyboard. Correct as needed, and then click **Next**.
14. To indicate that this virtual machine is using an evaluation copy, wait for the Type your product key for activation dialog box, clear the **Automatically activate Windows when I'm online** check box, click **Next,** and, if necessary, then click **No**.

15. When the Please read the license terms dialog box opens, check the **I accept the license terms** check box, and then click **Next**.
16. When the Choose a user name and picture dialog box opens, type **Student1** in the Type a user name (for example, John) text box, press **Tab**, type **Secret1** in the Type a password (recommended) text box, press **Tab**, type **Secret1** in the Retype your password text box, and then click **Next**.
17. When the Type a computer name and choose a desktop background dialog box opens, type **Client-01** in the Type a computer name (for example, Office-PC) text box, and then click **Next**.
18. When the Help protect Windows automatically dialog box opens, click **Ask me later**.
19. When the Review your time and date settings dialog box opens, review the settings and correct as needed, and then click **Next**.
20. When the Select your computer's current location dialog box opens, click **Work**.
21. When the Thank you dialog box opens, click the **Start** button.
22. Log on to your Client-01 virtual machine with a username of **Student** and a password of **Secret1**.
23. If the Welcome Center window opens, close the Welcome Center window.
24. To provide an IP configuration, click **Start**, click **Control Panel**, click the View **network status and tasks** link under Network and Internet, click the View **status** link under Network (Private network), and then click the **Properties** button.
25. When the User Account Control dialog box opens, click the **Continue** button.
26. Clear the **Internet Protocol Version 6 (TCP/IPv6)** check box, click Internet Protocol Version 4 (TCP/IPv4), click the **Properties** button, click the Use the following IP address option button, type **192.168.0.111** in the IP address text box, press **Tab** twice, type **192.168.0.1** in the Default gateway text box, press **Tab** twice, type **192.168.0.101** in the Preferred DNS server text box, click **OK**, and then click **Close** twice.
27. Close the Network and Sharing Center window.
28. To save the current state of the client, press right **Alt**, and click the **Save State** icon (first icon on the Console Manager toolbar).

Configuring Client-02

29. Repeat Steps 3 through 23 using Client-02 in place of Client-01.
30. To provide an IP configuration, click **Start**, click **Control Panel**, click the View **network status and tasks** link under Network and Internet, click the View **status** link under Network (Private network), and then click the **Properties** button.
31. When the User Account Control dialog box opens, click the **Continue** button.
32. Clear the **Internet Protocol Version 6 (TCP/IPv6)** check box, click Internet Protocol Version 4 (TCP/IPv4), click the **Properties** button, click the Use the following **IP address** option button, type **192.168.0.112** in the IP address text box, press **Tab** twice, type

192.168.0.1 in the Default gateway text box, press **Tab** twice, type **192.168.0.101** in the Preferred DNS server text box, click **OK**, and then click **Close** twice.

33. Close the Network and Sharing Center window.

34. To save the current state of the server, press right **Alt**, click the **Save State** icon (first icon on the Console Manager toolbar).

35. Leave the computer logged on for the next activity.

Virtual Machine Additions

Virtual Machine Additions (VMA) can only be added after the operating system is installed and configured. For this reason, when working with differencing virtual hard disks, it is recommended to install Virtual Machine Additions in the child virtual machines. You will be installing VMA in Activity 8-7.

Activity 8-7: Installing Virtual Machine Additions

Time Required: 25 minutes

Objective: Install Virtual Machine Additions for the virtual machines.

Requirements: Completion of Activities 8-1 through 8-6.

Description: In this activity, you will install Virtual Machine Additions into each virtual machine. This activity is useful if you want to use the features of Virtual Machine Additions.

1. If necessary, log on to your Host PC with a username of **Administrator** and a password of **Secret1**.

2. If necessary, to launch VMRCplus, double-click the **VMRCplus** icon on the desktop.

Installing Virtual Machine Additions in Server Virtual Machines

3. To start the first server virtual machine, click **Server-01**, and then click the **Turn On** icon.

4. To view the display for the virtual machine, click on the **VM Console** icon.

5. Wait for the Console Manager to open.

6. If necessary, log on with a username of **Administrator** and a password of **Secret1**.

7. Wait for the Server Manager window to open, and then minimize the Server Manager window.

8. To mount the Virtual Machine Additions, click the **Media** menu, press right **Alt**, click the **Media** menu, and then click **Load ISO Image**.

9. If necessary, double-click **Computer**, double-click **New Volume (C:)**, double-click **Program Files**, double-click **Microsoft Virtual Server**, and then double-click **Virtual Machine Additions**. Click **VMAdditions.iso**, and then click **Open**.

10. Wait for the Autoplay window to open, click in the Server-01 virtual machine window, and then click **Run setup.exe**.

11. Click in the Server-01 virtual machine, click **Next**, wait for the installation to complete, and then click **Finish**.
12. When requested to restart your system, click **Yes**.
13. Wait for Server-01 to restart.
14. Log on to your virtual machine with a username of **Administrator** and a password of **Secret1**.
15. Wait for the Server Manager window to open.
16. To save the current state of the server, click the **Save State** icon.
17. Repeat Steps 3 through 16 for Server-02 and Server-03.

Installing Virtual Machine Additions in Client Virtual Machines

18. To start the client virtual machine, click **Client-01**, and then click the **Turn On** icon.
19. To view the display for the virtual machine, click on the **VM Console** icon.
20. Wait for the Console Manager to open.
21. To mount the Virtual Machine Additions, click the **Media** menu, press right **Alt**, click the **Media** menu, and then click **Load ISO Image**.
22. If necessary, double-click **Computer**, double-click **New Volume (C:)**, double-click **Program Files**, double-click **Microsoft Virtual Server**, and then double-click **Virtual Machine Additions**.
23. Click **VMAdditions.iso**, and then click **Open**.
24. Wait for the Autoplay window to open, click in the Client-01 virtual machine window, and then click **Run setup.exe**.
25. When the User Account Control dialog box opens, click the **Continue** button.
26. Click **Next**, wait for the installation to complete, and then click **Finish**.
27. When requested to restart your system, click **Yes**.
28. Wait for Client-01 to restart.
29. Log on to your virtual machine with a username of **Student** and a password of **Secret1**.
30. Wait for the Welcome Center to open, and then close the Welcome Center window.
31. To save the current state of the client, click the **Save State** icon.
32. Repeat Steps 18 through 31 for Client-02.
33. Leave the computer logged on for the next activity.

Verifying the IP Addressing on the Classroom Network

If the IP configurations are not correct, the virtual machines will not communicate with each other. You learned how to check the IP configuration for each virtual machine and the host computer in Chapter 4.

In Activity 8-8, you will check the IP configuration against the values in Table 8-2.

Activity 8-8: Verifying IP Configurations

Time Required: 10 minutes

Objective: Verify the IP configurations for the virtual machines.

Requirements: Completion of Activities 8-1 through 8-7.

Description: In this activity, you will use the ipconfig command to verify that the IP configuration is correct on each virtual machine.

1. If necessary, log on to your host PC with a username of **Administrator** and a password of **Secret1**.
2. If necessary, to launch VMRCplus, double-click the **VMRCplus** icon on the desktop.

Checking IP Configuration for Servers

3. To start the Server-01 virtual machine, click **Server-01**, and then click the **Turn On** icon.
4. To view the display for the virtual machine, click on the **VM Console** icon.
5. Wait for the Console Manager to open.
6. If necessary, log on to your virtual machine with a username of **Administrator** and a password of **Secret1**.
7. To open a command prompt window, click **Start**, and then click **Command Prompt**.
8. To execute the ipconfig command, type **ipconfig /all**, and then press **Enter**.
9. Scroll the window and verify that the IP configuration matches Table 8-2 for the IP addresses. If there are discrepancies for the IP addresses, contact your instructor.

To see more of the ipconfig results, drag the bottom of the command prompt window down.

10. To close the command prompt window, type **exit**, and then press **Enter**.
11. To save the state of the virtual machine, click the **Control** menu from the Console Manager window, click **Saved State Options**, and then click **Save State**.

Performance will be enhanced by placing virtual machines that are not needed in the Saved State.

12. Return to the VM Manager window.
13. Repeat Steps 3 through 12 for Server-02 and Server-03.

Checking IP Configuration for Clients

14. To start the Client-01 virtual machine, click **Client-01**, and then click the **Turn On** icon.
15. To view the display for the virtual machine, click on the **VM Console** icon.

16. Wait for the Console Manager to open.
17. If necessary, log on to your virtual machine with a username of **Student** and a password of **Secret1**.
18. To open a command prompt window, click **Start**, type **cmd** in the **Start Search** text box, and then press **Enter**.
19. To execute the ipconfig command, type **ipconfig /all**, and then press **Enter**.
20. Scroll the window and verify that the IP configuration matches Table 8-2 for the IP addresses. If there are discrepancies for the IP addresses, contact your instructor.
21. To close the command prompt window, type **exit**, and then press **Enter**.
22. Repeat Steps 14 through 21 for Client-02.

Checking IP Configuration for the Host

23. To open a command prompt window on the host computer, click **Start**, and then click **Command Prompt**.
24. To execute the ipconfig command, type **ipconfig /all**, and then press **Enter**.
25. Scroll the window and verify that the IP configuration resembles Table 8-2.

The IP addresses for the host network were provided for illustration purposes only. The IP configuration for your host computer will be determined by your physical network IP addressing scheme.

26. To close the command prompt window, type **exit**, and then press **Enter**.
27. Leave the computer logged on for the next activity.

Configuring the Windows Firewall

You learned about the Windows Firewall in Chapter 4. Windows Firewall provides protection against network attacks for computers on which it is enabled by checking all communications that cross the network connection and selectively blocking certain communications.

The default behavior of the Windows Firewall is to:

- Block all incoming traffic unless it is solicited or it matches a configured rule.
- Allow all outgoing traffic unless it matches a configured rule.

The blocking of unsolicited incoming traffic can cause problems. The Echo Request is an Internet Control Message Protocol (ICMP) message, which sends a packet of data to another computer and expects that data to be sent in return in an Echo Reply. The Windows Firewall rejects this Echo Request because this is unsolicited data. This Echo Request/Echo Reply is used by the ping command, which checks connectivity between the two computers.

You must change a rule in the Windows Firewall to permit the ICMP Request to be accepted. Figure 8-5, on the next page, shows the configuration tool for the Windows Firewall. To open the Windows Firewall with the Advanced Security snap-in, click Start, click Control Panel, click Control Panel Home, click the System and Maintenance link, click the Administrative Tools link, and double-click the Windows Firewall with Advanced Security shortcut.

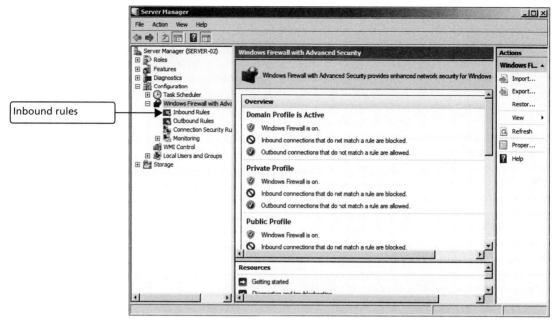

Figure 8-5 Windows Firewall with Advanced Security window

The rule that you must set is the File and Printer Sharing (Echo Request–ICMPv4-In) rule, as shown in Figure 8-6. Notice that the pane was scrolled down. In Activity 8-9, you will enable this rule for your five virtual machines and the host computer.

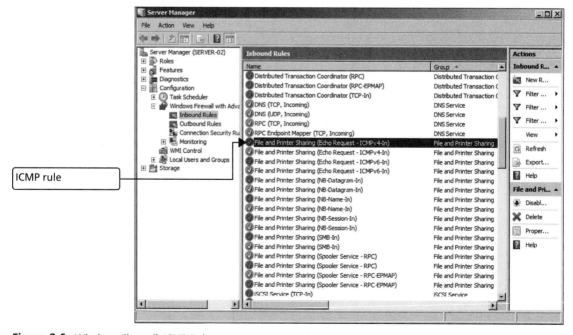

Figure 8-6 Windows Firewall–ICMP Rule

Activity 8-9: Setting the ICMP Rules

Time Required: 20 minutes

Objective: Set the ICMP rules to permit the Echo Request.

Requirements: Completion of Activities 8-1 through 8-8. The virtual machines were running in Activity 8-8.

Description: In this activity, you will enable the Echo Request rule in Windows Firewall, which permits the ping command to function correctly.

Setting ICMP Rules for Server Virtual Machines

1. To access the Server-01 virtual machine, click the **localhost/Server-01** tab (located on the Console Manager).
2. If necessary, log on to the virtual machine with a username of **Administrator** and a password of **Secret1**.
3. If necessary, to open the Server Manager, click **Start,** point to **Administrative Tools,** and then click **Server Manager.**
4. To open the Windows Firewall with Advanced Security snap-in, click the **Go to Windows Firewall** link, and then expand the **Windows Firewall with Advanced Security** node.
5. To modify the inbound rule for ICMP, click **Inbound Rules** in the left pane, scroll and double-click the **File and Printer Sharing (Echo Request–ICMPv4-In)** rule (the one with the gray checkmark), click the **Enabled** check box, click OK, and then click **Server Manager (SERVER-01)** in the left pane.
6. Repeat Steps 1 through 5 for Server-02 and Server-03.

Setting ICMP Rules for Client Virtual Machines

7. To access the Client-01 virtual machine, click the **localhost/Client-01** tab.
8. If necessary, log on to the virtual machine with a username of **Student** and a password of **Secret1.**
9. To open the Windows Firewall with Advanced Security snap-in, click **Start,** click **Control Panel,** click the **System and Maintenance** link, scroll and click the **Administrative Tools** link, and double-click the **Windows Firewall with Advanced Security** shortcut.
10. When the User Account Control dialog box opens, click the **Continue** button.
11. To modify the inbound rule for ICMP, click **Inbound Rules** in the left pane, scroll and double-click the first **File and Printer Sharing (Echo Request–ICMPv4-In)** rule (the one with the gray checkmark), click the **Enabled** check box, and then click **OK.**
12. Close the open windows.
13. Repeat Steps 7 through 12 for Client-02.
14. Minimize the open virtual machine windows.

Setting ICMP Rules for the Host

15. If necessary, to open the Server Manager, click **Start,** point to **Administrative Tools,** and then click **Server Manager.**

16. To open the Windows Firewall with Advanced Security snap-in for the host computer, click the **Go to Windows Firewall** link, and then expand the **Windows Firewall with Advanced Security** node.

17. To modify the inbound rule for ICMP, click **Inbound Rules** in the left pane, scroll and double-click the **File and Printer Sharing (Echo Request–ICMPv4-In)** rule (the one with the gray checkmark), click the **Enabled** check box, and then click **OK**.

18. Close the Server Manager window.

19. Leave the virtual machines running.

20. Leave the computer logged on for the next activity.

Verifying IP Connectivity

Now that the Windows Firewall rules are set, you can test IP connectivity between the three virtual machines servers and the host computer. For this test, you use the ping command. You then test the client virtual machines.

Figure 8-7 shows a test of Client-02's connectivity. To perform such a test, you issue a ping command to the remaining machines in sequence—Server-01 (ping 192.168.0.101), Server-02 (ping 192.168.0.102), Server-03 (ping 192.168.0.103).

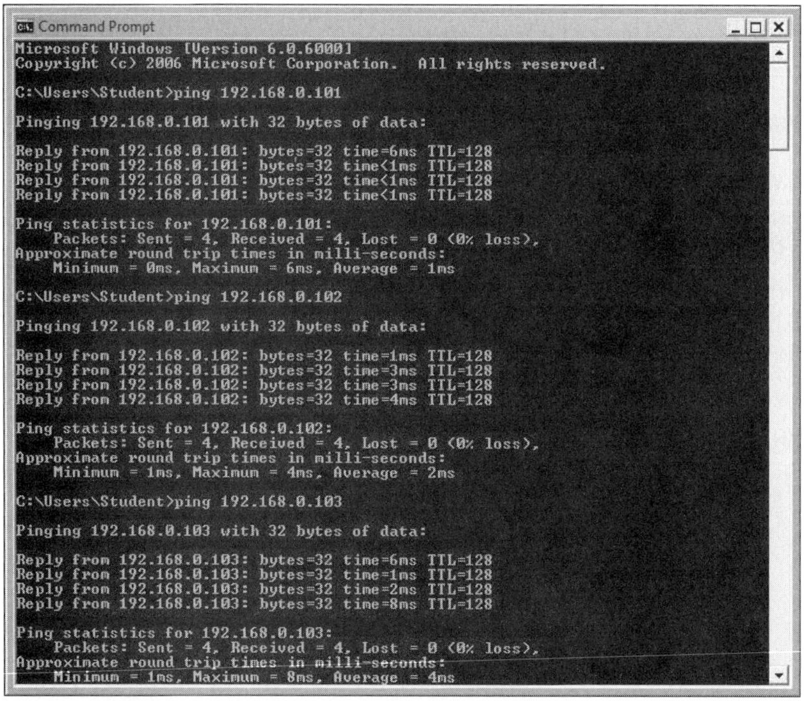

Figure 8-7 Results of pings to servers from Client-02

Continue the connectivity testing—by pinging the host (ping 192.168.0.1) and then Client-01 (ping 192.168.0.111). There is no need to issue a ping 192.168.0.112 because this would be contacting the Client-02 virtual machine. The results are shown in Figure 8-8.

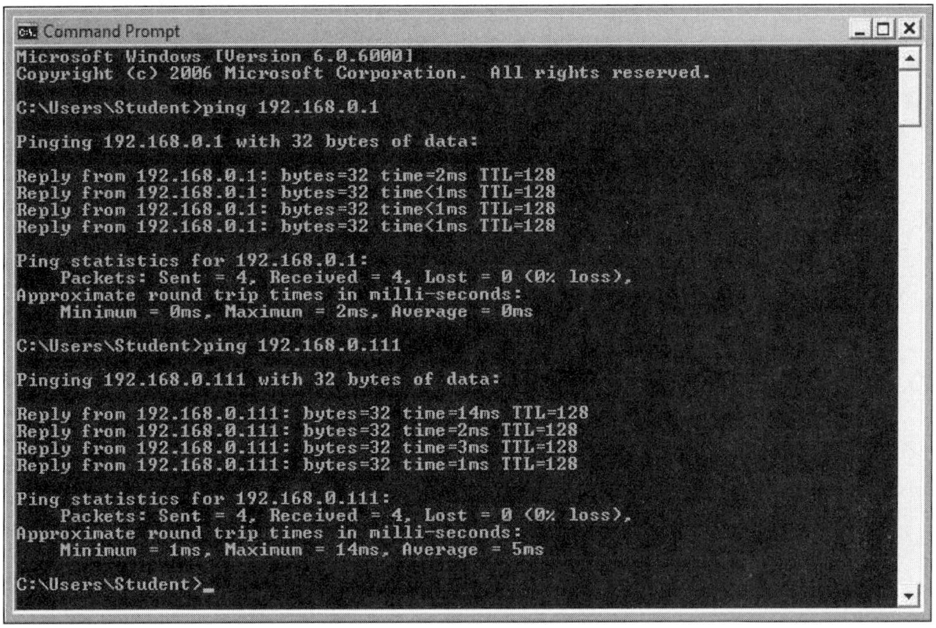

Figure 8-8 Results of pings to clients

Activity 8-10: Verifying IP Connectivity

Time Required: 5 minutes

Objective: Verify IP connectivity from the Client-02 virtual machine.

Requirements: Completion of Activities 8-1 through 8-9. The virtual machines should be running.

Description: In this activity, you will verify IP connectivity from the Client-02 virtual machine to the other virtual machines and the host computer.

1. If necessary, to restore the Server-01 virtual machine, right-click the saved virtual machine, and then click **Turn On**.
2. If necessary, wait for the Server-01 virtual machine to have the Running status.
3. If necessary, to access the Server-01 virtual server, click the **localhost/Server-01** tab.
4. If necessary, complete Steps 1 through 3 for the remaining virtual machines in a saved state.
5. To access the Client-02 virtual machine, click the **localhost/Client-02** tab.
6. If necessary, log on to the Client-02 virtual machine with a username of **Student** and a password of **Secret1**.

7. To open a command prompt window, click **Start**, type **cmd** in the Start Search text box, and then press **Enter**.

8. To verify connectivity to Server-01, type **ping 192.168.0.101**, and then press **Enter**. Verify that you can ping Server-01. If you cannot reach Server-01, contact your instructor.

9. To verify connectivity to Server-02, type **ping 192.168.0.102**, and then press **Enter**. Verify that you can ping Server-02. If you cannot reach Server-02, contact your instructor.

10. To verify connectivity to Server-03, type **ping 192.168.0.103**, and then press **Enter**. Verify that you can ping Server-03. If you cannot reach Server-03, contact your instructor.

11. To verify connectivity to Client-01, type **ping 192.168.0.111**, and then press **Enter**. Verify that you can ping Client-01. If you cannot reach Client-01, contact your instructor.

12. To verify connectivity to the host, type **ping 192.168.0.1**, and then press **Enter**. Verify that you can ping the gateway. If you cannot reach the gateway, contact your instructor.

13. Leave the computer logged on for the next activity.

Implementing Active Directory Domain Services

Active Directory Domain Services (AD DS), which you learned about in Chapter 4, provides the directory service that you use for management of your network. When Active Directory Domain Services is installed, your Server-01 becomes the domain controller for the Classroom.local network. With AD DS, Classroom administrators can assign policies, control infrastructure services, and manage the network resources. AD DS stores information and settings relating to Classroom's resources in a central, organized, and accessible database.

You will create a domain controller on Server-01 in Activity 8-11.

To create the role and promote Server-01 to a domain controller, you will need to complete these general steps (these steps are included in Activity 8-11):

- Pause the virtual machines other than Server-01—Pause from Virtual Machine Manager.
- Add Active Directory Domain Services—Run the Add Roles Wizard within Server Manager.
- Promote to a domain controller—Run the Active Directory Domain Services Installation Wizard.
- Install and configure DNS—This is accomplished using the Active Directory Domain Services Installation Wizard.

Pausing the virtual machines, other than Server-01, will make additional processor cycles available for the installation of Active Directory Domain Services.

Activity 8-11: Creating a Domain Controller

Time Required: 45 minutes

Objective: Promote a virtual machine to a domain controller.

Requirements: Completion of Activities 8-1 through 8-10 and the Windows Server 2008 DVD. The virtual machines should be running, as in Activity 8-10.

Description: In this activity, you will change the role of Server-01, establishing it as a domain controller.

1. To gain additional cycles for the installation of Active Directory Domain Services, return to the Virtual Machine Manager, right-click **Client-01**, and then click **Pause**.
2. Repeat Step 1 for the remaining virtual machines with the exception of Server-01.
3. To access Server-01, click the **Console Manager**, click the **localhost/Server-01** tab, and then click in the Server-01 virtual machine.
4. If necessary, log on to the Server-01 virtual machine with a username of **Administrator** and a password of **Secret1**.
5. Insert the Windows Server 2008 DVD. When the Autoplay window opens, close the window.
6. To start the installation of Active Directory Domain Services, click the **Roles** node in the Server Manager window, click the **Add Roles** link, click **Server Roles**, check the **Active Directory Domain Services** check box, and then click **Next**.
7. Review the Introduction to Active Directory Domain Services, and then click **Next**.
8. Review the Confirm Installation Selections, and then click **Install**.
9. Review the Installation Results, and then click **Close**.
10. When the roles are displayed, click the **Go to Active Directory Domain Services** link.
11. When the Active Directory Domain Services is displayed, click the **Run the Activity Directory Domain Services Installation Wizard (dcpromo.exe)** link.
12. Review the Welcome to the Active Directory Domain Services Installation Wizard dialog box, and then click **Next**.
13. To specify the forest and domain, click the **Create a new domain in a new forest** option button, and then click **Next**.
14. Type **Classroom.local** in the FQDN of the forest root domain name text box, and then click **Next**.
15. Wait for the forest name and NetBIOS name to be verified.
16. Click the **Forest functional level** drop-down list arrow, click **Windows Server 2008**, and then click **Next**.
17. Wait for the DNS check.
18. Retain the **DNS Server** check box, and then click **Next**.
19. Wait for the configuration DNS check.

20. Review the delegation message, and then click **Yes**.
21. Review the file locations, and then click **Next**.
22. To set the Directory services restore password, type **Secret1** in the Password text box, press **Tab**, type **Secret1** in the Confirm password text box, and then click **Next**.
23. Review the summary, and then click **Next**.
24. Review the text messages indicating the progress of the installation, and wait for the installation to complete.
25. Review the Completing the Active Directory Domain Services Installation Wizard, and then click **Finish**.
26. When requested, click the **Restart Now** button.
27. Wait for the virtual machine to restart.
28. Press right **Alt+Delete**, and log on to the Server-01 virtual machine with a username of **Administrator** and a password of **Secret1**.
29. To verify the correctness of your domain controller, click **Start**, click **Command Prompt**, type **dcdiag /fix**, and then press **Enter**.
30. Scroll to the line Doing Primary tests, and look for tests that were passed.

If you have questions about the results, discuss these with your instructor.

31. Close the command prompt window.
32. To view the domain controller, expand **Roles**, expand **Active Directory Domain Services**, expand **Active Directory Users and Computers**, expand **Classroom.local**, and then double-click **Domain Controllers**.
33. To view the users and security groups, click **Users**, and then review users and security groups.
34. Click the **Server Manager (Server-01)** node.
35. Leave the computer logged on for the next activity.

Joining the Domain

To access the network resources of the Classroom.local domain, each virtual machine must be a member of the domain. This process is called "joining a domain." In this process, you will contact the domain controller from a virtual machine and request to become a member.

The process varies with the operating system. In each case, you will use the Computer Name/Domain Changes dialog box, as shown in Figure 8-9, entering the name of the desired domain you want to join.

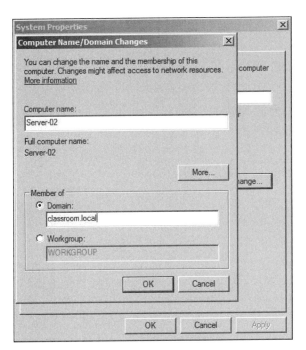

Figure 8-9 Entering the domain name

To join the virtual machine to the domain, you will need to know the user ID and password for an account that has privileges permitting it to join the domain. The Adminstrator account with password of Secret1 has these privileges. This information will be requested from a logon box. After a brief wait, you will receive a "Welcome to the domain" message.

After you have joined all of the virtual machines to the domain, you can see the computer accounts in Active Directory Users and Computers. Clicking the Computers node in the left pane displays details about the members of the domain. See Figure 8-10.

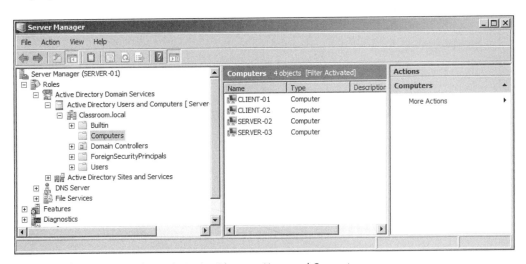

Figure 8-10 Computers shown in Active Directory Users and Computers

Activity 8-12: Joining Computers to the Domain

Time Required: 20 minutes

Objective: Join virtual machines to the Classroom.local domain.

Requirements: Completion of Activities 8-1 through 8-11. With the exception of Server-01, the virtual machines should remain paused.

Description: In this activity, you will add the virtual machines to the Classroom.local domain.

Joining Server Virtual Machines to the Domain

1. Return to Virtual Machine Manager. Right-click **Server-02**, and then click **Resume**.
2. Return to the Console Manager and click the **localhost/Server-02** tab.
3. If necessary, log on to the Server-02 virtual machine with a username of **Administrator** and a password of **Secret1**.
4. To change the domain name, click the **Change System Properties** link, click the **Change** button, click the **Domain** option button, type **Classroom.local** in the Domain text box, and then click **OK**.
5. When the Windows Security dialog box opens, type **Administrator**, enter a password of **Secret1**, and then click **OK**.
6. Wait for the Welcome to the Classroom.local domain message, and then click **OK**.
7. To restart the virtual machine, click **OK**, click **Close**, and then click the **Restart Now** button.
8. Wait for the virtual machine to restart.
9. Log on to Server-02 with a username of **classroom\Administrator** and a password of **Secret1**.

If you cannot log on, contact your instructor.

10. Repeat Steps 1 through 9 for **Server-03**.

Joining Client Virtual Machines to the Domain

11. Return to Virtual Machine Manager. Right-click **Client-01**, and then click **Resume**.
12. Return to the Console Manager and click the **localhost/Client-01** tab.
13. If necessary, log on to the Client-01 virtual machine with a username of **Student** and a password of **Secret1**.
14. To open the System Properties dialog box, click **Start**, right-click **Computer**, click **Properties**, and then click the **Advanced system settings** link.
15. When the User Account Control dialog box opens, click the **Continue** button.

16. To change the domain name, click the **Computer Name** tab, click the **Change** button, click the **Domain** option button, type **Classroom.local** in the Domain text box, and then click **OK**.

17. When the Windows Security dialog box opens, type **Administrator** and a password of **Secret1**, and then click **OK**.

18. Wait for the Welcome to the Classroom.local domain message to appear, and then click **OK**.

19. To restart the virtual machine, click **OK**, click **Close**, and then click the **Restart Now** button.

20. Wait for the virtual machine to restart.

21. Log on to Client-01 with a username of **classroom\Administrator** and a password of **Secret1**.

22. Repeat Steps 11 through 21 for **Client-02**.

23. Leave the virtual machines running.

24. Leave the computer logged on for the next activity.

Configuring DNS Services for Classroom.local

As a part of the installation of Active Directory Domain Services, the DNS role was added to Server-01. In the following sections, you will complete the configuration of DNS services. In addition, you will add the DNS role to Server-02.

Overview of DNS Queries

DNS is an abbreviation for Domain Name System, a system for naming computers and network services that is organized into a hierarchy of domains. DNS maintains databases of IP addresses for host names. DNS naming is used in TCP/IP networks, such as the Internet. When a user enters a DNS name in an application, DNS services can resolve the name to other information associated with the name, such as an IP address. Figure 8-11 shows a basic use of DNS, finding the IP address of a computer based on its name.

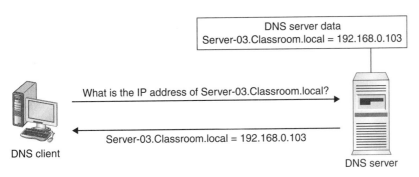

Figure 8-11 Finding the IP address of Server-03

In this example, the Client-01 computer queries a DNS server, asking for the IP address of a computer configured to use Server-03.Classroom.local as its DNS domain name. Because the DNS server can answer the query based on its local database, it replies with an answer containing the requested information, which is a host (A) resource record that contains the IP address information for Server-03.Classroom.local. The A record (address record, or host record) maps a host name to an IP address.

DNS queries resolve in a number of different ways:

- A DNS client can sometimes answer a query locally using cached information obtained from a previous query.
- The local DNS server can use its own cache of resource record information to answer a query.
- A local DNS server can also query or contact other DNS servers on behalf of the requesting client to fully resolve the name, then send an answer back to the client. This process is known as **recursion**.

In general, the DNS query process occurs in three parts:

1. A name query begins at a client computer and is passed to a **resolver**, the DNS Client service, for resolution.
2. When the query cannot be resolved locally (using previously cached resolutions), the local DNS server can be queried as needed to resolve the name.
3. When the query cannot be resolved by the local DNS server, the local DNS server can forward the query to a designated DNS server for resolution.

More information on the query process is presented in the next three sections.

DNS Cache Figure 8-12 shows the DNS cache entry for the Server-01.Classroom.local host in the client's DNS cache. If the client needs the IP address for the Server-01 virtual machine, the IP address would be returned from the DNS cache. The entry exists in the cache because this resolution occurred previously.

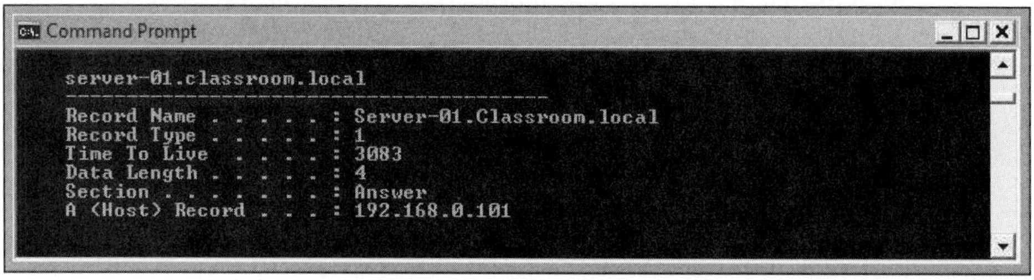

```
server-01.classroom.local
----------------------------------------
Record Name . . . . . : Server-01.Classroom.local
Record Type . . . . . : 1
Time To Live  . . . . : 3083
Data Length . . . . . : 4
Section . . . . . . . : Answer
A (Host) Record . . . : 192.168.0.101
```

Figure 8-12 DNS cache entry for Server-01.Classroom.local

Local DNS Server If the resolver cannot locate the host name in the DNS cache, the query is then passed to the preferred DNS server (or local server) for resolution. You have learned to designate the IP address of the preferred DNS server by entering the IP address in the Internet Protocol Version 4 (TCP/IPv4) Properties dialog box, as shown in Figure 8-13.

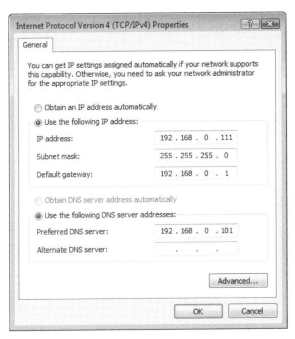

Figure 8-13 Entering the IP address for the DNS server

Designated DNS Server If the local DNS server cannot resolve the query, the query is then passed to the DNS server designated in the configuration of the local DNS server. A common use of this forwarding is the resolution of Internet host addresses. For example, there is no DNS host (A) resource record for *www.microsoft.com* in the local DNS server. Therefore, the request must be passed to another server—namely, the designated DNS server to respond to the query. In reality, the query will be passed in turn to numerous DNS servers to locate the IP address for this host. When the IP address is located and then resolved, the IP address will be returned.

Forwarding Name Resolution Requests

To set up the designated DNS server, a forwarding entry is made in the local DNS server. Figure 8-14 shows the forwarding entry to the Host01 computer. Note that 192.168.0.1 is the IP address for the Microsoft Loopback Adapter. You will configure this forwarding entry in Activity 8-13.

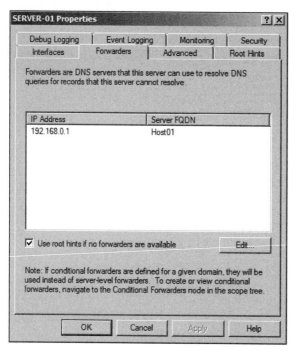

Figure 8-14 Forwarders tab showing host IP address

DNS Zones

Figure 8-15 shows the forward lookup zones for the DNS server. You can access the reverse lookup zones through the same screen. These zones contain records that match host name to IP address and IP address to host name. Forward lookup zones allow computers to resolve host names to IP addresses, and reverse lookup zones resolve IP addresses to DNS names.

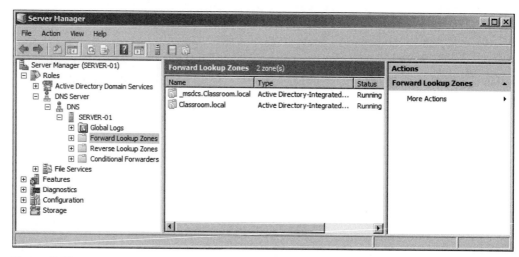

Figure 8-15 Forward lookup zones and reverse lookup zones for the DNS server

Forward Lookup Zones For DNS services to work (and Active Directory Domain Services as well), at least one forward lookup zone must be configured on your server. Installation and configuration of DNS during the installation of Active Directory Domain Services automatically configures a forward lookup zone. Forward lookup zones allow forward lookup queries, the standard method of name resolution in DNS, to work. Forward lookup zones allow computers to resolve host names to IP addresses.

Figure 8-15 shows the two zones in the forward lookup zones. In addition to the Classroom.local entry, an _msdcs.Classroom.local was added during the installation of Active Directory Domain Services. Sometimes clients might need to contact a Microsoft-hosted service. For that reason, the DNS has an _msdcs.Classroom.local that hosts only SRV records that are registered by Microsoft-based services. **SRV** records are often used by Microsoft Windows 2008 clients to find the domain controller.

Reverse Lookup Zones A reverse lookup zone is not required for DNS services to function. However, you will want to create a reverse lookup zone to resolve IP addresses to host names. Troubleshooting tools such as NSLOOKUP that can resolve host names from IP addresses require a reverse lookup zone to work properly.

Unlike naming a forward lookup zone, you name a reverse lookup zone by its IP address. Using the New Zone Wizard, you type your network ID into the first field and the reverse lookup zone name automatically is created, as shown in Figure 8-16. You will create the reverse lookup zone in Activity 8-13.

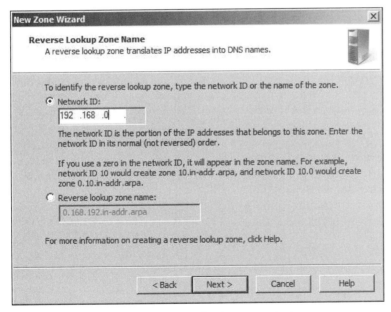

Figure 8-16 Entering the network ID for the reverse lookup zone

DNS Record Types The two most prevalent DNS records are the A record (or Address record) found within the forward lookup zone and the PTR record (or Pointer record) found in the reverse lookup zone. The A record maps a host name to an IP address. The pointer records work in reverse—mapping an IP address to a host name. Table 8-3 describes these two and other record types that you might encounter when working with DNS lookup zones.

Table 8-3 Common DNS record types

Type	Description
A	IPv4 address record maps a host name to a 32-bit IPv4 address
AAAA	IPv6 address record maps a host name to a 128-bit IPv6 address
CNAME	Canonical name record is an alias of one name to another; useful for providing multiple names for a single Web server
MX	Mail exchange record maps a domain name to a list of mail exchange servers for that domain
PTR	Pointer record maps an IPv4 address to the name for that host
NS	Name server record maps a domain name to a list of DNS servers authoritative for that domain
SOA	Start of authority record specifies the DNS server providing authoritative information about an Internet domain, the e-mail of the domain administrator, the domain serial number, and several timers related to refreshing the zone
SRV	Record is a generalized service location record; used by Microsoft clients to locate domain controllers

Dynamic Update

Dynamic update enables DNS client computers to register and dynamically update their resource records with a DNS server whenever computers are moved around the network. The dynamic update feature reduces the need for manual administration of zone records, especially for clients that frequently move or change locations and use DHCP to obtain an IP address.

By itself, dynamic update is not secure; any client can modify DNS records. Secure dynamic update is available only on Active Directory-integrated zones. When secure dynamic update is configured, computers that have joined the domain are permitted to update their host records. To configure secure dynamic updates, you use the secure dynamic update located on the zone property dialog box, as shown in Figure 8-17.

Three choices exist for dynamic update:

- None—No updates are accepted.
- Nonsecure and secure—All updates are accepted.
- Secure—Only secure updates are permitted.

In addition to computers using dynamic updates, computers that are configured with static IP addresses also attempt to dynamically register resource records. By default, all computers register records based on their fully qualified domain name (FQDN). Figure 8-18 shows the host records dynamically updated by the virtual machines on the Classroom.local domain. Dynamic records are time stamped when they are updated.

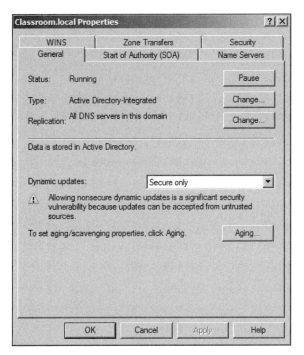

Figure 8-17 Dynamic update showing secure status

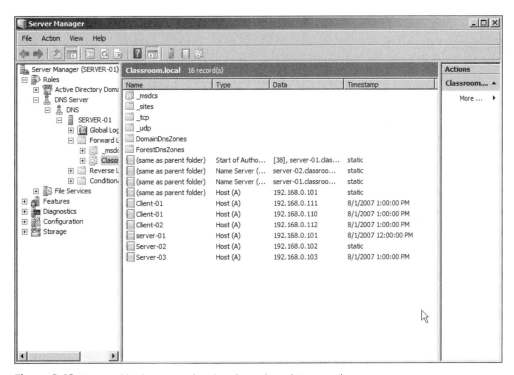

Figure 8-18 Forward lookup zone showing dynamic update records

Creating a Secondary DNS Server

Domain Name System (DNS) design specifications recommend that at least two DNS servers be used to host each zone. See Figure 8-19. For active directory-integrated primary zones, secondary servers are supported. An **Active Directory-integrated primary zone** is an authoritative primary (forward lookup) zone in which all of the zone data is stored in Active Directory. Secondary servers support read-only copies of zones, called **secondary zones**.

Secondary servers can be used to off-load DNS query traffic in areas of the network where a zone is heavily queried. In addition, if a primary server is unavailable to a client, a secondary server (alternate DNS server) can provide some name resolution in the zone until the primary server (preferred DNS server) is available.

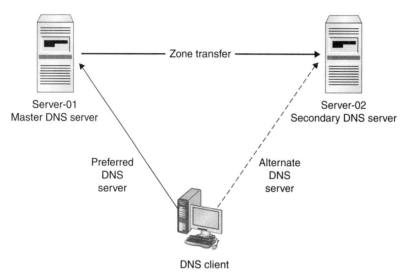

Figure 8-19 Primary/secondary DNS servers

Because a primary server always maintains the master copy of updates and changes to the zone, a secondary server relies on DNS zone transfer mechanisms to obtain its information and keep the information current. Figure 8-20 shows the secondary zone file on Server-02 that was transferred from the DNS on Server-01. Two zone transfer methods—using either **full zone transfers** (all records) or **incremental zone transfers** (only new or changed records)—are used.

To add a secondary server to an existing zone, you must have network access to the server that acts as the master server for the secondary server Also, for security reasons, you must identify the servers that can request zone transfers—the secondary server must be identified to the master server. This is done by adding the secondary server with a name server record to the master server. The master server acts as the source for zone data. It is contacted periodically to assist in renewing the zone and to transfer zone updates whenever they are needed.

You will create a secondary zone on Server-02 for the Classroom.local network in Activity 8-14.

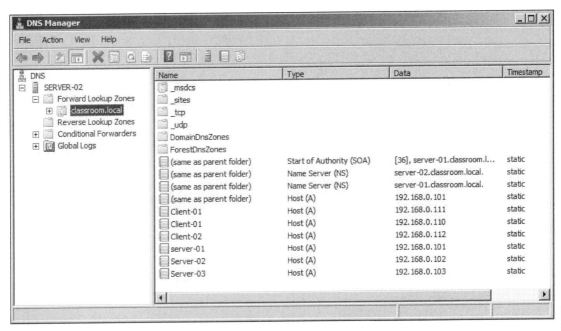

Figure 8-20 Secondary zone file on Server-02

Activity 8-13: Configuring DNS on Server-01

Time Required: 10 minutes

Objective: Configure DNS on Server-01.

Requirements: Completion of Activities 8-1 through 8-12. The virtual machines should remain running.

Description: In this activity, to resolve host names on the Internet, you will add the forwarder to the Internet. You will also add the reverse lookup zone and then identify Server-02 as a potential secondary server.

1. Return to the Console Manager and click the **localhost/Server-01** tab.

2. If necessary, log on to the Server-01 virtual machine with a username of **Administrator** and a password of **Secret1**.

3. To enable Internet host names to be resolved, expand the **Roles** node, expand the **DNS Server** node, expand the **DNS** node, expand the **Server-01** node, right-click the **SERVER-01** node in the left pane, click **Properties**, click the **Forwarders** tab, click the **Edit** button, type **192.168.0.1** over the <click here to add an IP address or DNS Name> message and then click **OK** twice.

4. To add the reverse lookup zone for Classroom.local, expand the reverse lookup zone, right-click **Reverse Lookup Zones** in the left pane, click **New Zone**, click **Next**, retain the **Primary zone** option button, click **Next** twice, retain the **IPv4 Reverse Lookup Zone**, click **Next**, type **192.168.0** in the Network ID text box, click **Next** twice, and then click **Finish**.

5. To add a record for the DNS server, double-click **0.168.192.in-addr.arpa**, right-click in the white space in the center pane, click **New Pointer (PTR)**, type **101** after 192.168.0 in the Host IP Address text box, click the **Browse** button, double-click **Server-01**, double-click **Forward Lookup Zones**, double-click **Classroom.local**, scroll and click **Server-01**, and then click **OK** twice.

6. Verify that 192.168.0.101 was added as a Pointer (PTR) record.

7. To add a record for Server-02, double-click **0.168.192.in-addr.arpa**, right-click in the white space in the center pane, click **New Pointer (PTR)**, type **102** after 192.168.0 in the Host IP Address text box, type **Server-02** in the Host name text box, and then click **OK**.

8. Verify that 192.168.0.102 was added as a Pointer (PTR) record.

9. To enable Server-02 to be a DNS server, expand **Forward Lookup Zones**, right-click **Classroom.local** in the left pane, click **Properties**, click the **Name Servers** tab, click the **Add** button, type **server-02.Classroom.local** in the Server fully qualified domain name (FQDN) text box, click the **<click here to add an IP address>** message, type **192.168.0.102** over the <click here to add an IP address> message, press **Enter**, and then click **OK** twice.

10. To allow zone transfers to other DNS servers, expand **Forward Lookup Zones**, right-click **Classroom.local**, click **Properties**, click the **Zone Transfers** tab, click the **Allow zone transfers** check box, click the **Only to servers listed on the Name Servers tab** option button, and then click **OK**.

11. Leave the virtual machines running.

12. Leave the computer logged on for the next activity.

Activity 8-14: Configuring DNS on Server-02

Time Required: 15 minutes

Objective: Add a secondary DNS service on Server-02.

Requirements: Completion of Activities 8-1 through 8-13. The virtual machines should remain running.

Description: In this activity, you will add Server-02 as a secondary DNS server to the primary DNS on Server-01.

1. Return to the Console Manager and click the **localhost/Server-02** tab.

2. If necessary, log on to the Server-02 with a username of **Administrator** and a password of **Secret1**.

3. Wait for the Server Manager window to open.

4. To add the DNS server role, click the **Roles** node, click the **Add Roles** link, click the **Server Roles** link, check the **DNS Server** check box, click **Next** twice, and then click **Install**.

5. Wait for the installation to complete, and then click **Close**.

6. To verify connectivity to the master DNS server, click **Start**, click **Command Prompt**, type **nslookup server-01**, and then press **Enter**. If you see error messages, contact your instructor.
7. Close the command prompt window.
8. To launch the DNS Manager, click **Start**, point to **Administrative Tools**, and then click **DNS**.
9. To set up the secondary zone file, expand **SERVER-02**, expand **Forward Lookup Zones**, right-click **Forward Lookup Zones**, click **New Zone**, click **Next**, click the **Secondary Zone** option button, click **Next**, type **Classroom.local** in the Zone name text box, click **Next**, type **192.168.0.101** over the <click here to add an IP address or DNS Name> message, press **Enter**, click **Next**, and then click **Finish**.
10. To refresh the zone, expand the **Forward Lookup Zone**, click **Refresh**, and then click **Classroom.local**. If Classroom.local is not displayed, contact your instructor.
11. Return to the Virtual Machine Manager.
12. Right-click **Client-01**, and then click **Save State**.
13. Repeat Step 12 for the remaining virtual machines with the exception of Server-01.
14. To shut down Server-01, return to the Console Manager, click **localhost/Server-01**, logon if necessary, click **Start**, click the arrow next to the lock, click **Shut Down**, click the **Option** drop-down list arrow, click **Operating System: Reconfiguration (Planned)**, and then click **OK**.
15. Close the open windows.
16. Log off and shut down the host computer.

Chapter Summary

- You created the Classroom.local network as a demonstration network for use in learning more about managing and expanding a virtual network based on guidelines and requirements outlined in the initial network diagram. You designated the three server and two client roles to help determine the necessary operating systems, which then determined the RAM and hard disk requirements for each of the computers in the network.
- You installed operating systems and defined a communications scheme to implement the Classroom.local virtual network. For each computer to access the Classroom.local network, it must be a member of the domain.
- Installation of Active Directory Domain Services (AD DS) included DNS and established the virtual network's domain controller. Active Directory Domain Services provided the directory service for centralized, secure management of the network.
- For DNS to work properly, a forward lookup zone was configured. The reverse lookup zone is not required for DNS is work properly, but is necessary for some troubleshooting tools.

Key Terms

Active Directory-integrated primary zone—The primary DNS zone file stored in Active Directory and replicated when the Active Directory Domain Services exchanges information.

full zone transfers—The transmission by the master server for a zone of the entire zone database to the secondary server for that zone.

incremental zone transfer—The transmission of parts of a DNS zone from a primary DNS server to a secondary. Only changes to the zone need be transferred.

infrastructure server—A computer or program that responds to requests from a client and provides services, specifically network services, such as DNS and DHCP.

recursion—A process in which a DNS server answers queries for names outside of its authoritative zones by sending a query on to the "closest" DNS server to the queried name that it knows. The process continues (if necessary) until the DNS server gets a response back for the original query.

resolver—A set of software routines used for making, sending, and interpreting query and reply messages with Internet domain name servers.

secondary zones—Zones that are replicated from another server, the master server.

SRV—A DNS resource record intended to provide information on available services.

.vsv—A temporary file that contains information about a virtual machine's state when the virtual machine is placed in a saved state.

Review Questions

1. When configuring parent/child virtual machines, _____. (Choose all that apply.)
   a. Use a dynamic expanding disk for the parent
   b. Use a differencing disk for the child
   c. Use a dynamic expanding disk for the child
   d. Use a differencing disk for the parent

2. Installation of the servers in the Classroom.local network was reduced by _____ of the time through use of parent cloning.
   a. One-half
   b. One-third
   c. One-fourth
   d. One-fifth

3. /oobe _____. (Choose all that apply.)
   a. Is a switch that instructs the Windows installation to run Windows Welcome the next time the computer boots
   b. Stands for out-of-box experience
   c. Is required by Microsoft when a manufacturer markets a personal computer with a preinstalled Windows product
   d. Is a switch that instructs Sysprep to remove system-specific data, including unique security identifiers (SIDs)

4. /generalize _____.
   a. Is a switch that instructs the Windows installation to run Windows Welcome the next time the computer boots
   b. Stands for out-of-box experience
   c. Is required by Microsoft when a manufacturer markets a personal computer with a preinstalled Windows product
   d. Is a switch that instructs Sysprep to remove system-specific data, including unique security identifiers (SIDs)

5. When using Sysprep, you will need to repeat the _____ task for each child. (Choose all that apply.)
   a. Copy the files from the DVD for the operating system
   b. Provide a product key
   c. Accept the license terms
   d. Name the computer

6. When using the Saved State, _____. (Choose all that apply.)
   a. You save the current state of the virtual machine
   b. You stop the virtual machine from running
   c. You pause the virtual machine
   d. You can restore the saved virtual machine

7. Virtual Machine Additions (VMA) _____. (Choose all that apply.)
   a. Can only be added after the operating system is installed and configured
   b. Can be added at any time during the operating system installation
   c. Should be installed in the parent virtual machines
   d. Should be installed in the child virtual machines

8. The Windows Firewall _____. (Choose all that apply.)
   a. Must be changed to permit the ICMP Request to be accepted
   b. Has a default behavior to block all incoming traffic unless it is solicited or it matches a configured rule
   c. Has a default behavior to allow all outgoing traffic unless it matches a configured rule
   d. Is no problem for the Classroom.local network
9. The implementation of Active Directory Domain Services and DNS _____.
   a. Provides centralized file sharing
   b. Provides communication utilities
   c. Allows Internet access
   d. Provides security management of the virtual machines and other network objects
10. Active Directory Domain Services _____. (Choose all that apply.)
    a. Assigns policies
    b. Controls infrastructure services
    c. Manages network resources
    d. Is installed with the Domain Name Services Installation Wizard
11. To join a computer to a domain, _____. (Choose all that apply.)
    a. Configure the client with the IP address of a DNS server
    b. Use a user account with privileges to join a computer to a domain
    c. Use the System properties dialog box
    d. Type the domain name in the Domain text box
12. DNS _____. (Choose all that apply.)
    a. Is an abbreviation for Domain Name System
    b. Maintains databases of IP addresses for host names
    c. Is used in networks using TCP/IP
    d. Is installed with Active Directory Domain Services
13. A resolver _____. (Choose all that apply.)
    a. Is a DNS client service that is used to locate an IP address of a computer based on its name
    b. Is located locally in the client computer
    c. Uses previously cached resolutions to help locate the IP addresses
    d. Is a DNS server

14. Forward lookup zones _____. (Choose all that apply.)
    a. Must be configured for DNS services to work
    b. Are not required for DNS services to function
    c. Enable forward lookup queries, the standard method of name resolution of DNS to work
    d. Allow computers to resolve host names to IP addresses
15. Reverse lookup zones _____. (Choose all that apply.)
    a. Must be configured for DNS services to work
    b. Are not required for DNS services to function
    c. Are needed for some troubleshooting tools to work properly
    d. Allow computers to resolve IP addresses to host names
16. Dynamic update _____. (Choose all that apply.)
    a. Enables DNS client computers to register host records
    b. Reduces the need for administrators to add/remove host records
    c. Simplifies the movement of computers
    d. Supports secure dynamic updates
17. Primary DNS servers _____. (Choose all that apply.)
    a. Support forward lookup zones
    b. Support reverse lookup zones
    c. Transfer zone records to secondary DNS servers
    d. Receive zone transfers from secondary DNS servers
18. Secondary DNS servers _____. (Choose all that apply.)
    a. Support forward lookup zones
    b. Support reverse lookup zones
    c. Transfer zone records to secondary DNS servers
    d. Receive zone transfers from secondary DNS servers
19. Full zone transfers _____. (Choose all that apply.)
    a. Copy all records
    b. Copy new or changed records
    c. Transfer records from the primary DNS server to the secondary DNS server
    d. Transfer records from the secondary DNS server to the primary DNS server

20. ICS _____. (Choose all that apply.)
   a. Is software that the host computer runs
   b. Enables virtual machines to connect to the Internet using the IP address provided by the host computer
   c. Routes packets between the two network adapters on the host, the physical network adapter, and the Microsoft Loopback adapter
   d. Supports DNS name resolution, which is used to resolve the computers on the Internet to IP addresses

Case Projects

Case 8-1: Procedure to Create Virtual Machines Using Parent/Child
The student lab supervisor Ted is pleased with the progress you have made with the new virtual machines. Now, he needs a procedure written for future technicians with the steps to create parent virtual machines. Outline this procedure in a document. You will also need to include the steps to create child virtual machines.

Case 8-2: Saved State Problems
Saved state can cause problems in virtual machine computers used as domain controllers. Describe a saved state that you would not want your domain controller to revert back to. Why would you want to avoid this situation?

Case 8-3: Configuring Domain Name System
Rachel is the networking administrator for a medium-sized organization that has recently added a connection to the Internet. The computers in the local network can resolve host names. However, the local computers receive error messages indicating that Internet host names are not resolvable. What will you do to correct this problem?

chapter 9

Classroom.local Virtual Network Infrastructure

After reading this chapter and completing the exercises, you will be able to:

- Analyze traffic with Microsoft Network Monitor
- Install the Dynamic Host Configuration Protocol
- Implement routing

In Chapter 8, you built a demonstration network called Classroom.local with Active Directory Domain Services and Domain Name System. In this chapter, you will continue building the network infrastructure.

You will download a tool from Microsoft that lets you access detailed information about the contents of packets, which helps you troubleshoot the network. To reduce the administration burden and complexity of configuring hosts on a TCP/IP-based network, you will add a role to support dynamic IP addressing.

Finally, you will implement **routing**, which is the process of moving a data packet from its local network to a remote network based on the address of the remote network. Routing supports future growth of the network.

Analyzing Traffic

Microsoft Network Monitor (also called a **protocol analyzer**) is a network diagnostic tool that monitors local area networks and provides a graphical display of network traffic. Network Monitor only allows you to monitor packets transmitted to or from the machine on which it is installed. A protocol analyzer decodes the network traffic using a set of rules. These rules are used in communications by endpoints in a telecommunication connection.

You can use this analysis to perform routine troubleshooting tasks, such as solving problems with network protocols. While collecting information from the network's data stream, Network Monitor displays the following types of information:

- The source IP address of the computer that sent a packet onto the network
- The destination IP address of the computer that received the packet
- The protocols used to send the frame
- The data or a portion of the message being sent

The process by which Network Monitor collects this information is called **capturing**. During capturing, data is transferred into a file for later analysis. By default, Network Monitor gathers all the frames it detects on the network into a capture buffer, which is a reserved storage area in memory. To capture packets on only a specific subset of frames, you can single out these frames by designing a capture filter. For example, you can capture only frames that originate from a particular IP address.

Figure 9-1 shows the results of a capture. Three buttons that you will find useful when working with captures are the Start Capture (F10), Pause/Resume Capture (F9), and Stop Capture (F11) buttons. The middle pane shows the alias list. The **alias list** is a file used by Network Monitor to store the associations between an IP address and a computer name. The bottom pane shows the frame summary. Each line represents a frame. A **frame** is data that is transmitted between two computers as a complete unit.

You can use the function keys to control the capture process. For example, to start a capture, press the F10 key.

Analyzing Traffic   **351**

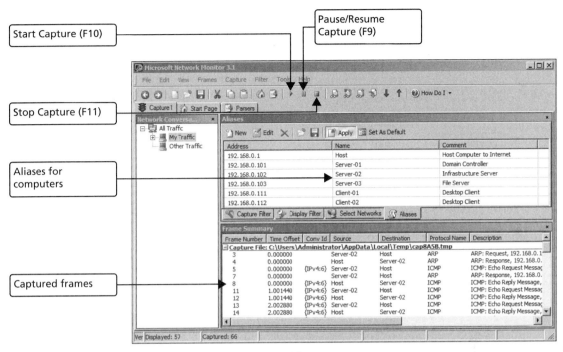

Figure 9-1 Microsoft Network Monitor showing captured frames

Creating an Alias List

To use aliases in Microsoft Network Monitor, you should first build an alias list. Microsoft Network Monitor uses the alias listed in the file to identify computers by name, which makes it easier to work with the captured frame. An alias list for the Classroom.local virtual network is shown in Figure 9-2. You will build an alias list in Activity 9-2.

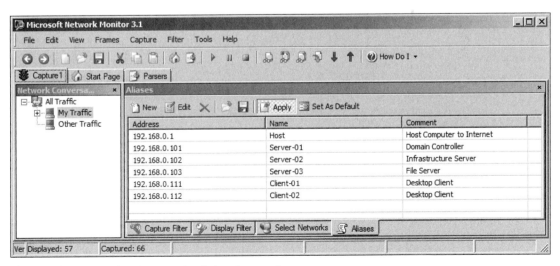

Figure 9-2 Alias list for Classroom.local virtual network

Filtering Packets

When you have finished capturing information, you can design a display filter to specify how much of the information that you have captured will be displayed in Microsoft Network Monitor's Frame Viewer window. Figure 9-3 illustrates the filtering accomplished through Network Monitor.

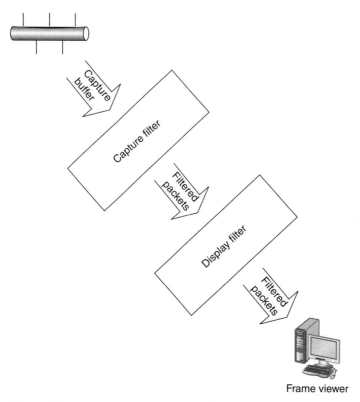

Figure 9-3 Filtering frames in Microsoft Network Monitor

Microsoft Network Monitor allows you to select from standard built-in filters, or you can create your own. Any filter can be applied either as a capture filter or a display filter. When a **capture filter** is applied, Microsoft Network Monitor only captures frames that meet the filter criteria. When a **display filter** is applied, Microsoft Network Monitor still captures frames that don't meet the criteria, but it doesn't display them.

You select a filter template by clicking Filter, pointing to Capture Filter or Display Filter, pointing to Load Filter, pointing to Standard Filters, and then clicking the filter type. Next, you edit the filter template in the Capture Filter or Display Filter pane. After you create or customize a filter, you can validate it to ensure that it works. Filters can be saved and loaded again later.

Capturing Data Between Two Computers

To monitor traffic between two computers, create a capture filter in Microsoft Network Monitor. A capture filter can be applied to the capture itself, avoiding the collection of data that is not needed to diagnose your problem. A capture filter specifies the type of data you want to monitor. To do this, you must load the filter by clicking the Load Filter button (the yellow folder with the green arrow) and then set the capture filter in the Capture Filter pane by clicking the Apply button. After the filter is set here, it remains active for all subsequent captures and must be either removed by choosing the Remove button or set to a new filter when it is no longer needed. Figure 9-4 shows the capture filter for the traffic between Server-02 and Client-01.

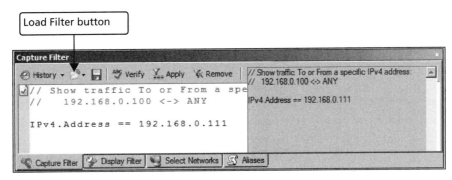

Figure 9-4 Capture Filter pane

Figure 9-5 shows the packets exchanged between Server-02 and Client-01 when the ping command was issued from Client-01. The ping command is a computer network tool used to test whether a particular host is reachable across an IP network. It works by sending ICMP "echo request" packets to the target host and listening for ICMP "echo response" replies. Ping estimates the round-trip time, generally in milliseconds, and records any packet loss, and prints a statistical summary when finished. Ping uses the **Internet Control Messaging Protocol (ICMP)**—an error reporting and diagnostic utility, which is considered a required part of any IP implementation. The **Address Resolution Protocol** (**ARP**) is the standard method for finding a host's hardware address when only its IP address is known.

Frame Number	Time Offset	Conv Id	Source	Destination	Protocol Name	Description
Capture File: C:\Users\Administrator\AppData\Local\Temp\capB0AA.tmp						
1	0.000000				NetmonFilter	NetmonFilter: Updated Captu
2	0.000000				NetworkInfoEx	NetworkInfoEx: Network info
3	5.958568	{IPv4...	Client-01	Server-02	ICMP	ICMP: Echo Request Message
4	5.968582	{IPv4...	Server-02	Client-01	ICMP	ICMP: Echo Reply Message, T
5	6.980037	{IPv4...	Client-01	Server-02	ICMP	ICMP: Echo Request Message
6	6.980037	{IPv4...	Server-02	Client-01	ICMP	ICMP: Echo Reply Message, T
7	7.971462	{IPv4...	Client-01	Server-02	ICMP	ICMP: Echo Request Message

Figure 9-5 Captured network traffic pane

After you have captured packets, you can isolate the captured frames with a display filter. To quickly create a display filter, right-click on the item that you want to filter by, and click Add Cell to Display Filter. To see the results of your display filter, click the Apply button. Figure 9-6, on the next page, shows the results of the ICMP display filter.

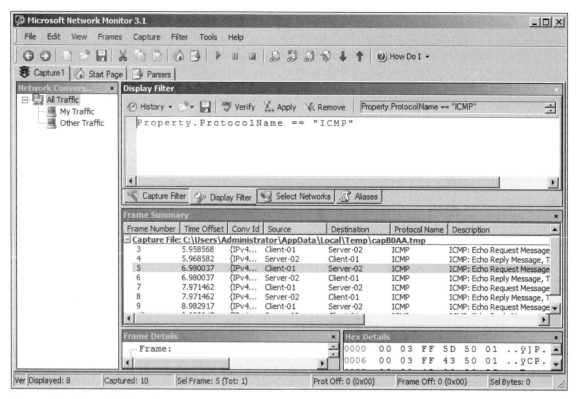

Figure 9-6 Filtered ICMP packets

Activity 9-1: Installing Microsoft Network Monitor

Time Required: 15 minutes

Objective: Install Microsoft Network Monitor.

Requirements: Completion of Activities 8-1 through 8-14.

Description: In this activity, you will download and install Microsoft Network Monitor.

1. Log on to your Host PC with a username of **Administrator** and a password of **Secret1**.
2. To launch VMRCplus, double-click the **VMRCplus** icon on the desktop.
3. To start Server-01, click **Server-01**, click **Turn On**, and then click **VM Console**.
4. Log on to Server-01 with a username of **Administrator** and a password of **Secret1**.
5. If necessary, to start Server-02, return to the Virtual Machine Manager, click **Server-02**, click **Turn On**, and then click **VM Console**.
6. If necessary, log on to Server-02 with a username of **Administrator** and a password of **Secret1**.
7. If Server Manager does not appear, click **Start** on the host computer, point to **Administrative Tools**, and then click **Server Manager**.

8. To set security for Microsoft Internet Explorer on Server-02, click **Server Manager (SERVER-02)**, click the **Configure IE ESC** link, click the **Off** option button under Administrators, and then click **OK**.
9. To launch Internet Explorer, click **Start**, and then click **Internet Explorer**.
10. To search for Network Monitor, type **Download Network Monitor 3.1** in the Live Search text box, and then press **Enter**.
11. To open the download Web page, scroll and click the link for the Network Monitor download.

There are many entries for Network Monitor 3.1 on Microsoft's site; you will need to locate a link that will lead to the Network Monitor download.

12. Scroll and click the download button for the proper version (x64 for 64-bit processors or x86 for 32-bit processors).
13. When the File Download - Security Warning dialog box opens, click the **Run** button.
14. When the Do you want to run this software? message appears, click the **Run** button, and then click **Next**.
15. Check the **I accept the terms in the License Agreement** option button and then click **Next**.
16. Click the **I do not want to use Microsoft Update** option button, and then click **Next**.
17. Click the **I do not want to participate in the program at this time** option button, and then click **Next**.
18. Click the **Typical** icon, and then click **Install**.
19. Wait for the installation to complete, and then click **Finish**.
20. Close the Internet Explorer window.
21. Leave the computer logged on for the next activity.

Next, you will investigate Network Monitor by capturing data traveling between two computers.

Activity 9-2: Capturing Packets

Time Required: 15 minutes

Objective: Capture packets between two computers with Microsoft Network Monitor.

Requirements: Completion of Activity 9-1. Server-01 and Server-02 are logged on.

Description: In this activity, you will create an alias list that will enable Network Monitor to identify the computers. Then, you will capture packets between the two computers.

1. Repeat Steps 1 through 6 from the previous activity.
2. Return to the Virtual Machine Manager window.

3. To start Client-01, return to the Virtual Machine Manager, click **Client-01**, click **Turn On**, and then click **VM Console**.

4. If necessary, log on to Client-01 with a username of **Classroom\Administrator** and a password of **Secret1**.

5. Return to Server-02.

6. To launch Network Monitor, double-click the **Microsoft Network Monitor 3.1** icon on the desktop.

7. When the Check for Microsoft Update Opt-In message appears, clear the **Microsoft Network Monitor updates at startup** check box, and then click **No**.

8. Verify that the **Local Area Connection** check box in the Select Networks pane is checked, and then click the **X** to close the Select Networks pane.

9. To enable conversations, check the **Enable Conversations (consumes more memory)** check box.

10. To display the Network Monitor panes, click the **Create a new capture tab** button.

11. To enter aliases for IP addresses, click the **Aliases** tab, click the **New** button in the Alias pane, type **192.168.0.1** in the Address text box, press **Tab**, type **Host** in the Name text box, and then click **OK**.

12. Repeat Step 11 using these associations:
    - 192.168.0.101 – Server-01
    - 192.168.0.102 – Server-02
    - 192.168.0.103 – Server-03
    - 192.168.0.111 – Client-01
    - 192.168.0.112 – Client-02

13. To save the alias definitions, click the **Disk** icon in the Aliases pane, type **Single Network** in the File name text box, and then click the **Save** button.

14. To create a capture filter, click the **Capture Filter** tab, click the **Load Filter** button (the yellow folder with the green arrow), point to **Standard Filters**, click **IPv4Address**, click in the text window, scroll and edit the IP address to be **192.168.0.111**, click the **Verify** button (if needed, correct the IP address), and then click **Apply**.

15. To start a capture, click the **Start Capture (F10)** button (the green Play button on the toolbar).

16. Return to Client-01.

17. To open a command prompt window, click **Start**, type **cmd** in the Start Search text box, and then press **Enter**.

18. To generate network traffic, type **ping 192.168.0.102**, and then press **Enter**.

19. Return to Server-02.

20. Wait for network traffic to appear, and click the **Stop Capture (F11)** button (the blue box on the toolbar).

21. To create a display filter, right-click **ICMP** in the Protocol Name column (located in the Frame Summary pane), click **Add Cell to Display Filter**, click the **Verify** button (if needed, correct the rule), and then click the **Apply** button.
22. Verify that any records other than the protocol ICMP disappear.
23. Close the Microsoft Network Monitor 3.1 window, and then click **No**.
24. Leave the computer logged on for the next activity.

Reconfiguring a Virtual Network

To properly implement the server roles in this chapter, you must revise the configuration of each network adapter. Currently, the network adapters are configured to use the Microsoft Loopback Adapter in the host computer. The host computer is configured to provide ICS for the virtual machines. ICS provides a number of services that will be implemented in this chapter. To avoid this duplication, you must move the network adapters in the Classroom.local network virtual machines to a new virtual network. These changes are illustrated in Figure 9-7.

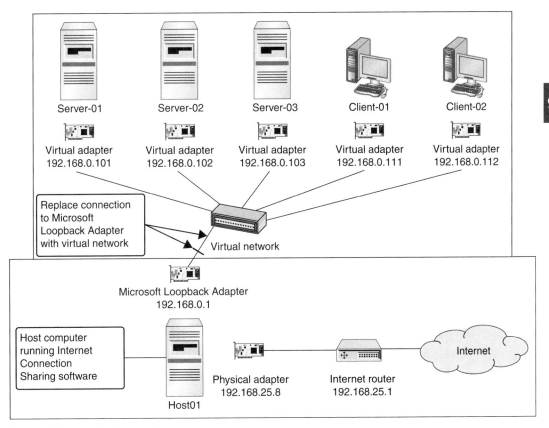

Figure 9-7 Required network changes

The creation of the new virtual network and the reconfiguration of the network occur in Activity 9-3.

Activity 9-3: Reconfiguring the Network for Classroom.local

Time Required: 10 minutes

Objective: Create a new virtual network and reconfigure the network adapters for each virtual machine.

Requirements: Completion of Activities 9-1 and 9-2.

Description: In this activity, you will create a new virtual network called Virtual Network 0. Then you will reconfigure each virtual machine to use this new virtual network.

1. If necessary, log on to your Host PC with a username of **Administrator** and a password of **Secret1**.
2. If necessary, to launch VMRCplus, double-click the **VMRCplus** icon on the desktop.
3. To create a new virtual network, click the **Tools** menu, click **Virtual Networks**, click the **Create** button, type **Virtual Network 0** in the Network Name text box, and then click **OK**.
4. To change the network adapter for Client-01, right-click **Client-01**, click **Settings**, click the **Connected to** drop-down list arrow, click **Virtual Network 0**, and then click **OK**.

You can change the virtual network setting "on the fly." Doing so saves the time required to shut down and restart the virtual machine as with the other virtual machine configuration options.

5. Repeat Step 4 for the remaining virtual machines.
6. Leave the computer logged on for the next activity.

You have changed the network adapter to isolate the virtual machines from the public network. Next, you will learn about the installation of one of the services for a TCP/IP network.

Installing the Dynamic Host Configuration Protocol

You will further enhance the flexibility of your Classroom.local virtual network by installing the Dynamic Host Configuration Protocol (DHCP). DHCP reduces the administration burden and complexity of configuring hosts on a TCP/IP-based network, such as Classroom.local. Three basic components make up DHCP in Windows Server 2008:

- DHCP servers—The Microsoft DHCP Server service includes the DHCP snap-in, which is an easy-to-use graphical user interface management tool that allows network administrators to define DHCP client configurations. The DHCP server also includes a database for managing assignment of IP addresses and other configuration parameters.

- DHCP clients—Operating systems running TCP/IP provide the software to support the DHCP clients.
- DHCP Relay Agents—DHCP relies on network broadcasts to communicate with clients. Routers in normal routed environments do not automatically forward broadcasts from one network to another. A DHCP Relay Agent must forward these messages. A router or a host computer configured to listen for DHCP broadcast messages and direct them to a specific server running DHCP can act as a **DHCP Relay Agent**. Using relay agents eliminates the necessity of having a server running DHCP on each physical network segment. Relay agents direct local DHCP client requests to remote DHCP servers and also return remote DHCP server responses to the DHCP clients.

You will be installing a DHCP Relay Agent in Activity 9-13 after routing has been installed.

Authorizing a DHCP Server

When configured correctly and authorized for use on a network, DHCP servers provide their intended administrative service. However, when a misconfigured or unauthorized DHCP server is introduced into a network, it can cause problems. For example, if an unauthorized DHCP server starts, it might begin leasing incorrect IP addresses to clients (duplicate IP addresses).

To resolve these issues, DHCP servers running Windows Server 2008 are verified as authorized in Active Directory Domain Services (AD DS) before they can service clients. This avoids most of the accidental damage caused by running DHCP servers with incorrect configurations or correct configurations on the wrong network. You authorize the DHCP server when the DHCP role is added. You will authorize your DHCP server in Activity 9-4.

DHCP Process

To simplify IP addressing tasks for the network administrator, you can now manually configure just one computer—the DHCP server. Whenever a new computer starts on a network segment that is served by the DHCP server (or an existing computer is restarted), the computer asks for a unique IP address and the DHCP server assigns one from the pool of available addresses.

As Figure 9-8 (on the next page) shows, this process requires only four steps:

1. **DHCP discover** message—Packet where the DHCP client asks for an IP address
2. **DHCP offer** message—Packet where the DHCP server offers a lease and IP configuration
3. **DHCP request** message—Packet where the DHCP client accepts the offer and requests the IP configuration
4. **DHCP acknowledge** message—Packet where the DHCP server officially assigns the address to the client for the lease period

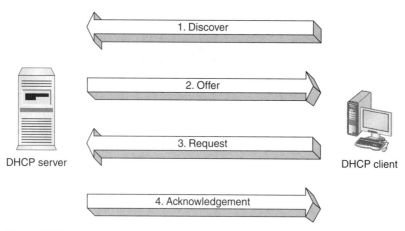

Figure 9-8 DHCP process

Managing DHCP

The DHCP snap-in helps network administrators configure and monitor DHCP servers. See Figure 9-9. You can define global and scope-specific configuration settings to identify routers and set DHCP client configurations. A **scope** is an administrative grouping of TCP/IP addresses with associated information about those addresses. You must define a scope before DHCP clients can use the DHCP server for dynamic TCP/IP configuration.

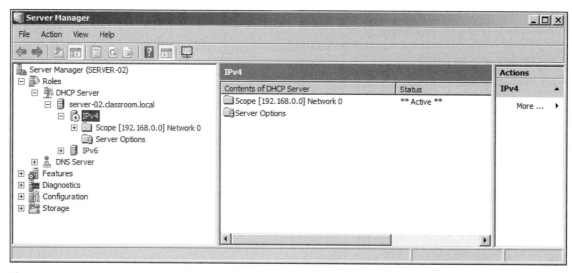

Figure 9-9 DHCP in Server Manager

A computer running Windows Server 2008 and TCP/IP automatically creates a DHCP server database on installation of the DHCP Server service. After installation, changing the parameters in Table 9-1 can further customize the service.

Table 9-1 DHCP customization parameters

Parameter	Description
Scope	The consecutive range of possible IP addresses for a network. Scopes typically define a single physical subnet on the network to which DHCP services are offered.
Superscope	An administrative grouping of scopes that can be used to support multiple logical IP subnets on the same physical subnet.
Exclusion range	A limited sequence of IP addresses within a scope, excluded from DHCP service offerings. Exclusion ranges permit static addresses to be assigned by a network administrator.
Address pool	The collection of addresses within a scope that remain after you define a DHCP scope and apply exclusion ranges. Pooled addresses are eligible for dynamic assignment by the server to DHCP clients on your network.
Lease	A length of time that a DHCP server specifies, during which a client computer can use an assigned IP address.
Reservation	A permanent address lease assignment by the DHCP server. Reservations ensure that a specified hardware device on the subnet can always use the same IP address.

Creating Scopes

Administrators plan scopes based on the needs of specific groups of computers, with appropriate lease durations defined for the related scopes. You create a scope with the DHCP snap-in and specify the following information:

- A range of possible IP addresses from which to include or exclude addresses used in DHCP service lease offerings
- A unique subnet mask to determine the subnet related to a given IP address
- A scope name assigned when the scope is created
- Lease duration values to be assigned to DHCP clients that receive dynamically allocated IP addresses
- Reservations for computers and printers requiring specific individual IP address
- Configuration options such as IP addresses for gateways and DNS servers

As shown in Figure 9-10 on the next page, DHCP scope consists of a pool of IP addresses on a subnet, such as 192.168.0.1 through 192.168.0.254, that the DHCP server can lease to DHCP clients. Each physical network can have only one DHCP scope.

Larger networks might require the following configuration steps to assign several address ranges within a single scope or subnet for DHCP service:

- Define the scope by using the entire range of consecutive IP addresses that make up the local IP subnet.
- Set exclusion ranges, which define the IP addresses within the scope that the DHCP server does not lease. For example, to exclude the first 10 addresses in the previous sample scope to be assigned to servers and routers, you must exclude 192.168.0.1 through 192.168.0.10. Doing so specifies that no DHCP clients ever receive these addresses for leased configuration.

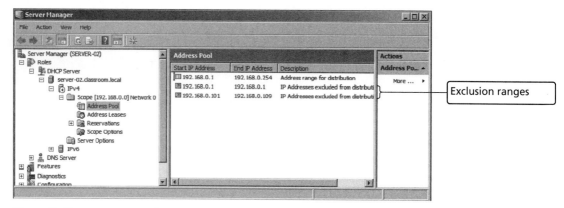

Figure 9-10 DHCP scope with exclusion ranges

Depending on the complexity of your network, a defined scope might require the following additional configuration steps:

- Select additional exclusion ranges to further exclude any IP addresses that are not to be leased to DHCP clients. Exclusions should include all devices that cannot use DHCP, such as printers.

- Create reservations by reserving some IP addresses for permanent lease assignment to specified computers or devices on a network. Reservations should be made only for devices that use DHCP and have a specialized function on the network, such as special server computers (servers used for DHCP, WINS, or DNS) and routers. Figure 9-11 shows the New Reservation dialog box.

- Adjust the duration of leases. Note that the default lease duration of eight days might not require adjustment.

- After defining and configuring a scope as outlined previously, you must activate the scope before dynamic service begins for DHCP-enabled clients. After you do this, the server can begin processing IP address lease requests and offering leases to DHCP-enabled clients on the network.

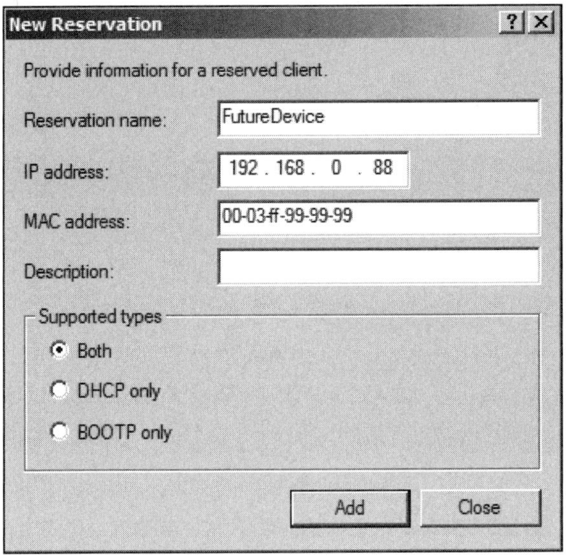

Figure 9-11 DHCP reservation

Scope Options

The DHCP installation adds a number of scope options. With the scope options, you can specify IP configuration information to be assigned to the client. Figure 9-12 shows the scope options for the Classroom.local domain. These three items will be provided to each client when a lease is requested.

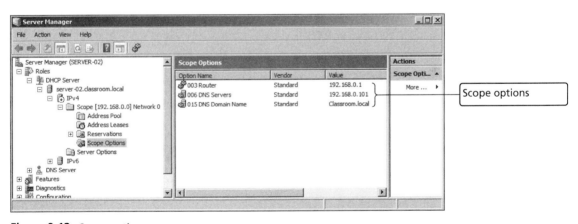

Figure 9-12 Scope options

Table 9-2 lists some of the more common scope options that can be assigned by DHCP servers.

Table 9-2 Common scope options

Code	Option name	Option description
2	Time Offset	Specifies the offset of the client's subnet in seconds from UTC
3	Router	Specifies a list of IP addresses for routers on the client's subnet
4	Time Server	Specifies a list of time servers available to the client
6	DNS Servers	Specifies a list of DNS servers available to the client
15	DNS Domain Name	Specifies the domain name that the client should use when resolving host names via DNS

Viewing DHCP Traffic in Microsoft Network Monitor

In addition to using Microsoft Network Monitor to capture network traffic coming to and from a computer, you can use it to view and analyze traffic between a DHCP server and DHCP clients. Observing the IP address lease process is an example of how Network Monitor can provide information about DHCP. Figure 9-13 shows the traffic between a DHCP client and DHCP server as a lease occurs.

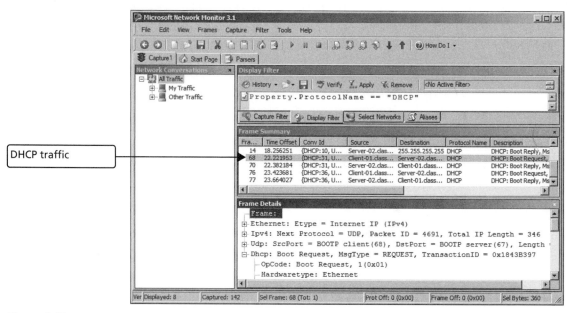

Figure 9-13 DHCP traffic in Network Monitor

Activity 9-4: Adding and Authorizing a DHCP Service

Time Required: 15 minutes

Objective: Add the DHCP Service and authorize its use in AD DS.

Requirements: Completion of Activity 9-1.

Description: In this activity, you will install the DHCP service. Then, you will authorize its use in AD DS.

1. If necessary, log on to your Host PC with a username of **Administrator** and a password of **Secret1**.
2. If necessary, to launch VMRCplus, double-click the **VMRCplus** icon on the desktop.
3. If necessary, to start Server-01, click **Server-01**, click **Turn On**, and then click **VM Console**.
4. If necessary, log on to Server-01 with a username of **Administrator** and a password of **Secret1**.
5. If necessary, to start Server-02, return to the Virtual Machine Manager, click **Server-02**, click **Turn On**, and then click **VM Console**.
6. If necessary, log on to Server-02 with a username of **Administrator** and a password of **Secret1**.
7. If necessary, to launch Server Manager, click **Start**, point to **Administrative Tools**, and then click **Server Manager**.
8. To start the addition of the DHCP role, click the **Roles** node, click the **Add Roles** link, click **Server Roles**, click the **DHCP Server** check box, and then click **Next** twice.
9. To verify the network bindings, retain the existing IP address check box, and then click **Next**.
10. To assign the DNS server address, type **192.168.0.101** in the Preferred DNS server IP address text box, click the **Validate** button, and then click **Next** twice.
11. To add the initial scope, click the **Add** button, type **Virtual Network 0** in the Scope Name text box, type **192.168.0.1** in the Starting IP Address text box, type **192.168.0.254** in the Ending IP Address text box, type **255.255.255.0** in the Subnet Mask text box, type **192.168.0.1** in the Default Gateway (optional) text box, click **OK**, and then click **Next**.
12. To not use DHCPv6 stateless operation, click the Disable DHCPv6 stateless mode for this server option button, and then click **Next**.

DHCPv6 stateless operation is beyond the scope of this text.

13. To authorize the DHCP server, click the **Use alternate credentials** option, click the **Specify** button, log on with a username of **Administrator** and a password of **Secret1**, click **OK**, and then click **Next**.
14. Verify the DHCP Server feature settings, and then click **Install**.
15. Wait for the installation to be completed, and then click **Close**.
16. To view the DHCP console, click **Start**, point to **Administrative Tools**, and then click **DHCP**.
17. To view the DHCP configuration, expand the **server-02.classroom.local** node, and then expand the **IPv4** node.

The Scope (192.168.0.0) Virtual Network 0 may have a red down arrow. This is OK. You will complete the configuration of this scope in the next activity.

18. Leave the DHCP console open for the next activity.

Do not remove the DHCP server role. At the time that this text was written, there was no provision to unauthorize the DHCP server in Windows Server 2008.

Activity 9-5: Configuring DHCP Scopes

Time Required: 20 minutes

Objective: Complete the configuration of the scope for Virtual Network 0 and activate the scope.

Requirements: Completion of Activities 9-1 through 9-4.

Description: In this activity, you will continue the configuration of the scope for Virtual Network 0. Also, you will activate the scope.

1. If necessary, log on to your Host PC with a username of **Administrator** and a password of **Secret1**.
2. If necessary, to launch VMRCplus, double-click the **VMRCplus** icon on the desktop.
3. If necessary, to start Server-01, click **Server-01**, click **Turn On**, and then click **VM Console**.
4. If necessary, log on to Server-01 with a username of **Administrator** and a password of **Secret1**.
5. If necessary, to start Server-02, return to the Virtual Machine Manager, click **Server-02**, click **Turn On**, and then click **VM Console**.

6. If necessary, log on to Server-02 with a username of **Administrator** and a password of **Secret1**.
7. If necessary, to view the DHCP console, click **Start**, point to **Administrative Tools**, and then click **DHCP**.
8. To see the address pool, expand **Scope (192.168.0.0) Virtual Network 0**, and then click the **Address Pool** node.
9. To add an exclusion for the gateway, right-click in the white space in the right pane, click **New Exclusion Range**, type **192.168.0.1** in the Start IP address text box, and then click **Add**.
10. To add exclusions for the existing virtual machine, type **192.168.0.101** in the Start IP address text box, type **192.168.0.109** in the End IP address text box, click **Add**, and then click **Close**.
11. To practice adding a reservation for a future device, click the **Reservations** node, click the **Action** menu, click **New Reservation**, type **FutureDevice** in the Reservation name text box, type **192.168.0.88** in the IP address text box, type **00-03-FF-99-99-99** in the MAC address text box, click **Add**, and then click **Close**.
12. To view the scope options, click the **Scope Options** node in the left pane and note the options that are configured.
13. Close the DHCP console window.
14. Leave the computer logged on for the next activity.

Activity 9-6: Viewing DHCP Traffic in Network Monitor

Time Required: 10 minutes

Objective: View DHCP traffic in Network Monitor.

Requirements: Completion of Activities 9-1 through 9-5.

Description: In this activity, you will configure Client-01 to use dynamic addressing. Then, you will monitor the DHCP records exchanged between the DHCP service on Server-02 and DHCP client on Client-01.

1. If necessary, log on to your Host PC with a username of **Administrator** and a password of **Secret1**.
2. If necessary, to launch VMRCplus, double-click the **VMRCplus** icon on the desktop.
3. If necessary, to start Server-01, click **Server-01**, click **Turn On**, and then click **VM Console**.
4. If necessary, log on to Server-01 with a username of **Administrator** and a password of **Secret1**.
5. If necessary, to start Server-02, return to the Virtual Machine Manager, click **Server-02**, click **Turn On**, and then click **VM Console**.

6. If necessary, log on to Server-02 with a username of **Administrator** and a password of **Secret1**.
7. If necessary, to start Client-01, return to the Virtual Machine Manager, click **Client-01**, click **Turn On**, and then click **VM Console**.
8. If necessary, log on to **Client-01** with a username of **Classroom\Administrator** and a password of **Secret1**.
9. Switch to Server-02.
10. To launch Microsoft Network Monitor, double-click the **Microsoft Network Monitor** icon on the desktop.
11. To start a capture, click the **Create a new capture tab** button, click the **Start Capture (F10)** button (the green arrowhead on the toolbar).
12. Switch to Client-01.
13. To open the Local Area Connection Properties dialog box, click **Start**, click **Control Panel**, click the **View network status and tasks** link under Network and Internet, click the **View status** link under Classroom.local (Domain network), and then click the **Properties** button.
14. If the User Account Control dialog box opens, click the **Continue** button.
15. To configure Client-01 to obtain an IP address automatically, click **Internet Protocol Version 4 (TCP/IPv4)**, click the **Properties** button, click the **Obtain an IP address automatically** option button, click **OK**, click **Close** twice, and then close the Network and Sharing Center window.
16. Return to Server-02.
17. Wait for network traffic to appear and click the **Stop Capture (F11)** button (the blue box on the toolbar).

To change the size of the display panes, click and drag the borders.

18. To create a display filter, click the **Display Filter** tab, scroll and locate a DHCP protocol, right-click **DHCP** in the Protocol Name column, click **Add Cell to Display Filter**, click the **Verify** button (if needed, correct the rule), and then click the **Apply** button.
19. Scroll the Frame Summary pane to locate the first record that appears in the set of records with a protocol name of DHCP.
20. To view the DHCP discover message, click the first record, close the **Hex Details** pane, expand the **Dhcp: Boot Request** node, and then scroll to view the remainder of the Frame Details to see the remaining fields.
21. To view the DHCP offer message, click the Frame Summary pane to display the next record, expand the **Dhcp: Boot Reply** node, and then scroll to view the remainder of the Frame Details to see the remaining fields.

22. To view the DHCP request message click the next record, expand the **Dhcp: Boot Request** node, and then scroll to view the remainder of the Frame Details to see the remaining fields.

23. To view the DHCP acknowledge message, click the next record, expand the **Dhcp: Boot Reply** node, and then scroll to view the remainder of the Frame Details to see the remaining fields that contain the IP configuration for Client-01.

24. Close the Microsoft Network Monitor 3.1 window, and then click **No**.

25. Leave the computer logged on for the next activity.

Implementing Routing

As you learned earlier, routing is the process of moving information across a network from a source to a destination. Routing involves two basic activities—determining optimal routing paths and transporting packets through a network. A **router** is a network device that connects two or more networks and routes incoming data packets to the appropriate network.

You will learn more about routing in the sections that follow.

Routing Tables

A **routing table** is a set of rules, often viewed in table format, that all IP-enabled devices, including computers and routers, use to determine where data packets traveling over a network will be directed.

A routing table contains the information necessary to forward a packet along the best path toward its destination. The **best path** is identified by the lowest routing metric. A **routing metric** is a standard of measurement, such as hop count, that is used by routing algorithms to determine the best path to a destination. Each packet contains information about its origin and destination. When a router receives a packet, the router examines the packet and matches it to the routing table entry providing the best match for its destination. The table then provides the router with instructions for sending the packet to the next hop on its route across the network.

Administrators can maintain routing tables manually or dynamically. Tables for static network devices do not change unless you manually change them. In dynamic routing, devices build and maintain their routing tables automatically by using routing protocols. **Routing protocols** facilitate the exchange of routing information between networks, allowing routers to build routing tables dynamically.

Figure 9-14, on the next page, shows a basic routing table. The routing table for TCP/IPv4 is listed by typing the command route print -4 at a command prompt. To implement IP routing, you need to understand the configuration of the routing table. Every computer that runs the TCP/IP protocol makes routing decisions that are determined by the IP routing table.

The columns in a basic routing table include the following information:

- Network destination—Entries are checked for a match to the destination IP address. Entries in this column can be individual addresses, network addresses, or gateways.

- Netmask—Entries are used in much the same way as the subnet mask, though it isn't precisely the same thing. It tells you which part of the network address is important for the match.

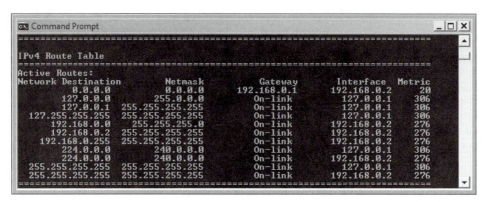

Figure 9-14 Basic routing table

- Gateway—Entries specify where packets are sent that match the rule specified by the network destination and the netmask.
- Interface—Entries specify which network connection to use when sending to the destination IP address.
- Metric—Entries specify a cost (ranging from 1 to 9999) to each available route so that the most cost-effective path can be chosen.

Each line in a routing table constitutes a routing rule. Table 9-3 shows examples of routing rules.

Table 9-3 Routing rules

Routing rules	Network destination	Netmask	Gateway	Interface	Metric
1	0.0.0.0	0.0.0.0	192.168.0.1	192.168.0.2	20
2	127.0.0.0	255.0.0.0	On-link	127.0.0.1	306
3	127.0.0.1	255.255.255.255	On-link	127.0.0.1	306
4	127.255.255.255	255.255.255.255	On-link	127.0.0.1	306
5	192.168.0.0	255.255.255.0	On-link	192.168.0.2	276
6	192.168.0.2	255.255.255.255	On-link	192.168.0.2	276
7	192.168.0.255	255.255.255.255	On-link	192.168.0.2	276
8	224.0.0.0	240.0.0.0	On-link	127.0.0.1	306
9	224.0.0.0	240.0.0.0	On-link	192.168.0.2	276
10	255.255.255.255	255.255.255.255	On-link	127.0.0.1	306
11	255.255.255.255	255.255.255.255	On-link	192.168.0.2	276

Now let's look at some individual entries. There are four individual IP addresses listed in the route table (Lines 6, 7, 10, and 11). Look at the Netmask column—a netmask of 255.255.255.255 means that every single bit of the network address must be considered for a match. 192.168.0.2 is the IP address of the network card on this computer. 192.168.0.255 is a special-purpose IP address used for broadcasts to the 192.168.0.x network. The two 255.255.255.255 entries are two network-limited broadcasts. Because of the metrics for these network-limited broadcasts, the broadcasts will be forwarded to the 192.168.0.2 interface.

There are three network addresses in the list: 192.168.0.0, 127.0.0.0, and 224.0.0.0 (Lines 2, 5, 8, and 9). The first is the network to which 192.168.0.2 belongs; the second is a special-use address for local loopback. When used on any computer anywhere, the **local loopback** address always refers to the current computer. In particular, the address 127.0.0.1 is defined as the local loopback address, and means "this computer right here." The last two iterations of 224.0.0.0 are reserved numbers for multicasting. A use for multicasting is broadcasting big events over the Internet. **Multicasting** allows a single computer to create the content (concert, film, and so on) and many computers to play the same single stream.

There are three entries of interest:

- The first is the individual address, 192.168.0.2 (Line 6), which is the IP address of the current computer.
- The interface IP address of 127.0.0.1 tells you that any packet with that destination is looped back to this computer.
- The local network address is 192.168.0.0. A packet from an application on the local computer addressed to any address in the 192.168.0.x group (except for 192.168.0.1) is passed on to the network card.

Routing Protocols

The routing protocol also specifies how routers in a network share information with each other and report network changes. Routers monitor activity on the network and respond to occurrences such as communication failures and network congestion. The routing protocol enables a network to make dynamic adjustments to its conditions, so routing decisions do not have to be predetermined and static.

Routing protocols use metrics to evaluate the best path for a packet to travel. To aid the process of path determination, routing algorithms initialize and maintain routing tables, which contain route information. Route information varies depending on the routing algorithm used.

Static Routing

With **static routing**, you maintain the routing table manually using the route command. Static routing is practical for a single network communicating with one or two other networks, such as Classroom.local.

The steps to implement static routing are as follows:

1. Open a command prompt on each virtual machine.
2. Display the routing table by executing the route print -4 command.
3. Determine the networks that exist.
4. Add static routes for the missing routes with the route add command.

Figure 9-15 shows the routing table for Client-01. There is a routing table entry for the 192.168.0.0 network on which Client-01 resides. Two network entries are missing—192.168.1.0 and 192.168.2.0.

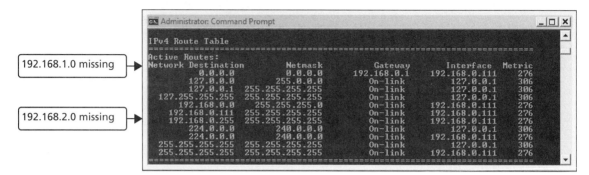

Figure 9-15 Routing table for Client-01

You will need two route add statements, as shown in Figure 9-16.

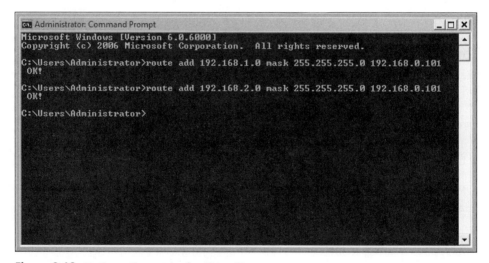

Figure 9-16 Static routing entries for Client-01

The format for the route add statement is as follows:
Route add *destinationnetwork* mask *nnn.nnn.nnn.nnn gateway*

The *destinationnetwork* is the network that packets will be routed to. You enter a network mask where the *nnn.nnn.nnn.nnn* appears. The gateway is the IP address on the "other end" of the network segment where packets are forwarded to a router.

You will enter a route add statement for your network in Activity 9-10. Routing statements are removed with the Route remove *destinationnetwork* command.

Dynamic Routing

Routing Information Protocol (RIP) is a widely used protocol for managing router information within a small, self-contained network such as a corporate network. Using RIP, a gateway router sends its entire **dynamic routing table** (which lists all the other networks it knows about) to its closest neighbor router every 30 seconds. The neighbor router, in turn, passes the information on to its next neighbor and so on until all routers within the network have the same knowledge of routing paths, a state known as **network convergence**. RIP uses a hop count as a way to determine network distance. (Other protocols use more sophisticated algorithms that include bandwidth as well.) Each router in the network uses the routing table information to determine the next router to route a packet to for a specified destination.

Network Policy and Access Services

Network Policy and Access Services (NPAS) is a service within Windows Server 2008 that allows you to provide local and remote network access and to define and enforce policies for network access authentication, authorization, and client health. NPAS includes a full-featured software router in the **Routing and Remote Access Service (RRAS)**, which offers routing services to businesses in local area network (LAN) and wide area network (WAN) environments.

After adding Network Policy and Access Services in Server Manager, you can install the Routing and Remote Access Service. In the Server Manager main window, under Roles Summary, click Add Roles. From the Add Roles Wizard, select Network Policy and Access Services. In the list of role services, select Routing and Remote Access Services. Activity 9-9 provides detailed instructions on the installation of RRAS.

After installing RRAS, you need to enable the service to configure your server for routing and remote access. Follow the instructions in the Routing and Remote Access Server Setup Wizard to select RIP routing. Figure 9-17 shows the selection of RIP as a routing protocol. Follow the steps in Activity 9-12 to configure RIP routing.

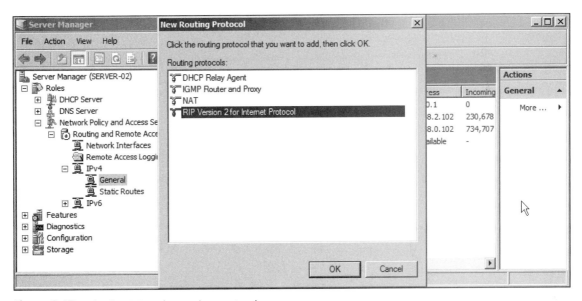

Figure 9-17 Selecting RIP as the routing protocol

RIP is a **distance-vector routing protocol**. It advertises the number of hops to a network destination (the distance) and the direction in which a packet can reach a network destination (the vector). The distance-vector algorithm, also known as the **Bellman-Ford algorithm**, enables a router to pass route updates to its neighbors at regularly scheduled intervals, as shown in Figure 9-18. Each neighbor then adds its own distance value and forwards the routing information on to its immediate neighbors. The result of this process is a table containing the cumulative distance to each network destination.

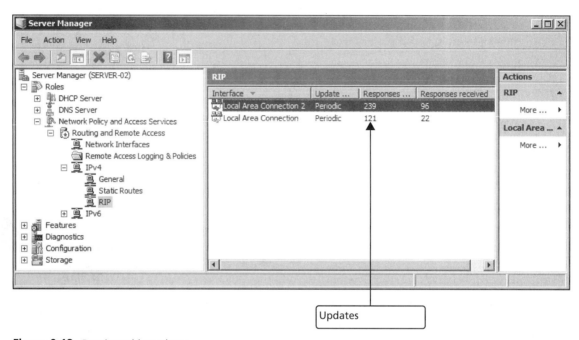

Figure 9-18 Routing table updates

Reconfiguring the Classroom.local Virtual Network for Routing

To implement routing, two additional networks—Virtual Network 1 and Virtual Network 2—need to be added to the Classroom.local network, as shown in Figure 9-19.

Server-01 and Server-02 will be configured to support routing. Client-01 and Client-02 will test routing—from Virtual Network 0 to Virtual Network 1 through Virtual Network 2.

Figure 9-19 shows three virtual networks—Virtual Network 0, Virtual Network 1, and Virtual Network 2. There are two routers in this network—Server-02 and Server-03. These two routers have two network adapters, or interfaces. Server-02 has an interface on Virtual Network 0 and Virtual Network 2 and must be configured to route packets between these two interfaces. This requires the addition of an additional server role for Server-02—the Network Policy and Access Services role.

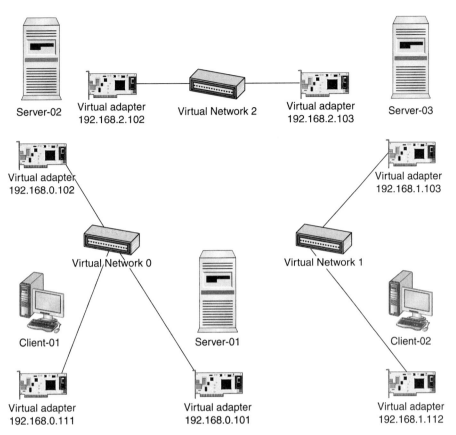

Figure 9-19 Classroom.local virtual network reconfigured for routing

Figure 9-20 shows Routing and Remote Access—one of the services provided by Network Policy and Access Services. As needed, packets will be routed between Local Area Connection (Virtual Network 0) to Local Area Connection 2 (Virtual Network 2).

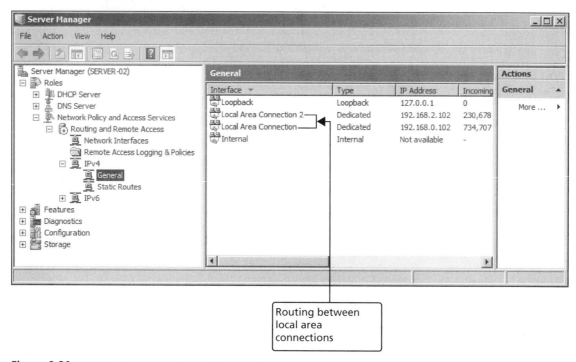

Figure 9-20 LAN routing on Routing and Remote Access service

Table 9-4 shows the IP configurations for the network adapters in the virtual machines. You will use this information in Activity 9-7.

Table 9-4 IP addresses for reconfigured Classroom.local network

Virtual Machine	Network	Network adapter	Interface IP address	Gateway IP address	DNS IP address
Server-01	Virtual Network 0	Local Area Connection	192.168.0.101	192.168.0.102	192.168.0.101
Server-02	Virtual Network 0	Local Area Connection	192.168.0.102		192.168.0.102
Server-02	Virtual Network 2	Local Area Connection 2	192.168.2.102	192.168.2.103	192.168.0.101
Server-03	Virtual Network 1	Local Area Connection	192.168.1.103		192.168.0.101
Server-03	Virtual Network 2	Local Area Connection 2	192.168.2.103	192.168.0.102	192.168.0.101
Client-01	Virtual Network 0	Local Area Connection	192.168.0.111	192.168.0.102	192.168.0.102
Client-02	Virtual Network 1	Local Area Connection	192.168.1.112	192.168.1.103	192.168.0.101

Activity 9-7: Reconfiguring the Classroom.local Virtual Network for Routing

Time Required: 15 minutes

Objective: Reconfigure the Classroom.local network for routing.

Requirements: Completion of Activities 9-1 through 9-6.

Description: In this activity, you will add two more virtual networks—Virtual Network 1 and Virtual Network 2. Next, you will adjust the virtual machines to connect to the three networks. You will add an additional network adapter to Server-01 and Server-02. The last task is to reconfigure the IP addresses on the virtual machines to connect to the proper network.

1. If necessary, log on to your Host PC with a username of **Administrator** and a password of **Secret1**.
2. If necessary, to launch VMRCplus, double-click the **VMRCplus** icon on the desktop.
3. Switch to the Virtual Machine Manager window.

Creating Virtual Networks

4. To create a new virtual network, click the **Tools** menu, click **Virtual Networks**, click the **Create** button, type **Virtual Network 1** in the Network Name text box, and then click **OK**.
5. Repeat Step 4 using Virtual Network 2 in place of Virtual Network 1.

Configuring Virtual Machines to Use Virtual Network 1 and Virtual Network 2

6. To shut down Server-02, return to the Console Manager in VMRCplus, click **localhost/Server-02**, click **Start**, click the arrow next to the lock, click **Shut Down**, click the **Option** drop-down list arrow, click **Hardware Installation (Planned)**, and then click **OK**.
7. If necessary, repeat Step 6 using Server-03 in place of Server-02.

Server-02 and Server-03 must be off. A second network adapter cannot be added to a virtual machine that is in a Saved or Running state.

8. To add a second network adapter to Server-02, return to the Virtual Machine Manager, right-click **Server-02**, click **Settings**, click the **NIC 2** check box, click the **Connected to** drop-down list arrow, click **Virtual Network 2**, and then click **OK**.
9. To change the first network adapter for Server-03, right-click **Server-03**, click **Settings**, click the **Connected to** drop-down list arrow for NIC 1, click **Virtual Network 1**, and then click **Apply**.
10. To add a second network adapter network for Server-03, click the **NIC 2** check box, click the **Connected to** drop-down list arrow, click **Virtual Network 2**, and then click **OK**.

11. To change the network adapter for Client-02, right-click **Client-02**, click **Settings**, click the **Connected to** drop-down list arrow, click **Virtual Network 1**, and then click **OK**.
12. To start Server-02, click **Server-02**, click **Turn On**, and then click **VM Console**.
13. Log on to Server-02 with a username of **Administrator** and a password of **Secret1**.
14. If necessary, to launch Server Manager, click **Start**, point to **Administrative Tools**, and then click **Server Manager**.
15. To view the Network Connections window, click **Server Manager (SERVER-02)**, and then click the **View Network Connections** link.
16. To configure the IP address for the Local Area Connection, right-click **Local Area Connection**, click **Properties**, click the **Internet Protocol Version 4 (TCP/IPv4)** line, click **Properties**, type **192.168.0.102** in the IP address text box, press **Tab** twice, clear the Default gateway text box, press **Tab** twice, type **192.168.0.101** in the Preferred DNS server text box, click **OK**, and then click **Close**.
17. To configure the IP address for the Local Area Connection 2, right-click **Local Area Connection 2**, click **Properties**, clear the **Internet Protocol Version 6 (TCP/IPv6)** check box, click the **Internet Protocol Version 4 (TCP/IPv4)** line, click **Properties**, click the **Use the following IP address** option button, type **192.168.2.102** in the IP address text box, press **Tab** twice, type **192.168.2.103** in the Default geteway text box, press **Tab** twice, type **192.168.0.102** in the Preferred DNS server text box, click **OK**, click **Close**, and then close the Network Connections window.
18. Switch to the Virtual Machine Manager window.
19. To start Server-03, click **Server-03**, click **Turn On**, and then click **VM Console**.
20. Log on to Server-03 with a username of **Administrator** and a password of **Secret1**.
21. If necessary, to launch Server Manager, click **Start**, point to **Administrative Tools**, and then click **Server Manager**.
22. To view the Network Connections window, click **Server Manager (SERVER-03)**, and then click the **View Network Connections** link.
23. To configure the IP address for the Local Area Connection, right-click **Local Area Connection**, click **Properties**, click the **Internet Protocol Version 4 (TCP/IPv4)**, click **Properties**, type **192.168.1.103** in the IP address text box, press **Tab** twice, clear the Default gateway text box, type **192.168.0.101** in the Preferred DNS server text box, click **OK**, and then click **Close**.
24. To configure the IP address for the Local Area Connection 2, right-click **Local Area Connection 2**, click **Properties**, clear the **Internet Protocol Version 6 (TCP/IPv6)** check box, click **Internet Protocol Version 4 (TCP/IPv4)**, click **Properties**, click the **Use the following IP address** option button, type **192.168.2.103** in the IP address text box, press **Tab** twice, type **192.168.2.102** in the Default geteway text box, press **Tab** twice, type **192.168.0.101** in the Preferred DNS server text box, click **OK**, click **Close**, and then close the Network Connections window.
25. To start Client-01, return to the Virtual Machine Manager, click **Client-01**, if necessary, click **Turn On**, and then click **VM Console**.

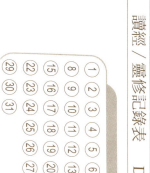

我靠著那加給我力量的，凡事都能作。（腓 Php 4:13）
I can do everything through him who gives me strength. (腓 Php 4:13)

26. If necessary, log on to Client-01 with a username of **Classroom\Administrator** and a password of **Secret1**.

27. To provide an IP configuration for Client-01, click **Start**, click **Control Panel**, click the **View network status and tasks** link under Network and Internet, click the **View status** link, and then click the **Properties** button.

28. If the User Account Control dialog box opens, click the **Continue** button.

29. Click **Internet Protocol Version 4 (TCP/IPv4)**, click the **Properties** button, click the **Use the following IP address** option button, type **192.168.0.111** in the IP address text box, press **Tab** twice, type **192.168.0.102** in the Default gateway text box, press **Tab** twice, type **192.168.0.102** in the Preferred DNS server text box, click **OK**, click **Close** twice, and then close the Network and Sharing window.

If the Set Network Location window opens, click Work, and then click Close.

30. To start Client-02, return to the Virtual Machine Manager, click **Client-02**, click **Turn On**, and then click **VM Console**.

31. If necessary, log on to Client-02 with a username of **Student** and a password of **Secret1**.

32. To provide an IP configuration, click **Start**, click **Control Panel**, click the **View network status and tasks** link under Network and Internet, click the **View status** link, and then click the **Properties** button.

33. When the User Account Control dialog box opens, click the **Continue** button.

34. Click **Internet Protocol Version 4 (TCP/IPv4)**, click the **Properties** button, type **192.168.1.112** in the IP address text box, press **Tab** twice, type **192.168.1.103** in the Default gateway text box, press **Tab** twice, type **192.168.0.101** in the Preferred DNS server text box, click **OK**, click **Close** twice, and then close the Network and Sharing window.

Activity 9-8: Interpreting Routing Tables

Time Required: 15 minutes

Objective: Interpret the entries in the routing table on Client-01.

Requirements: Completion of Activities 9-1 through 9-7.

Description: In this activity, you will display the routing table for Client-01. Next, you will answer questions related to the entries in the routing table. This activity is useful because you must be able to interpret routing tables to add static routing entries and perform routing.

1. If necessary, log on to your Host PC with a username of **Administrator** and a password of **Secret1**.

2. If necessary, to launch VMRCplus, double-click the **VMRCplus** icon on the desktop.

3. If necessary, to start Client-01, return to the Virtual Machine Manager, click **Client-01**, click **Turn On**, and then click **VM Console**.
4. If necessary, log on to Client-01 with a username of **Student** and a password of **Secret1**.
5. To open a command prompt window, click **Start**, type **cmd** in the Start Search text box, and then press **Enter**.
6. To display the routing table, type **route print -4** and then press **Enter**.
7. Using the information generated by the route print command, complete Table 9-5.
8. Leave the computer logged on for the next activity.

Table 9-5 Routing table details

Reference number	Item	Answer
1	IP address for network adapter	
2	Gateway IP address	
3	Network	
4	Netmask for network in #3	
5	Broadcast to network in #3	
6	Loopback address	

Activity 9-9: Implementing LAN Routing

Time Required: 20 minutes

Objective: Implement LAN routing for routers on the Classroom.local network.

Requirements: Completion of Activities 9-1 through 9-8.

Description: In this activity, you will turn on routing on Server-02 and Server-03.

1. If necessary, log on to your Host PC with a username of **Administrator** and a password of **Secret1**.
2. If necessary, to launch VMRCplus, double-click the **VMRCplus** icon on the desktop.
3. If necessary, to start Server-02, return to the Virtual Machine Manager, click **Server-02**, click **Turn On**, and then click **VM Console**.
4. If necessary, log on to Server-02 with a username of **Administrator** and a password of **Secret1**.
5. To add the Network Policy and Access Services, click **Roles** in Server Manager, click the **Add Roles** link, click **Server Roles**, click the **Network Policy and Access Services**, click **Next** twice, click the **Routing and Remote Access Services** check box, click **Next**, and then click **Install**.
6. Wait for Network Policy and Access Services to install, and then click **Close**.

7. To add LAN routing for Routing and Remote Access Services, expand **Roles**, expand **Network Policy and Access Services**, right-click **Routing and Remote Access Services**, click **Configure and Enable Routing and Remote Access**, click **Next**, click the **Custom configuration** option button, click **Next**, click the **LAN routing** check box, click **Next**, and then click **Finish**.
8. To start the Routing and Remote Access Service, click the **Start service** button, and then wait for the service to start.
9. To view the LAN routing interfaces, expand **Routing and Remote Access**, expand **IPv4**, and then click **General**.
10. Repeat Steps 3 through 9 using Server-03 in place of Server-02.
11. Leave the computer logged on for the next activity.

Activity 9-10: Configuring the Static Routing Protocol

Time Required: 20–30 minutes

Objective: Implement the static routing protocol for the routers on the Classroom.local virtual network.

Requirements: Completion of Activities 9-1 through 9-9.

Description: In this activity, you will enter static routes for the missing routes in each of the five virtual machines. Recall that each virtual machine must have routes to the 192.168.0.0, 192.168.1.0, and 192.168.2.0 networks.

1. If necessary, log on to your Host PC with a username of **Administrator** and a password of **Secret1**.
2. If necessary, to launch VMRCplus, double-click the **VMRCplus** icon on the desktop.

Entering the Static Routes for Server-01

3. If necessary, to start Server-01, return to the Virtual Machine Manager, click **Server-01**, click **Turn On**, and then click **VM Console**.
4. If necessary, log on to Server-01 with a username of **Administrator** and a password of **Secret1**.
5. To display the routing table, click **Start**, click **Command Prompt**, type **route print -4**, and then press **Enter**.
6. Observe the routing statements for the missing routing rule.
7. To add the route to Virtual Network 1, type **route add 192.168.1.0 mask 255.255.255.0 192.168.0.102**, and then press **Enter**.

To reuse a command from this session, press the Up arrow and edit the previous command.

8. To add the route to Virtual Network 2, type **route add 192.168.2.0 mask 255.255.255.0 192.168.0.102**, and then press **Enter**.

9. Leave the command prompt window open.

Entering the Static Routes for Server-02

10. If necessary, to start Server-02, return to the Virtual Machine Manager, click **Server-02**, click **Turn On**, and then click **VM Console**.

11. If necessary, log on to Server-02 with a username of **Administrator** and a password of **Secret1**.

12. To display the routing table, click **Start**, click **Command Prompt**, type **route print -4**, and then press **Enter**.

13. Observe the routing statements for the missing routing rule.

14. To add the route to Virtual Network 1, type **route add 192.168.1.0 mask 255.255.255.0 192.168.2.103**, and then press **Enter**.

15. Leave the command prompt window open.

Entering the Static Routes for Server-03

16. If necessary, to start Server-03, return to the Virtual Machine Manager, click **Server-03**, click **Turn On**, and then click **VM Console**.

17. If necessary, log on to Server-03 with a username of **Administrator** and a password of **Secret1**.

18. To display the routing table, click **Start**, click **Command Prompt**, type **route print -4**, and then press **Enter**.

19. Observe the routing statements for the missing routing rules.

20. To add the route to Virtual Network 0, type **route add 192.168.0.0 mask 255.255.255.0 192.168.2.102**, and then press **Enter**.

21. Leave the command prompt window open.

Entering the Static Routes for Client-01

22. If necessary, to start Client-01, return to the Virtual Machine Manager, click **Client-01**, click **Turn On**, and then click **VM Console**.

23. If necessary, log on to Client-01 with a username of **Student** and a password of **Secret1**.

24. To display the routing table, click **Start**, type **cmd** in the Start Search text box, right-click **cmd**, and then click **Run as Administrator**.

25. When the User Account Control dialog box opens, click the **Continue** button.

26. Type **route print -4**, and then press **Enter**.

27. Observe the routing statements for the missing routing rules.

28. To add the route to Virtual Network 1, type **route add 192.168.1.0 mask 255.255.255.0 192.168.0.102**, and then press **Enter**.

29. To add the route to Virtual Network 2, type **route add 192.168.2.0 mask 255.255.255.0 192.168.0.102**, and then press **Enter**.
30. Leave the command prompt window open.

Entering the Static Routes for Client-02

31. If necessary, to start Client-02, return to the Virtual Machine Manager, click **Client-02**, click **Turn On**, and then click **VM Console**.
32. If necessary, log on to Client-01 with a username of **Student** and a password of **Secret1**.
33. To display the routing table, click **Start**, type **cmd** in the Start Search text box, right-click **cmd**, and then click **Run as Administrator**.
34. When the User Account Control dialog box opens, click the **Continue** button.
35. Type **route print -4**, and then press **Enter**.
36. Observe the routing statements for the missing routing rules.
37. To add the route to Virtual Network 0, type **route add 192.168.0.0 mask 255.255.255.0 192.168.1.103**, and then press **Enter**.
38. To add the route to Virtual Network 2, type **route add 192.168.2.0 mask 255.255.255.0 192.168.1.103**, and then press **Enter**.
39. Leave the command prompt window open.

Activity 9-11: Testing Static Routing

Time Required: 15–20 minutes

Objective: Test the routing statements for the routers on the Classroom.local virtual network.

Requirements: Completion of Activities 9-1 through 9-10.

Description: In this activity, you will test routing for the routers by incrementally verifying that each virtual machine can be reached. Also, you will remove the static routing statements in preparation for configuring RIP routing.

1. If necessary, log on to your Host PC with a username of **Administrator** and a password of **Secret1**.
2. If necessary, to launch VMRCplus, double-click the **VMRCplus** icon on the desktop.
3. If necessary, to start Server-01, return to the Virtual Machine Manager, click **Server-01**, click **Turn On**, and then click **VM Console**.
4. If necessary, log on to Server-01 with a username of **Administrator** and a password of **Secret1**.
5. If necessary, complete Steps 3 and 4 using Server-02 and Server-03 in place of Server-01.

6. If necessary, log on to Client-01 with a username of **Student** and a password of **Secret**.
7. If necessary, log on to Client-02 with a username of **Student** and a password of **Secret**.

Incrementally Testing Static Routing with ping

8. Switch to Client-01.
9. If necessary, log on to Client-01 with a username of **Student** and a password of **Secret**.
10. To test routing to the near side of Server-02, type **ping 192.168.0.102**, and then press **Enter**.

If you cannot ping to the indicated interface, consult with your instructor.

11. To test routing to the far side of Server-02, type **ping 192.168.2.102**, and then press **Enter**.
12. To test routing to the near side of Server-03, type **ping 192.168.2.103**, and then press **Enter**.
13. To test routing to the far side of Server-03, type **ping 192.168.1.103**, and then press **Enter**.
14. To test routing to Client-02, type **ping 192.168.1.112**, and then press **Enter**.

Removing the Static Routes

You will need to remove the static routes because static routes have priority over routes established by the RIP routing protocol.

15. Remain at Client-01.
16. To delete the route to Virtual Network 1, type **route delete 192.168.1.0**, and then press **Enter**.
17. To delete the route to Virtual Network 2, type **route delete 192.168.2.0**, and then press **Enter**.
18. Switch to Server-01.
19. To delete the route to Virtual Network 1, type **route delete 192.168.1.0**, and then press **Enter**.
20. To delete the route to Virtual Network 2, type **route delete 192.168.2.0**, press **Enter**, type **exit**, and then press **Enter**.
21. Switch to Server-02.
22. To delete the route to Virtual Network 1, type **route delete 192.168.1.0**, press **Enter**, type **exit**, and then press **Enter**.
23. Switch to Server-03.

24. To delete the route to Virtual Network 0, type **route delete 192.168.0.0**, press **Enter**, type **exit**, and then press **Enter**.
25. Switch to Client-02.
26. To delete the route to Virtual Network 0, type **route delete 192.168.0.0**, and then press **Enter**.
27. To delete the route to Virtual Network 2, type **route delete 192.168.2.0**, press **Enter**, type **exit**, and then press **Enter**.
28. Leave the computer logged on for the next activity.

Activity 9-12: Configuring the RIP Routing Protocol

Time Required: 15 minutes

Objective: Implement the RIP routing protocol for routers on the Classroom.local virtual network.

Requirements: Completion of Activities 9-1 through 9-11.

Description: In this activity, you will configure Server-02 and Server-03 to function as LAN routers using the RIP routing protocol. Also, you will systematically test the routing on the Classroom.local virtual network.

1. If necessary, log on to your Host PC with a username of **Administrator** and a password of **Secret1**.
2. If necessary, to launch VMRCplus, double-click the **VMRCplus** icon on the desktop.

Configuring RIP Routing Statements

3. If necessary, to start Server-02, return to the Virtual Machine Manager, click **Server-02**, click **Turn On**, and then click **VM Console**.
4. If necessary, log on to Server-02 with a username of **Administrator** and a password of **Secret1**.
5. If necessary, to launch Server Manager, click **Start**, point to **Administrative Tools**, and then click **Server Manager**.
6. To add the RIP protocol, expand **IPv4**, right-click **General**, click **New Routing Protocol**, click **RIP Version 2 for Internet Protocol**, and then click **OK**.
7. To add the first LAN routing interface, click **RIP** under IPv4 in the left pane, right-click the right pane, click **New Interface**, click **Local Area Connection**, click **OK**, review the default RIP Properties, and then click **OK**.
8. To add the second LAN routing interface, right-click the right pane, click **New Interface**, click **Local Area Connection 2**, click **OK**, then review the default RIP Properties.
9. To add the neighboring router, click the **Neighbors** tab, click the **Use neighbors in addition to broadcast or multicast** option button, type **192.168.2.103** in the IP address text box, click the **Add** button, and then click **OK**.
10. Repeat Steps 3 through 8 using Server-03 in place of Server-02.

11. To add the neighboring router, click the **Neighbors** tab, click the **Use neighbors in addition to broadcast or multicast** option button, type **192.168.2.102** in the IP address text box, click the **Add** button, and then click **OK**.

12. Wait for the Responses sent and Responses received for Local Area Connection to appear.

13. Press the **F5** key to refresh the screen.

Incrementally Testing RIP Routing with ping

14. Switch to Client-01.

15. If necessary, log on to Client-01 with a username of **Student** and a password of **Secret**.

16. If necessary, to display the command prompt, click **Start**, type **cmd** in the Start Search text box, right-click **cmd**, and then click **Run as Administrator**.

17. If necessary, when the User Account Control dialog box opens, click the **Continue** button.

18. To test routing to the near side of Server-02, type **ping 192.168.0.102**, and then press **Enter**.

If you cannot ping the indicated interface, consult with your instructor.

19. To test routing to the far side of Server-02, type **ping 192.168.2.102**, and then press **Enter**.

20. To test routing to the near side of Server-03, type **ping 192.168.2.103**, and then press **Enter**.

21. To test routing to the far side of Server-03, type **ping 192.168.1.103**, and then press **Enter**.

22. To test routing to Client-02, type **ping 192.168.1.112**, and then press **Enter**.

23. Leave the computer logged on for the next activity.

Revising the DHCP Relay Agent

Because of the network changes required to implement routing, Client-02's connection to the DHCP Server-02 has been blocked by a router—Server-03. Recall that DHCP relies on network broadcasts to communicate with clients. Routers in normal routed environments do not automatically forward broadcasts from one network to another. A relay agent must forward these messages. A router (Server-03) is configured to listen for DHCP broadcast messages and direct them to a specific server running DHCP (Server-02). To enable Client-02 to receive an IP configuration from Server-02, these tasks must be completed:

1. Create and activate a scope for the 192.168.1.0 network.

2. Install and configure a DHCP Relay Agent on Server-03.

3. Reconfigure Client-02 to use dynamic IP addressing.

You will complete these three tasks in Activity 9-13.

Activity 9-13: Configuring DHCP Relay Agent

Time Required: 15 minutes

Objective: Implement DHCP Relay Agent for the virtual machines on Virtual Network 1.

Requirements: Completion of Activities 9-1 through 9-12.

Description: In this activity, you will add a scope for the Virtual Network 1. Next, you will implement the DHCP Relay Agent on Server-02 and then test from Client-02.

1. If necessary, log on to your Host PC with a username of **Administrator** and a password of **Secret1**.
2. If necessary, to launch VMRCplus, double-click the **VMRCplus** icon on the desktop.

Adding a DHCP Scope for the 192.168.1.0 Network

3. If necessary, to start Server-02, return to the Virtual Machine Manager, click **Server-01**, click **Turn On**, and then click **VM Console**.
4. If necessary, log on to Server-02 with a username of **Administrator** and a password of **Secret1**.
5. If necessary, to launch Server Manager, click **Start**, point to **Administrative Tools**, and then click **Server Manager**.
6. To add a new scope with the New Scope Wizard, expand **DHCP Server**, expand **server-02.classroom.local**, expand **IPv4**, right-click the **IPv4** node, click **New Scope**, click **Next**, type **Virtual Network 1** in the Name text box, click **Next**, type **192.168.1.1** in the Start IP address text box, type **192.168.1.254** in the End IP address text box, and then click **Next**.
7. To add exclusions for the existing servers, type **192.168.1.101** in the Start IP address text box, type **192.168.1.109** in the End IP address text box, click **Add**, and then click **Next** three times.
8. To specify the router (default gateway), type **192.168.1.103** in the IP address text box, click **Add**, and then click **Next**.
9. To specify the domain name and DNS servers, type **Classroom.local** in the Parent domain text box, type **Server-01** in the Server name text box, click the **Resolve** button, click the **Add** button, click **Next** three times, and then click **Finish**.
10. To view the address pool, expand **Scope [192.168.1.0] Virtual Network 1**, and then click **Address Pool**.
11. To view the scope options, click the **Scope Options** node and note the options that are configured.
12. Switch to Server-03.

13. If necessary, log on to Server-03 with a username of **Administrator** and a password of **Secret1**.
14. If necessary, to launch Server Manager, click **Start**, point to **Administrative Tools**, and then click **Server Manager**.
15. To add the DHCP Relay Agent protocol, expand **IPv4**, right-click **General**, click **New Routing Protocol**, click **DHCP Relay Agent**, and then click **OK**.
16. To indicate the interface for the DHCP Relay Agent, right-click **DHCP Relay Agent**, click **New Interface**, click **Local Area Connection**, and then click **OK** twice.
17. To specify the DHCP server, right-click **DHCP Relay Agent**, click **Properties**, type **192.168.0.102** in the Server address text box, click **Add**, and then click **OK**.
18. Switch to Client-02.
19. If necessary, log on to Client-02 with a username of **Student** and a password of **Secret**.
20. To provide an IP configuration, click **Start**, click **Control Panel**, click the **View network status and tasks** link under Network and Internet, click the **View status** link, and then click the **Properties** button.
21. When the User Account Control dialog box opens, click the **Continue** button.
22. Click **Internet Protocol Version 4 (TCP/IPv4)**, click the **Properties** button, click the **Obtain an IP address automatically** option button, click the **Obtain DNS Server address automatically** option button, click **OK**, click **Close** twice, and then close the Network and Sharing Center window.
23. To display the IP configuration, click **Start**, type **cmd** in the Start Search text box, right-click **cmd**, and then click **Run as Administrator**.
24. When the User Account Control dialog box opens, click the **Continue** button.
25. Type **ipconfig /all** and then press **Enter**.
26. Verify that the IPv4 Address resembles 192.168.1.2(Preferred). If it does not, consult with your instructor.
27. Type **exit** and press **Enter**.
28. Return to the Virtual Machine Manager.
29. Right-click **Client-02**, and then click **Save State**.
30. Repeat Step 30 for the remaining virtual machines with the exception of Server-01.
31. To shut down Server-01, return to the Virtual Machine Manager, click **localhost/Server-01**, click **Control**, click **Shutdown**, and then click **Yes**.
32. Close the open windows.
33. Log off and shut down the host computer.

Chapter Summary

- Also known as the protocol analyzer, Microsoft Network Monitor is a network diagnostic tool that monitors local area networks and provides a graphical display of the network traffic. Routine troubleshooting tasks can be performed, such as locating a server that is down or solving network protocol problems. Information that is collected and displayed from the network data stream by Network Monitor includes the source IP address of the computer that sent a packet onto the network, the destination of the computer that received the packet, the protocols used to send the frame, and the data or portion of data from the message that was sent.

- The installation of the Dynamic Host Configuration Protocol, or DHCP, reduces the administrative burden and complexity of configuring hosts on a TCP/IP-based network. The DHCP servers need to be configured correctly and authorized for use on a network to be useful and not cause major problems. When a computer asks for an IP address, the DHCP server will assign one from a pool of available addresses using a four-step process. The DHCP snap-in helps administrators configure and monitor DHCP servers; after installation of the DHCP service, further customization can occur to help administrators configure and monitor DHCP servers. Administrators also create scopes or administrative groupings of customers based on the needs of the specific groups of computers. Larger, more complex networks might need further scope defined and reservations. Network Monitor can be used to view and analyze the traffic between a DHCP server and DHCP clients.

- You reconfigured the Classroom.local network for routing, adding two networks. The Network Policy and Access Services was added in Server Manager so the Routing and Remote Access Service could be installed. You configured RIP routing and also installed and configured a DHCP Relay Agent. After the network was reconfigured for routing, you examined the routing tables and implemented LAN routing on the Classroom.local virtual network.

Key Terms

Address Resolution Protocol (ARP)—The protocol used by the Internet Protocol (IP) to map IP network addresses to the hardware addresses. The term *address resolution* refers to the process of finding an address of a computer in a network.

alias list—A file that is used by Network Monitor to store IP addresses and their associated computer names.

Bellman-Ford algorithm—Also known as the Bellman-Ford distance-vector routing algorithm, a procedure that determines the shortest route between two nodes on a network. This algorithm is used in the Routing Information Protocol (RIP).

best path—A method used to determine the most optimal network path to a specific remote destination when two or more diverse network paths are available.

capture filter—Similar in function to a database query, a filter that is used to specify types of network information you want to monitor. Information obtained from the filter can be saved to a file and then loaded for use later.

capturing—The transfer of received data into a file for archiving or later analysis.

DHCP acknowledge—The message that is generated when the DHCP server officially assigns the address to the client.

DHCP discover—The message that is generated when the DHCP client asks for an IP address.

DHCP offer—The message that is generated when the DHCP server offers an address.

DHCP Relay Agent—A router or a host computer that is configured to listen for DHCP/BOOTP broadcast messages and direct them to a specific DHCP server(s). Using relay agents eliminates the necessity of having a DHCP server on each physical network segment.

DHCP request—The message that is generated when the DHCP client accepts the offer and requests the address during the DHCP process.

display filter—Similar in function to a database query, a filter that allows you to single out specific types of network information, such as source or destination address from a captured network frame.

distance-vector routing protocol—A protocol that requires a router to inform its neighbors of network changes periodically and, in some cases, when a change is detected in the topology of a network. A distance-vector routing protocol uses the Bellman-Ford algorithm to calculate paths. *See* Bellman-Ford algorithm.

dynamic routing table—Table containing routing information that adjusts automatically to the current conditions of the network. Dynamic routing typically uses one of several dynamic-routing protocols such as RIP.

frame—A data packet of fixed or variable length.

Internet Control Messaging Protocol (ICMP)—An extension to the Internet Protocol that allows for the generation of error messages, test packets, and informational messages related to IP.

local loopback—The special network address, 127.0.0.1, defined by the Internet Protocol as a local loopback address. Hosts use local loopback addresses to send messages to themselves.

Microsoft Network Monitor—Software that can intercept and log traffic passing over a digital network or part of a network. Also known as a protocol analyzer.

multicasting—The delivery of information to a group of destinations simultaneously using the most efficient strategy to deliver the messages over each link of the network only once.

network convergence—The state that occurs when the routing tables for all routers in the network are in agreement.

Network Policy and Access Services (NPAS)—A service within Windows Server 2008 that delivers a variety of methods to provide local and remote network connectivity, to connect network segments, and to allow network administrators to centrally manage network access and client health policies.

protocol analyzer—Software that captures data packets and decodes and analyzes their content. *See* Microsoft Network Monitor.

router—An intermediary device on a communications network that expedites message delivery. On a single network linking many computers through a mesh of possible connections, a router receives transmitted messages and forwards them to their correct destinations over the most efficent available route.

routing—The process of forwarding packets between networks from source to destination.

Routing and Remote Access Service (RRAS)—A service within Network Policy and Access Services used to manage remote access connections and devices.

Routing Information Protocol (RIP)—A widely used protocol for managing router information within a small, self-contained network such as a corporate network. Routers communicate network changes periodically to their neighbor routers, which helps routers dynamically adapt to changes of network connections.

routing metric—A standard of measurement, such as hop count, that is used by routing algorithms to determine the best path to a destination.

routing protocol—A convention or standard that specifies how routers communicate with each other to disseminate information that allows them to select routes between two nodes on a network. A routing protocol shares the information each router has about its immediate neighbors so other networks in a network topology have the information.

routing table—In data communications, a table of information that provides network devices with the directions needed to forward packets of data to locations on other networks. Routing tables are updated frequently as new or more current information becomes available.

scope—An administrative grouping of computers running the DHCP Client service. You create a scope for each subnet on the network to define parameters for that subnet.

static routing—Routing based on a fixed forwarding path. Unlike dynamic routing, static routing does not adjust to changing network conditions.

Review Questions

1. _____ is the process of moving a data packet from its local network to a remote network based on the address of the remote network.
    a. Networking
    b. Remote access
    c. Routing
    d. Monitoring

2. A network diagnostic tool that monitors local area networks and provides a graphical display of network traffic is known as _____. (Choose all that apply.)
    a. A protocol analyzer
    b. A protocol monitor
    c. A network analyzer
    d. Network Monitor

3. Network Monitor is used _____. (Choose all that apply.)
    a. To locate a server that is down
    b. To solve problems with network protocols
    c. To improve the performance of the computer monitor
    d. For routing troubleshooting tasks

4. The information collected from the network's data stream by Network Monitor includes the _____. (Choose all that apply.)
   a. Source IP address for the computer that sent a packet onto the network
   b. Destination IP address of the computer that received the packet
   c. Protocols used to send the frame
   d. Data or a portion of the message being sent
5. To improve the results of data capture when Network Monitor is used, it is recommended that you use a(n) _____ file.
   a. Encrypted
   b. Alias
   c. Packet
   d. Display
6. By default, Network Monitor captures _____ frame(s) it detects on the network into a capture buffer.
   a. Every other
   b. No
   c. The first and last
   d. All
7. To monitor traffic between two computers on a network, you should create _____.
   a. A buffer file
   b. A display file
   c. A capture filter
   d. An alias list
8. DHCP _____. (Choose all that apply.)
   a. Is designed to reduce the administration burden and complexity of configuring hosts on a TCP/IP-based network
   b. Is designed to decrease the administration burden and complexity of configuring virtual machines on a TCP/IP-based network
   c. Relies on network broadcasts to perform their work
   d. Can act as a DHCP Relay Agent
9. Relay agents _____. (Choose all that apply.)
   a. Eliminate the necessity of having a server running DHCP on each physical network segment
   b. Direct local DHCP client requests to remote DHCP servers
   c. Return remote DHCP server responses to DHCP clients
   d. Direct remote DHCP server requests to DHCP clients

10. The process of a computer asking for a unique IP address requires _____ step(s).
    a. One
    b. Two
    c. Three
    d. Four
11. DHCP customization parameters include a(n) _____. (Choose all that apply.)
    a. Lease
    b. Address pool
    c. Exclusion range
    d. Superscope
12. The DHCP customization parameter scope is the _____.
    a. Administrative grouping of scopes that can be used to support multiple logical IP subnets on the same physical subnet
    b. Addresses remaining from the available address pool within the scope
    c. Permanent address lease assignment of the DHCP server
    d. Consecutive range of possible IP addresses for a network
13. When scopes are created by administrators, properties that are considered include _____. (Choose all that apply.)
    a. The range of possible IP addresses from which to include or exclude addresses used in DHCP service lease offerings
    b. A unique subnet mask to determine the relation to a given IP address
    c. A scope name when the scope is created
    d. Reservations
14. The network device that connects two or more networks and routes incoming data packets to the appropriate network is known as a _____.
    a. Hub
    b. Gateway
    c. Router
    d. Bridge
15. A set of rules, often in table format, used to determine where data packets that travel over a network are to be directed is known as a(n) _____.
    a. Address table
    b. Data table
    c. Routing table
    d. Network table

16. A basic routing table includes _____. (Choose all that apply.)
    a. Network destination
    b. Netmask
    c. Gateway
    d. Subnet mask
17. A _____ is used by a router to determine the appropriate path to transmit the packets.
    a. Packet locator
    b. Routing protocol
    c. Metric
    d. Route marker
18. NPAS in Windows Server 2008 _____. (Choose all that apply.)
    a. Allows you to provide local and remote network access, where you can define and enforce network access authentication, authorization, and client health
    b. Has a full-featured software router in the Routing and Remote Access Service that offers routing services to businesses in local area networks only
    c. Has a full-featured software router in the Routing and Remote Access Service that offers routing services to businesses in wide area networks only
    d. Has a full-featured software router in the Routing and Remote Access Service that offers routing services to businesses in local area networks and wide area network environments
19. RIP is _____. (Choose all that apply.)
    a. An acronym for Routing Information Protocol
    b. A widely used protocol for managing routing information within a small, self-contained network, such as a corporate network
    c. A distance-vector routing protocol that advertises the number of hops to a network destination
    d. Automatically installed when the Routing and Remote Access Service is installed
20. The distance-vector routing protocol _____. (Choose all that apply.)
    a. Uses RIP
    b. Is also known as the Bellman-Ford algorithm
    c. Enables a router to pass routes to its neighbors at regularly scheduled intervals
    d. Creates a table that contains the cumulative distance of each network destination

Case Projects

Case 9-1: DHCP Scope and Reservations for a Larger Network

The student lab network needs to expand. Work has already begun on the new network and your task is to define the DHCP scope and exclusions for the new larger and more complex tutoring network, which includes 120 desktop computers. There are 10 special server computers that use DHCP that will need static IP addresses. Also, there are six printers that require DHCP reservations. The current network is 192.168.233.0. The DNS server is at IP address 192.168.233.254 and supports the StudentLab.local domain. Prepare a detailed list of the information that must be entered to define the DHCP scope.

Case 9-2: Studying RIP Routing Updates

Using Microsoft Network Monitor, study the RIP routing updates between the two routers (Server-02 and Server-03). Write a one-page summary of your findings.

Case 9-3: Studying Network Traffic

You have been asked to help resolve a problem for the Web programmers and database administrators using the student lab. The Web programmers are developing a Web application that stores data in the tables on a database server. The Web programmers and database administrators are at an impasse—the Web programmers are confident that they are accessing the database with the proper commands. Likewise, the database administrators are equally certain that the database system is furnishing the correct information. However, the data that is returned to the Web application from the database table is not complete. Your task is to describe the use of a Microsoft program to study the problem and assist the Web programmers and database administrators in resolving this problem.

chapter 10

Implementing Security for the Classroom.local Virtual Network

After reading this chapter and completing the exercises, you will be able to:

- Use Active Directory Domain Services for a virtual network
- Apply Group Policy for a virtual network
- Implement IPSec for a virtual network

In Chapter 8 you installed Active Directory Domain Services (AD DS) for the Classroom .local domain. In this chapter, you will expand your use of AD DS.

Users often cause problems on a network through inadvertent errors, such as modifying system configuration files and rendering a computer unworkable. The presence of nonessential applications and features on the desktop can also lead to lost productivity. **Group Policy** is a tool within AD DS that defines the settings and allowed actions for users and computers. Administrators can use Group Policy to create desktops that are tailored to users' job responsibilities and level of experience with computers while keeping users away from areas of the system where they can cause trouble for the entire network. You can manage computers centrally with Active Directory Domain Services and Group Policy. Using Group Policy to deliver managed computing environments allows you to work more efficiently because of the centralized, one-to-many management it enables.

Without security, both public and private networks are susceptible to unauthorized monitoring and access. Internal attacks might be a result of minimal or nonexistent internal security. Risks from outside the private network originate from connections to the Internet. Password-based user access controls alone do not protect data transmitted across a network. **Internet Protocol security (IPSec)** is a framework of open standards for ensuring private, secure communications over Internet Protocol (IP) networks through the use of **cryptographic security services**, which is the ability to scramble data so that only the sender and the designated receiver can read the contents.

Using Active Directory Domain Services

A major part of network administration involves management of users, computers, and security groups. **Security groups** are collections of users who share the same minimum permissions. AD DS plays several major roles in providing security. Among these roles are the efficient and effective management of user logon authentication and user authorization. Both are central features of the Windows Server 2008 security subsystem and both are fully integrated with Active Directory.

Active Directory **user authentication** confirms the identity of any user trying to log on to a domain and lets users access resources (such as data, applications, or printers) located anywhere on the network. A key feature of Windows Server 2008 user authentication is its single sign-on capability, which makes multiple applications and services available to the user over the network without the user having to provide credentials more than once.

Active Directory **user authorization** protects resources from unauthorized access. After a user account has received authentication and can potentially access a network resource, the type of access actually granted is determined by the user privileges that are assigned to the user and the access control permissions that are attached to the objects the user wants to access. An object is a distinct, named set of attributes, and includes shared resources such as servers, shared folders, and printers; network user and computer accounts; as well as domains, applications, services, and security policies.

Active Directory Concepts

The following definitions will help you understand the basic concepts that are used throughout this chapter:

- **User rights**—Privileges (such as Back Up Files and Directories) and logon rights (such as Access this Computer from the Network) assigned to groups (or users).

- **Access control permissions** (such as Read, Write, Full Control, or No Access)—Permissions attached to Windows Server 2008 objects.
- **Security identifier (SID)**—Code that uniquely identifies a specific user, group, or computer to the Windows Server 2008 security system. A user's own SID is always attached to the user's access token. When a user is made a member of a group, the SID for that group is also attached to the user's access token.
- **Access control list (ACL)**—A list that includes all of the security permissions that apply to an object. Access control lists are either discretionary or system.
- **Access token**—A representation of the user account created by Windows each time a user logs on; contains the following elements:
    - Individual SID—Represents the logged-on user
    - Group SID—Represents the logged-on user's group memberships
    - User rights—Privileges (associated with each SID) granted to the user or to groups to which the user belongs

The contents of the access token can be displayed with the whoami command. Figure 10-1 shows the contents of the access token for the student user on the Client-01 virtual machine.

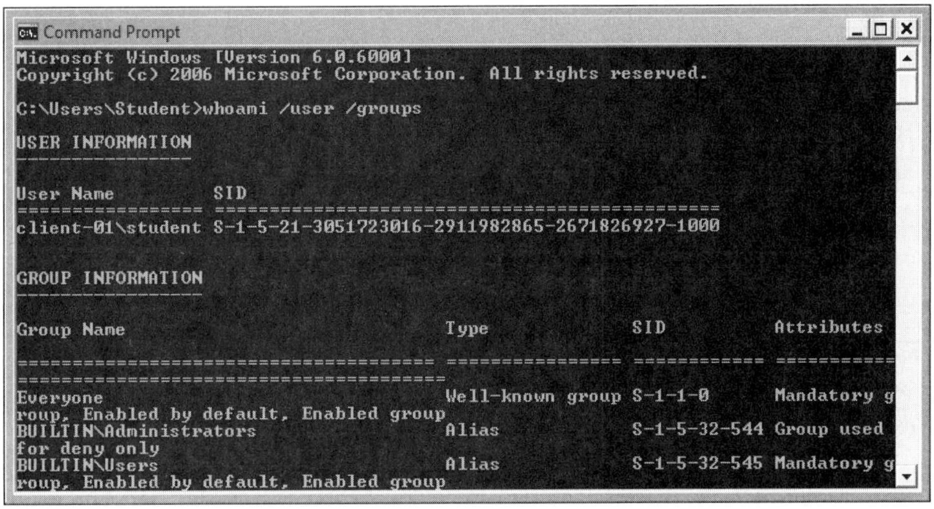

Figure 10-1 Contents of an access token

When the user tries to access an object, Windows compares each SID in the user's access token with entries in an object's discretionary access control list (described in the following list) to determine whether the user has permission to access the object and, if access is allowed, what type of access it is.

An access token is not updated until the next logon, which means that if you add a user to a group, the user must log off and log on before the access token is updated.

Each Active Directory object (as well as each file, Registry key, and so on) has two associated ACLs:

- **Discretionary access control list (DACL)**—Lists user accounts, groups, and computers that are allowed (or denied) access to the object
- **System access control list (SACL)**—Defines which events (such as file access) are audited for a user or group

A DACL or SACL consists of a list of **access control entries (ACEs)**, where each ACE lists the permissions granted or denied to the users, groups, or computers listed in the DACL or SACL. An ACE contains a SID with a permission, such as Read access or Write access. Windows combines access permissions; if you have Read access to an object because you are a member of Group A and if you have Write access because you are a member of Group B, you have both Read and Write access to the object. However, if you have No Access as a member of Group C, you will not have access to the object. Figure 10-2 illustrates this combination of the access permissions.

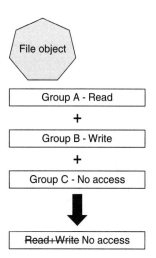

Figure 10-2 Access control entries

Active Directory User and Computer Accounts

The Windows operating system uses a user or computer account to authenticate the identity of the user or computer and to authorize or deny access to domain resources. For example, users who are members of the Domain Administrators group are, by default, granted permission to log on at any domain controller in the domain. Administrators can audit actions performed by user or computer accounts.

You add, disable, reset, or delete user and computer accounts using the Active Directory Users and Computers console. Figure 10-3 shows the Active Directory Users and Computers console.

To access the Active Directory Users and Computers console, click Start, point to Administrative Tools, and then click Active Directory Users and Computers. To view the objects in the Classroom.local domain, expand Classroom.local. To view the objects in a particular container, expand the container. Computer objects appear in the Computers containers after the computers are joined to the domain.

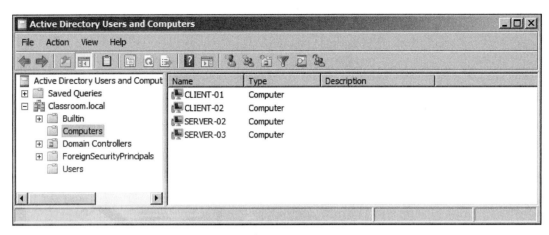

Figure 10-3 Active Directory Users and Computers console showing computers

User Accounts A user account defines the actions a user can perform in Windows. On a stand-alone computer or a computer that is a member of a workgroup, a user account establishes the privileges assigned to each user. On a computer that is part of a network domain, such as Classroom.local, a user must be a member of at least one security group. The permissions and rights granted to a group are assigned to its members.

A user requires an Active Directory user account to log on to a computer or to a domain. The account establishes an identity for the user; the operating system then uses this identity to authenticate the user and to grant him or her authorization to access specific domain resources.

To add a new user to the domain, click the Users container, click the Action menu, point to New, and then click User. Figure 10-4 shows a completed New Object – User dialog box.

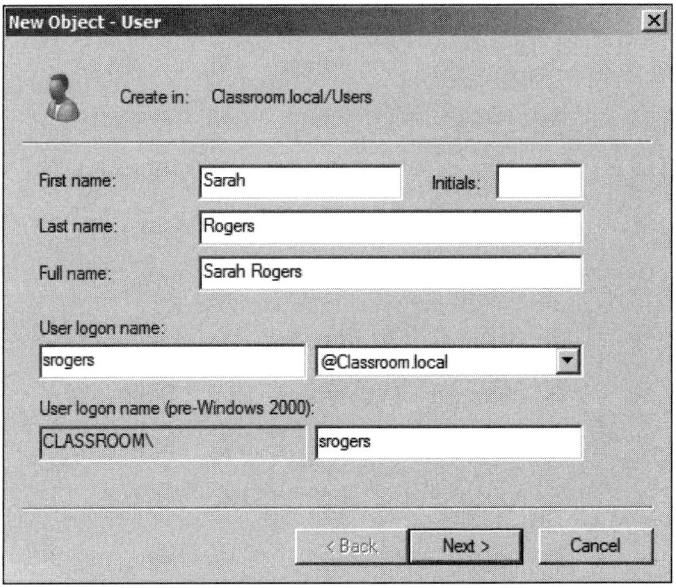

Figure 10-4 Adding a new user

Click Next for the dialog box to specify password-related entries. Figure 10-5 shows this completed dialog box. When the User must change password at next logon check box is checked, the user will set a new password after the initial logon, which shifts responsibility for password management to the user. The User cannot change password check box is used for applications, rather than users, that require a password. The Password never expires check box simplifies the retention of passwords. When a user account is disabled, the user account is suspended—this is handy for disabling accounts for employees who have left the organization.

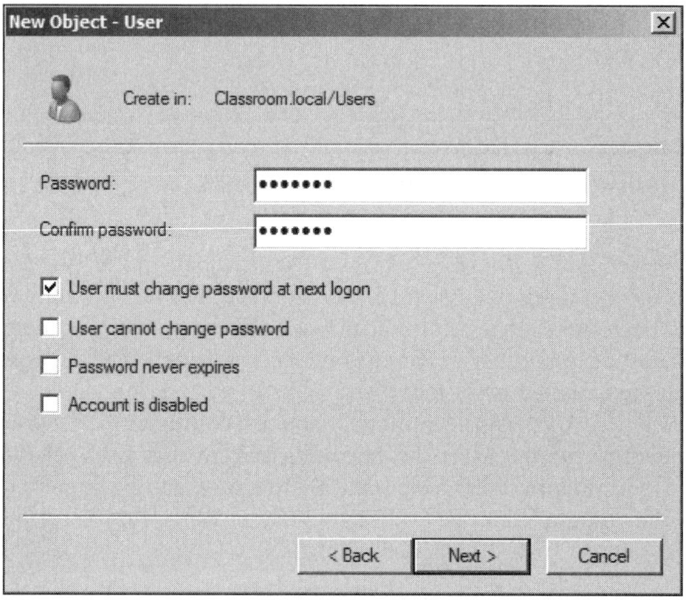

Figure 10-5 Specifying password options

Computer Accounts Like user accounts, Windows computer accounts provide a means for authenticating and auditing the computer's access to the network and its access to domain resources. Each Windows computer to which you want to grant access to resources must have a unique computer account.

Computers running Windows 98 and Windows 95 do not have the advanced security features of those running Windows 2000 and later operating systems, and they cannot be assigned computer accounts in Windows domains. However, you can log on to a network and use Windows 98 and Windows 95 computers in Active Directory domains.

There are two ways to create computer accounts:

1. Create a computer account in the Active Directory Users and Computers console. To add a new computer to the domain, click the Computers container, click the Action menu, point to New, and then click Computer.

2. Join the computer to the domain. From the client computer, click Start, right-click Computer, click Properties, click the Change settings link, click the Continue button, click the Change button, click the Domain option button, type the domain name, click OK, log on using an administrator account on the domain, and when requested, restart the computer.

Active Directory Security Groups

In the Windows Server 2008 operating system, security groups are an essential component of the relationship between users and security. Security groups have one primary function: to manage user and computer access to shared resources.

You collect users, computers, and other groups into a security group and then assign appropriate permissions to specific resources (such as file shares and printers) to the security group. This simplifies administration by letting you assign permissions once to the group instead of multiple times to each individual user. When you add a user to an existing group, the user automatically gains the rights and permissions already assigned to that group.

Recall that an access token contains the security information for a logon session. Windows creates an access token when a user logs on, and every process started on behalf of the user has a copy of the token. A process is an application that is currently running.

The access token identifies the user, the security groups to which the user belongs, and the privileges granted to the user and to the user's security groups. The system uses the token to control access to securable objects and to control the ability of the user to perform various system-related operations on the local computer.

Using Global Groups Groups with global scope help you manage Active Directory objects that require frequent maintenance, such as user and computer accounts. Use global groups to collect users or computers that are in the same domain and share the same job, organizational role, or function. For example, "Full-time employees," "Managers," and "File Servers" are all examples of global groups.

To add a global group to the domain, click the Users container, click the Action menu, point to New, and then click Group. Figure 10-6 shows a completed New Object – Group dialog box.

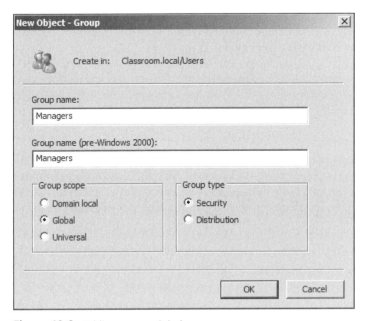

Figure 10-6 Adding a new global group

Security groups are groups of users who need to have the same levels of permission for the same objects. **Distribution groups** are mail-enabled Active Directory group objects that are created to expedite the mass sending of e-mail messages.

Using Domain Local Groups Domain local groups are designed to be used in discretionary access control lists (DACLs) on a domain's resources. That is, domain local groups help you define and manage access to resources within a single domain.

For example, to give five users access to a particular folder, you could add all five user accounts, one at a time, to the folder permissions list. Later, if you wanted to give the same five users access to a new folder, you would again have to specify all five accounts in the permissions list for the new folder. Or, you could take advantage of groups with domain local scope. To do so, you would perform the following steps:

1. Create a group with domain local scope, and assign it permission to access the folder (this is the Resource group).
2. Put the five user accounts into a group with global scope (this is the Accounts group), and add this global group to the group having domain local scope.

To create a domain local group, follow the steps to create a global group but click the Domain local option button rather than the Global option button.

Now, when you want to give another five users access to this folder, you can simply add them to the global group that is a member of the domain local group that has permission to access the folder, and you are done. Doing so gives all five new members of the group access to the folder in one step.

To add users to a global group, right-click the global group in the Active Directory Users and Computers console, click Properties, click the Members tab, click the Add button, click the Advanced button in the Select Users, Contacts, Computers, and Groups dialog box, click the Object Types button, clear the Other objects and Groups check boxes, click OK, click the Find Now button, scroll and select the user accounts, and then click OK twice. Figure 10-7 shows the users accounts that were added to the Managers global group.

To search for specific users, type the first few characters of the user's name in the text box following the Starts with in the Common Queries section.

To add the global group to domain local group, continue from the Managers Properties dialog box. Click the Member Of tab, click the Add button, click the Advanced button in the Select Groups dialog box, click the Find Now button, scroll and select the user accounts, and then click OK twice. Figure 10-8 shows the Managers global group added to the Performance domain local group.

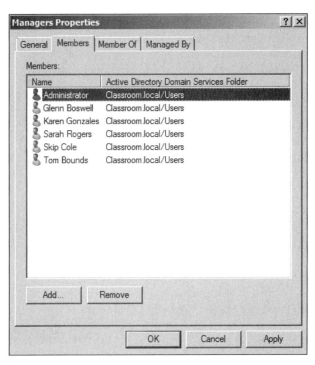

Figure 10-7 Managers Properties with added users

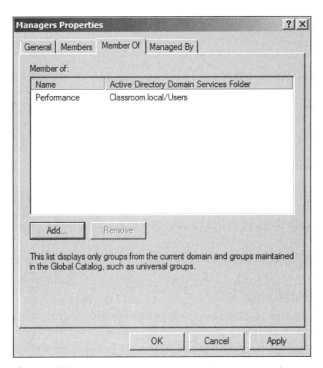

Figure 10-8 Managers global group added to the Performance domain local group

 Active Directory provides another type of security group, the Universal group, which is beyond the scope of this text.

Active Directory Organizational Units

Organizational units (OUs) are administrative-level containers within Active Directory that allow you to organize groups of users together so that any changes, security privileges, or any other administrative tasks can be accomplished more efficiently.

You will typically create organizational units that resemble your company's business organization. You can set up an OU for each department, as shown in Figure 10-9. Within that department OU, you can have user accounts, security groups, or even computers and printers on the network.

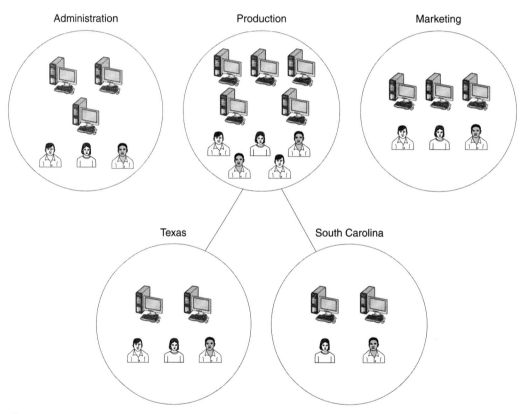

Figure 10-9 Organizational units

Applying a set of policies or restrictions to an organizational unit applies it to all subsets within that organizational unit. An object, placed into a new organizational unit, inherits all the policies and rights associated with that organizational unit. Figure 10-10 illustrates inheritance. The Texas OU and South Carolina OU inherit all the policies and rights associated with Production.

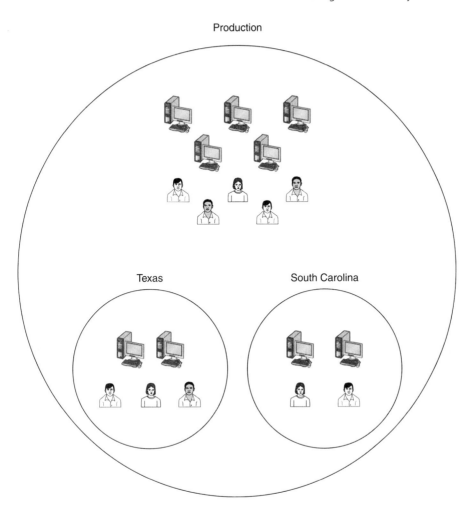

Figure 10-10 Inheritance

To create an OU, select the domain, click the Action menu, point to New, and then click Organizational Unit. To prevent accidental deletion of an OU in Windows Server 2008, you can select the Protect object against accidental deletion check box (the default) when you create the OU, or you can select this check box on the Object tab of the Properties dialog box for an existing OU.

Active Directory Sites

A **site** is a region of your network with high bandwidth connectivity that, by definition, is a collection of well-connected computers—based on Internet Protocol (IP) subnets. Multiple sites are connected for replication by **site link objects**.

Sites are used in Active Directory to do the following:

- Enable clients to discover network resources (file servers, printers, domain controllers) that are close to the physical location of the client, reducing network traffic over wide area network (WAN) links.
- Optimize replication between domain controllers.

The primary purpose of the Windows Server 2008 Active Directory Sites and Services console is to administer the replication between domain controllers both within a site in a LAN and between sites by a WAN. To open the Windows Server 2008 Active Directory Sites and Services console, click the Start button, point to Administrative Tools, and then click Active Directory Sites and Services. Figure 10-11 shows the Active Directory Sites and Services console. To see the SERVER-01 domain controller in Classroom.local, expand Sites, expand Default-First-Site-Name, expand Servers, and then click SERVER-01.

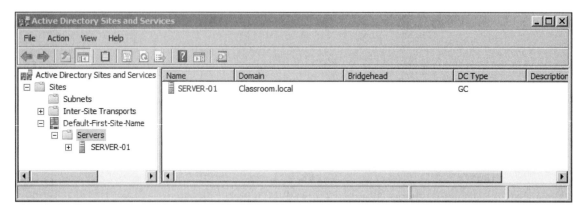

Figure 10-11 Active Directory Sites and Services console

 To rename the Default-First-Site-Name, right-click Default-First-Site-Name, click Rename, and then type the new site name.

To identify the subnets to Active Directory, click the Subnets folder, click the Action menu, click New Subnet, type the subnet number followed by the prefix length, select the site object, and then click OK. A completed New Object – Subnet dialog box is shown in Figure 10-12. The **prefix** is the network address that identifies the range of IP addresses in this subnet. For example, the 192.168.0.0 subnet has a 24-bit subnet mask, which is entered as a prefix of /24.

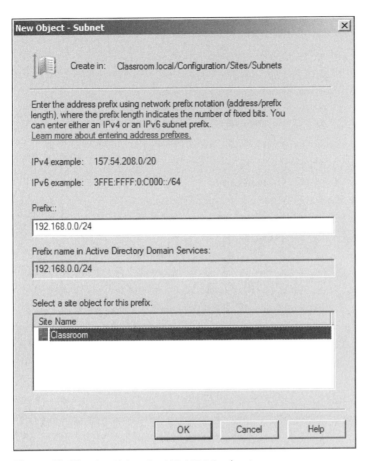

Figure 10-12 Identifying the 192.168.0.0 subnet

Figure 10-13, on the next page, shows the relationships between sites, domains, or organizational units. Within the Parts.com domain are a number of Active Directory objects. The company sites (shaded ellipses in the figure) are located at Headquarters, Texas, and South Carolina. The OUs are located at the indicated sites. Domains and OUs are logical. The three sites are physical.

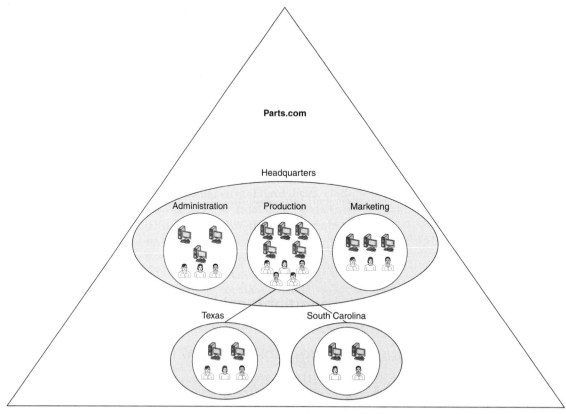

Figure 10-13 Relationship between sites, domains, or organizational units

Activity 10-1: Creating User Accounts

Time Required: 10 minutes

Objective: Create domain user accounts.

Description: In this activity, you will launch the Active Directory Users and Computers console and create five user accounts.

1. If necessary, log on to your Host PC with a username of **Administrator** and a password of **Secret1**.
2. If necessary, to launch VMRCplus, double-click the **VMRCplus** icon on the desktop.
3. To start Server-01, click **Server-01**, click **Turn On**, and then click **VM Console**.
4. Log on to Server-01 with a username of **Administrator** and a password of **Secret1**.
5. To launch the Active Directory Users and Computers console, click **Start**, point to **Administrative Tools**, and then click **Active Directory Users and Computers**.
6. To open the New Object – User dialog box, expand the **Classroom.local** node, click the **Users** folder in the left pane, click the **Action** menu, point to **New**, and then click **User**.

7. To enter the user account information, type **Glenn** in the First name text box, type **Boswell** in the Last name text box, type **GBoswell** in the User logon name text box, and then click **Next**.
8. To set the initial password, type **Password1** in the Password text box, press **Tab**, type **Password1** in the Confirm password text box, retain the **User must change password at next logon** check box, and then click **Next**.
9. Review the user account summary, and then click **Finish**. If necessary, click **Back** to correct the user account.
10. Repeat Steps 6 through 9 for the following users: **Karen Gonzales, Sarah Rogers, Skip Cole,** and **Tom Bounds**.
11. Leave the computer logged on for the next activity.

Activity 10-2: Displaying the Access Token

Time Required: 15 minutes

Objective: Display and interpret an access token.

Description: In this activity, you will open a command prompt and display the access token for the current local user. After logging off and logging on to the Classroom.local domain, display the access token for the current domain user.

1. If necessary, log on to your Host PC with a username of **Administrator** and a password of **Secret1**.
2. If necessary, to launch VMRCplus, double-click the **VMRCplus** icon on the desktop.
3. If necessary, to start Server-01, click **Server-01**, click **Turn On**, and then click **VM Console**.
4. If necessary, log on to Server-01 with a username of **Administrator** and a password of **Secret1**.
5. To start Client-01 in the Virtual Machine Manager, click **Client-01**, click **Turn On**, and then click **VM Console**.
6. Log on to Client-01 with a username of **Student** and a password of **Secret1**.
7. To open a command prompt, click **Start**, and then click **Command Prompt**.
8. To display the access token, type **whoami /user /groups** and then press **Enter**.
9. Locate the User Name entry and record the user account and user SID.
10. Locate the Group Name entries and record the group name and SID for Everyone, Administrators, and Users.
11. To close the command prompt window, type **exit**, and then press **Enter**.
12. Log off the Client-01 virtual machine.
13. To switch users, press right **Alt+Del**, and then click the **Switch User** button. Click the **Other User** button.
14. Log on to Client-01 with a username of **SRogers** and a password of **Password1**.

15. When The user's password must be changed before logging on the first time message appears, click **OK**, type **Secret1**, press **Tab**, type **Secret1**, and then click the arrow button.
16. When the Your password has been changed message appears, click **OK**.
17. To open a command prompt, click **Start**, type **cmd** in the Start Search text box, and then click **cmd**.
18. To display the access token, type **whoami /user /groups**, and then press **Enter**.
19. Locate the User Name entry and record the user account and user SID.
20. Locate the Group Name entries and record the group name and SID for Everyone.
21. To close the command prompt window, type **exit**, and then press **Enter**.
22. Leave the computers logged on for the next activity.

Activity 10-3: Creating Security Groups

Time Required: 10 minutes

Objective: Create global and domain local groups.

Description: In this activity, you will launch the Active Directory Users and Computers console, create a global group, add existing users to the global group, create a domain local group, and link the global group to the domain local group.

1. If necessary, log on to your Host PC with a username of **Administrator** and a password of **Secret1**.
2. If necessary, to launch VMRCplus, double-click the **VMRCplus** icon on the desktop.
3. If necessary, to start Server-01, click **Server-01**, click **Turn On**, and then click **VM Console**.
4. If necessary, log on to Server-01 with a username of **Administrator** and a password of **Secret1**.
5. If necessary, to launch the Active Directory Users and Computers console, click **Start**, point to **Administrative Tools**, and then click **Active Directory Users and Computers**.
6. To open the New Object – Group dialog box, click the **Users** folder in the left pane, click the **Action** menu, point to **New**, and then click **Group**.
7. To create the Managers global group, type **GG-Managers** in the Group name text box, and then click **OK**.
8. To create the DL-Production domain local group, click the **Action** menu, point to **New**, and then click **Group**, type **DL-Production** in the Group name text box, click the **Domain local** option button, and then click **OK**.
9. To add the user accounts to the Managers global group, double-click the **GG-Managers** global group, click the **Members** tab, click the **Add** button, click the **Object Types** button, clear the **Other objects** and **Groups** check boxes, click **OK**, click the **Advanced** button, click the **Find Now** button, click **Karen Gonzales**, press and hold **Shift**, click **Tom Bounds**, and then click **OK**.

10. To add the GG-Managers global group to the Production domain local group, click the **Member Of** tab, click the **Add** button, type **DL-Production** in the Enter the object names to select text box, click the **Check Names** button, and then click **OK** twice.

11. Leave the computers logged on for the next activity.

Activity 10-4: Creating an Organizational Unit

Time Required: 10 minutes

Objective: Create an organizational unit.

Requirements: Completion of Activity 10-3.

Description: In this activity, you will create an OU and move users to the organizational unit.

1. If necessary, log on to your Host PC with a username of **Administrator** and a password of **Secret1**.
2. If necessary, to launch VMRCplus, double-click the **VMRCplus** icon on the desktop.
3. If necessary, to start Server-01, click **Server-01**, click **Turn On**, and then click **VM Console**.
4. If necessary, log on to Server-01 with a username of **Administrator** and a password of **Secret1**.
5. If necessary, to launch the Active Directory Users and Computers console, click **Start**, point to **Administrative Tools**, and then click **Active Directory Users and Computers**.
6. To open the New Object – Organizational Unit dialog box, click the **Classroom.local** domain, click the **Action** menu, point to **New**, and then click **Organizational Unit**.
7. To create an OU for the Professional OU unit, type **Professional** in the Name text box, and then click **OK**.
8. To move users to the Professional OU, click **Users**, click the **View** menu, click **Filter Options**, click the **Show only the following types of objects** option button, click the **Users** check box if necessary, click **OK**, expand the **Users** folder, click **Karen Gonzales**, press and hold the **Shift** key, click **Tom Bounds**, right-click the marked group, click **Move**, click **Professional**, and then click **OK**.
9. To view the members of the Professional OU, click the **Professional** OU.
10. Leave the computers logged on for the next activity.

Activity 10-5: Managing a Site

Time Required: 10 minutes

Objective: Manage a physical site.

Description: In this activity, you will rename a site and add subnets to the site.

1. If necessary, log on to your Host PC with a username of **Administrator** and a password of **Secret1**.

414 Chapter 10   Implementing Security for the Classroom.local Virtual Network

2. If necessary, to launch VMRCplus, double-click the **VMRCplus** icon on the desktop.
3. If necessary, to start Server-01, click **Server-01**, click **Turn On**, and then click **VM Console**.
4. If necessary, log on to Server-01 with a username of **Administrator** and a password of **Secret1**.
5. To launch the Active Directory Sites and Services console, click **Start**, point to **Administrative Tools**, and then click **Active Directory Sites and Services**.
6. To rename the Default-First-Site-Name, expand **Sites**, right-click **Default-First-Site-Name**, click **Rename**, type **Classroom**, and then press **Enter**.
7. To identify the subnets, click **Subnets**, click the **Action** menu, click **New Subnet**, type **192.168.0.0/24** in the Prefix text box, click **Classroom**, and then click **OK**.
8. Repeat Step 7 for **192.168.1.0/24** and **192.168.2.0/24**.
9. Close the Active Directory Sites and Services console.
10. Leave the computers logged on for the next activity.

Applying Group Policy

You use Group Policy to define specific configurations for groups of users and computers by creating Group Policy settings. These settings are specified through the Group Policy Object Editor tools and are contained in a Group Policy Object (GPO), which is, in turn, linked to Active Directory containers, such as domains or OUs, as shown in Figure 10-14. GPOs are applied to domains and the OUs beneath them. Here, OU1 is affected by GPO1 and GPO2. OU2 is affected by all three GPOs.

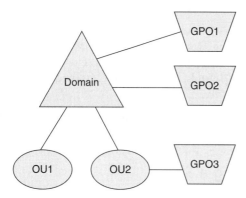

Figure 10-14 GPOs applied

In this way, Group Policy settings are applied to the users and computers in those Active Directory containers. You can configure the users' work environment once and rely on the system to enforce the policies as defined.

Group Policy Objects, other than the local Group Policy Object stored on local computers, are virtual objects. The policy setting information of a GPO is actually stored in two locations:

1. Group Policy container—An Active Directory container that stores GPO properties, including information on version, GPO status, and a list of components that have settings in the GPO.
2. Group Policy template—A folder structure that stores Administrative Template-based policies, security settings, script files, and information regarding applications that are available for Group Policy software installation.

Through Group Policy, you define the policies that determine how applications and operating systems are configured and keep users and systems secure. Table 10-1 describes the key features of Group Policy.

Table 10-1 Key features of Group Policy

Feature	Description
Registry-based policy	Define Registry-based policies for applications, the operating system, and its components. For example, an administrator can enable a policy setting that removes the Run command from the Start menu for all affected users.
Security settings	Set security options for computers and users within the scope of a GPO. For added protection, apply software restriction policies that prevent users from running files. Make exceptions to this default security level by creating rules for specific software.
Software restrictions	Defend against viruses, unwanted applications, and attacks on running computers. Use policies to identify software running in a domain and control its ability to execute.
Software distribution and installation	Manage application installation, updates, and removal centrally with Group Policy.
Computer and user scripts	Use scripts to automate tasks at computer startup and shutdown and user logon and logoff.
Roaming user profiles	Provide the ability to store user profiles centrally on a server and load them when a user logs on.
Redirected folders	Allow centralized management of these folders and give an IT group the capability to easily back up and restore these folders on behalf of users.
Offline folders	Provide access to network files and folders from a local disk.

Group Policy settings define the various components of the user's desktop environment that you need to manage, for example, the programs that are available to users, the programs that appear on the user's desktop, and options for the Start menu. Group Policy settings that you specify are contained in a Group Policy Object (GPO), which, in turn, is associated with selected Active Directory objects—sites, domains, or organizational units (OUs).

Group Policy applies not only to users and client computers, but also to member servers, domain controllers, and any other Windows Server 2008 computers within the scope of management. By default, Group Policy that is applied to a domain (that is, applied at the domain level just above the root of Active Directory Users and Computers) affects all computers and users in the domain. Active Directory Users and Computers also provides a built-in Domain Controllers OU. If you keep your domain controller accounts there, you can use the GPO Default Domain Controllers Policy to manage domain controllers separately from other computers.

Security Group Filtering

A GPO can be used to filter objects based on security group membership, which allows administrators to manage computers and users in either a centralized or a decentralized manner. To do this, administrators can use filtering based on security groups to define the scope of Group Policy management, so that Group Policy can be applied centrally at the domain level. Or, it can be applied in a decentralized manner at the OU level and can then be filtered again by security groups. Administrators can use security groups in Group Policy to do the following:

- Filter the scope of a GPO—This defines which groups of users and computers a GPO affects.
- Delegate control of a GPO—There are two aspects to managing and delegating Group Policy: managing the Group Policy links and managing who can create and edit GPOs.

With the Delegation of Control Wizard, you delegate control of Active Directory objects. You can grant a user permission to manage users, groups, and organizational units. This wizard is frequently used to delegate permission to reset passwords to a user.

Policy Inheritance

GPOs are linked to site, domain, and OU containers in Active Directory. Figure 10-15 shows the default order of precedence that follows the hierarchical nature of Active Directory: This order means that the local GPO is processed first, and GPOs that are linked to the organizational unit of which the computer or user is a direct member are processed last, which overwrites settings in the earlier GPOs if there are conflicts. (If there are no conflicts, then the earlier and later settings are merely aggregated.)

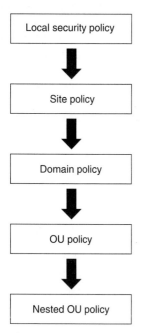

Figure 10-15 Default order of precedence

In general, Group Policy is passed down from parent to child containers within a domain. If you assign a specific Group Policy setting to a high-level parent container, that Group Policy setting applies to all containers beneath the parent container, including the user and computer objects in each container. However, if you explicitly specify a Group Policy setting for a child container, the child container's Group Policy setting overrides the parent container's setting.

If a parent OU has policy settings that are not configured, the child OU does not inherit them. Policy settings that are disabled are inherited as disabled. In addition, if a policy setting is configured (enabled or disabled) for a parent OU and the same policy setting is not configured for a child OU, the child inherits the parent's enabled or disabled policy setting.

If a policy setting that is applied to a parent OU and a policy setting that is applied to a child OU are compatible, the child OU inherits the parent policy setting, and the child's setting is also applied.

If a policy setting that is configured for a parent OU is incompatible with the same policy setting that is configured for a child OU (because the setting is enabled in one case and disabled in the other), the child does not inherit the policy setting from the parent. The policy setting in the child is applied.

Blocking Inheritance and No Override

The Block Policy inheritance option blocks GPOs that apply higher in the Active Directory hierarchy of sites, domains, and OUs. It does not block GPOs if they have No Override enabled. The Block Policy inheritance option is set only on sites, domains, and OUs, not on individual GPOs. These settings provide complete control over the default inheritance rules.

For example, you set up a GPO in the Professional OU, which applies by default to the users (and computers) in all child objects within the Professional OU. You then establish another GPO in the Professional OU and set it as No Override. These settings will apply to all child objects even if settings conflict with other settings applied through a GPO. You will then use the Block inheritance feature to prevent group policies set in a parent site, domain, or OU (in this case, the Professional OU) from being applied to the Professional OU.

Using the Group Policy Management Console

The Microsoft **Group Policy Management Console (GPMC)** helps you manage your group policies effectively. The GPMC is available as a separate feature in Windows Server 2008. To use the GPMC, add the feature from Server Manager. To do this, click the Add Features link on Server Manager, click the Group Policy Management check box, click Next, and then click Install.

To launch the GPMC, click Start, point to Administrative Tools, and click Group Policy Management. Figure 10-16, on the next page, shows the Group Policy Management Console.

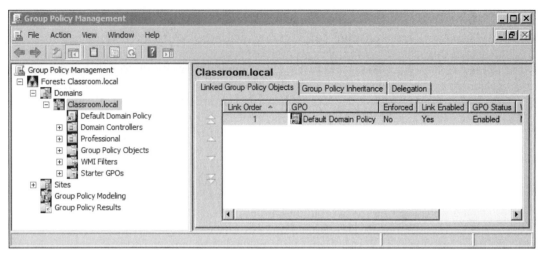

Figure 10-16 Group Policy Management Console

Using Resultant Set of Policy

Resultant Set of Policy (RSoP) makes policy implementation and troubleshooting easier. RSoP is a query engine that polls existing policies and planned policies, and then reports the results of those queries. It polls existing policies based on site, domain, domain controller, and organizational unit. RSoP collects policy information and provides details about all policy settings that you configured, including Administrative Templates, Folder Redirection, Internet Explorer Maintenance, Security Settings, Scripts, and Group Policy Software Installation. Figure 10-17 shows RSoP.

Figure 10-17 Resultant Set of Policy

When policies are applied on multiple levels (for example, site, domain, domain controller, and organizational unit), the results can conflict. RSoP can help you determine a set of applied policies and their precedence (the order in which policies are applied).

RSoP consists of two modes: planning mode and logging mode. With planning mode, you can simulate the effect of policy settings that you want to apply to a computer and user. Logging mode reports the existing policy settings for a computer and user that is currently logged on.

Activity 10-6: Using the Group Policy Management Editor to Create a Domain Security Policy

Time Required: 10 minutes

Objective: Create and test a domain security policy.

Description: In this activity, you will create an interactive logon policy to require the classic logon and then test the policy.

1. If necessary, log on to your Host PC with a username of **Administrator** and a password of **Secret1**.
2. If necessary, to launch VMRCplus, double-click the **VMRCplus** icon on the desktop.
3. If necessary, to start Server-01, click **Server-01**, click **Turn On**, and then click **VM Console**.
4. If necessary, log on to Server-01 with a username of **Administrator** and a password of **Secret1**.
5. If necessary, to launch Server Manager, click **Start**, point to **Administration Tools**, and then click **Server Manager**.
6. If necessary, to add the Group Policy Management Console, click **Features**, click the **Add Features** link, click the **Group Policy Management** check box, click **Next**, and then click **Install**.
7. Wait for Group Policy Management to install and then click **Close**.
8. To access the Group Policy Management Console, click **Start**, point to **Administrative Tools**, and then click **Group Policy Management**.

Creating a Domain Security Policy

9. To set Microsoft Internet Explorer security settings to work with GPMC, expand **Forest: Classroom.local**, expand **Domains**, expand **Classroom.local**, double-click **Default Domain Policy**, click **OK**, click the **Settings** tab, click the **Add** button, click the **Add** button, and then click **Close**.
10. To edit the Default Domain Policy, right-click **Default Domain Policy** in the left pane, and then click **Edit**.
11. To view the contents of Security Options node, click **Computer Configuration** in the left pane, expand **Windows Settings**, expand **Security Settings**, expand **Local Policies**, and then click **Security Options**.

12. To use the classic logon, scroll and double-click **Interactive logon: Do not display last user name**, click the **Define this policy setting** check box, click the **Enabled** option button, and then click **OK**.
13. Close the Group Policy Management Editor.

Testing the Domain Security Policy

14. If necessary, log on to Client-01 with a username of **SRogers** and a password of **Secret1**.
15. If the user's password must be changed before logging on the first time, click **OK**, type **Secret1**, press **Tab**, type **Secret1**, and then click **OK** twice.
16. To open a command prompt, type **cmd** in the Start Search text box, and then click **cmd**.
17. To update the policy on the local computer, type **gpupdate**, and then press **Enter**.
18. Wait for the Group Policy update to complete.
19. To close the command prompt window, type **exit**, and then press **Enter**.
20. Log off the Client-01 computer.
21. To log on using the classic logon box, press right **Alt+Del**, type **srogers**, press **Tab**, type **Secret1**, and then press **Enter**.
22. Leave the computers logged on for the next activity.

Activity 10-7: Using the Group Policy Management Editor to Create a Policy for an Organizational Unit

Time Required: 10 minutes

Objective: Create and test a security policy.

Requirements: Completion of Activities 10-3, 10-4, and 10-6.

Description: In this activity, you will create an interactive logon policy to require the classic logon and then test the policy.

1. If necessary, log on to your Host PC with a username of **Administrator** and a password of **Secret1**.
2. If necessary, to launch VMRCplus, double-click the **VMRCplus** icon on the desktop.
3. If necessary, to start Server-01, click **Server-01**, click **Turn On**, and then click **VM Console**.
4. If necessary, log on to Server-01 with a username of **Administrator** and a password of **Secret1**.
5. If necessary, to launch Server Manager, click **Start**, click **Administrative Tools**, and then click **Server Manager**.

Creating an Organizational Security Policy

6. If necessary, to access the Group Policy Management Console, click **Start**, point to **Administrative Tools**, and then click **Group Policy Management**.

7. To create a link to a GPO, right-click **Professional**, click **Create a GPO in this domain, and Link it here**, type **GP-Professionals** in the Name text box, and click **OK**.
8. To edit the GPO, expand the **Professional** node, right-click **GP-Professionals**, and click **Edit**.
9. To view the administrative templates, click **User Configuration**, and then expand **Administrative Templates**.
10. To view the Start menu and taskbar policies, click **Start Menu and Taskbar**.
11. To remove the Music icon from the Start menu, scroll and double-click **Remove Music icon from Start menu**, click the **Enabled** option button, and then click **OK**.
12. To remove the Pictures icon from the Start menu, double-click **Remove Pictures icon from Start menu**, click the **Enabled** option button, and then click **OK**.

Testing the Organizational Unit Security Policy

13. If necessary, log on to Client-01 with a username of **SRogers** and a password of **Password1**.
14. If the user's password must be changed before logging on the first time, click **OK**, type **Secret1**, press **Tab**, type **Secret1**, and then click **OK** twice.
15. To open a command prompt, type **cmd** in the Start Search text box, and then click **cmd**.
16. To update the policy on the local computer, type **gpupdate**, and then press **Enter**.
17. Wait for the Group Policy update to complete.
18. To close the command prompt window, type **exit**, and then press **Enter**.
19. To verify that the two icons have been removed, click **Start**, and look for the Music and Pictures icons.
20. Leave the computers logged on for the next activity.

Activity 10-8: Using the Resultant Set of Policy

Time Required: 15 minutes

Objective: Use the RSoP to verify the status of security policies.

Requirements: Completion of Activities 10-3, 10-4, 10-6, and 10-7.

Description: In this activity, you will verify the status of the security policies on Server-01 and Client-01.

1. If necessary, log on to your Host PC with a username of **Administrator** and a password of **Secret1**.
2. If necessary, to launch VMRCplus, double-click the **VMRCplus** icon on the desktop.
3. If necessary, to start Server-01, click **Server-01**, click **Turn On**, and then click **VM Console**.
4. If necessary, log on to Server-01 with a username of **Administrator** and a password of **Secret1**.

5. To create a console for the RSoP, click **Start**, click **Run**, type **mmc** in the Open text box, press **Enter**, click the **File** menu, click **Add/Remove Snap-in**, scroll and click **Resultant Set of Policy**, click the **Add** button, and then click **OK**.

6. To save the console, click the **File** menu, click **Save As**, type **RSoP**, and then click the **Save** button.

Reviewing the Security Policy on Server-01

7. To launch the RSoP console, click **Start**, point to **All Programs**, click the **Administrative Tools** folder (not the Administrative Tools menu), and then click **RSoP**.

8. If necessary, to access the Resultant Set of Policy Wizard, click the **Resultant Set of Policy** node, click the **Action** menu, and then click **Generate RSoP Data**.

9. To generate data for the existing computer and the current user, click **Next** five times and then click **Finish**.

10. To view the user configuration, expand the **Administrator on Server-01 –RSoP** node, click **User Configuration**, expand **Windows Settings**, and then expand **Security Settings**.

11. Verify that the administrative templates are not present.

12. Close the RSoP window. Click **No** when asked to Save console settings for RSoP.

Reviewing the Security Policy on Client-01

13. To access the Resultant Set of Policy Wizard, click the **Resultant Set of Policy** node, click the **Action** menu, and then click **Generate RSoP Data**.

14. To start planning mode, click **Next**, click the **Planning mode** option button, and then click **Next**.

15. To specify the user, click the **User** option button, click the **Browse** button within User Information, type **srogers** in the Enter the object name to select text box, click the **Check Names** button, and then click **OK**.

16. To specify the computer, click the **Computer** option button, click the **Browse** button within Computer Information, type **Client-01** in the Enter the object name to select text box, click the **Check Names** button, click **OK**, click the **Skip to the final page of this wizard without collecting additional data** check box, and then click **Next**.

17. To start the simulation, click **Next**.

18. Wait for the progress to complete, and then click **Finish**.

19. To view the contents of the Security Options node, expand SRogers on Client-01, click **Computer Configuration**, expand **Windows Settings**, expand **Security Settings**, expand **Local Policies**, and then click **Security Options**.

20. Scroll and verify that the Interactive logon: Do not display last user name option is enabled, and then click **OK**.

21. To view the administrative templates, click **User Configuration**, and then expand **Administrative Templates**.

22. To view the Start menu and taskbar policies, click **Start Menu and Taskbar**.

23. Verify that the Remove Music icon from Start menu and Remove Picture icon from Start menu options are enabled.
24. Close the RSoP window.
25. Leave the computers logged on for the next activity.

Implementing IP Security

The Windows Server 2008 operating system simplifies deployment and management of network security with the **Internet Protocol security (IPSec)** for Windows Server 2008, a Microsoft implementation of the Internet Engineering Task Force (IETF) standards. The **Internet Engineering Task Force (IETF)** is a large, open, international community of network designers, operators, vendors, and researchers concerned with the evolution of the Internet architecture and the smooth operation of the Internet. It is open to any interested individual.

In today's interconnected business world of the Internet, internal networks, branch offices, and remote access, sensitive information constantly crosses networks—of which many are unprotected. Your challenge is to ensure that sensitive traffic is safe from the following:

- Data modification while in transit (**data integrity**)
- Being read and interpreted while in transit (**data confidentiality**)
- Being spoofed by unauthenticated parties (**data origin authentication**)
- Being resubmitted (replayed) to gain unauthorized access to protected resources (**replay protection**)

IPSec provides network-level data integrity, data confidentiality, data origin authentication, and replay protection for IP-based traffic. IPSec in Windows Server 2008 integrates with the inherent security of the Windows Server 2008 operating system to provide the platform for protecting network communications.

IPSec Protocols

IPSec provides its security services by wrapping the payload of an IP packet with an additional header or trailer that contains the information to provide data origin authentication, data integrity, data confidentiality, and replay protection. IPSec consists of the following:

- **Authentication header (AH)**—Provides data authentication, data integrity, and replay protection for an IP packet
- **Encapsulating Security Payload (ESP) header and trailer**—Provides data authentication, data integrity, replay protection, and data confidentiality for an IP packet payload

The result of applying the AH or the ESP header and trailer to an IP packet transforms the packet into a protected packet, as shown in Figure 10-18 on the next page.

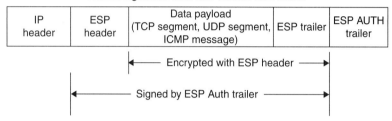

Figure 10-18 IPSec packet showing a protected packet

IPSec Modes

IPSec supports two modes—transport mode and tunnel mode—that transform the original IP packet into a protected packet.

Transport Mode Transport mode is the default mode for IPSec, and it is used between two communicating peer computers. Figure 10-19 shows the communications between a client and a server. When transport mode is used, IPSec encrypts only the IP payload.

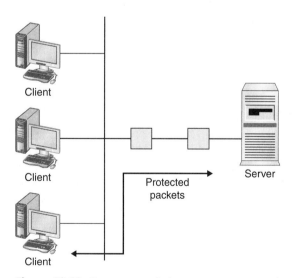

Figure 10-19 Transport mode between two communicating peer computers

Transport mode protects an IP payload through an AH or an ESP header. Typical IP payloads are TCP segments (which contain a TCP header and TCP segment data), UDP messages (which contain a UDP header and UDP message data), and Internet Control Message Protocol (ICMP) messages (which contain an ICMP header and ICMP message data).

AH in transport mode provides data origin authentication, data integrity, and anti-replay for the entire packet (both the IP header and the data payload carried in the packet, except for fields in the IP header that must change in transit). This type of protection does not provide confidentiality, which means that it does not encrypt the data. The data can be read but not easily modified or impersonated. AH uses a **cryptographic hash function** transformation that takes an input and returns a fixed-size number, which is called the hash value. This **hash value** is a sort of "digital fingerprint" of the larger document. This value is generated by imposing a hashing algorithm onto an input. The value is then transformed, or signed, by a private key to produce a digital signature.

For example, Computer01 sends data to Computer02. The IP header, the AH header, and the IP payload are protected with data integrity and data origin authentication. Computer02 can determine that Computer01 really sent the packet and that the packet was not modified in transit.

AH is identified in the IP header with an IP protocol ID of 51, as shown in Figure 10-20. The AH header contains a **security parameter index (SPI)** field that IPSec uses in combination with the destination address and the security protocol (AH or ESP) to identify the correct security association (SA) for the communication. The security association (SA) is explained in the Negotiation Phases section, later in this chapter.

Protocol of payload	Payload length	Reserved	SPI	Sequence number	Authentication data

Figure 10-20 IP header fields

IPSec at the receiver uses the SPI value to determine with which SA the packet is identified. To prevent replay attacks, the AH header also contains a **Sequence Number field** (an increasing number, used to prevent replay attacks).

An Authentication Data field in the AH header contains the **integrity check value (ICV)**, which is used to verify both data integrity and data origin authentication. The receiver calculates the ICV value and checks it against this value (which is calculated by the sender) to verify integrity. The ICV is calculated over the IP header, the AH header, and the IP payload.

AH authenticates the entire packet for data integrity and data origin authentication, with the exception of some fields in the IP header that might change in transit (for example, the Time to Live and Checksum fields). Figure 10-21, on the next page, shows the original IP packet and how it is protected with AH in transport mode.

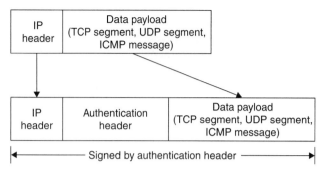

Figure 10-21 A packet protected with AH in transport mode

You can use AH alone or combine it with ESP. ESP in transport mode provides confidentiality (in addition to data origin authentication, data integrity, and anti-replay) for an IP packet payload. ESP in transport mode does not authenticate the entire packet. Only the IP payload (not the IP header) is protected. You can use ESP alone or combine it with AH. For example, consider two communicating peer computers, Computer01 sends data to Computer02. The IP payload is encrypted and authenticated. Upon receipt, IPSec verifies data integrity and data origin authentication and then decrypts the payload.

ESP is identified in the IP header with the IP protocol ID of 50 and consists of an ESP header that is placed before the IP payload, and an ESP and authentication data trailer that is placed after the IP payload.

Like the AH header, the ESP header contains SPI and Sequence Number fields. The Authentication Data field in the ESP trailer is used for message authentication and integrity for the ESP header, the payload data, and the ESP trailer.

Figure 10-22 shows the original IP packet and how it is protected with ESP. The authenticated portion of the packet indicates where the packet has been protected for data integrity and data origin authentication. The encrypted portion of the packet indicates what information is confidential.

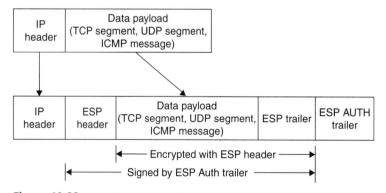

Figure 10-22 A packet protected with ESP in transport mode

The IP header is not authenticated and is not protected from modification. To provide data integrity and data origin authentication for the IP header, use ESP and AH.

Tunnel Mode IPSec tunnel mode is useful for protecting traffic between different networks, when traffic must pass through an intermediate, untrusted network. Figure 10-23 shows the use of tunnel mode between two networks using the Internet for communication.

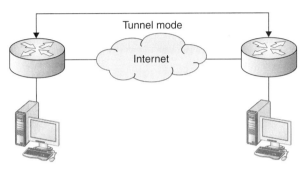

Figure 10-23 Tunnel mode between two communicating networks

Tunnel mode helps protect an entire IP packet by treating it as an AH or ESP payload. With tunnel mode, an IP packet is encapsulated with an AH or an ESP header and an additional IP header. The IP addresses of the outer IP header are the tunnel endpoints (routers between the two respective networks), and the IP addresses of the encapsulated IP header are the original source and final destination addresses.

As Figure 10-24 shows, AH tunnel mode encapsulates an IP packet with an AH and an IP header and authenticates the entire packet for data integrity and data origin authentication.

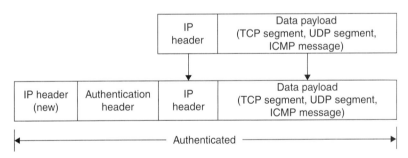

Figure 10-24 A packet protected with AH in tunnel mode

As Figure 10-25 (on the next page) shows, ESP tunnel mode encapsulates an IP packet with both an ESP and IP header and an ESP authentication trailer.

Because a new header for tunneling is added to the packet, everything that comes after the ESP header is authenticated (except for the ESP Authentication Data field) because it is now encapsulated in the tunneled packet. The original header is placed after the ESP header. The entire packet is appended with an ESP trailer before encryption occurs. Everything that follows the ESP header is encrypted, including the original header that is now part of the data portion of the packet but not including the ESP Authentication Data field.

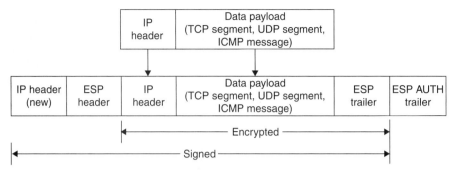

Figure 10-25 A packet protected with ESP in tunnel mode

The entire ESP payload is then encapsulated within a new IP header, which is not encrypted. The information in the new IP header is used only to route the packet through the unsecured network(s) to the tunnel endpoint.

If the packet is being sent across a public network, the packet is routed to the IP address of the tunnel server for the receiving network. The tunnel server decrypts the packet, discards the ESP header, and uses the original IP header to route the packet to the destination computer.

In tunnel mode, you can combine ESP with AH, providing both confidentiality for the tunneled IP packet and data integrity and data origin authentication for the entire packet.

Negotiation Phases

Before two communicating peer computers can exchange protected data, they must establish a contract—called a security association (SA)—in which both communicating peer computers agree on how to protect information. A **security association (SA)** is a combination of a negotiated encryption key, security protocol, and SPI, which together define the security used to protect the communication from sender to receiver. The SPI is a unique, identifying value in the SA that is used to distinguish among multiple SAs that exist at the receiving computer.

For example, multiple SAs might exist if a computer using IPSec protection is communicating with multiple computers at the same time. This situation occurs frequently when the computer is a file server that serves multiple clients. In these situations, the receiving computer uses the SPI to determine which SA the computer should use to process the incoming packets.

To build this contract between the two computers, the IETF has defined **Internet Key Exchange (IKE)** as the standard method of SA and key determination. IKE does the following:

- Centralizes SA management, reducing connection time
- Generates and manages shared, secret keys that help protect the information

Phase I or Main Mode Negotiation To help ensure successful and protected communication, IKE performs a two-phase operation. IKE helps ensure confidentiality and authentication during each phase by using encryption and authentication algorithms that the two communicating peer computers agree on during security negotiations. With the duties split between two phases, keys can be created rapidly.

During the first phase, the two communicating peer computers establish a protected, authenticated channel. This phase is called the phase I SA or main mode SA. IKE automatically protects the identities of the two communicating peer computers during this exchange.

The first step in main mode negotiation is policy negotiation. The following four mandatory parameters for the Windows implementation of IPSec are negotiated as part of the main mode SA:

1. The encryption algorithm (two options)

    - **Data Encryption Standard (DES)** is a **cipher** (a method for encrypting information) selected as an official Federal Information Processing Standard (FIPS) for the United States in 1976, and which has subsequently enjoyed widespread use internationally. DES uses the same algorithm and key for encryption and decryption and is now considered to be insecure for many applications. This is chiefly due to the 56-bit key size being too small; DES keys have been broken in less than 24 hours.
    - **Triple-DES (3DES)**—three 56-bit DES keys—was chosen as a simple way to enlarge the key space without a need to switch to a new algorithm.

2. The hash algorithm (two options)

    - **Message Digest 5 Hashed Message Authentication Code (MD5-HMAC)**—Widely used cryptographic hash function with a 128-bit hash value. MD5 has been employed in a wide variety of security applications, and is also commonly used to check the integrity of files. An MD5 hash is typically expressed as a 32-character hexadecimal number.
    - **Secure Hash Algorithm 1-HMAC (SHA1-HMAC)**—Considered to be the successor to MD5. SHA-1 produces a hash value that is 160 bits long.

3. The authentication method (three options)

    - **Kerberos V5**—Primary security protocol for authentication within a domain. The KerberosV5 network authentication protocol verifies both the identity of the user that is requesting authentication as well as the server providing the requested authentication. This dual verification is also known as **mutual authentication**.
    - **Certificate**—Should be used in situations that include Internet access, remote access to corporate resources, external business partner communications, or computers that do not run the Kerberos V5 security protocol. This requires that at least one trusted certificate authority (CA) and associated certificate have been configured. A **certificate authority (CA)** is an entity that issues digital certificates for use by other parties. It is an example of a trusted third party. There are many commercial CAs that charge for their services. Institutions and governments might have their own CAs.
    - **Preshared key**—Simple to use and does not require the client to run the Kerberos V5 protocol or have a public key certificate. Both parties must manually configure IPSec to use this preshared key.

4. The **Diffie-Hellman (DH) group** to be used for the base keying material. The DH group sets the length of the base prime numbers used during the key exchange process. For maximum security, Windows Server 2008 uses Group 2048 (high), which provides 2048 bits of keying strength. Strong Diffie-Hellman groups combined with longer key lengths increase the computational difficulty of determining a secret key.

Diffie-Hellman Exchange The Diffie-Hellman exchange is a cryptographic protocol that allows two communicating peer computers that have no prior knowledge of each other to jointly establish a shared secret key over an insecure communications channel. At no time do the two communicating peer computers exchange actual keys. The communicating peer computers exchange only the base information that the DH key determination algorithm requires to generate the shared, secret key. This key can then be used to encrypt subsequent communications. After this exchange, the IKE service on each computer generates the master key that the communicating peer computers use for subsequent communications.

Authentication The communicating peer computers attempt to authenticate the DH key exchange. A DH key exchange without authentication is vulnerable to a man-in-the-middle attack. A **man-in-the-middle attack** occurs when a computer masquerades as the endpoint between two communicating peer computers. Without successful authentication, communication cannot proceed. The communicating peer computers use the master key, in conjunction with the negotiation algorithms and methods, to authenticate their identities. The communicating peer computers encrypt the entire identity payload (including the identity type, port, and protocol) using the keys generated from the DH exchange. The identity payload, regardless of which authentication method is used, is protected from both modification and interpretation. The initiator offers a potential SA to the receiver. The responder cannot modify the offer. Should the offer be modified, the initiator rejects the responder's message. The responder sends either a reply accepting the offer or a reply with alternatives.

Phase II or Quick Mode Negotiation

In this phase, the communicating peer computers negotiate the SAs to protect the actual data sent between them. A quick mode negotiation consists of the following steps:

1. Security policy negotiation occurs.
    The IPSec peer computers exchange the following requirements to protect the data transfer:

    - The IPSec protocol (AH or ESP)
    - The hash algorithm (MD5-HMAC or SHA1-HMAC)
    - The encryption algorithm, if requested (DES or 3DES)

    The computers reach a common agreement and establish two SAs on each computer. One SA is for inbound communication, and the other is for outbound communication.

2. Session key material is refreshed or exchanged.
    IKE refreshes the keying material, and new shared keys are generated for data integrity, data origin authentication, and encryption (if negotiated). If rekeying is required, either a second DH exchange (as described in main mode negotiation) occurs, or a refresh of the original DH key is used.

The main mode SA helps protect the quick mode negotiation of security settings and keying material (for the purpose of securing data). The first phase helped protect the computers' identities, and the second phase helps protect the keying material by refreshing it before sending data. IKE can accommodate a key exchange payload for an additional DH exchange if a rekey is necessary. Otherwise, IKE refreshes the keying material from the DH exchange completed in main mode.

How IPSec Works

In the example illustrated in Figure 10-26, a user on Computer A is sending a message to a user on Computer B. IPSec for Windows Server 2008 policies have been deployed on both computers. At the user level, the process of securing the IP packets is transparent.

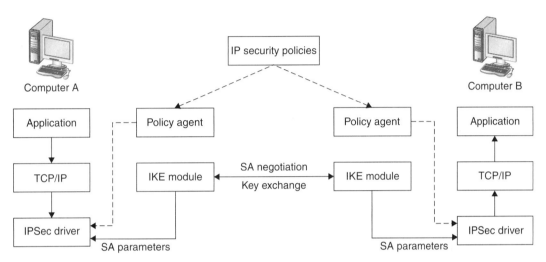

Figure 10-26 How IPSec works

The IPSec policies assigned to the domain system containers of Computer A and Computer B determine the level of security for the communication. The IPSec policies are retrieved by the IPSec Policy Agent and passed to the IKE module and the IPSec driver. The IKE module on each computer uses the negotiation settings of the IPSec policy to perform computer-level authentication, determine the secret key, and how to negotiate the protection of IPSec traffic and IPSec-secured traffic. The IPSec driver uses the IP filter settings of the IPSec policy to determine what types of traffic are to be protected.

Assuming that Computer A and Computer B are not already communicating securely and a message that Computer A sends to Computer B must be secured, IPSec works in the following way:

1. The user on Computer A sends a message to the user on Computer B. The message is passed to TCP/IP and is intercepted by the IPSec driver on Computer A.

2. The IPSec driver on Computer A checks its outbound IPSec filter list and determines that the message should be secured.

3. The action is to negotiate security, so the IPSec driver notifies the IKE module to begin negotiations.

4. The two computers use IKE to authenticate each other and determine secret keying material, the type of protection for future IKE traffic, and the type of protection for the message that is being sent.

5. The sets of parameters that determine the protection, known as security associations (SAs), are sent to the IPSec driver. The IPSec driver uses SA information to protect the message.

6. The IPSec-protected message is forwarded to Computer B.
7. The IPSec driver on Computer B receives the IPSec-protected message.
8. The IPSec driver on Computer B validates authentication and integrity and, if required, decrypts the message.
9. The IPSec driver passes the validated and decrypted message to the TCP/IP driver, which passes it to the receiving application on Computer B.

End-to-End Security Between Specific Hosts

IPSec establishes trust and security from a unicast source IP address to a unicast destination IP address (end-to-end). For example, IPSec can secure traffic between Web servers and database servers or domain controllers in different sites. As shown in Figure 10-26, only the sending and receiving computers need to be aware of IPSec. Each handles security at its respective end and assumes that the medium over which the communication takes place is not secure. The two computers can be located near each other, as on a single network segment, or across the Internet. Computers or network elements that route data from source to destination are not required to support IPSec.

Creating IPSec Policies

An IPSec policy is a collection of general settings and rules that are used to configure IPSec services and that determine IPSec behavior. To initiate the creation of an IPSec rule, click Start, point to Administrative Tools, and then click Local Security Policy. You create rules with the IP Security Policy Wizard. Start by right-clicking the IP Security Policies on Local Computer, and select Create IP Security Policy.

One or more IPSec rules determine which traffic IPSec examines, how that traffic is secured and encrypted, and how IPSec peers are authenticated.

An IPSec policy consists of one or more rules that determine IPSec behavior. Each IPSec rule contains the following primary configuration items—filters, filter actions, and authentication methods.

Filters A single filter list is selected that contains one or more predefined packet filters that describe the types of traffic to which the configured filter action for this rule is applied.

Figure 10-27 shows the completed IP filter list. With the wizard, you make decisions about the source and destination addresses, ports, and protocols. With the mirrored check box, packets are matched with the exact opposite source and destination IP addresses.

Filter Actions A single filter action is selected that includes the type of action required (permit, block, or secure) for packets that match the filter list. For the secure filter action, the negotiation data contains one or more security methods that are used (in order of preference) during IKE negotiations and other IPSec settings. Each security method determines the security protocol (such as AH or ESP), the specific cryptographic algorithms, and session key regeneration settings. Figure 10-28 shows a completed filter action.

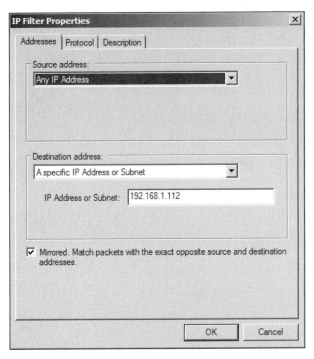

Figure 10-27 Completed IP filter list

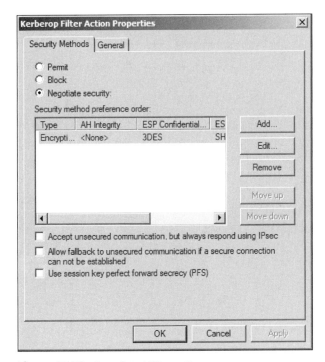

Figure 10-28 Completed filter action

Authentication Methods One or more authentication methods are configured (in order of preference) and used for authentication of IPSec peers during main mode negotiations. The available authentication methods are the Kerberos V5 protocol (used in Active Directory environments), use of a certificate issued from a specified certificate authority (CA), or a preshared key. Figure 10-29 shows a completed authentication method.

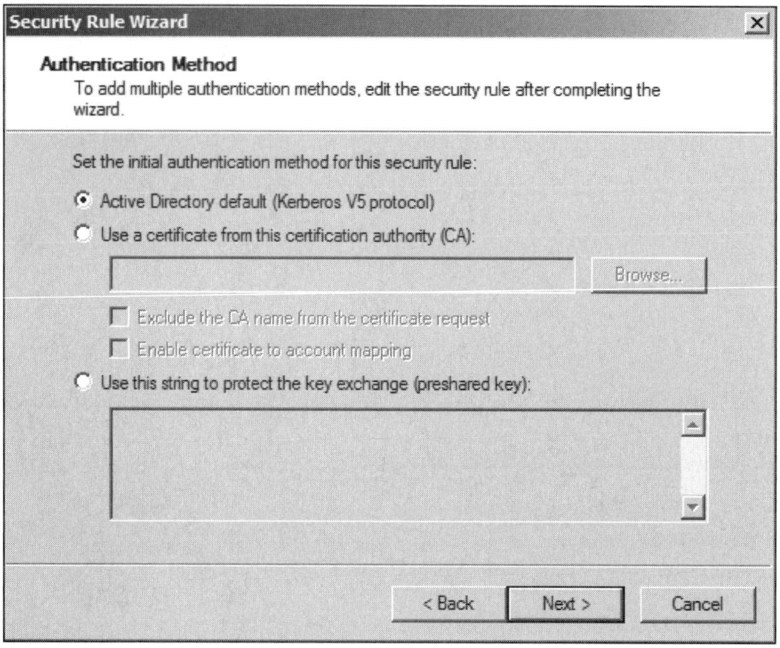

Figure 10-29 Authentication method

IP Security Monitor IP Security Monitor is a Windows-based tool used to confirm whether your secured, IP-based communications are successful by displaying the active security associations on local or remote computers. For example, you can use IP Security Monitor to determine whether there has been a pattern of authentication or security association failures, possibly indicating incompatible security policy settings. Figure 10-30 shows the Quick Mode associations in IP Security Monitor. When these Quick Mode Security Associations are displayed, you are assured that the transmissions between the transport pair are secured.

Implementing IP Security **435**

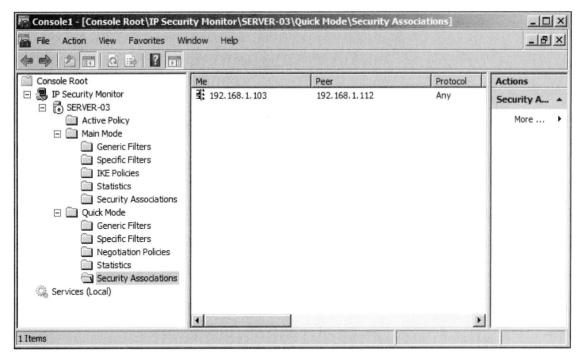

Figure 10-30 IP Security Monitor

Activity 10-9: Creating IPSec Policies

Time Required: 20 minutes

Objective: Use the IP Security Policy Wizard to create an IPSec policy.

Description: In this activity, you will create IPSec security policies using Kerberos authentication on Server-02 and Client-01.

1. If necessary, log on to your Host PC with a username of **Administrator** and a password of **Secret1**.
2. If necessary, to launch VMRCplus, double-click the **VMRCplus** icon on the desktop.

Creating the IP Security Policy on the File Server

3. To start Server-02, click **Server-02**, click **Turn On**, and then click **VM Console**.
4. Log on to Server-02 with a username of **Server-02\Administrator** and a password of **Secret1**.
5. To launch Local Security Policy on Server-02, click **Start**, point to **Administrative Tools**, and then click **Local Security Policy**.
6. To start the IP Security Policy Wizard, right-click the **IP Security Policies on Local Computer** node, click **Create IP Security Policy**, and then click **Next**.
7. To name the security policy, type **Kerberos Policy** in the Name text box, click **Next** twice, and then click **Finish**.

8. To specify the Security Rule, click the **Add** button, click **Next** three times, click the **Add** button, type **Kerberos Filter List** in the Name text box, and then click **Add**. Click **Next** three times, click the **Destination Address** drop-down list arrow, click the **A specific IP address or subnet** entry, type **192.168.0.111** in the IP Address or Subnet text box, click **Next** twice, click **Finish**, and then click **OK**.

9. To add the filter action, click the **Kerberos IP Filter List** option button, click **Next**, click the **Add** button, click **Next**, type **Kerberos Filter Action** in the Name text box, click **Next**, retain the **Negotiate security** option button, click **Next** three times, and then click **Finish**.

10. To specify the authentication method, click the **Kerberos Filter Action** option button, click **Next**, retain the **Active Directory default (Kerberos V5 Protocol)** option button, click **Next**, click **Finish**, and then click **OK**.

11. To assign the security policy, click the **IP Security Policies on Local Computer** node, right-click **Kerberos Policy**, and then click **Assign**.

Creating the IP Security Policy on the Client

12. If necessary, to start Client-01, click **Client-01**, click **Turn On**, and then click **VM Console**.

13. If necessary, log on to Client-01 with a username of **client-01\student** and a password of **Secret1**.

14. To launch the Local Security Policy tool, click **Start**, click **Control Panel**, click **Classic View**, double-click **Administrative Tools**, right-click **Local Security Policy**, and then click **Run as administrator**.

15. When the User Account Control dialog box opens, click the **Continue** button.

16. To launch the IP Security Policy Wizard, right-click **IP Security Policies on Local Computer**, click **Create IP Security Policy**, and then click **Next**.

17. To name the security policy, type **Kerberos Policy** in the Name text box, click **Next** twice, and then click **Finish**.

18. To specify the Security Rule, click the **Add** button, click **Next** three times, click the **Add** button, type **Kerberos Filter List** in the Name text box, and then click **Add**. Click **Next** three times, click the **Destination Address** drop-down list arrow, click the **A specific IP address or subnet** entry, type **192.168.0.102** in the IP Address or Subnet text box, click **Next** twice, click **Finish**, and then click **OK**.

19. To add the filter action, click the **Kerberos IP Filter List** option button, click **Next**, click the **Add** button, click **Next**, type **Kerberos Filter Action** in the Name text box, click **Next**, retain the **Negotiate security** option button, click **Next** three times, and then click **Finish**.

20. To specify the authentication method, click the **Kerberos Filter Action** option button, click **Next**, retain the **Active Directory default (Kerberos V5 Protocol)** option button, click **Next**, click **Finish**, and then click **OK**.

21. To assign the security policy, click the **IP Security Policies on Local Computer** node, right-click **Kerberos Policy**, and then click **Assign**.
22. Leave the computers logged on for the next activity.

Activity 10-10: Testing IPSec Policies

Time Required: 20 minutes

Objective: Test the IPSec policies.

Requirements: Completion of Activities 9-7 through 9-9, 9-12, and 10-9. Server-01 must be running.

Description: In this activity, you will test the security policies created in Activity 10-9.

1. If necessary, log on to your Host PC with a username of **Administrator** and a password of **Secret1**.
2. If necessary, to launch VMRCplus, double-click the **VMRCplus** icon on the desktop.
3. To start Server-02, click **Server-02**, click **Turn On**, and then click **VM Console**.
4. Log on to Server-02 with a username of **Administrator** and a password of **Secret1**.
5. If necessary, to start Server-02, click **Server-02**, click **Turn On**, and then click **VM Console**.
6. If necessary, log on to Server-02 with a username of **Server-02\Administrator** and a password of **Secret1**. If necessary, to enable network discovery and file sharing, click **Start**, right-click **Network**, click **Properties**, click the **Network discovery** drop-down list arrow, click the **Turn on network discovery** option button, click the **Apply** button, click the **No, make the network that I am connected to a private network** link, click the **File sharing** drop-down list arrow, click the **Turn on file sharing** option button, click the **Apply** button, and then close the Network and Sharing Center window.
7. To share a folder, click **Start**, click **Computer**, double-click **Local Disk (C:)**, right-click in the right-pane, point to **New**, click **Folder**, type **Shared Files**, press **Enter**, right-click **Shared Files**, click **Properties**, click the **Sharing** tab, click the **Advanced Sharing** button, click the **Share this folder** check box, click the **Permissions** button, click the **Allow Full Control** check box, click **OK** twice, and then click **Close**.
8. To create the IP Security Monitor console, click **Start**, click **Run**, type **mmc**, click **OK**, click the **File** menu, click **Add/Remove Snap-in**, click **IP Security Monitor**, click the **Add** button, click **Services**, click the **Add** button, click **Finish**, and then click **OK**.
9. To restart the IPSec Policy Agent, double-click **Services**, scroll and right-click the **IPSec Policy Agent**, click **Restart**, and then wait for the policy to restart.
10. Expand IP Security Monitor.
11. If necessary, to reconnect to Server-02, right-click **Server-02**, and then click **Reconnect**.
12. To verify that the Kerberos policy is active, expand **Server-02**, and then click **Active Policy**.
13. If necessary, log on to Client-01 with a username of **client-01\student** and a password of **Secret1**.

14. To provide an IP configuration, click **Start**, and then click **Network**. If the Network Discovery and file sharing are turned off message appears, click the message, and then click **Turn on network discovery and file sharing**.

15. When the User Account Control dialog box opens, click the **Continue** button. Click **No, make the network that I am connected to a private network**.

16. Click **Network and Sharing Center**, click the **View status** link, and then click the **Properties** button.

17. When the User Account Control dialog box opens, click the **Continue** button.

18. Click **Internet Protocol Version 4 (TCP/IPv4)**, click the **Properties** button, click the **Use the following IP address** option button, type **192.168.0.111** in the IP address text box, press **Tab** twice, type **192.168.0.102** in the Default gateway text box, press **Tab** twice, type **192.168.0.101** in the Preferred DNS server text box, click **OK**, click **Close** twice, and then click the **View computers and devices** link.

19. Wait for the computers on the virtual network to be listed.

20. To restart the IPSec service, click **Start**, click **Control Panel**, click **Classic View**, double-click **Administrative Tools**, and then double-click **Services**.

21. When the User Account Control dialog box opens, click the **Continue** button.

22. Scroll and right-click **IPSec Policy Agent**, click **Restart**, wait for the policy to restart.

23. Close the open windows.

24. To access the Network, click **Start**, and then double-click **Network**.

25. If the Network discovery and file sharing are turned off message appears, click the message, and then click **Turn on network discovery and file sharing**. When the User Account Control dialog box opens, click the **Continue** button. Click **No, make the network that I am connected to a private network**.

26. To connect to the Shared Files Folder on Server-02, double-click **SERVER-02**, log on with a username of **Administrator** and a password of **Secret1**, and double-click the **Shared Files** folder.

27. Return to the Server-02 virtual machine.

28. To review the negotiation security associations, expand **Main Mode**, and then click on **Security Associations**.

29. To review the security associations, expand **Quick Mode**, and then click on **Security Associations**. Verify that Security Association exists. If not, contact your instructor.

30. Return to the Virtual Machine Manager.

31. Right-click **Client-01**, and then click **Save State**.

32. Repeat Step 23 for the remaining virtual machines with the exception of Server-01.

33. To shut down Server-01, return to the Virtual Machine Manager, right-click **Server-01**, and then click **Shut Down**.

34. Close the open windows.

35. Log off and shut down the host computer.

Chapter Summary

- To provide a public and private network that is not susceptible to unauthorized monitoring and access, administrators can manage networks using Active Directory Domain Services (AD DS). These services enable an administrator to centrally manage computers using Active Directory and Group Policy to work more efficiently by using one-to-many management. Access control lists (ACLs) provide information on user accounts and groups and computers that are allowed or denied access to Active Directory objects as well as those events that are audited for a user or group. Accounts are established to provide user rights and access control permissions; security identifiers are established to confirm the authentication and authorization of users and access to resources. These accounts can be disabled or suspended when a user's status with a company changes. The security groups function to ensure that shared resources are secure. In addition, user groups can be organized into organizational units.

- To create Group Policy settings, the Group Policy Object Editor tools were used to define specific configurations for groups of users. These settings were contained in a Group Policy Object and linked to Active Directory containers, such as domains or organizational units (OUs). Through Group Policy, the policies are defined that determine how applications and operating systems are configured. The policies also specify how you keep your users and systems secure in a virtual network. Group Policy applies to the user and client computers as well as member servers, domain controllers, and any other Window Server 2008 computers within the scope of management. The Group Policy Management Console (GPMC) helps you manage your group policies and the RSoP makes policy and troubleshooting easier.

- The Internet Protocol security for Windows Server 2008 simplifies the deployment and management of network security. IPSec is implemented by using the IP Security Wizard. IPSec consists of an authentication header (AH) and Encapsulating Security Payload (ESP) header and trailer. The AH and ESP transform the packet into a protected packet. Two modes are supported by IPSec, transport and tunnel. Transport mode is the default mode and is used between two communicating peer computers. Tunnel mode is used when the traffic in different networks must pass through an intermediate, untrusted network. Two computers negotiate security to build a security association (SA). SA management is centralized using the IKE method, which also generates and manages shared, secret keys that help protect the information. To ensure successful, protected communications in IPSec, different algorithms and protocols such as DES, Triple-DES, MD5-HMAC, SHA1-HMAC, Kerberos V, and Diffie-Hellman exchange are used in different negotiation phases. The IPSec behavior and services are created with the IP Security Policy Wizard.

Key Terms

access control entries (ACEs)—An entry in an access control list (ACL). An ACE contains a set of access rights and a security identifier (SID) that identifies a trustee for whom the rights are allowed, denied, or audited.

access control list (ACL)—A list of security protections that applies to an object. There are two types of access control lists: discretionary and system.

access control permissions—Permissions that define the type of access granted to a user or group for an object or object property. The common permissions are Read, Write, Full Control, or No Access.

access token—A token containing security information that is created by the system when a user logs on. Every process executed on behalf of the user has a copy of the token. The token identifies the user, the user's groups, and the user's privileges.

authentication header (AH)—Header that provides authentication, integrity, and replay protection for the whole packet (both the IP header and the data carried in the packet).

certificate—A security technique used in situations that include Internet access, remote access to corporate resources, external business partner communications, or computers that do not run the Kerberos V5 security protocol. This requires that at least one trusted certificate authority (CA) and associated certificate have been configured.

certificate authority (CA)—An entity that issues digital certificates for use by other parties.

cipher—An algorithm for performing encryption or decryption. It will consist of a series of well-defined steps that follow a procedure.

cryptographic hash function—An algorithm or formula that takes an input to generate a hash value and digital signatures.

cryptographic security services—A service that has the ability to scramble data so that only the sender and the designated receiver can read the contents.

data confidentiality—The protection of data from being read and interpreted while in transit.

Data Encryption Standard (DES)—A block cipher that encrypts data in 64-bit blocks. DES is a symmetric algorithm that uses the same algorithm and key for encryption and decryption.

data integrity—The protection of data from being modified while in transit.

data origin authentication—The protection of data from being spoofed by unauthenticated parties.

Diffie-Hellman (DH) group—A group that sets the length of the base prime numbers used during the key exchange process. The cryptographic strength of any key derived depends, in part, on this length.

Diffie-Hellman exchange—A cryptographic protocol that allows two parties that have no prior knowledge of each other to jointly establish a shared secret key over an insecure communications channel. This key can then be used to encrypt subsequent communications using a symmetric key cipher.

discretionary access control list (DACL)—An access control list that lists user accounts, groups, and computers that are allowed (or denied) access to the object.

distribution groups—Mail-enabled Active Directory groups created to expedite the mass sending of e-mail messages.

Encapsulating Security Payload (ESP) header and trailer—A security protocol that provides confidentiality, authentication, integrity, and replay protection for an IP packet payload.

Group Policy—A tool within AD DS that defines the settings and allowed actions for users and computers.

Group Policy Management Console (GPMC)—A new Group Policy management solution that unifies management of Group Policy for managing all Group Policy-related tasks. It lets administrators manage Group Policy for multiple domains and sites within one or more forests using a a simplified user interface (UI) with drag-and-drop support.

hash value—A value used in creating digital signatures. This value is generated by imposing a hashing algorithm onto an input. The value is then transformed, or signed, by a private key to produce a digital signature.

integrity check value (ICV)—A value found in the Authentication Data field in the AH header. It is used to verify both data integrity and data origin authentication.

Internet Engineering Task Force (IETF)—An open community of network designers, operators, vendors, and researchers concerned with the evolution of Internet architecture and the smooth operation of the Internet.

Internet Key Exchange (IKE)—The standard method of SA and key determination that centralizes SA management to reduce connection time. It also generates and manages shared, secret keys that help protect the information.

Internet Protocol security (IPSec)—A framework of open standards for ensuring private, secure communications over Internet Protocol (IP) networks. IPSec also includes protocols for cryptographic key establishment.

IP Security Monitor—A Microsoft tool that provides information about which IPSec policy is active and whether a secure channel between computers is established.

Kerberos V5—A network authentication protocol that authenticates the identity of the user that is requesting authentication as well as the server providing the requested authentication.

man-in-the-middle attack—An attack that occurs when a computer masquerades as the endpoint between two communicating peer computers.

Message Digest 5 Hashed Message Authentication Code (MD5-HMAC)—A hashing algorithm in which the HMAC protocol uses a 128-bit hash value. An MD5 hash is typically expressed as a 32-character hexadecimal number.

mutual authentication—A security feature in which a client process must prove its identity to a service, and the service must prove its identity to the client, before any application traffic is transmitted over the client/service connection.

organizational units (OUs)—Active Directory containers into which you can place users, groups, computers, and other organizational units. Organizational units can be created to mirror your organization's functional or business structure.

prefix—The network address that identifies the range of IP addresses in the subnet.

preshared key—An encryption option that requires both partities to share a key. The option is used when the client does not use the Kerberos V5 protocol or have a public key certificate.

replay protection—Protection from an attacker maliciously replaying messages.

Resultant Set of Policy (RSoP)—A query engine that polls existing policies and planned policies, and then reports the results of those queries. It polls existing policies based on site, domain, domain controller, and organizational unit.

Secure Hash Algorithm 1-HMAC (SHA1-HMAC)—Security protocol considered to be the successor to MD5. SHA-1 produces a hash value that is 160 bits long.

security association (SA)—A security definition that is the combination of a negotiated key, a security protocol, and the security parameter index (SPI).

security groups—Collections of users who share the same minimum permissions.

security identifier (SID)—A unique value used to identify a user or security group in Windows operating systems.

security parameter index (SPI)—A unique, identifying value in the security association that is used to distinguish among multiple security associations that exist at the receiving device.

Sequence Number field—A field in the AH header that provides replay protection for the packet.

site—The region of the network with high bandwidth connectivity that, by definition, is a collection of well-connected computers based on IP subnets. Active Directory uses sites to enable clients to discover network resources and optimize replication between domain controllers.

site link objects—Active Directory objects that are used to connect multiple sites of a network for replication.

system access control list (SACL)—An ACL that defines which events (such as file access) are audited for a user or group.

Triple-DES (3DES)—A variation of the DES block cipher algorithm that encrypts plain text with one key, encrypts the resulting cipher text with a second key, and finally, encrypts the result of the second encryption with a third key. Triple DES is a symmetric algorithm that uses the same algorithm and keys for encryption and decryption.

user account—Definition of the actions a user can perform in Windows.

user authentication—The confirmation of the identity of the user trying to log on to a domain. After authenticating, Active Directory will let the user access resources, such as data, applications, or printers.

user authorization—The ability of Active Dirctory to ensure that only those users who are authenticated and then authorized to a resource are actually the ones accessing the resource.

user rights—Privileges (such as Back Up Files and Directories) and logon rights (such as Access this Computer from the Network) assigned to groups (or users).

Review Questions

1. Cryptographic security services is used by _____.
    a. SID
    b. PUID
    c. IPSec
    d. CSS

2. Collections of users who share the same minimum permissions are known as _____.
    a. AD DS
    b. Security groups
    c. User accounts
    d. Computer accounts
3. The confirmation of the identity of any user to log on to a domain and let users access resources is known as _____.
    a. User verification
    b. User authorization
    c. User confirmation
    d. User authentication
4. The verification of a user's access privileges and their access control permissions to resources is known as _____.
    a. User authorization
    b. User verification
    c. User confirmation
    d. User authentication
5. The security identifier (SID) is a code used in the Windows Server 2008 security system to uniquely identify _____. (Choose all that apply).
    a. A group
    b. A specific user
    c. A computer
    d. An application
6. The access token _____. (Choose all that apply.)
    a. Has the user's SID attached to it
    b. Has the user's group attached to it when they are made a member of a group
    c. Contains the user rights
    d. Can display its contents with the whoami command
7. The list that contains the user accounts, groups, and computers that are allowed or denied access to a network resource is called the _____.
    a. Discretionary access control list
    b. System access control list
    c. Access control list
    d. Permissions list

8. The list that defines which events (such as file access) are audited for a user or group is called the _____.
   a. Discretionary access control list
   b. System access control list
   c. Access control list
   d. Permissions list
9. The access control entries (ACEs) _____. (Choose all that apply.)
   a. Are found in both the DACL and SACL
   b. Do not list the permissions granted or denied to users, groups, or computers listed in the SACL
   c. List the permissions granted or denied to users, groups, or computers listed in the DACL
   d. Contain the SID with a permission, such as Read access or Write access
10. A user _____. (Choose all that apply.)
    a. Can access their account even when their account is disabled
    b. Must be a member of at least one security group when the computer is part of a network domain
    c. Requires an Active Directory user account to log to a computer or a domain
    d. Is authenticated by the operating system and privileges are assigned through the user account
11. The primary function of security groups is to _____.
    a. Identify users
    b. Identify resources
    c. Organize secure groups
    d. Manage user and computer access to shared resources
12. Group Policy _____. (Choose all that apply.)
    a. Defines the policies that determine how applications and operating systems are configured
    b. Keeps users and systems secure
    c. Applies to users, client computers, member servers, domain controllers, and any other Windows Server 2008 computers within the scope of management
    d. Contains objects that are all virtual objects
13. Group Policy Objects _____. (Choose all that apply.)
    a. Can be used to filter objects based on security group membership
    b. Are linked to site, domain, and organization containers in Active Directory
    c. Contain the Group Policy settings you specify
    d. Can be managed and controlled with the Delegation of Control Wizard

14. The query engine that polls existing policies and planned policies and reports the results is known as _____.
    a. GPMC
    b. RSoP
    c. OU
    d. GPO

15. An IP packet is transformed into a protected packet by applying an _____. (Choose all that apply.)
    a. Authentication header
    b. Encapsulating Security Payload (ESP) header and trailer
    c. IP header
    d. Authorization header

16. The integrity check value is a(n) _____.
    a. Authentication Data field in the ESP
    b. Field in the IP header
    c. Authentication Data field in the AH
    d. Authorization Data field in the AH

17. The IPSec tunnel mode _____. (Choose all that apply.)
    a. Is useful for protecting traffic between different networks
    b. Helps protect an entire IP packet by treating it as an AH or ESP payload
    c. Allows you to combine ESP with AH to provide both confidentiality for the tunneled IP packet and data integrity and data origin authentication for the entire packet
    d. Adds new headers for tunneling so everything after that comes after the ESP header is authenticated

18. The mandatory parameters for Windows implementation of IPSec include the _____. (Choose all that apply.)
    a. Authorization method
    b. Encryption algorithm
    c. Hash algorithm
    d. Authentication method

19. The Diffie-Hellman exchange _____. (Choose all that apply.)
    a. Is a cryptographic protocol
    b. Allows two communication peer computers with no prior knowledge of each other to jointly establish a shared key over a secure communications channel
    c. Allows two communication peer computers with no prior knowledge to jointly establish a shared key over an unsecured communications channel
    d. Requires that the computers exchange the actual keys

20. A situation in which a computer masquerades as the midpoint between two communicating peer computers is known as _____.
    a. An attempt to network
    b. A peer-to-peer DH key exchange
    c. A user authentication process
    d. A man-in-the-middle attack

Case Projects

Case 10-1: Using Active Directory
Your lab supervisor, Rita, asked you to provide the Active Directory design for the IT Academy. To get you started, Rita gives you the organizational chart, shown in Figure 10-31, for the IT Academy. The organizational chart depicts the shared folders for each organizational group.

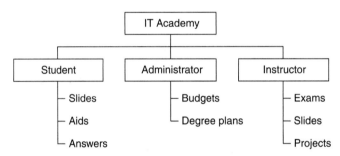

Figure 10-31 IT Academy organizational chart

You will need to identify the necessary organizational groups, global groups, and local domain groups. Indicate the necessary permissions for the shared resources. Provide a report of your findings to Rita.

Case 10-2: Using RSoP to Plan Group Policy
You need to study the group policies for the following Active Directory objects: Default Domain Policy, Professionals OU, and the Accountants OU. Describe how you will use the tools provided in Windows Server 2008 to plan for the following entities: Test_Account_Computer and Test_Account_User.

Case 10-3: Setting IPSec Policies
You need to protect packets sent from the headquarters of Golf, Inc., to the company's retail stores. These packets contain confidential information that must not be altered in transit. Describe the IPSec policies that are required.

Glossary

.vhd The file extension for the virtual hard disk file. This special file contains multiple files typically found on a computer system, including OS files, personal settings, Windows Registry, menus, programs, and data files.

.vsv A temporary file that contains information about a virtual machine's state when the virtual machine is placed in a saved state.

.vud The extension for the temporary file used as an undo disk. This file allows you to commit changes to the .vhd file, save the changes for later, or delete the changes and remove the .vud file.

access control entries (ACEs) An entry in an access control list (ACL). An ACE contains a set of access rights and a security identifier (SID) that identifies a trustee for whom the rights are allowed, denied, or audited.

access control list (ACL) A list of security protections that applies to an object. There are two types of access control lists: discretionary and system.

access control permissions Permissions that define the type of access granted to a user or group for an object or object property. The common permissions are Read, Write, Full Control, or No Access.

access token A token containing security information that is created by the system when a user logs on. Every process executed on behalf of the user has a copy of the token. The token identifies the user, the user's groups, and the user's privileges.

Active Directory Domain Services (AD DS) The native directory service included with Microsoft Windows Server 2008.

Active Directory-integrated primary zone The primary DNS zone file stored in Active Directory and replicated when the Active Directory Domain Services exchanges information.

Address Resolution Protocol (ARP) The protocol used by the Internet Protocol (IP) to map IP network addresses to the hardware addresses. The term *address resolution* refers to the process of finding an address of a computer in a network.

alias list A file that is used by Network Monitor to store IP addresses and their associated computer names.

authentication header (AH) Header that provides authentication, integrity, and replay protection for the whole packet (both the IP header and the data carried in the packet).

basic disk A physical disk that can be accessed by MS-DOS and all Windows-based operating systems. Basic disks can contain up to four primary partitions, or three primary partitions and an extended partition with multiple logical drives.

Bellman-Ford algorithm Also known as the Bellman-Ford distance-vector routing algorithm, a procedure that determines the shortest route between two nodes on a network. This algorithm is used in the Routing Information Protocol (RIP).

best path A method used to determine the optimal network path to a specific remote destination when two or more diverse network paths are available.

capture filter Similar in function to a database query, a filter that is used to specify types of network information you want to monitor. Information obtained from the filter can be saved to a file and then loaded for use later.

capturing The transfer of received data into a file for archiving or later analysis.

certificate A security technique used in situations that include Internet access, remote access to corporate resources, external business partner communications, or computers that do not run the Kerberos V5 security protocol. This requires that at least one trusted certificate authority (CA) and associated certificate have been configured.

certificate authority (CA) An entity that issues digital certificates for use by other parties.

child A new virtual hard disk that stores the changes when using differencing disks.

cipher An algorithm for performing encryption or decryption. It consists of a series of well-defined steps that follow a procedure.

cloning The process of replicating or copying the entire contents of a partition on a hard disk drive (or the virtual hard disk .vhd file) by creating an image of the hard disk drive.

clustering Linking two or more computer systems (generally, servers) that work together to handle variable workloads or to provide continued operation in case one fails.

consolidation Combining multiple OSs on a single computer system, resulting in higher rates of utilization.

cryptographic hash function An algorithm or formula that takes an input to generate a hash value and digital signatures.

cryptographic security services A service that has the ability to scramble data so that only the sender and the designated receiver can read the contents.

data confidentiality The protection of data from being read and interpreted while in transit.

Data Encryption Standard (DES) A block cipher that encrypts data in 64-bit blocks. DES is a symmetric algorithm that uses the same algorithm and key for encryption and decryption.

data integrity The protection of data from being modified while in transit.

data origin authentication The protection of data from being spoofed by unauthenticated parties.

DHCP acknowledge The message that is generated when the DHCP server officially assigns the address to the client.

DHCP discover The message that is generated when the DHCP client asks for an IP address.

DHCP offer The message that is generated when the DHCP server offers an address.

DHCP Relay Agent A router or a host computer that is configured to listen for DHCP/BOOTP broadcast messages and direct them to a specific DHCP server(s). Using relay agents eliminates the necessity of having a DHCP server on each physical network segment.

DHCP request The message that is generated when the DHCP client accepts the offer and requests the address during the DHCP process.

Diffie-Hellman exchange A cryptographic protocol that allows two parties that have no prior knowledge of each other to jointly establish a shared secret key over an insecure communications channel. This key can then be used to encrypt subsequent communications using a symmetric key cipher.

Diffie-Hellman (DH) group A group that sets the length of the base prime numbers used during the key exchange process. The cryptographic strength of any key derived depends, in part, on this length.

directory services A service on a network that acts as a repository of information about users, devices, and other services on a network.

discretionary access control list (DACL) An access control list that lists user accounts, groups, and computers that are allowed (or denied) access to the object.

display filter Similar in function to a database query, a filter that allows you to single out specific types of network information, such as source or destination address from a captured network frame.

distance-vector routing protocol A protocol that requires a router to inform its neighbors of network changes periodically and, in some cases, when a change is detected in the topology of a network. A distance-vector routing protocol uses the Bellman-Ford algorithm to calculate paths. *See* Bellman-Ford algorithm.

distribution groups Mail-enabled Active Directory groups created to expedite the mass sending of e-mail messages.

domain A collection of computers that shares access to network resources with centralized administration and security policies.

domain controller A server that responds to security requests within a domain.

Domain Name System (DNS) A system for converting host names and domain names into IP addresses on the Internet or on local networks that use the TCP/IP protocol.

dynamic disk A disk initialized for dynamic storage.

Dynamic Host Configuration Protocol (DHCP) Protocol for assigning dynamic IP addresses to computers on a network.

dynamic routing table Table containing routing information that adjusts automatically to the current conditions of the network. Dynamic routing typically uses one of several dynamic-routing protocols such as RIP.

emulated hardware system Duplicates the functions of one system with a different system.

Encapsulating Security Payload (ESP) header and trailer A security protocol that provides confidentiality, authentication, integrity, and replay protection for an IP packet payload.

fault tolerance The ability of a computer or an operating system to respond to a catastrophic event or fault, such as a power outage or hardware failure, in a way that ensures that no data is lost and any work in progress is not corrupted.

file server A file storage device on a local area network that is accessible to all users on the network.

forest A logical collection of domains.

frame A data packet of fixed or variable length.

full zone transfers The transmission by the master server for a zone of the entire zone database to the secondary server for that zone.

Group Policy A tool within AD DS that defines the settings and allowed actions for users and computers.

Group Policy Management Console (GPMC) A new Group Policy management solution that unifies management of Group Policy for managing all Group Policy-related tasks. It lets administrators manage Group Policy for multiple domains and sites within one or more forests using a simplified user interface (UI) with drag-and-drop support.

guest operating system An operating system running within a virtual machine.

hash value A value used in creating digital signatures. This value is generated by imposing a hashing algorithm onto an input. The value is then transformed, or signed, by a private key to produce a digital signature.

heartbeat A regular signal sent to Virtual Server that allows the virtual machine to report that it is still functioning.

host operating system The OS that controls the physical computer system on which the virtual environment runs.

incremental zone transfers The transmission of parts of a DNS zone from a primary DNS server to a secondary. Only changes to the zone need be transferred.

infrastructure server A computer or program that responds to requests from a client and provides services, specifically network services, such as DNS and DHCP.

integrity check value (ICV) A value found in the Authentication Data field in the AH header. It is used to verify both data integrity and data origin authentication.

Internet Connection Sharing (ICS) Allows the sharing of a single computer's Internet connection with other computers on the same local area network. With VMs, ICS enables one or more VMs to connect to the Internet using the connection provided by the host computer.

Internet Control Message Protocol (ICMP) A message control and error-reporting protocol used to announce network errors, time-outs, and congestion. It also allows for the generation of error messages, test packets, and informational messages related to IP. ICMP is the basis of the ping command.

Internet Engineering Task Force (IETF) An open community of network designers, operators, vendors, and researchers concerned with the evolution of Internet architecture and the smooth operation of the Internet.

Internet Key Exchange (IKE) The standard method of SA and key determination that centralizes SA management to reduce connection time. It also generates and manages shared, secret keys that help protect the information.

Internet Protocol security (IPSec) A framework of open standards for ensuring private, secure communications over Internet Protocol (IP) networks. IPSec also includes protocols for cryptographic key establishment.

IP Security Monitor A Microsoft tool that provides information about which IPSec policy is active and whether a secure channel between computers is established.

ISO image (.iso) A copy or duplicate of an ISO 9600 file system.

ISO 9660 file system An international format standard for CD-ROM and DVD-ROM media adopted by the International Organization for Standardization (ISO).

Kerberos authentication protocol A computer network identity authentication protocol; the default protocol for computers in Active Directory domains.

Kerberos V5 A network authentication protocol that authenticates the identity of the user that is requesting authentication as well as the server providing the requested authentication.

local loopback The special network address, 127.0.0.1, defined by the Internet Protocol as a local loopback address. Hosts use local loopback addresses to send messages to themselves.

man-in-the-middle attack An attack that occurs when a computer masquerades as the endpoint between two communicating peer computers.

Message Digest 5 Hashed Message Authentication Code (MD5-HMAC) A hashing algorithm in which the HMAC protocol uses a 128-bit hash value. An MD5 hash is typically expressed as a 32-character hexadecimal number.

Microsoft Loopback Adapter Built-in network interface driver shipped with Microsoft Windows Vista that allows the creation of a local-only network interface device and is useful when creating multiple virtual networks.

Microsoft Network Monitor Software that can intercept and log traffic passing over a digital network or part of a network. Also known as a protocol analyzer.

mirrored volume A hard drive or other form of storage media that stores an exact copy of the data from another volume. It is used for fault tolerance, which means a mirrored volume serves as a backup device in case the primary device fails.

multicasting The delivery of information to a group of destinations simultaneously using the most efficient strategy to deliver the messages over each link of the network only once.

mutual authentication A security feature in which a client process must prove its identity to a service, and the service must prove its identity to the client, before any application traffic is transmitted over the client/service connection.

Network Address Translation (NAT) Conversion of an Internet Protocol address (IP address) used within one network to a different IP address known within another network.

network convergence The state that occurs when the routing tables for all routers in the network are in agreement.

Network Policy and Access Services (NPAS) A service within Windows Server 2008 that delivers a variety of methods to provide local and remote network connectivity, to connect network segments, and to allow network administrators to centrally manage network access and client health policies.

organizational units (OUs) Active Directory containers into which you can place users, groups, computers, and other organizational units. Organizational units can be created to mirror your organization's functional or business structure.

parent An existing virtual hard disk. When using differencing, the parent is used to start the VM with changes made to the differencing disk.

parent-child relationship A differencing virtual hard disk is a virtual hard disk associated with another virtual hard disk in a parent-child relationship. The differencing disk is the child and the associated virtual disk is the parent.

parity A calculated value that can be used to reconstruct data after a failure.

PowerShell A command-line shell designed and developed by Microsoft for system administrators that includes an interactive prompt and a scripting environment.

Preboot Execution Environment (PXE) The environment that allows a workstation to boot from a server on a network prior to booting the operating system on the local hard drive.

prefix The network address that identifies the range of IP addresses in the subnet.

preshared key An encryption option that requires both partities to share a key. The option is used when the the client does not use the Kerberos V5 protocol or have a public key certificate.

protocol analyzer Software that captures data packets and decodes and analyzes their content. *See* Microsoft Network Monitor.

RAID (Redundant Array of Independent Disks) A disk subsystem that is used to increase performance or provide fault tolerance or both.

RAID-1 A storage scheme using disk mirroring, which provides 100 percent duplication of data. Offers highest reliability, but doubles storage cost. RAID-1 is widely used in business applications.

RAID-5 A storage scheme in which data is striped across three or more drives for performance, and parity bits are used for fault tolerance. RAID-5 is widely used in servers.

recursion A process in which a DNS server answers queries for names outside of its authoritative zones by sending a query on to the "closest" DNS server to the queried name that it knows. The process continues (if necessary) until the DNS server gets a response back for the original query.

Remote Desktop A Windows feature that allows a machine to be run remotely from another Windows machine.

replay protection Protection from an attacker maliciously replaying messages.

resolver A set of software routines used for making, sending, and interpreting query and reply messages with Internet domain name servers.

Resultant Set of Policy (RSoP) A query engine that polls existing policies and planned policies, and then reports the results of those queries. It polls existing policies based on site, domain, domain controller, and organizational unit.

router An intermediary device on a communications network that expedites message delivery. On a single network linking many computers through a mesh of possible connections, a router receives transmitted messages and forwards them to their correct destinations over the most efficent available route.

routing The process of forwarding packets between networks from source to destination.

Routing and Remote Access Service (RRAS) A service within Network Policy and Access Services used to manage remote access connections and devices.

Routing Information Protocol (RIP) A widely used protocol for managing router information within a small, self-contained network such as a corporate network. Routers communicate network changes periodically to their neighbor routers, which helps routers dynamically adapt to changes of network connections.

routing metric A standard of measurement, such as hop count, that is used by routing algorithms to determine the best path to a destination.

routing protocol A convention or standard that specifies how routers communicate with each other to disseminate information that allows them to select routes between two nodes on a network. A routing protocol shares the information each router has about its immediate neighbors so other networks in a network topology have the information.

routing table In data communications, a table of information that provides network devices with the directions needed to forward packets of data to locations on other networks. Routing tables are updated frequently as new or more current information becomes available.

scope An administrative grouping of computers running the DHCP Client service. You create a scope for each subnet on the network to define parameters for that subnet.

secondary zones Zones that are replicated from another server, the master server.

Secure Hash Algorithm 1-HMAC (SHA1-HMAC) Security protocol considered to be the successor to MD5. SHA-1 produces a hash value that is 160 bits long.

security association (SA) A security definition that is the combination of a negotiated key, a security protocol, and the security parameter index (SPI).

security groups Collections of users who share the same minimum permissions.

security identifiers (SIDs) A unique alphanumeric string that identifies user accounts or security groups in Windows operating systems. These are not changed when the computer name is changed or the computer is cloned unless the operating system is prepared prior to cloning.

security parameter index (SPI) A unique, identifying value in the security association that is used to distinguish among multiple security associations that exist at the receiving device.

Sequence Number field A field in the AH header that provides replay protection for the packet.

server roles A description of one or more functions of the server.

site The region of the network with high bandwidth connectivity that, by definition, is a collection of well-connected computers based on IP subnets. Active Directory uses sites to enable clients to discover network resources and optimize replication between domain controllers.

site link objects Active Directory objects that are used to connect multiple sites of a network for replication.

SRV A DNS resource record intended to provide information on available services.

stateful firewall A firewall that keeps track of the state of network connections (such as TCP streams) traveling across it. Only packets that match a known connection state are allowed by the firewall; others are rejected.

static IP addressing An addressing scheme in which the computer uses the IP address assigned by an administrator. Each virtual machine is assigned a unique, unchanging IP address.

static routing Routing based on a fixed forwarding path. Unlike dynamic routing, static routing does not adjust to changing network conditions.

storage area network (SAN) A high-speed subnetwork of shared storage devices.

striped The spreading out of the blocks of each file across multiple disk drives.

Sysprep A software tool used to prepare a Windows operating system for duplication. It removes all system-specific information from an installed Windows image, including the computer security identifier (SID).

system access control list (SACL) An ACL that defines which events (such as file access) are audited for a user or group.

Triple-DES (3DES) A variation of the DES block cipher algorithm that encrypts plain text with one key, encrypts the resulting cipher text with a second key, and finally, encrypts the result of the second encryption with a third key. Triple DES is a symmetric algorithm that uses the same algorithm and keys for encryption and decryption.

unsolicited request Incoming traffic that does not correspond to either traffic sent in response to a request by the computer or unsolicited traffic that has been specified as allowed.

user account Definition of the actions a user can perform in Windows.

user authentication The confirmation of the identity of the user trying to log on to a domain. After authenticating, Active Directory will let the user access resources, such as data, applications, or printers.

user authorization The ability of Active Dirctory to ensure that only those users who are authenticated and then authorized to a resource are actually the ones accessing the resource.

user rights Privileges (such as Back Up Files and Directories) and logon rights (such as Access this Computer from the Network) assigned to groups (or users).

video RAM (VRAM) A special type of RAM (DRAM) used in high-speed video applications. Video RAM uses separate pins for the processor and the video circuitry, providing the video circuitry with a back door to the video RAM.

virtualization The use of software to allow physical hardware to run multiple OS images in VMs at the same time.

virtual machine (VM) The software that simulates enough hardware to allow multiple OSs to be set up on a host OS.

Virtual Machine Additions Software that increases performance and adds important features to the guest machine; one of the most important features in Virtual PC 2007 that is not installed by default.

virtual machine configuration (.vmc) file The file that stores the VM configuration information.

Virtual Machine Network Services Driver Driver installed during the installation of Microsoft Virtual PC 2007 that routes Ethernet frames between VMs; frames can optionally be routed to the host computer's network.

Virtual Machine Remote Control (VMRC) client A Virtual Server client application that allows a running virtual machine to be managed remotely.

Virtual Machine Remote Control (VMRC) server A Virtual Server server application that manages virtual machines by using a Virtual Machine Remote Control protocol to interact with the machines using the keyboard and mouse.

virtual networking The ability to connect a VM to another VM to share files, surf the Web, and more.

Virtual Server Administration Web site A Web site created with the installation of Virtual Server that administrators use to run virtual machines, virtual networks, and virtual hard disks.

Virtual Server service A service that creates the virtual machines and provides all virtual machine functionality.

VMRC ActiveX plug-in A plug-in that supports the use of the VMRC client from within Internet Explorer.

VMRCplus A client application for creation and configuration management of Virtual Server and remote control of virtual machines. VMRCplus is an alternative to the Virtual Server Administration Web site.

VMRC protocol A remote presentation and control protocol that administrators use to view and control virtual machines across networked environments.

volume A fixed amount of storage on a disk. The term volume is often used as a synonym for the storage medium itself, but it is possible for a single disk to contain more than one volume or for a volume to span more than one disk.

Windows NT LAN Manager (NTLM) protocol A protocol used to authenticate logons to stand-alone computers. The default for network authentication in the Windows NT 4.0 operating system, it is retained for compatibility with down-level clients and servers.

Windows Preinstallation Environment (WinPE) A basic version of the operating system that is loaded into RAM when Windows Vista is first installed. It provides a basic GUI for the first phase of setup and is built from Windows Vista components.

Windows service A program that starts when the Microsoft Windows operating system is booted and runs in the background as long as Windows is running.

Index

A

access control entries (ACEs), **400, 440**
access control lists (ACLs)
   described, **399, 440**
   discretionary (DACLs), **400, 440**
   system (SACLs), **400, 442**
access control permissions, **399, 440**
access tokens
   displaying, 411–412
   use described, **399**–400, 403, **440**
accessing files on host using shared folders, 92–93
ACEs (access control entries), **400, 440**
ACLs. *See* access control lists
Active Directory
   sites, **406**–409
   user and computer accounts, 400–402
Active Directory Domain Services (AD DS)
   described, **150**
   in Dovercorp.local virtual network, 111–112
   implementing in Classroom.local virtual network, 328–333
   implementing in Dovercorp.local virtual network, 132–150
   using in network administration, 398–414
Active Directory Domain Services Installation Wizard, 134–143
Active Directory-integrated primary zone, **340, 344**
Active Directory security groups, 403–406
Active Directory Sites and Services console, 408
Add Roles Wizard, 132–134
adding
   users to domains, 401–402
   virtual machines, 40–42, 65–66, 177, 271–272
Address Resolution Protocol. *See* ARP
administration, network. *See* network administration

AHs (authentication headers), **423, 441**
alias lists
   creating, 351
   described, **350, 389**
applications
   See also specific application
   development and testing with virtualization, 6
   installing in virtual machines, 165–166
   Virtual PC and Virtual Server support, 207
architecture, Virtual Server, 202–203
Armstrong, Ben, 26
ARP (Address Resolution Protocol)
   described, **389**
   finding host's address with, 353
audio. *See* sound
authentication
   data origin, **423, 440**
   Kerberos authentication protocol, **214, 244**
   man-in-the-middle attack vulnerability, 430
   methods, 434
   mutual, **429, 441**
   user, **398, 442**
authentication headers (AHs), **423, 440**
Automatically detect floppy disk option, VPC settings, 56–57

B

backups, restoring Directory Services databases from, 141
basic disks, **194**
   converting to dynamic disks, 180–182
   and dynamic disks, **179**
basic hard drives, converting to dynamic, 189
Bellman-Ford algorithm, **374, 389**
best path, routing and, **369, 389**
Block Policy inheritance option, Group Policy, 417
blogs, exploring Virtual PC 2007, 26

C

capture filters, **352, 389**
capturing
   data between two computers, 352–354
   described, **390**
CD/DVD drive controllers, VPC settings, 56
certificate authorities (CAs), **429, 440**
certificates, and authentication, **429, 440**
child clients, configuring, 318–320
child servers, configuring, 309–310, 314–316
child virtual hard disks, **12, 27**
child virtual machines
   creating, 287–288
   creating and running, 176–178
ciphers described, **429, 440**
Classroom.local virtual network
   analyzing traffic, 350–358
   configuring DNS services for, 333–343
   implementing, 308–328
   implementing AD DS, 328–333
   implementing routing, 369–388
   installing DHCP, 358–369
   network diagram (fig.), 308
   overview and setup of, 302–308
Clipboard
   copying and pasting on virtual machines, 95–96
   integration with VMA, 17
cloning
   described, **102**
   virtual machines, **98**–102
close options for VMs (VPC settings), 63–64
closing virtual machines, 97
clustering
   computer systems, **244**
   Virtual Server support for, **209**
COM ports, VPC settings, 57–58
compacting hard disks, 163–165
compressing virtual hard drives, 160
computer accounts and Active Directory, 402

453

computers
  See also virtual machines
  capturing data between two, 352–354
  clustering, **244**
  joining domains, 147–150, 330–333
  performance options, studying effects of, 167–168
confidentiality, data, **423, 440**
configuring
  Administration Web site properties, 216–217
  child clients, 318–320
  child servers, 314–316
  DHCP scopes, 366–367
  Internet Connection Sharing (ICS), 222–223
  Microsoft Loopback Adapter, 221–222
  network adapters for VMs, 221
  RIP, 385–386
  RIP routing, 373–374
  servers for Remote Desktop access, 242–243
  static routing protocol, 381–383
  virtual hard disks, 11–13
  virtual machines, 34–39
  virtual networks, 223–227
  Virtual PC 2007 global settings, 42–51
  Virtual Server 2005, 212–220
  VMRCplus, 253–256
  Windows Firewall, 127–130, 323–324
connecting to network, Vista setup, 85–86
connection sharing. See Internet Connection Sharing
Console Manager, 264, 281–287
consolidation of systems through virtualization, **5, 27**
Control menu, Console Manager, 281
converting
  basic to dynamic disks, 180–182, 233
  basic to dynamic hard drives, 189
copying
  with Clipboard on virtual machines, 95–96
  files on virtual machines, 94–95
CPU (central processing unit)
  allocation, configuring, 217–218

allocation, and Virtual Server, 208
virtual machine optimization, 158–159
Create New Virtual Machine window, 257–259
creating
  child virtual machines, 176–178
  computer accounts, 402
  differencing disks, 170–171
  differencing virtual hard disks, 289
  domain controllers, 144–146, 329–330
  domain local groups, 404
  dynamically expanding virtual disks, 288–289
  forests and domains, 137–139
  IPSec policies, 432–437
  organizational security policies, 420–421
  organizational units (OUs), 406, 413
  parent virtual machines, 175–176
  scopes, 361–364
  security groups, 412–413
  user accounts, 410–411
  virtual disks, 230–233, 283–287
  virtual hard disks, 38–39, 259–260
  virtual machines, 34–40, 65–66, 234–236, 239
  virtual machines for Dovercorp.local, 114–115
  virtual machines using VMRCplus, 257–266, 266–280
  virtual networks, 223–227
cryptographic hash functions, **425, 440**
cryptographic security services, and IPSec, **398, 440**
Ctrl+Alt+Delete on virtual machines, 47
customizing DHCP, 361

D

data confidentiality, **423, 440**
Data Encryption Standard (DES), **429, 440**
data integrity, **423, 440**
data origin authentication, **423, 440**
defragmenting hard drives, 160, 161–162, 165
delegation, 140
deleting VMs using VMRCplus, 272

DES (Data Encryption Standard), **429, 440**
desktop clients
  in Classroom.local virtual network, 304
  creating VMs for, 306–308
  in Dovercorp.local virtual network, 112
devices
  emulated in Virtual Server, 205
  emulated, in Virtual PC, 10
DHCP (Dynamic Host Configuration Protocol)
  described, **27, 389**
  installing, 358–369
DHCP acknowledge message, **359, 390**
DHCP discover message, **359, 390**
DHCP offer message, **359, 390**
DHCP Relay Agent, **359, 386–387, 390**
DHCP request message, **359, 390**
DHCP scopes, configuring, 366–367
DHCP servers
  options, configuring, 226
  and shared networking, 15
  on virtual networks, 223
DHCP service, adding and authorizing, 365–366
differencing disks
  hard disks, 12–13
  and parent-child relationships, **295**
  using in Virtual Server, 231
differencing virtual hard disks
  described, 170–171
  using in Virtual Server, 228–229
Diffie-Hellman (DH) groups, **429, 440**
Diffie-Hellman exchange, **430, 440**
directory services
  described, **150**
  use in virtual network, **110**
discretionary access control lists (DACLs), **400, 404, 440**
Disk Fragmenter, 161–162
Disk Management tool, 180–182, 189–192
disks
  See also hard disks, virtual hard disks
  basic, dynamic, **179, 194**

implementing advanced disk
    options, 168–179
undo. *See* undo disks
display for virtual machines (VPC
    settings), 62–63
display filters, **352**, **353**, **390**
Display menu, Console Manager,
    281
displaying
    access tokens, 411–412
    messages, VPC setup options, 46–47
distance-vector routing protocol,
    374, **390**
distribution groups, **404**, **440**
DNS. *See* Domain Name System
DNS cache, 334–335
DNS lookup zones, 336–338
DNS record types, 338
DNS servers, creating and
    configuring, 340–343
DNS services
    configuring for Classroom.local
        virtual network, 333–343
    overview of DNS queries, 333–334
domain controllers, **150**
    in Classroom.local virtual network,
        303–304
    creating, 144–146, 329–330
    in Dovercorp.local virtual network,
        111–112
domain local groups, 404–405
Domain Name System (DNS),
    150
    See also DNS services
    and Active Directory Domain
        Services, **112**
    and forest creation, 137
domain security policies, 420
domains
    described, **111**, **150**
    and forests, creating, 137–139
    joining computers to, 147–150,
        330–333
    and sites and OUs, 410
Dover Leasing company, 110
Dovercorp.local virtual network
    diagram of devices on, 115
    implementing, 115–131
    implementing AD DS, 132–150
    memory requirements for, 160
    overview and setup of, 110–115

drag and drop
    copying files on virtual machines,
        94–95
    VMA feature, 17
drivers
    custom video, 97
    Intel 440BX chipset, 194
    using virtual machine's, 205
    video, 17
    Virtual Machine Network Services
        Driver, 13–14, 223
DVDs, using to install operating
    systems, 261
dynamic disks
    converting basic disks to, 180–182
    and fault tolerance, **179**
dynamic hard drives, converting
    basic to, 189
Dynamic Host Configuration
    Protocol. *See* DHCP
dynamic routing tables, **373**, **390**
dynamically expanding virtual
    disks, 227–228, 230, 288–289

E

Echo Request (File and Printer
    Sharing), 128
echo response, ICMP replies, 353
emulated hardware systems, **2–3**, **27**
    emulated devices in Virtual Server,
        205
    emulated devices in VPC, 10
Enable undo disks option, Virtual
    Server, 229–230
enabling
    undo disks, 13
    VPC security, 49–50
Encapsulating Security Payload
    (ESP) header and trailer,
    423–424, **441**
error messages, troubleshooting
    Virtual PC installations,
    192–194
ESP (Encapsulating Security
    Payload), **423–424**, **441**
Ethernet frames and network
    adapter, 14
event logging
    viewing with Event Viewer,
        217–218

Virtual Server support, 208
Event Viewer, accessing event logs,
    217–218

F

fault tolerance
    described, **194**
    dynamic disks and, **179–192**
    implementing storage options,
        182–188
File and Printer Sharing rule,
    128
file paging, and performance
    optimization, 161
file servers, **150**
    in Classroom.local virtual network,
        304
    in Dovercorp.local virtual network,
        112
files
    accessing on host using shared
        folders, 92–93
    dragging and dropping on virtual
        machines, 94–95
filters
    capture filters, **352**, **389**
    display, **352**, **353**, **390**
    IPSec, 432–434
firewalls
    See also Windows Firewall
    stateful, described, **127**, **151**
floppy disks
    Automatically detect floppy disk
        option, 56–57
    virtual, 230, 232
folders, shared. *See* shared folders
forests
    described, **150**
    and domains, creating, **137–139**
forward lookup zones, 336–338
forwarding Name Resolution
    Requests, 335–336
frames
    described, **390**
    and traffic analysis, 350
full-screen mode, starting VM
    in, 63
Full-Screen Mode option,
    coordinating with OS, 44–45
full zone transfers, 340, 344

G

global security groups, Active Directory, 403–404
global settings, configuring Virtual PC 2007, 42–51
GPMC (Group Policy Management Console), 417–418, 441
Group Policy
    described, **398**, 441
    features, applying, 414–423
Group Policy Management Console (GPMC), **417–418**, 441
Group Policy Management Editor, 419–421
Group Policy Objects (GPOs), 414–417
guest operating systems in virtual systems, **2**, 27

H

hard disks
    defragmenting, 161–162
    performance optimization, 160
    virtual. *See* virtual hard disks
    virtual machine settings, 54–55
hard drives
    converting basic disks to dynamic disks, 180–182
    implementing additional, 188
hardware
    configuration for Virtual Server host, 216
    operating systems default selections (table), 37
    virtual machines components, 9–10
    virtualization, and utilization of, 4–5
    virtualization benefits, 6, 44
hash values, **425**, 441
heartbeats, **244**
    virtual machines', and Virtual Server, **206**
    and VMA, 205
Help
    Console Manager menu, 282
    Virtual PC 2007, 24–25
    Virtual Server, 211–212
help desks, virtualization benefits, 7
host operating systems in virtual systems, **2**, 27

I

ICMP (Internet Control Message Protocol)
    described, **151**, **390**
    and ping command, **353**
    rules, setting for VMs, 325–326
    unsolicited requests, and Windows Firewall, **127**
ICS (Internet Connection Sharing), 27
    installing, **19–22**
    use in Dovercorp.local virtual network, 116
ICV (integrity check value), **425**, 441
IDE controllers, 11
IKE (Internet Key Exchange), **428**, 441
image files, capturing, 162–163
implementing
    Active Directory Domain Services, 132–150, 328–333
    additional hard drives, 188
    Classroom.local virtual network, 308–328
    Dovercorp.local virtual network, 115–131
    IPSec (Internet Protocol security), 423–435
    LAN routing, 380–381
    RAID-1 volume, 189–190
    RAID-5 volume, 190–191
    routing in virtual network, 369–374
    virtual machines with Virtual Server, 234–243
    virtual networks, 220–223, 289–293
incremental zone transfers, **340**, 344
infrastructure servers
    in Classroom.local virtual network, 303, **304**
    described, **344**
inheritance in Active Directory, 416–417
initializing hard disks, 181
installing
    Active Directory Domain Services, overview, 132–144
    applications in virtual machines, 165–166
    Domain Name System (DNS) on Dovercorp.local, 139–140
    Internet Connection Sharing (ICS), **19–22**, 209–210
    Microsoft Vista Business into VMs, 86–88, 119–121
    Network Monitor, 354–355
    operating systems in Virtual PC 2007, 72–74
    operating systems, overview, 75–86
    Virtual Machine Additions, 17, 90–92, 121–122, 241–242, 320–321
    Virtual PC 2007, 22–24
    Virtual Server 2005, 209–212, 210–211
    VMRCplus, 253–256
    Windows Server 2008 into VMs, 88–90, 312–313
    Windows Vista Business, 75–77, 316–318
integrity check value (ICV), **425**, 441
Integrity Engineering Task Force (IETF), **423**, **428**, 441
Intel 440BX chipset drivers, troubleshooting, 194
Internet, accessing with virtual machines, 19
Internet Connection Sharing (ICS), 27
    configuring, 222–223
    installing, **19–22**, 209–210
Internet Control Message Protocol. *See* ICMP
Internet Engineering Task Force (IETF), **423**, 441
Internet Explorer (IE)
    launching, 23
    Phishing Filter, 165
Internet Key Exchange (IKE), **428**, 441
Internet Protocol security. *See* IPSec
IP addresses
    and shared networking, 59–60
    of virtual machines, 15
IP addressing
    for Classroom.local virtual network, 309
    creating scopes, 361–364
    static, **116**, **151**
    verifying configuration in Classroom.local virtual network, 321–323

Index **457**

verifying configuration in Dovercorp.local, 122–126
IP connectivity, verifying in virtual network, 130–131, 326–328
IP Security Monitor, using, 434–435, **441**
IPSec (Internet Protocol security), **398**, **441**
  creating and testing policies, 432–438
  overview, negotiation phases, **423–430**
  process described, 431–432
ISO 660 file system
  described, **102**
  and operating system installation, 75
ISO image (.iso), **75**, **102**

J

joining domains, 147–150, 330–333, 401, 402

K

Kerberos authentication protocol, **214**, **244**
Kerberos V5, **429**, **441**
keyboard
  Ctrl+Alt+Delete on VMs, 47
  control on virtual machines, 93
Keyboard option, VPC setup, 47–48

L

LAN routing, implementing, 380–381
language, VPC setup options, 50–51
launching Internet Explorer, 23
license validation for Vista, 77, 80
linked disk option, Virtual Disk Wizard, 171–172
linked virtual hard disks, 231
Linux
  Virtual Server support, 206
  and VPC configuration, 11
Local Area Connection Properties dialog box, 14
local loopbacks, **371**, **390**
local networking and virtual machines, 15
locking down virtual machines (VMs), 49
Longhorn Server, 110
Loopback Adapter, **16**, 21, 22, **27**, 116, 124
LPT1 printer ports, VPC settings, 58

M

MAC addresses, removing from .vmc files, 193
man-in-the-middle attacks, **430**, **441**
managing
  Active Directory sites, 413–414
  DHCP, 360–361
  virtual disks with Virtual Disks Manager, 283–287
  virtual hard disks on VMs, 54–55
Master Status pane, Virtual Server, 236–237
MD5-HMAC (Message Digest 5 Hashed Message Authentication Code), **429**, **441**
Media menu, Console Manager, 281
memory
  See also RAM, storage
  needed for machines in Dovercorp.local virtual network, 112–113
  required for virtual machines, 236
  virtual machine optimization, 159–160
  virtual machine settings, 52–53
Message Digest 5 Hashed Message Authentication Code (MD5-HMAC), **429**, **441**
message display, VPC setup options, 46–47
Microsoft
  See also specific products
  virtualization products and options, 7–18
Microsoft Download Center, 23
Microsoft Loopback Adapter, 21, 22, 116, 124
  configuring, 221–222
  described, **16**, **27**
Microsoft Network Monitor. *See* Network Monitor
Microsoft Server 2008, installing into VMs, 117–119, 240–241
Microsoft Virtual Server. *See* Virtual Server 2005
Microsoft Vista Business, installing into VMs, 86–88, 119–121
mirrored volumes, **183**, **195**
modems and COM port (VPC settings), 57–58
mouse
  control with VMA, 17, 61, 205
  drag and drop restrictions, 94–95
  integration with VMs, 93–94
  Virtual PC setup options, 48–49
multicasting, **371**, **390**
multithreading, Virtual Server support, 208
muting sound on virtual machines, VPC settings, 45–46
mutual authentication, **429**, **441**

N

naming
  domains, 112
  guest computers, 83
  virtual hard disks, 260
  virtual machines, 52, 235
NAT (Network Address Translation)
  described, **27**
  and shared networking, **15**
  Virtual PC settings, 59
negotiation phases, IPSec, 428–430
network adapters
  configuring for virtual machines, 15–16, 59–60
  configuring for virtual networks, 221
  selecting, 21
  virtualized, 234
network administration
  using Active Directory Domain Services, 398–414
  DHCP servers, 359–360
  Run as Administrator option, Virtual Disk Wizard, 171–172
  Virtual Server Administration Web site, **203**, 212, **244**
Network Address Translation (NAT), **27**
  and shared networking, **15**
  VPC settings, 59

network convergence, **373, 390**
Network Monitor, 356, 389, **390**
  creating alias lists, 351
  installing, 354–355
  using, 350–351
  viewing DHCP traffic in, 364, 367–369
Network Policy and Access Services (NPAS), **373, 390**
Network Properties page, configuring for virtual networks, 223–225, 243
networking
  shared. *See* shared
  virtual, **13–14**
  VPC settings, 59–60
networks
  analyzing traffic, 350–358
  connecting to, choosing location (Vista), 85–86
  and routing, 369
New Virtual Machine Wizard, 34–39, 65–66, 193
NPAS (Network Policy and Access Services), **373, 390**
NTLM protocol, **214, 244**

O

operating systems
  guest and host, 2
  installing in Virtual PC 2007, 72–74
  installing Microsoft Server 2008, 240–241
  overview of installation, 75–86
  requirements for Classroom.local virtual network, 304–305
  supported by Virtual Server, 205–206
  supported by Virtual PC, 11
  system requirements for virtual networks, 112–113
optimizing performance, on virtual machines, 158–168
OUs (organizational units), **441**
  in Active Directory, **406–407**
  creating, 413
  creating policies for, 420–421
  and sites and domains, 410
out of box experience, sysprep option, 173, 311

P

packets
  capturing, 355–357
  filtering, 352
  and routing, 369
page file, eliminating, 161
parent-child relationships between virtual machines, **268, 295**
parent virtual hard disks, **12, 27**
parent virtual machines, creating, 175–176
parity
  described, **195**
  and RAID-5, 185
partitioning
  dynamic disks and fault tolerance, 179
  installation, 80–82
passwords, entering for Vista installation, 83
pasting with Clipboard on virtual machines, 95–96
paths, best path for routing, **369, 389**
performance
  optimization on virtual machines, 158–168
  options, studying effects of, 167–168
  virtualization benefits, 5
  and VMA, 17
  Virtual PC settings, 43–44
permissions, access control, **440**
Phishing Filter (IE), 165
ping command, **353, 386**
policies, IPSec, **431–438**
policy inheritance in Active Directory, 416–417
ports, COM and LPT1 (VPC settings), 57–58
power options, changing for VMs, 276
PowerShell, **158, 195**
  running script, 166–167
  using, 165
Preboot Execution Environment (PXE), **73, 102**
prefixes (in network addresses), **408, 441**
preshared keys, **429, 441**

product activation, product key, Windows Vista, 77–79
protocol analyzers, **350, 390**
protocols
  See also specific protocol
  routing, **369, 371**
  provisioning with virtualization, 5
PXE (Preboot Execution Environment), **73, 102**

R

RAID described, **195**
RAID-1, **195**
  implementing volume, 189–190
  mirroring hard drives using, 183–185
RAID-5, **195**
  implementing fault tolerance using, 185–188
  implementing volume, 190–191
  Virtual Server support for, 232
RAM (random access memory)
  and performance optimization, 159–160
  Virtual Server support, 208
reconfiguring
  Classroom.local virtual network for routing, 374–379
  virtual networks, 357–358
recursion
  described, **344**
  and DNS query resolution, 334
Redundant Array of Independent Disks. *See* RAID-1, RAID-5
Remote Desktop, **236, 244**
  configuring server for access, 242–243
  running Windows Server 2008 using, 238–239
removing
  existing virtual machines in network, 113
  virtual machines, 41–42, 272
renaming virtual machines, 52
repairing fault-tolerant volumes, 191–192
replay protection, **423, 441**
requests
  DHCP, **390**
  unsolicited, **127, 151**
resizing windows of virtual machines, 96–97

resolution
  Full-Screen Mode option (VPC settings), 44–45
  video, 17, 96
resolvers and DNS query resolution, 334, 344
Restore at Start option, VPC settings, 42–43
Restore Mode Administrator account, 141
restoring Directory Services databases from backup, 141
Resultant Set of Policy (RSoP)
  described, **441**
  using, 418–419, 421–423
reverse lookup zones, 336–338
RIP (Routing Information Protocol), **391**
  configuring, 385–386
  and dynamic routing, 373–374
routers, 369, 390
routing, **390**
  dynamic, 373
  implementing in Classroom.local virtual network, 369–388
  implementing LAN, 380–381
  metrics, 369, **391**
  protocols, 369, **391**
  static, **391**
Routing and Remote Access Server (RRAS), 373, **390**
Routing Information Protocol. See RIP
routing tables, 369, 379, **391**
RRAS (Routing and Remote Access Server), 373, **390**
RSoP (Resultant Set of Policy)
  described, **441**
  using, 418–419, 421–423
rules
  routing, 370–371
  Windows Firewall, 129–130
Run as Administrator option, 171–172

S

sales demonstrations using virtualization, 7
SAN (storage area network), **232**, **244**
SAs (security associations), **428**, **442**

Saved State option, 311
saving
  changes to undo disks, 229–230
  PowerShell scripts, 166
scalability, virtualization benefits, 6
scopes, **360**
  adding, 387–388
  configuring DHCP, 366–367
  creating, 361–364
  in DHCP Client service, **391**
scripts
  managing Virtual Server using, 208
  running PowerShell, 166–167
  Virtual Server, 215
SCSI adapters
  virtual hard disks on, 232–233
  Virtual Server support, 208
search paths, Virtual Server, 215–216
secondary zones, 340, 344
Secure Hash Algorithm 1-HMAC (SHA1-HMAC), **429**, **442**
Secure Sockets Layer (SSL) security, 208
security
  cryptographic security services, **440**
  enabling (VPC settings), 49–50
  groups. See security groups
  Virtual Server administration settings, 213–214
  VMRC server settings, 254
security associations (SAs), **428**, **442**
security groups, **398**, **442**
  in Active Directory, 403–406
  creating, 412–413
  viewing in virtual network, 144
security identifiers (SIDs), 98, 102, 399, **442**
security parameter index (SPI), **425**, **442**
Sequence Number field, **425**, **442**
Server Properties, Virtual Server administration settings, 213
server roles in Windows Server 2008, **110**, **151**
servers
  authorizing DHCP, 359
  configuring for Remote Desktop access, 242–243
  domain controllers, 150
  file, 150
  infrastructure, 344

in shared networks, 15
viewing properties of virtual, 253–255
VMRC, **202**, **244**
Settings menu, Console Manager, 282
shared folders
  using between virtual machines, 61–62
  using to access files on host, 92–93
  and VMA, 17
shared networking
  adapter configurations, problems with, 59–60
  and virtual machines, 15
shutting down virtual machines, 102
SIDs (security identifiers), 98, 102, 399, **442**
site link objects, **406**, **442**
sites, **442**
  Active Directory, 406–409
  and domains and OUs, 410
  managing, 413–414
sound, controlling virtual machines, 45–46, 60–61
speakers, controlling virtual machine, 45–46
Special menu, Console Manager, 282
SPI (security parameter index), **425**, **442**
SRV records, using in forward lookup zones, 337, 344
SSL security, 208
stateful firewalls, **127**, **151**
static IP addressing, **116**, **151**, 178
static routing, **391**
  configuring protocol, 381–383
  implementing for Classroom.local virtual network, 371–372
  testing, 383–385
storage
  dynamic, 179
  fault tolerant, 182–188
  virtual hard disks, 11–13
storage area network (SAN), **232**, **244**
striped data, and RAID-5, **185**, **195**
subnets, identifying to Active Directory, 408–409

Sysprep, **102**
    running from command prompt, 173
    using, 310–311
    using for cloning, **98–102**
system access control lists (SACLs), **400**, **442**
system event logging, Virtual Server 2005, 208
System Preparation tool. *See* Sysprep
systems
    consolidation through virtualization, **5**, 27
    ISO 660 file, 102
    virtualized, 2

T

TCP/IP, and scope, 360
testing
    domain security policies, 420
    IPSec policies, 437–438
    organizational unit security policies, 421
    static routing, 383–385
time and date settings, Vista, 85
time, currency formats, Vista, 77
time synchronization
    and VMA, 205–206
    virtual machine with host, 96
Tools menu, Virtual Machine Manager, 273
traffic
    analyzing, 350–358
    viewing DHCP, in Network Monitor, 364, 367–369
training, virtualization benefits, 6
transport mode, IPSec, 424–426
Triple-DES (3DES), **429**, **442**
troubleshooting
    repairing fault-tolerant volumes, 191–192
    viewing event logs, 217–218
    Virtual PC 2007 problems, 26
    Virtual PC installations, 192–194
tunnel mode, IPSec, 427–428

U

undo disks
    advanced disk options, implementing, 168–170

Enable undo disks option, Virtual Server, 229–230
    enabling, 13
    using, 55–56, 168–170, 174
    virtual machine settings option, 55–56
unsolicited requests, and Windows Firewall, **127**, **151**
updates, Vista settings, 83–84
updating VMRC Server security settings, 254
user accounts, **442**
    and Active Directory, **400–402**
    creating, 410–411
user authentication, **398**, **442**
user authorization, **398**, **442**
user rights in Active Directory, **398–399**, **442**
usernames, entering for Vista installation, 83
users, viewing in virtual network, 144

V

verifying
    IP configuration on Dovercorp.local network, 122–126
    IP connectivity in virtual network, 130–131
VHD file storage, 160
.vhd files, **11–12**, 27, 35, 234
    compacting, 163–165
    storing, 160–161
    zeroing free space, 162–163
video
    drivers, 17, 97
    resolution on VMs, 96
video RAM (VRAM), **97**, **102**
View menu, Virtual Machine Manager, 272–273
viewing
    DHCP traffic in Network Monitor, 364, 367–369
    users, security groups, 144
    Virtual PC 2007 Help, 24–25
    virtual machine properties, 273–275
    VMRC Server settings, 253
Virtual Disk Precompactor, 162–163

Virtual Disk Wizard, 49, 170–171
    compact option, 164
    creating virtual hard disks using, 179–180
    implementing additional hard drives using, 188
virtual disks
    creating, 230–233
    options in Virtual Server, 227–234
Virtual Disks Manager, 259–260, 283–287
virtual floppy disks, 230, 232
virtual hard disks, 11–13, 160
    associating with virtual machines, 235–236
    creating, 38–39, 259–260, 289
    differencing, 170–171
    dynamic disks and fault tolerance, 179–192
    implementing advanced disk options, 168–179, 243
    partitions, Vista install settings, 80
    specifying for new virtual machines, 35
    undo disks. *See* undo disks
    zeroing free space, 162–163
Virtual Machine Additions (VMA), **17**, **28**
    installing, 90–92, 241–242
    installing into VMs, 121–122, 320–321
    and Virtual Server, 205
virtual machine configuration (.vmc) files, **35**, **66**
Virtual Machine Manager, 264–280
Virtual Machine Network Services Driver, **13–14**, **28**, 223
Virtual Machine Remote Control server properties, 214
Virtual Machine Remote Control (VMRC) clients, 237–238, **244**
    for access to virtual machines, 236
    and Virtual Server, **203**
Virtual Machine Remote Control (VMRC) servers, **202**, **244**
virtual machines (VMs), **2**, **28**
    See also virtualization technology
    adding, 40–42, 65–66, 177
    additions. *See* Virtual Machine Additions

associating virtual hard disks with, 235–236
cloning, 98–102
closing, 97
components, settings, 9–10
controlling with mouse, 93–94
creating, 34–40, 65–66, 234–236, 239
creating and running child, 176–178, 287–288
creating Dovercorp.local, 114–115
creating parent, 175–176
creating, running with VMRCplus, 257–280
in Dovercorp.local virtual network, 110–113
drag and drop copying on, 94–95
guests running on top of hosts, 4
how VPC works with, 11–16
implementing with Virtual Server, 234–243
installing applications in, 165–166
installing Microsoft Server 2008 into, 117–119
installing Vista Business into, 86–88, 119–121
installing VMA into, 121–122
installing Windows Server 2008 into, 88–90
managing settings, 51–64
memory settings, 52–53
performance optimization, 158–168
removing, 41–42, 113
resizing windows, 96–97
setting configuration using VPC, 64–65
setting global options, 51
shutting down, 102
time synchronization, 96
viewing settings, properties, 277–280
and Virtual Server, 203–204
virtual networking
described, 13–14, 28
Virtual Server support, 209
virtual networks
Classroom.local. *See* Classroom.local virtual network
creating, 223–227
Dovercorp.local. *See* Dovercorp.local virtual network
implementing, 220–223, 289–293

reconfiguring, 357–358
Virtual PC 2007
exploring blog, 26
global settings, configuring, 42–51
Help pages, viewing, 24–25
history, 7–8
installing, 22–24
installing operating systems in, 72–74
local and shared networking, 15
managing virtual machine settings, 51–66
performance optimization, 158–168
researching, 18–19
settings for new VM, 9–10
supported OSs, storage, 11–13
troubleshooting installations, 192–194
virtual networking, 13–14
vs. Virtual Server, 207–209
Virtual PC 2007 Console, 34
Virtual Server 2005
configuring, 212–220
creating, implementing virtual networks, 220–227
Help, 211–212
history, 7–8
installing, 209–212
overview, features, 202–209
researching, 206–207
virtual disks in, 227–234
vs. Virtual PC 2007, 207–209
Virtual Server 2008, 8
Virtual Server Administration Web site, **203, 244**
accessing, 212
configuring settings, 216–217
Virtual Server Manager window, 254–255
Virtual Server menu, Virtual Machine Manager, 273
Virtual Server service, **202, 244**
virtual servers, 253–255
virtualization described, **2, 28**
virtualization technology
introduction to, 2–4
uses of, 4–7
Vista (Windows)
30-day evaluation, 79
different operating systems running on, 2–3

Internet Connection Sharing. *See* ICS
installing in virtual machines, 75–77
versions, selecting, 79
virtual machine configuration, 36
Vista Business, installing into VMs, 86–88, 119–121
VMA. *See* Virtual Machine Additions
.vmc files, 35, 66, 215, 234
VMRC ActiveX plug-in, **203, 244**
VMRC protocol and Virtual Server, **202, 244**
VMRC servers, 214, 253–255
VMRCplus, **236, 244**, 289–293
Console Manager, using, 281–287
installing, configuring, 253–256
overview, features of, **250–253**
Virtual Machine Manager, using, 266–280
VMs. *See* virtual machines
.vnc files, 234
volume (storage), **195**
See also RAID
dynamic disks and fault tolerance, **179**
mirrored, 183, **195**
repairing fault-tolerant, 191–192
VPC. *See* Virtual PC 2007
VRAM (video RAM), **97, 102**
.vsv files, **311, 344**

W

Web sites
Virtual Server 2005, 207
Virtual Server Administration Web site, **203, 244**
windows, resizing virtual machine, 96–97
Windows Firewall
configuring, 127–129, 323–324
setting rules, 129–130
Windows Genuine Advantage add-on, 165
Windows Management Instrumentation (WMI), 208
Windows NT LAN Manager (NTML) protocol, **214, 244**
Windows Preinstallation Environment (WinPE)
described, **102**
usage, 75–77

Windows Server 2003, functional levels, and Windows Server 2008, 137
Windows Server 2008
  and Dovercorp.local virtual network, 110
  installing DHCP, 358–364
  installing evaluation copy, 178
  installing in VMs, 88–90, 312–313
  preinstallation, 72–74
Windows Server 2008 Active Directory Sites and Services console, 408
Windows service in Virtual Server, **202**, **244**
Windows Vista. *See* Vista
WinPE. *See* Windows Preinstallment Environment